A DICTIONARY OF SPANISH LITERATURE

DICTIONARY OF SPANISH LITERATURE

by MAXIM NEWMARK, Ph.D.

Author of

TWENTIETH CENTURY MODERN LANGUAGE TEACHING

DICTIONARY OF FOREIGN WORDS AND PHRASES

DICTIONARY OF SCIENCE AND TECHNOLOGY IN ENGLISH, FRENCH, GERMAN, SPANISH

PHILOSOPHICAL LIBRARY • NEW YORK

15 East 40th Street, New York 16, N. Y.

Printed in the United States of America

PREFACE

The primary aim of *A Dictionary of Spanish Literature* is to serve as a convenient reference work for American students of Spanish and Spanish American literature. This aim has determined the scope of the dictionary as a whole and the treatment of the separate articles. The scope is limited to those names and topics usually represented in standard textbooks and outlines of Spanish and Spanish American literature, as checked by a comparison of tables of contents and indices. The treatment is concise, factual and objective, the endeavor being to present a maximum of data with a modicum of critical commentary, and to make the latter representative rather than subjective.

Within the limits mentioned, the coverage includes the great anonymous masterpieces, the major and minor novelists, poets, dramatists, essayists and literary critics, both of Spain and of Spanish America. Also included are eminent Spanish literary scholars as well as outstanding hispanists of other countries, but especially those of the United States. In addition to biographies, critical evaluations, chief works and critical references for the above, the dictionary contains articles on significant movements, schools, and literary genres. Definitions of terms in Spanish metrics, philology and linguistics are given, but these are limited to their significance with respect to Spanish literature in general. There are also entries on scholarly journals, source works, text collections, bibliographies, and literary, cultural and educational institutions. Wherever pertinent, the interrelationships of Spanish literature with that of other countries is treated in appropriate detail. The entire dictionary is thoroughly cross-referenced with respect to titles of representative works, famous literary characters and pseudonyms of authors.

Entries are arranged in strict alphabetical order, whether they comprise one or more words or names. Consultants unfamiliar with Spanish alphabetization should note that *ch*, *ll*, and *ñ* are separate letters, both initially and intermedially. To prevent searching, abbreviations have been kept to a minimum; in particular, the titles of periodicals are given in full. Those few abbreviations which are used, if not self-explanatory, will be found as separate entries in the body of the dictionary.

MAXIM NEWMARK

ACKNOWLEDGMENTS

It would be impractical at this point to list the many references consulted by the author. They are given in detail at the end of articles throughout the dictionary. However, a special word of acknowledgment is due to certain works which have been of particular value in compiling this dictionary. They are: Romera-Navarro, M., *Historia de la literatura española,* 2a. ed., Boston, 1949 (bibliographical references, summaries of masterpieces); Río, Ángel del, *Historia de la literatura española,* 2 vols., N. Y., 1948 (historical, philosophical and cultural backgrounds, foreign influences, combined index and glossary); Northup, G. T., *An Introduction to Spanish Literature,* 2nd ed., Chicago, 1936 (history of scholarship in early Spanish literature); Boggs, R. S., *Outline History of Spanish Literature,* Boston, 1937 (chronological tables, historical periods); Brenan, G., *The Literature of the Spanish People,* 2nd ed., Cambridge, 1953 (glossary of medieval verse forms, *aljamiada* literature); Sáinz de Robles, F. C., *Ensayo de un diccionario de la literatura,* II, *Escritores españoles e hispanoamericanos,* 2a. ed., Madrid, 1953 (biographical data); Bleiberg, G. & Marías, J., (Editors), *Diccionario de literatura española,* 2a. ed., Madrid, 1953 (criticism, biographical data); Sánchez, L. A., *Historia de la literatura americana,* 2a. ed., Santiago de Chile, 1940 (general reference); Hespelt, E. H., (Editor), *An Outline History of Spanish American Literature,* 2nd ed., N. Y., 1942 (biographical data, bibliography); Lázaro Carreter, F., *Diccionario de términos filológicos,* Madrid, 1953 (metrics, linguistics); Shipley, J .T., (Editor), *Encyclopedia of World Literature,* N. Y., 1946 (general reference); Real Academia Española, *Diccionario manual e ilustrado de la lengua española,* Madrid, 1950 (general reference). In addition, acknowledgment is due to the many American scholars in the hispanic field for their co-operation in filling out and forwarding the personal data sheets sent to them. Where this was neglected, the compiler had recourse to biographical reference works, but must disclaim responsibility for any discrepancies or omissions.

A

A.A.T.S. See *American Association of Teachers of Spanish.*

Abad, Pero. The same as Per Abbat. See under *Abbat.*

Abbat, Per. The medieval author or copyist whose name appears on the manuscript of the *Poema del Cid* (1307). See under *Cantar de Mío Cid.*

Abenalcotía. See under *cantar de gesta; Ribera, Julián.*

Abencerraje y la hermosa Jarifa. An anonymous narrative of the early 16th century, based on a theme from the Moorish romance cycle and relating events which probably occurred in about 1485. The tale occurs in three sources: the *Inventario* (1565) of Antonio de Villegas; the fourth book of Montemayor's *Diana* (1561); and a chronicle by Fernando de Antequera (1650?). It is the story of the Moor, Abindarráez of Granada, and his bride, Jarifa. The other chief figure is the Spanish knight, Narváez of Antequera, who captures Abindarráez while the latter is on his way to wed the lovely Jarifa. The Moor gives and keeps his pledge to return three days after his wedding, and is magnanimously liberated by Narváez. *El Abencerraje* marks the beginning of the *novela.*

Cf. Text, in *BAE,* III; Menéndez y Pelayo, M., "Orígenes de la novela," *NBAE,* I; Mérimée, H., "El Abencerraje d'après diverses versions publiées au 16e siècle," *Bulletin hispanique,* XXX; Crawford, J. P. W., "Un episodio de 'El Abencerraje' y una novela de Ser Giovanni," *Revista de filología española,* X; Deferrari, H. A., *The Sentimental Moor in Spanish Literature Before 1600,* U. of P. Press, Philadelphia, 1927.

Aben Humeya. See under *Martínez de la Rosa.*

Abiel Smith. See under *Smith Professorship.*

Abindarráez. The noble Moor who weds Jarifa by permission of the Spanish knight, Narváez de Antequera, who then magnanimously grants the Moor his freedom. The theme occurs in the Moorish romance cycle, and particularly in an anonymous narrative of the 16th century, *Abencerraje y la hermosa Jarifa.* See under *Abencerraje . . . ; Montemayor, Jorge de.*

Abravanel, Judas. See *Hebreo, León.*

abulia. A term used in psychopathology to indicate loss of will-power. The term was introduced by Unamuno *(Ensayos,* I, 207, 1890) to indicate a Spanish trait which accounts for Spain's decadence. The expression *abulia* was given wider currency by Ganivet in his *Idearium español* (1897), where he opposes to it the notion of *voluntad* as an antidote.

Academia de la Historia. See *Real Academia de la Historia.*

Academia del buen gusto. See under *Montiano y Luyando.*

Academia de letras humanas. A literary academy founded in 1793 by the leaders of the 18th century Sevillan school. The orientation of the academy was neoclassic. Among the chief members were: Lista, Reinoso, Arjona and Blanco White. See under *Escuela sevillana.*

Academia de los árcades. See under *Cruz, Ramón de la.*

Academia de los nocturnos. Famous Valencian literary academy (1591-1594). See under *Castro, Guillén de.*

Academia Española. See *Real Academia Española.*

Acción Española. See under *Maeztu, Ramiro de.*

Aceitunas (Las). See under *Rueda, Lope de; paso.*

Acero de Madrid (El). See under *Vega, Lope de.*

Acevedo Díaz, Eduardo (1851-1924). Uruguayan political journalist, politician and novelist. A political refugee at various stages in his career, he wrote all of his work in exile, beginning with a trilogy of patriotic novels inspired by the Uruguayan wars of independence *(Himno de sangre).* Chiefly noted as a pioneer of the gaucho genre, his style alternated between naturalistic and romantic extremes. His indigenous themes and characters influenced the development of Uruguayan gaucho literature. Among his chief works were: *Ismael,* 1888; *Nativa,* 1890; *Grito de gloria,* 1894; *Soledad,* 1894.

Cf. Zum Felde, A., *Proceso intelectual del Uruguay,* Montevideo, 1930.

Acuña, Manuel (1849-1873). Mexican poet. A suicide at the age of twenty-four. Author of a romantic drama *(El pasado,* 1872) and of a single volume of poetry which has gone through many editions (*Poesías,* Paris, 1884; *Poesías completas,* Paris, 1911). Of romantic disposition, his early medical studies led him to a rationalistic philosophy. The distinctive lyrical effect of these antithetical traits is shown in his much-anthologized poem, *Ante un cadáver.*

Cf. González Peña, C., *Historia de la literatura mexicana,* Mexico, 1940.

Adams, Nicholson Barney (1895). American hispanist. Professor of Spanish, University of North Carolina, since 1924. Visiting professor at the Universities of Wisconsin, Chicago, and New Mexico. Author of *The Romantic Dramas of García Gutiérrez,* N. Y., 1922; *The Heritage of Spain,* N. Y., 1943; *España,* N. Y., 1947.

adónico. A pentasyllabic verse which concludes the *estrofa sáfica.* See under *sáfico.*

Agonía del Cristianismo. See under *Unamuno.*

aguda. See *rima aguda; oxítona.*

agudeza. See under *conceptismo.*

Agudeza y arte de ingenio. Gracián's exposition of the literary theories of *conceptismo;* published in 1648. It was a sequel to his *Arte de ingenio* (1642) and incorporates the latter work together with examples from *conceptista* writers. See under *Gracián y Morales.*

Aguja de navegar cultos. See under *Quevedo.*

Agustini, Delmira (1886-1914). Uruguayan poetess. Her brilliant literary career ended tragically when she was murdered by her estranged husband, who then committed suicide. Gifted with extraordinary sensitivity, her bold sincerity and impassioned lyrical utterance ranks her among the outstanding early modernist poets. She has few equals among the feminine poets of Latin America. Among her chief works were: *El libro blanco,* 1907; *Cantos de la mañana,* 1910; *Los cálices vacíos,* 1913; *El osario de Eros,* 1914; *Los astros del abismo* (posthumous, 1924); *Poesías completas* (Zum Felde, A., ed., Buenos Aires, 1944).

Cf. Zum Felde, A., *Crítica de la literatura uruguaya,* Montevideo, 1930; Miranda, E., *Poetisas de Chile y Uruguaya,* Santiago, 1937.

Ajuda. See under *cancionero.*

Alarcón, Juan Ruiz de. See *Ruiz de Alarcón.*

Alarcón y Ariza, Pedro Antonio (1833-1891). Novelist and short-story writer. Born in Guadix, Granada; died in Madrid. After studying law, he went to Cádiz, where he was active as a journalist. Later, in Madrid, he became editor of *El látigo,* an anti-royalist journal. In 1860 he served as a volunteer in Africa. His experiences of the African campaign and of a subsequent trip to Italy are recorded in two volumes of newspaper dispatches, memoirs and travel narratives *(Diario de un testigo de la guerra de África,* 1859-1860; *De Madrid a Nápoles,* 1861). Ranked with the outstanding representatives of the 19th century regionalist novel, Alarcón began at the age of eighteen with a juvenile work entitled *El final de Norma* (1855). Although a radical in his youth, he became conservative with increasing maturity. His religious convictions are argued in *El niño de la bola* (1880). He reached his peak as a writer in the delightfully humorous *El sombrero de tres picos* (1874), based on a popular ballad, *El molinero de Arcos.* Although the theme is little else but a variation of the bedroom farce, Alarcón's treatment is highly original. Manuel de Falla's famous ballet was inspired by it. Uneven in structure, Alarcón's novels and tales nevertheless reveal him as one of the great Spanish masters of humor. His chief works were: (tales) *El carbonero alcalde,* 1859; *Cuentos amatorios,* 1881; *Historietas nacionales,* 1881; *Narraciones inverosimiles,* 1882; (novels) *El final de Norma,* 1855; *El sombrero de tres picos,* 1874; *El escándalo,* 1875; *El niño de la bola,* 1880; *El capitán Veneno,* 1881; *La pródiga,* 1882.

Cf. "Historia de mis libros," in *Obras completas,* Madrid, 1899; Romano, J., *Pedro Antonio de Alarcón, el novelista romántico,* Madrid, 1933.

Alarcos (El conde). See under *Castro, Guillén de.*

Alas, Leopoldo. See under *Clarín.*

alba. (From Provençal "dawn"). A song or poem at dawn when lovers must part. The genre was cultivated by Provençal troubadours and was adopted by Gallego-Portuguese and early Castilian poets. The Spanish terms *albada* and *alborada* occur with the same meaning as *alba.* Medieval *albas* were largely inspired by Ovid, who in his poetry frequently laments the approach of dawn and the end of a lovers' tryst. Spanish poets applied the form to other themes besides love.

Cf. Schevill, R., *Ovid and the Renaissance in Spain,* Berkeley,

1913; *Dictionary of World Literature,* (Ed. Shipley, J. T.), N. Y., 1943.

albada. The same as *alba.*

Alberti, Rafael (1902). Postmodernist lyric poet. Born near Cádiz. He attended a Jesuit college but did not complete his studies for a degree. In 1917 he established himself in Madrid intent on becoming a cubist painter, but he soon turned to poetry. He first achieved fame in 1925 when a volume of his verse, *Marinero en tierra,* was awarded the National Prize for Literature. During the Spanish Civil War, he aligned himself with the Communists and, at its conclusion, went into exile in South America. Influenced by Góngora among earlier Spanish poets, and by Juan Ramón Jiménez among the moderns, Alberti's earlier manner was a mingling of gongoresque diction with modernistic expression. His versatility in adopting new styles and themes has been remarkable. He went from a subtle and ironic "popularism" *(La amante,* 1925; *El alba del alhalí,* 1926), through baroque neogongorism *(Cal y canto,* 1927) and surrealism *(Sobre los ángeles,* 1929) into the more intimate and spiritual poetry of his later period *(Entre el clavel y la espada,* 1941).

Cf. *Antología poética,* Buenos Aires, 1945; Proll, E., *"Popularismo* and *Barroquismo* in the Poetry of Rafael Alberti," *Bulletin of Spanish Studies,* XIX, 1942.

alborada. The same as *alba.*

Album Cubano. See under *Gómez de Avellaneda.*

Album de un loco. See under *Zorrilla y Moral.*

Alcalde de Zalamea (El.). See under *Calderón.*

Alcayaga, Lucila Godoy. See *Mistral, Gabriela.*

Alcázar, Baltasar del. See under *Escuela sevillana.*

Aldea perdida (La). See under *Palacio Valdés* .

Alegría, Ciro (1909). Peruvian novelist. Born in Trujillo. One of the leaders of the *aprista* movement, he was imprisoned (1931-1933) and exiled to Chile (1934) for his pro-Indian, socialistic agitation. Beginning as a writer of verse and short stories, he soon turned to the novel. The three novels for which he is best known all received literary prizes. Their titles are: *La serpiente de oro* (1935), *Los perros hambrientos* (1939) and *El mundo es ancho y ajeno* (1941). All portray the community life of the Indians in various remote regions of Peru, depicting their struggles against the forces of nature and protesting against the injustices perpetrated by man. One of the best of the *criollista* writers, *Alegría* frequently attains lyrical heights as a stylist, but his chief merit lies in the intensity of his social compassion.

Cf. Spell, J. R., *Contemporary Spanish-American Fiction,* Chapel Hill, N. C., 1944.

Aleixandre, Vicente (1900). Modern lyric poet. Born in Seville. He completed his studies at Málaga and then became a lawyer in Madrid. His first volume of verse, *Ambito,* appeared in Málaga in 1928. In 1933 he was awarded the National Prize for Literature, for his book of poetry, *La destrucción o el amor,* and he subsequently became a member of the *Academia Española.* The best known of his later works is *Sombra del paraíso* (1944). Aleixandre's poetry has been called a blend of romanticism and surrealism. He sings of human discontent and aspiration expressed in metaphors of earth and nature. He has shown a penchant for free verse and conceptual language; however, his own conception of the nature of poetry as "a flight toward supra-sensory reality" subordinates the importance of form and language to metaphysical emphasis.

Cf. Alonso, D., "La poesía de Vicente Aleixandre," *Ensayos sobre poesía española,* Madrid, 1944; Gómez de la Serna, R., "Gerardo Diego y Vicente Aleixandre," *Revista Nacional de Cultura,* Caracas, May-June, 1954.

Alemán, Mateo (1547-1614?). Classical writer of the Spanish picaresque novel. Born in Seville; died in Mexico. Son of a prison doctor, he became familiar with criminal types while accompanying his father on visits to the Seville prison. He began, but did not complete, the study of medicine at the Universities of Salamanca and Alcalá. After a long career as a government clerk in Madrid, he went to Mexico (1608), where he spent the rest of his life. The first part of his masterpiece, *Guzmán de Alfarache* (pt. 1, 1599; pt. 2, 1604), appeared some fifty years after the great anonymous prototype of the picaresque novel, *Lazarillo de Tormes,* since clerical authorities frowned on the glorification of the rogue. The influence of clerical censorship is also reflected indirectly in the long moralizing passages of *Guzmán de Alfarache.* The novel is remarkable not only for its vivid narration of adventures and its philosophical observations, but also for its evocation of the life, morals and manners of the period of the Counter Reformation in Spain and in Italy. *Guzmán* attained a phenomenal popularity, going through 26 editions in its first six years, even exceeding the vogue of *Don Quijote* in its day. The success of the first part prompted a spurious second part (1602) attributed to a Seville lawyer, Juan José Martí. The authentic second part appeared in Lisbon, in 1604. Mateo's *Guzmán* exercised an important influence on the development of the picaresque novel not only in Spain but also in France and in Germany, where Lessing recognized its greatness.

Cf. García Blanco, M., *Mateo Alemán y la novela picaresca alemana,* Madrid, 1930; Rodríguez Marín, V. F., *Documentos referentes a Mateo Alemán,* Madrid, 1933; Espinosa, C., *La novela picaresca y el "Guzmán de Alfarache,"* Habana, 1935; Moreno Báez, E., *Guzmán de Alfarache,* Madrid, 1948.

alexandrine. See under *cuaderna vía.*

Alfonsi, Petrus. See under *Disciplina clericalis.*

Alfonso VII. See under *Sandoval, Prudencio de.*

Alfonso X, el Sabio (1220?-1284). The son and successor of Fernando III, and for a time Holy Roman Emperor, he was not as successful politically as his illustrious father, his reign (1252-1284) being marred by a disastrous civil war over the succession to the throne. Despite his political misfortunes, Alfonso's place in history is assured for his cultural achievements. He was the greatest medieval patron of letters, an encyclopedic scholar and a poet. He exercised great influence on the development of Castilian prose through his sponsorship of the codification of the ancient Gothic Laws *(Las siete partidas,* ca. 1256) and his compilations of medieval lore, especially in the field of history *(La crónica general,* 1270 *et seq.; General estoria,* 1270-1280) and astronomy *(Libros del saber de astronomía,* ca. 1277). Also interesting is his work on precious stones *(Lapidario,* 1279). The *Crónica* is of particular significance in the history of Spanish literature because it contains prose versions of the epic *cantares de gesta.* Alfonso was also a lyric poet in his own right, choosing the literary Galician dialect for his *Cantigas de Santa María,* a collection of 420 songs, set to music and glorifying the miracles performed by the Virgin Mary.

Cf. Valmar, Marqués de, (Ed.), *Cantigas de Santa María,* Real

Academia Esp., Madrid, 1889; Menéndez Pidal, R., (Ed.), "La primera crónica general," *NBAE,* V. Madrid, 1906; Solalinde, A. G., (Ed.), *Alfonso X, el Sabio, Antología de sus obras,* Madrid, 1923; Trend, J. B., *Alfonso the Sage and other essays,* London, 1926.

Alfonso XI. See under *Poema de Alfonso Onceno.*

Alfonso, Pedro. The same as Alfonsi, Petrus. See under *Disciplina clericalis.*

Alhambra (The). See under *Irving, Washington.*

Alianza Popular Revolucionaria Americana. See *Aprismo.*

Alixandre. See *Libro de Alexandre.*

aljamiada literature. Early Spanish literature written in Castilian but using the Arabic or Hebrew alphabet. The term *aljamiada* is derived from the Arabic word for the Castilian language *(aljamía).* The principal example of this literature is *El Poema de Yuçuf* (early 14th century). Modern research has expanded the scope of *aljamiada* literature through the discovery of some 40 *jarchas,* Spanish lyrics embedded in Hebrew and Arabic poetry of the 11th century.

Cf. Menéndez Pidal, R., "Poema de Yuçuf: materiales para su estudio," *Revista de Archivos, Bibliotecas y Museos,* VII, 1902; Stern, S. M., "Les vers finaux en espagnol dans les muwassahas hispano-hébraïques," *Al-Andalus,* XIII, 1948; García Gómez, E., "Más sobre las jarchas romances en muwassahas hebreas," *Al-Andalus,* XIV, XV, 1949, 1950; Spitzer, L., "The Mozarabic Lyric," *Comparative Literature,* IV, 1952; Brenan, G., *The Literature of the Spanish People,* 2nd ed., Cambridge University Press, London, 1953.

Almanaques. See under *Torres Villarroel.*

Almogáver. See *Boscán, Juan.*

Alonso, Amado (1896-1952). Linguistic scientist and literary critic. Born in Lerín, Navarra; died in Cambridge, Mass. He was a pupil and collaborator of Menéndez Pidal and Navarro Tomás at the *Centro de Estudios Históricos* in Madrid, specializing in phonetics. He occupied professorial posts at the Universities of Hamburg, Buenos Aires and Harvard. At the University of Buenos Aires he was for many years Director of the *Instituto de Filología,* where he founded and edited the monumental *Biblioteca de Dialectología Hispanoamericana* and other series of philological studies. In 1939 he founded the *Revista de Filología Hispánica,* which rapidly became a leading periodical in its field. Among his other publications were: *El problema de la lengua en América* (1935); *Castellano, español, idioma nacional* (1942); *Poesía y estilo de Pablo Neruda* (1940); *Estudios lingüísticos,* Madrid, 1953; *De la pronunciación,* (Ed. Lapesa, R.), Madrid, 1955.

Cf. *Revista de Filología Española,* I, 1952; *Homenaje a Amado Alonso,* Mexico, 1954; Lapesa, R., "Amado Alonso (1896-1952)," *Hispania,* XXXVI, 1953; "Homenaje a Amado Alonso," *Nueva Revista de Filología Hispánica,* VII, 1953.

Alonso, Dámaso (1898). Romance philologist, critic and poet. Born in Madrid. A pupil of the great Menéndez Pidal, he himself became a noted philologist, literary critic and lecturer, occupying through the years professorial posts at Valencia, Madrid, Berlin, Cambridge, Stanford, Columbia and Harvard. Most responsible for the renewed understanding and revaluation of Góngora, his *La lengua poética de Góngora* (1935) was awarded the National Prize for Literature. Another of his works, *La poesía de San Juan de la Cruz* (1942), received an award from the *Academia Española;* and he himself was elected to that august body in 1945. He has contributed to the leading periodicals in the hispanic field, and has prepared annotated editions of Spanish classics (Góngora, Gil Vicente, San Juan de la Cruz, *etc.)* His anthology of medieval Spanish poetry is a standard work in the field *(Poesía de la Edad Media y poesía de tipo tradicional,* 1935). Among his many historical and stylistic studies on Spanish poetry are: *Ensayos sobre la poesía española,* 1944; *Poesía española,* 1950; and *Poetas españoles contemporáneos,* 1952. The most original work among the several volumes of his own poetry is *Hijos de la ira* (1944), a collection of religious and metaphysical poems.

Cf. Valbuena Prat, A., *Historia de la literatura española,* Barcelona, 1946; Del Río, A., *Historia de la literatura española,* N. Y., 1948.

Alonso Cortés, Narciso (1875). Literary historian, poet and critic. Member of the *Real Academia Española.* Professor at the *Instituto de Valladolid.* Principal works: *Romances populares de Castilla; Artículos histórico-literarios; Sumandos biográficos; Espronceda; Zorrilla, su vida y sus obras.*

Cf. *Hispania,* XXXVI, 1953.

Alphabeta exemplorum. See under *ejemplo.*

Alphabeta narrationum. See under *ejemplo.*

Alsino. See under *Prado, Pedro.*

Altamira, Rafael (1866-1951). Historian and critic. Born in Alicante; died in Mexico. He studied law at the University of Madrid, where he later became Professor of History. Other professorships which he held were at Oviedo, at the Sorbonne, and at the *Institución Libre de Enseñanza.* In addition to his teaching and writing, he traveled and lectured throughout Europe and America. His specialty was the history of civil and political institutions of Spain and of America. He was also an authority on comparative and international law, serving as a Spanish delegate to the League of Nations and as a member of the International Court of Justice at the Hague. A disciple of Giner de los Ríos, Altamira was one of the modern Spanish historians who interpreted history as an organic cultural whole rather than in the light of traditional political history. His outstanding work was *Historia de España y de la civilización española* (1900-1911).

Altamirano, Ignacio Manuel (1834-1893). Mexican teacher, journalist, poet and novelist. A full-blooded Aztec, he was educated in Toluca and in Mexico City. He fought under Juárez against Maximilian. Following a meritorious career in journalism, literature and education, he was appointed Consul-General to Spain in 1889. After his death in San Remo, Italy, his remains were transferred to the Mexican Westminster Abbey, the "Rotunda de Hombres Ilustres." One of the outstanding figures of the romantic period in Mexico, he concentrated on local themes and national history, his novel *Clemencia* (1869) having the Maximilian regime as its background.

Cf. González Peña, C., *Historia de la literatura mexicana,* Mexico, 1940.

Altar mayor. See under *Espina, Concha.*

alumbrado. A derogatory name given by proponents of the Counter-Reformation to the followers of Erasmus. The same as *iluminista.* See also under *iluminismo; Reformation.*

Álvarez de Villasandino, Alfonso (d. 1425?). Castilian *trovador* from Burgos, whose poems constitute one-third of the *Cancionero de Baena* (ca. 1445). Baena's extravagant praise merely points to Villasandino's exalted reputation in his day. However, he was nothing but a clever, facile and superficial poet who wrote on commission for various royal or wealthy patrons. Like the other poets in the *Cancionero de Baena,* Villasandino represents the transition between Gallego-Portuguese poetry (14th century) and Castilian court poetry (15th century).

Cf. *Poesías* in *Cancionero castellano del siglo XV,* (Ed. Foulché-Delbosc, R.), *NBAE,* XXII; Buceta, E., "Álvarez de Villasandino," *Revista Filológica Española,* 1928.

Álvarez Quintero, Serafín (1871-1938) and **Joaquín** (1873-1944). Born in Seville. Brothers and life-long collaborators in almost 200 plays. Local colorists of the Generation of 1898, their comedies, dramas and *zarzuelas* reflect the sunny atmosphere, gay humor and colloquial speech of their native Andalusia. Their aim was diversion rather than instruction, and in consequence, their work lacked dramatic intensity. However, their deft plots, vivid characterizations and wholesome sentimentality place them among the most charming of contemporary Spanish playwrights. Their most significant plays were *Los Galeotes* (1900), noted for its technical perfection, *El amor que pasa* (1904), a nostalgic comedy of lonely country girls dreaming of a Prince Charming who never comes, and *Doña Clarines* (1909), a dramatic portrait of a disillusioned girl with an embarrassing compulsion for telling the truth. Among their more serious plays was *Malvaloca* (1912), which received the prize of the *Real Academia.* Their chief works were: *El ojito derecho,* 1897; *Los Galeotes,* 1900; *El patio,* 1901; *Los flores,* 1901; *La reina mora,* 1903; *El amor que pasa,* 1904; *Mañana de sol,* 1905; *El genio alegre,* 1906; *Amores y amorios,* 1908; *Las de Caín,* 1908; *Malvaloca,* 1912; *Puebla de las mujeres,* 1912; *Cabrita que tira al monte,* 1916; *Doña Clarines,* 1909; *La calumniada,* 1919; *Cancionera,* 1924; *La boda de Quinita Flores,* 1925; *Mariquilla Terremoto,* 1930.

Cf. González Blanco, A., *Los dramaturgos españoles contemporáneos,* Valencia, 1917; Pérez de Ayala, R., *Las máscaras, ensayos de crítica teatral,* Madrid, 1917-1919; "Azorín," *Los Quintero y otras páginas,* Madrid, 1925; Mérimée, V. E., "Le théâtre des Alvarez Quintero," *Bulletin Hispanique,* XXVIII, 1926.

Amadís de Gaula. A cycle of the European chivalric romances which originated in the Middle Ages and reached its apogee during the Renaissance. Allusion to a medieval version of the *Amadís* occurs for the first time in Spain (in *Regimento de los príncipes,* Seville, 1350), proving that the work had existed in Spain prior to that date. However, the question as to whether it was in the Spanish or Portuguese language is undecided, although evidence seems to favor the latter. Be that as it may, the sole form in which it is preserved is the version of Montalvo: *Los quatro libros del virtuoso cauallero Amadís de Gaula* (Saragossa, 1508). It appears that the first three books were re-worked from a medieval prototype by Garci Rodríguez de Montalvo, who then added a fourth book, and who was probably also the author of a sequel: *Las sergas de Esplandián* (1510). The authorship is vague since early editions bear the name of Garci Ordóñez de Montalvo. The *Amadís* recounts the birth and childhood of a knight by that name, his love for Oriana, his penitence in an island hermitage, his combats with monstrous humans and beasts, and his fantastic dreams. Written in the effulgent prose style of the Renaissance, Montalvo's *Amadís* is the best of its many sequels. It exerted a widespread influence on the prose fiction of the 16th century. Although it has the defects of its period, *i.e.,* an excess of the supernatural and the fantastic, it had a wholesome effect on the thought and manners of its time, since it glorified the ideals of chivalry. See also under *Vicente, Gil.*

Cf. Gayangos, P. de, "Catálogo razonado de los libros de caballerías," *BAE,* XL; Menéndez y Pelayo, M., "Orígines de la novela," *NBAE,* I; Thomas, H., *Spanish and Portuguese Romances of Chivalry,* London, 1920; Williams, G. S., "The Amadis Question," *Revue hispanique,* XXI, 1909.

Amador de los Ríos, José (1818-1878). Medievalist and historian. Born in Baena; died in Seville. One of the great literary scholars of the 19th century, he wrote a compendious history of Spanish literature, including Latin, Mohammedan and Jewish writers, and covering the period from the beginnings to the end of the 15th century, *i.e.,* through the reign of Fernando and Isabel *(Historia crítica de la literatura española,* 7 vols., 1861-1865). Although the work has now been largely superseded, it is still available, especially in those volumes dealing with the medieval period. Ríos also edited the works of Santillana *(Obras del Marqués de Santillana,* 1853) and wrote a history of the Jews in the Iberian peninsula (*Historia social, política y religiosa de los judíos en España y Portugal,* 3 vols., 1875-1876).

Cf. Valbuena Prat, A., *Historia de la literatura española,* 3rd ed., Barcelona, 1950.

Amalia. See under *Mármol, José.*

Amante liberal (El.) See under *Cervantes.*

Amantes de Teruel (Los). See under *Tirso de Molina; Hartzenbusch, Juan Eugenio.*

Amarillis. See under *Vega, Lope de.*

Amar sin saber a quién. See under *Vega, Lope de.*

Amauta. The chief periodical of the *Aprista* movement; published in Lima, Peru (1926-1930). See under *"indianista" literature.*

American Association of Teachers of Spanish (A.A.T.S.). Founded in 1915-17 through the efforts of Lawrence A. Wilkins, John D. Fitzgerald, Aurelio Espinosa, and encouraged by Ramón Menéndez Pidal, among other noted Hispanists. The aim of the A.A.T.S. is to foster and improve Spanish teaching in the United States. First president, Lawrence A. Wilkins of New York City. First editor of *Hispania,* official publication of the A.A.T.S., Aurelio Espinosa of San Francisco. First honorary presidents, Archer M. Huntington and Juan C. Cebrián. First meeting, College of the City of New York, December, 1917. In December, 1944, the Association changed its name to The American Association of Teachers of Spanish and Portuguese (A.A.T.S.P.). The current president (1954) is Graydon S. De Land of Florida State University. Archer M. Huntington of the Hispanic Society of America is the honorary president. The present editor of *Hispania* is Donald Devenish Walsh of the Choate School, Wallingford, Conn.

Cf. Wilkins, Lawrence A., "On the Threshold," *Hispania,* I, November, 1917. Coester, Alfred, "The First Annual Meeting," *Hispania,* I, February, 1918. Wilkins, Lawrence A., "Haec olim meminisse," *Hispania,* XXV, February, 1942. Jones, Willis Knapp, "The A.A.T.S., Past and Future," *Hispania,* XXV, February, 1942.

Americas. A periodical. See under *Pan American Union.*

Ameto. See under *pastoral novel.*

AMGD. Abbreviation of the Jesuit motto, *Ad majorem gloriam Dei.* Title of a novel by *Pérez de Ayala, Ramón.*

Amor brujo (El). See under *Martínez Sierra.*

Amor de los amores. See under *León, Ricardo.*

anaptyctic vowel. (Sp. *vocal anaptíctica).* See under *epenthesis; anaptyxis.*

anaptyxis. (Sp. *anaptixis).* The development of an interpolated vowel in a word to facilitate pronunciation or to promote euphony. See also under *epenthesis.*

Anastasio el pollo. See *Campo, Estanislao del.*

Andalusian school. See *Escuela sevillana.*

Andersson, Theodore (1903). American Romance philologist and foreign language methodologist. Associate Professor at Yale University since 1946. Author of *Carlos María Ocantos, Argentine Novelist,* Yale University Press, 1934; *Carlos María Ocantos y su obra,* Madrid, 1935; *The Teaching of Foreign Languages in the Elementary School,* Boston, 1953; Editor and part author of the UNESCO publication, *The Teaching of Modern Languages,* Paris, 1954.

Andorran. See under *Spanish.*

Andrade, Olegario Victor (1841-1882). Argentine poet, government official and journalist. Born in the province of Entre Ríos and died in Buenos Aires. After a distinguished literary and journalistic career, in 1880 he was appointed Editor of *La tribuna nacional,* the official newspaper of the Argentine government. His poetry is epic in scope, often tending toward the philosophical and didactic, as in *Atlántida,* a poem of soaring optimism regarding the future of Latin America. Andrade has often been compared to Whitman because of his lack of literary finesse overshadowed by elemental creative power and an abiding faith in the perfectibility of man. His chief works were: *El nido de cóndores,* 1877; *Prometeo,* 1877; *San Martín,* 1878; *Victor Hugo,* 1881; *Atlántida,* 1881; *Obras poéticas,* Buenos Aires, 1915 *et seq.*

Cf. Rojas, R., *La literatura argentina,* Buenos Aires, 1924-1925; Menéndez y Pelayo, M., *Antología de poetas hispanoamericanos,* Madrid, 1927-1928.

Andrómeda. See under *Vega, Lope de.*

Anfriso. The key name of the Duke of Alba in Lope de Vega's pastoral novel, *Arcadia* (1598). See under *Vega, Lope de.*

Ángel Guerra. See under *Pérez Galdós.*

Ángeles, Juan de los. See under *mysticism.*

Aniceto el gallo. See *Ascasubi, Hilario.*

Anselm of Canterbury. See under *mysticism.*

tone, blending the sentimental and the ironic with impeccable technique. As a short-story writer he introduced a new genre, the so-called "psycho-zoological" tale. As a novelist he is one of the outstanding creators of contemporary fiction in South America. His chief works are: *Los atormentados,* 1914; *El hombre que parecía un caballo,* 1915; *El Señor Monitot,* 1922; *Las rosas de Engaddi,* 1927; *Llama,* 1934; *El mundo de los Maharachías,* 1938; *Viaje a Ipanda,* 1939.

Cf. Onís, F., "Resurrección de Arévalo Martínez," *Revista de estudios hispánicos,* I, 1928.

Argonautos. See under *Blasco Ibáñez.*

Arguedas, Alcides (1879-1946). Bolivian journalist, diplomat, sociologist, historian and novelist. Pursued social studies in Paris. Diplomatic representative of his country to France, England and Colombia. Prominent as a sociologist *(Pueblo enfermo)* and historian *(Historia general de Bolivia),* his chief literary significance derives from his novels which pioneered the "indianista" trend. Through his pitilessly true revelation of the Indian problem Arguedas raised the social thesis novel to a high literary plane. His chief works were: *Wuatu-Wuaru,* 1904; *Pueblo enfermo,* 1909; *Vida criolla,* 1912; *Raza de bronce,* 1919.

Cf. Guzmán, A., *Historia de la novela boliviana,* La Paz, 1938.

Arjona, Manuel María. See under *Escuela sevillana; pie quebrado.*

Arniches, Carlos. See under *género chico.*

Arrieta, Juan Emilio. See under *García Gutiérrez, Antonio.*

Arrieta, Rafael Alberto (1889). Argentine professor, literary critic and poet. Professor of European literature at various universities (La Plata, Buenos Aires). Editor of the review *Atenea.* Author of many critical essays on European writers (Dickens, Sarmiento). A collection of his poems appeared in Buenos Aires in 1923. His verse is simple in theme and traditional in form. He was awarded the National Philosophical Prize in 1942 for his work on South American bibliographers, *Don Gregorio Béeche.* Among his chief works are: *Alma y momento,* 1910; *Las noches de oro,* 1917; *Estío serrano,* 1927; *Don Gregorio Béeche y los bibliógrafos de Chile y del Plata,* 1942.

Cf. Torres Ríoseco, A., *Antología de la literatura hispanoamericana,* N. Y., 1941.

Arroz y Tartana. See under *Blasco Ibáñez.*

Arte de ingenio. Gracián's exposition of the literary theory of *conceptismo,* published in 1642. This work was later incorporated in a sequel entitled *Agudeza y arte de ingenio* (1648). The work contains examples from *conceptista* writers. See under *Gracián y Morales.*

Arte de la poesía castellana. See under *Encina; arte mayor.*

arte de maestría mayor. A verse form in which the same rhymes are repeated in all the strophes of a poem.

arte de maestría menor. A verse form in which the rhymes are varied from strophe to strophe in a poem.

arte mayor. A verse form consisting of octets of eleven or twelve syllabled verses, rhymed ABBAACCA. The *arte mayor* verse is based on a rhythmic rather than syllabic pattern and has four major stresses. A caesura divides the verse into hemistiches. Variations of the number of syllables and of the rhyme scheme are frequent. Often referred to as the Spanish alexandrine, this verse form gradually displaced *cuaderna vía* at the end of the 14th century. The theory of *arte mayor* was first discussed by Juan del Encina (1469-1529) in his *Arte de la poesía castellana* (1496), and with greater understanding, by Nebrija (1444-1522) in his *Gramática castellana* (1492). These *versos de arte mayor* were first used by the court poets of the 14th and 15th century, notably by Álvarez de Villasandino (1350?-1428?); and in the next generation it was adopted by the humanist poets under the influence of Latin and Italian masters (Lucan, Dante), notably by Juan de Mena (1411-1456), who used the form in his *Laberinto de Fortuna* (1489). Part of the description of the battle of la Higuera from this work is given below as an example of *arte mayor.*

Con dos quarentenas e mas de millares
le vimos de gentes armadas a punto,
sin otro mas pueblo ynerme alli junto,
entrar por la vega talando oliuares,
tomando castillos, ganando lugares,
faziendo por miedo de tanta mesnada
con todo su tierra tenblar a Granada,
tenblar las arenas fondon de los mares.
(Stanza 148)

Cf. Foulché-Delbosc, R., *Juan de Mena y el "Arte Mayor,"* Madrid, 1903; Morel-Fatio, "L'arte mayor et l'hendécasyllabe dans la poésie castillane du xv. siècle, *etc.*," *Romania,* XXIII.

arte menor. A general term for Spanish verse forms of from two to eight syllables and of one or two rhythmic stresses. *Arte menor* is distinguished from *arte mayor.*

Arte nuevo de hacer comedias . . . See under *Vega, Lope de.*

artículos de costumbres. See under *costumbrismo.*

Asbaje, Juana Inés. See *Cruz, Sor Juana Inés de la.*

Ascasubi, Hilario (1807-1875). Argentine journalist and poet. Born in the Argentine province of Córdoba and died in Buenos Aires. He led an eventful life at sea and in foreign countries, fought in the war against Brazil, and was imprisoned for two years by the dictator Rosas, finally escaping to Montevideo. He founded various periodicals, of which *Aniceto el gallo* (1852) is significant not only for its vivid contents but also because he adopted the title of the periodical as a pen name. Ascasubi is best known for his gaucho ballads, *Paulino Lucero* (1839-1851), and for his gaucho epic poem, *Santos Vega o los Mellizos de la Flor* (1851-1872). He is important in Argentine literature as one of the best of the early gaucho poets. He describes the life of the gaucho in barracks and in battle during the revolutionary wars. His conception of Santos Vega as a gaucho minstrel *(Santos Vega, el payador)* is typical of the gaucho spirit. His influence on subsequent gaucho writing, notably on the work of Estanislao del Campo, was considerable.

Cf. Rojas, R., *La literatura argentina,* Buenos Aires 1924-1925; Tiscornia, E. F., *Poetas gauchescos,* Buenos Aires, 1940.

asimilación. See *assimilation.*

Asmodeo. The imp in *El diablo cojuelo* (1641) by Luis Vélez de Guevara. See under *Vélez de Guevara.*

assimilation. (Sp. *asimilación.)* A phonetic process whereby two sounds acquire common characteristics or become identical. When the sounds are adjacent, the process is known as "contiguous assimilation" *(asimilación orgánica)*; when the sounds are separated, the process is known as "incontiguous assimilation" *(asimilación armónica).* The sound which causes this process is called the "assimilatory sound" *(sonido asimilador)*; the sound which changes is called the "assimilated sound" *(sonida asimilado).* If the assimilatory sound precedes the assimilated sound the process is called "progressive assimilation" *(asimilación progresiva)*; if the assimilatory sound follows the assimilated one, the process is called "regressive assimilation" *(asimilación regresiva).* If both sounds affect each other, the process is called "reciprocal assimilation" *(asimilación recíproca).* Examples (1) Progressive assimilation: mb > m: palumba > *paloma.* (2) Regressive assimilation: pt > tt > t: septe > *siete.* (3) Reciprocal assimilation: ai > ei > e: carraria > *carraira* > *carreira* > *carrera.*

Cf. Pei., M. A. and Gaynor, F., *A Dictionary of Linguistics,* N. Y., 1954; Lázaro Carreter, F., *Diccionario de términos filológicos,* Madrid, 1953.

Astrée. See under *Montemayor, Jorge de.*

Atalaya de las crónicas. See under *Arcipreste de Talavera.*

Atenea. An Argentine review. See under *Arrieta, Rafael Alberto.*

Ateneo. See under *tertulia.*

Atkinson, William C. (1902). British hispanist and literary scholar. Professor of Spanish, University of Glasgow. Editor of the *Bulletin of Spanish Studies.* Author of *Spain: A Brief History.* Translator of *The Lusiads of Camoens.*

Cf. *Hispania,* XXXVI, 1953.

Atlántida. See under *Andrade.*

Atlas lingüístico. See under *Navarro Tomás, Tomás.*

Auto da barca. See under *Vicente, Gil.*

Auto da Sibila Casandra. See under *Vicente, Gil.*

Auto de los Reyes Magos. The only example of the early Spanish liturgical drama written in the vernacular language. Although originally composed about the middle of the 12th century, the only extant manuscript dates from the 13th century and is still preserved in the *Biblioteca Nacional.* It consists of a fragment of 147 rhymed verses varying in length from six, eight, to twelve syllables. Evidence seems to indicate that it was inspired by a Latin prototype. The fragment relates three episodes of the Nativity: (1) the Magi test the Christ child by noting which of their gifts he will choose; (2) they inform Herod of the birth of the Christ; (3) Herod consults with his astrologers. Here the fragment ends. Although rather primitive in its characterization, the drama is sustained by an aura of clerical dignity.

Cf. Menéndez Pidal, R., (Ed.), "Auto de los Reyes Magos," *Revista de archivos, bibliotecas y museos,* IV; Crawford, J. P. W.,

Spanish Drama Before Lope de Vega, Philadelphia, 1922; Sturdervant, W., *The Misterio de los Reyes Magos,* Baltimore, 1927.

auto sacramental. A one-act religious play dealing with the theme of the Eucharist. *Autos sacramentales* were performed in the public squares of Spanish towns on the afternoon of Corpus Christi Day during the 13th through the 17th centuries. Symbolic and allegorical in character, they comprised religious, mythical and historical subjects. The *auto sacramental* generally ends with a glorification of the Eucharist. Early examples of this type of play are to be found in Rouanet, L., *Colección de autos, farsas y coloquios del siglo XVI* (4 vols., Madrid-Barcelona, 1901). The greatest writer of *autos sacramentales* was Calderón de la Barca (1600-1681).

Cf. Mariscal de Gante, J., *Los autos sacramentales desde sus orígines hasta mediados del siglo XVIII,* Madrid, 1911; Alenda, J., "Catálogo de autos sacramentales, históricos y alegóricos," *Boletín de la Real Academia Española,* 1916; Valbuena Prat, A., "Los autos sacramentales de Calderón, "*Revue hispanique,* LXI, 1924; Parker, A. A., *The Allegorical Drama of Calderon,* Oxford, 1943; Wardropper, B. W., "The search for a dramatic formula for the auto sacramental," *PMLA,* LXV, 1950.

Avellaneda. See *Gómez de Avellaneda; Fernández de Avellaneda.*

Aves sin nido. See under *Matto de Turner.*

Avrett, Robert William (1901). American hispanist, literary scholar, poet and translator. Associate Professor of Romance Languages and Literatures, University of Tennessee, since 1947. Authority on Spanish grammar, Latin American and Spanish literature. Author, articles on González Martínez de la Rosa, Leopoldo Alas, Tirso de Molina, *etc.,* in *Hispania, Romanic Review, etc.,* and of hundreds of books reviews, *Books Abroad, Hispanic American Historical Review, Modern Language Journal, etc.* Editor, *Entre Nosotros,* 1951-1952.

ayacucho. A Quechua dialect. See under *Quechua.*

Ayala (El Canciller). See *López de Ayala, Pero.*

Ayanque, Simón. See *Terralla y Landa.*

Ayguals de Izco, Wenceslao. See under *entrega.*

¡Ay panadera! See under *copla.*

Azorín (1873). The pen name of José Martínez Ruiz, impressionistic critic and novelist, born in Manóvar, Alicante. After studying law at the Universities of Valencia and Madrid, he devoted himself to a literary career. At first a liberal journalist and critic writing under various pseudonyms, his reputation under the name of Azorín was firmly established by 1900. Since then, his stream of literary production has continued unabated, at the rate of one or more works each year. Several times a legislative representative of conservative stamp, he also served as undersecretary of the Ministry of Education. He was elected to the *Academia Española* in 1924. One of the foremost of contemporary Spanish critics, he is noted as a novelist and as an interpreter of the Castilian spirit. As a critic he is extremely impressionistic, his critical canons being essentially those of the Generation of 1898 *(Los valores literarios, Al margen de los clásicos,* etc.). Among his idiosyncrasies are a dislike of the drama, occasional glorification of insignificant writers and rejection of the previous generation on principle. Opposed to the traditional novel as too artificial a genre, Azorín developed a type of essayistic novel devoid of plot and characterization, its sole content being his own impressionistic evocations of the past, of locales, persons, moods and atmosphere *(La voluntad, Antonio Azorín, Las confesiones de un pequeño filósofo,* etc.). Azorín's style is highly subjective, his short sentences lending a staccato swiftness to his prose. His rhetorical questions and repetitions are a deliberate mannerism, not always ingratiating. However, he has the knack of arousing enthusiasm by dint of his remarkable descriptive power, his vivid evaluations of literary figures and trends, and his personal charm and erudition. As an interpreter of the Castilian spirit *(El alma castellana, Castilla)* he has done a great deal to preserve the best traditions of Spanish culture. His chief works are: *El alma castellana,* 1900; *La fuerza del amor,* 1901; *La voluntad,* 1902; *Antonio Azorín,* 1903; *Las confesiones de un pequeño filósofo,* 1904; *Los pueblos,* 1905; *La ruta de Don Quijote,* 1905; *España,* 1909; *Lecturas españolas;* 1912; *Castilla,* 1912; *Clásicos y modernos,* 1913; *Los valores literarios,* 1914; *Al margen de los clásicos,* 1915; *El licenciado Vidriera,* 1915; *Rivas y Larra,* 1916; *El paisaje de España,* 1917; *Fantasías y devaneos,* 1920; *Los dos Luises,* 1921; *Don Juan,* 1922; *De Granada a Castelar,* 1922; *Una hora de España,* 1924; *Doña Inés,* 1925; *Españoles en Paris,* 1939; *Pensando en España,* 1940; *Valencia,* 1941; *Madrid,* 1941; *El escritor,* 1942; *Cavilar y contar,* 1942; *Sintiendo a España,* 1942; *El enfermo,* 1943; *Capricho,* 1943; *María Fontán,* 1944; *Salvadora de Olbena,* 1944; *Paris,* 1945; *Memorias inmemoriales,* 1946; *Con permiso de los cervantistas,* 1948.

Cf. Casares, J., *Crítica profana,* Madrid, 1916; *Henríquez Ureña,* P., "Azorín," *En la orilla: mi España,* Mexico, 1922; Mulerrt, V. W., *Azorín,* Halle, 1926 (trsl. Madrid, 1930); Diéz-Canedo, E., *Azorín: estudio crítico,* Madrid, 1930; Villalonga, L., *Azorín: su obra, su espíritu,* Madrid, 1931; Barja, C., "Azorín," in *Libros y autores contemporáneos,* Madrid, 1935; Essays on Azorín in *Cuadernos de literatura contemporánea,* XVI, XVII, Madrid, 1945.

Azuela, Mariano (1873-1952). Mexican physician and novelist. Studied medicine in Guadalajara. Served as an army doctor during the Mexican Revolution. A resident of Mexico City from 1916 until his death. Awarded the National Prize for Literature in 1949. Azuela is known as the chief literary portrayer of the Mexican Revolution. His greatest novel is *Los de abajo,* based on the brutality and corruption of the 1910 Revolution. It has become a modern classic and has been widely translated. Azuela's two following novels *(Los caciques* and *Las moscas)* are also based on the Revolution. His later works portray the life of the lower classes in Mexico City *(La luziérnaga)* and the social problems of the post-revolutionary period in Mexico *(La nueva burguesía).* In a style of great dramatic and lyrical power, he displays deep compassion for the Indians and the poor white class of Mexico. His humanitarian ardor, however, is tempered by a brooding pessimism regarding the possibility of social melioration. Among his chief works were: *Mala yerba,* 1909; *Los de abajo,* 1915; *Los caciques,* 1917; *Las moscas,* 1918; *La luziérnaga,* 1932; *El camarada Pantoja,* 1937; *San Gabriel de Valdivias,* 1938; *Regina Landa,* 1939; *Avanzada,* 1940; *La nueva burguesía,* 1941.

Cf. Spell, J. R., *Contemporary Spanish-American Fiction,* U. of North Carolina Press, Chapel Hill, N. C., 1944.

Azul. Darío's first book of poetry, published in 1888. See under *Darío.*

B

BAE. See *Biblioteca de Autores Españoles.*

Baena, Juan Alfonso de. See under *cancionero.*

balada. See *romance.*

Balbuena, Bernardo de (1568-1627). Mexican poet of the colonial period. Although born in Spain, he was brought to Mexico as a child. After serving as a minor church functionary, he pursued ecclesiastical studies in Spain, obtaining the degree of doctor of theology at the University of Sigüenza. In 1620 he was appointed Bishop of Puerto Rico. Many of his works were destroyed together with his library when San Juan was attacked by the Dutch in 1625. His chief work was *Bernardo o la victoria de Roncesvalles* (1624), an epic poem of 40,000 verses in octets, based on the legend of Bernardo del Carpio. Balbuena is noted for his narrative style, verbal power and perfection of form, but his work is full of allegorical and other extrinsic digressions. His other important writings were: *La grandeza mexicana* (1604), a lengthy descriptive narrative of Mexico City in the closing years of the 16th century; and, poetically more significant, *El siglo de oro en las selvas de Erífile* (1608), a collection of eclogues.

Cf. Van Horne, John, *Bernardo de Balbuena: Biografía y crítica,* Mexico, 1940.

Balearic. See under *Spanish.*

Balmes, Jaime (1810-1848). See under *Romanticism.*

Balseiro, José Agustín (1900). Authority on modern Spanish literature. Professor, University of Miami, Florida. Studies and honors in Spain and in Spanish America. Author of *Novelistas españoles modernos,* 1933; *Blasco Ibáñez, Unamuno, Valle-Inclán y Baroja: Cuatro individualistas de España,* 1949.

ballad. See *romance.*

Bances Candamo, F. A. See under *Candamo; zarzuela.*

Banchs, Enrique (1888). Argentine poet. Ranked as one of his country's most popular lyricists although his production has been very sparse since 1910. His verse is generally in traditional classic form and his themes are the eternal ones of love, death, beauty and nature. His style, however, shows traces of modernist influence. Among his chief works are: *Las barcas,* 1907; *El libro de los elogios,* 1908; *El cascabel del halcón,* 1909; *Oda a los padres de la patria,* 1910.

Cf. *Poemas selectos,* (Ed. Monterde, F., with introduction), Mexico, 1921.

Bandos de Castilla (Los). See under *López Soler.*

barba. A reference to the actor who played the role of the old man in the classical Spanish theater.

barca. Ship. The word occurs in the titles of Gil Vicente's religious plays; e.g. *Auto da barca do Inferno,* etc. See under *Vicente, Gil.*

Barja, César (1892-1952). Hispanist, literary critic, and professor at the University of Los Angeles, California. Among his many articles and studies is a trilogy of significant critical works on Spanish literature: *Libros y autores clásicos; Libros y autores modernos;* and *Libros y autores contemporáneos* (1922-1935). The last of these, in particular, is a much quoted source in critical studies of modern Spanish literature.

Barlaam y Josafat. An anonymous collection of oriental tales known since the 7th century in Greek, and since the 12th century, in Latin versions, although the first extant Spanish version is that of Juan de Arce (Madrid, 1608). Its influence is evident in Spanish literature as far back as Juan Manuel's (1282-1349?) *Libro de los estados.* The tales have been traced to a Sanscrit source, *Lalita Vistara,* a legendary account of Buddha's youth. They center about Josaphat (Buddha) and his tutor, a hermit named Barlaam. The 7th century Greek version was written by an eastern monk, who imparted ascetic, mystical and Christian overtones to the tales. Thus, after a sensual existence, Josaphat has allegorical encounters with old age, sickness, poverty and death, which, as interpreted by his tutor Barlaam, lead him to conversion to the Christian faith and to an ascetic life. The tales were extremely popular in the Middle Ages because they lent themselves to apologetics and moralizing. We find echoes of them in Boccaccio and in Lessing *(The Tale of the Three Rings),* and in classical

Spanish literature, in Lope de Vega *(Barlaam y Josafat)* and in Calderón *(La vida es sueño).*

Cf. Text ed. by Lauchert, *Romanische Forschungen,* VII, 1893; De Haan, "Barlaam and Josephat in Spain," *Modern Language Notes,* X, 1893; Moldenhauer, G., *Die Legende von Barlaam und Josaphat auf der Iberischen Halbinsel,* Halle, 1929.

Baroja, Pío (1872). After Galdós, the leading Spanish novelist of the 20th century. His full name is Pío Baroja y Nessi. Of Basque descent, he was born in San Sebastián. After studying medicine in Madrid, he practised for two years in the provinces, but then abandoned his medical career to take over the management of a bakery in Madrid. After eight years, the business failed, and Baroja, at the age of thirty, thenceforth devoted himself entirely to literature. An extraordinarily prolific writer, he has published some 100 novels, travel diaries and essay collections since the beginning of his literary career at the turn of the century. In 1936 he was elected a member of the *Academia Española.* The essence of Baroja's novelistic art is action, a restless dynamicism which takes precedence over plot and characterization. This element of incessant action, a picaresque trait, is to be found in every one of his works, whether he writes of the Basque region *(Tierra vasca),* of the lower classes *(La lucha por la vida),* of historical events *(Memorias de un hombre de acción),* of the inner life *(La vida fantástica),* or of the incongruities of modern civilization and ethics *(El árbol de la ciencia).* Like his contemporaries of the Generation of 1898, Baroja is critical of Spanish decadence. He does not believe in free will, or in the meaningfulness of existence, or in the possibility of social melioration. He sees no salvation in art or in religion. His only positive ideals are the intellect and nature. Philosophical speculation and science are to him the only possible roads to truth. Despite his dynamic style, his avidity for experience, and his relentless sincerity, Baroja's extreme pessimism and anarchism can scarcely be interpreted as mature and constructive. His chief works are: "Tierra vasca": *La casa de Aizgorri,* 1900; *El mayorazgo de Labraz,* 1903; *Zalacaín el aventurero,* 1909; "La vida fantástica": *Camino de perfección,* 1902; *Aventuras, inventos y mixtificaciones de Silvestre Paradox,* 1901; *Paradox, Rey,* 1906; "La lucha por la vida": *La busca,* 1904; *Mala hierba,* 1904; *Aurora roja,* 1904; "Memorias de un hombre de acción": *La ruta del aventurero,* 1916; *La nave de los locos,* 1925; "La raza": *La dama errante,* 1908; *La ciudad de la niebla,* 1909; *El árbol de la ciencia,* 1911; "Las ciudades": *El mundo es ansí,* 1912; *La sensualidad pervertida,* 1920; "Memorias": *Desde la última vuelta del camino: El escritor según los críticos,* 1944 et seq.

Cf. Peseux-Richard, H., "Un romancier espagnol: Pío Baroja," *Revue hispanique,* XXIII, 1910; Ortega y Gasset, J., "Ideas sobre Pío Baroja," *El espectador,* I, 1916; Pina, F., *Pío Baroja,* Valencia, 1928; Barja, C., *Libros y autores contemporáneos,* Madrid, 1935; Helmut, D., *Pío Baroja: Das Weltbild in seinen Werken,* Hagen, 1937; Pérez Ferrero, M., *Pío Baroja en su rincón,* Santiago de Chile, 1938; "Homenaje a Baroja," *Indice de artes y letras,* Año 9, núms. 70-71, Madrid, 1954.

baroque. See *barroco.*

Barraca. See under *Blasco Ibáñez.*

Barrios, Eduardo (1884). Chilean novelist and short-story writer. Attended the national military school in Valparaiso. Rejecting a military career, he led a checkered existence as merchant, bookkeeper, agent, rubber dealer and prospector in various South American countries before settling in Santiago. One time Minister of Education and Director of the National Library. Influenced by Zola and Bourget, Barrios devoted himself to the writing of psychological sketches and novels. He is not so much concerned with plot and action as he is with the delineation of his characters' minds and souls. In addition to his extraordinary power of psychological analysis and the creation of highly subjective, complex and even neurotic characters, he is noted for the subtle musical quality of his style. Among his chief works are: *Del natural,* 1907; *El niño que enloqueció de amor,* 1915; *Un perdido,* 1917; *El hermano asno,* 1922; *Páginas de un pobre diablo,* 1923; *Y la vida sigue,* 1925.

Cf. Spell, J. R., *Contemporary Spanish-American Fiction,* University of North Carolina Press, Chapel Hill, N. C., 1944.

barroco. (Eng. *baroque).* The predominance of the ornamental over the substantial in architecture, art, literature, and culture in general. In literature, the excessive preoccupation with form and stylistic details (language, figures of speech, allusions, etc.) to the detriment of content and readability. The baroque period in Spanish literature is the 17th century. The chief writers representative of the baroque style and spirit were: Góngora, in poetry; Calderón, in the drama; Gracián, the picaresque novels and novelists, in prose; and Quevedo, in several of these media. Spanish baroque literature is characterized by *conceptismo* and *culteranismo*. It is a literature of affectation, preciosity, exaggerated effects and violent contrasts. For all that, it was a true expression of its age and opened new avenues of expression to literature. See also under *conceptismo; culteranismo;* and under the respective authors mentioned above.

Cf. Díaz-Plaja, G., *El espíritu del barroco,* Barcelona, 1940; Del Río, A., "El barroco y la decadencia," *Historia de la literatura española,* Vol. I, N. Y., 1948.

Bastardo Mudarra (El). A play written in 1612 by Lope de Vega. It deals with a theme from the medieval legend of the *Infantes de Lara.* See under *Infantes de Lara.*

Bataillon, Marcel (1895). French Hispanist and literary scholar. Professor at the *Institut de France.* Author of innumerable studies and monographs, and contributor to Hispanic journals. Editor of *Bulletin Hispanique.* His specialties include humanism, mysticism and the picaresque novel. Among the Spanish writers whose works he has translated is Unamuno. His best known works are: *Le roman picaresque,* Paris, 1931; and *Erasme et l'Espagne,* Paris, 1937.

Batilo. The pastoral name adopted by Meléndez Valdés as a member of the *Parnaso salmantino.* See under *Escuela de Salamanca; Meléndez Valdés.*

Bécquer, Gustavo Adolfo (1836-1870). One of the greatest Spanish lyric poets of the 19th century. Born in Seville; died in Madrid. He was christened Gustavo Adolfo Domínguez Bastida, but later adopted his father's name of Bécquer. Orphaned at the age of ten, he was brought up by his godmother. In 1854, at the age of 18, he came to Madrid, hoping to achieve fame as a poet, but after struggling along as a journalist and translator, he was obliged to take a minor government post as censor (1864-1868). Burdened with poverty and disease, the hapless victim of an ill-fated love affair (with Julia Espín, the muse of his *Rimas)* and an unhappy marriage (1861) that ended in separation (1868), Bécquer was destined to an early, tragic end. He died of consumption at the age of 34. His greatness as a poet was not appreciated during his lifetime, most of his poems having appeared in periodicals (*El contemporáneo, El museo universal, La ilustración de Madrid,* etc.). The first collected edition of his works did not appear until 1871. Although influenced by the romanticists (Heine, Byron, Lamartine, De Musset), Bécquer's poetry cannot be classified as entirely romantic. Certainly his style lacks rhetorical abandon, a typical romantic trait. His language also is simple and restrained, emotion being transmitted through a kind of lyrical understatement. His themes, however, are decidedly romantic: frustration, melancholy, a yearning for the ideal and the infinite. He is essentially a poet of inner vision:

De la luz que entra el alma por los ojos,
los párpados velaban el reflejo,
mas otra luz el mundo de visiones
alumbrada por dentro.

Because of his abstractness Bécquer has been compared to Shelley and the German romanticists. However, his use of assonance rather than rhyme and his occasional metrical crudities, together with the simplicity of his language, are in the tradition of the Spanish *copla* rather than that of European romanticism. Also typically Spanish is his use of the dramatic reversal or paradox:

—Yo soy un sueño, un imposible
vano fantasma de niebla y luz;
soy incorpórea, soy intangible;
no puedo amarte.—¡Oh, ven; ven tú!

His *Rimas* (1860-1861), from which the above selections are taken, tell a tragic love story in about 80 short lyrics, undoubtedly the best of his poetic work. His best prose is seen in his *Leyendas* (1860-1864), romantic legends in the style of Hoffmann and Poe. Bécquer's stature as a poet has grown with the perspective of time, and his work has exercised a decisive influence on many modern poets (Darío, Ramón, Diego, Alberti, and others).

Cf. *Obras completas, Madrid,* 1934; López Núñez, J., *Bécquer: biografía anecdótica,* Madrid, 1915; Marroquín y Aguirre, P., *Bécquer, el poeta del amor y del dolor,* Madrid, 1927; Alonso, D., *Ensayos sobre poesía española,* Buenos Aires, 1944; Guillén, J.,

"La poética de Bécquer," *Revista Hispánica Moderna,* VIII, 1942.

Bédier, Joseph. See under *cantar de gesta.*

Béeche, Don Gregorio. See under *Arrieta, Rafael Alberto.*

Belardo. The key name of Lope de Vega in his pastoral novel, *Arcadia* (1598). See under *Vega, Lope de.*

Belarmino y Apolonio. See under *Pérez de Ayala.*

Belisa. See under *Vega, Lope de.*

Bell, Aubrey P. G. (1881-1950). British Hispanist. A specialist in both Spanish and Portuguese literature, particularly during the Renaissance. He was the author of *Studies in Portuguese Literature,* Oxford, 1922; and editor of the *Oxford Book of Portuguese Verse,* Oxford, 1925. His biographies of Spanish writers include *Gil Vicente,* Oxford, 1921; and *Luis de León: A Study of the Spanish Renaissance,* Oxford, 1925. His general works on Spanish literature are: *Contemporary Spanish Literature,* N. Y., 1925; and *Castilian Literature,* Oxford, 1938.

Bello, Andrés (1781-1865). Venezuelan philologist and poet. Born in Caracas; died in Santiago de Chile. He received a humanistic education, reading widely in the Latin, Greek and Spanish classics. During an extended sojourn in London (1810-1829), he continued his studies. At the invitation of the government he went to Chile in 1829. There he became Minister of Foreign Affairs, reorganized the educational system and was appointed the first president of the University of Chile. He also published a complete codification of Chilean law. The author of specialized treatises on Spanish verb tenses, orthology, and metrics, his greatest contribution to Hispanic philology was the *Gramática castellana* (1847), which, supplemented by the notes of Rufino José Cuervo (1844-1911), is still the standard work on the subject. Although an opponent of romanticism, as shown in his celebrated polemic against Sarmiento, Bello wrote excellent translations of Byron and Hugo; and his own poetry *(Silva a la agricultura de la zona tórrida,* 1826) has a great deal of romantic idealism, especially in the cause of freedom.

Cf. *Obras completas,* Santiago de Chile, 1881-1893; Amunátegui, M. L., *Vida de Don Andrés Bello,* Santiago de Chile, 1882; Castro, A., "En torno a la edición de la gramática de Bello," *Revista Nacional de Cultura,* Caracas, 1954; Torre, G. de, "Andrés Bello y la unidad del idioma," *Revista Nacional de Cultura,* Caracas, 1954.

Bello troyano. See under *Pérez de Hita.*

Benavente, Jacinto (1866-1954). Spain's foremost contemporary dramatist. Born and died in Madrid. His full name was Jacinto Benavente Martínez. The only son of a successful pediatrician, Dr. Mariano Benavente, he was educated at the San Isidro Institute and then began, but did not complete, the study of law at the University of Madrid. After a tour of Europe with a circus, he turned to acting, acquiring a practical knowledge of stagecraft and remaining an occasional actor for a good part of his career. Beginning with his first play in 1894 *(El nido ajeno),* he produced over 150 plays and was still actively writing at the age of 87, shortly before his death. Honors came to him early in his career. He was elected a member of the *Real Academia Española* in 1913, became director of the *Teatro Español* in 1920, and was awarded the Nobel Prize for Literature in 1922. In 1923 he toured the United States and South America with his own theatrical company. In addition to turning out a steady stream of plays, he also found time to write literary and political essays, to engage in politics, to edit a literary journal *(La vida literaria)* and to found a children's theater *(Teatro de los niños),* for which he wrote many delightful plays. Benavente's works are classified into (1) social satires *(Gente conocida);* (2) psychological dramas *(Señora ama);* (3) children's plays *(El príncipe que todo lo aprendió en los libros);* and (4) allegorical and morality plays *(Los intereses creados).* His most successful dramas are those in which he satirizes the aristocracy and upper middle classes of Madrid, their false standards, their worship of wealth and worldly status, and their social hypocrisy. This mocking, sceptical attitude, projected through sophisticated dialogue and with dramaturgical finesse, is most characteristic of Benavente and earned him the title of "the Bernard Shaw of Spain". Unlike Shaw, however, Benavente preaches no positive social message. He is content with exposing social folly and injustice without proposing any solutions, for his philosophy was essentially pessimistic. A note of ironic resignation emerges from the subtle allegory of his masterpiece in the conventionalized style of the *commedia dell'arte (Los intereses creados),* the thesis of which affirms the necessity of evil. Among his chief works were: *El nido ajeno,* 1894; *Gente conocida,* 1896; *Lo cursi,* 1901; *Los intereses creados,* 1907; *Señora ama,* 1908; *Por las nubes,* 1909; *La malquerida,* 1913; *La ciudad alegre y confiada,* 1916; *El príncipe que todo lo aprendió en los libros,* 1919; *Lecciones de buen amor,* 1924; *La mariposa que voló sobre el mar,* 1926; *Vidas cruzadas,* 1931; *La novia de nieve,* 1934; *Aves y pájaros,* 1940; *La infanzona,* 1946.

Cf. *Obras completas,* Madrid, 1940 *et seq.;* Onís, F. de, *Jacinto Benavente: estudio literario,* N. Y., 1923; Pérez de Ayala, R., *Las máscaras,* I, Madrid, 1924; Starkie, W., *Jacinto Benavente,* Oxford, 1924; Lázaro, A., *Jacinto Benavente: de su vida y de su obra,* Madrid, 1935; Córdoba, S., *Benavente desde le conocí,* Madrid, 1954; Estevan, I. S., *Jacinto Benavente y su teatro,* Barcelona, 1954.

Berceo, Gonzalo de (1195?-1265?). The earliest known poet in Spanish literature and the first representative of the *mester de clerecía* school. The exact dates of his birth and death are not known. He was probably born in the closing years of the 12th century, became a priest in the Benedictine monastery of San Millán de la Cogolla, situated in the community of Rioja, and, according to church records, was still living in 1264. His works were all written in *cuaderna vía.* The period of his major literary production was about 1230-1260. Berceo wrote three lives of saints, three poems about the Virgin Mary, three religious poems, and three hymns. His models were Latin *exempla* by medieval clerical writers. Outstanding among his saints' lives is his vivid account of the *Vida de Santo Domingo de Silos.* The best of his Virgin Mary poems is a collection of 25 tales entitled *Milagros de Nuestra Señora.* Also memorable is the descriptive power of his religious poem, *De los signos que aperecerán ante del juicio.* His other great religious poem is *El sacrificio de la misa.* Berceo wrote in an intimate, personal style, interspersing his narratives with simple humor and realistic, homely detail which accentuate his at times almost mystical reverence. Although not a great poet, his realistic treatment of the supernatural and projection of his own personality have struck a responsive chord in many modern Spanish poets, among them Darío, Machado, and Azorín.

Cf. Menéndez y Pelayo, M., *Antología de poetas líricos castellanos,* Madrid, 2nd ed., 1944; Fitzgerald, J. D., (Ed.), *Berceo:*

Vida de Santo Domingo de Silos, Paris, 1904; Solalinde, A. G., (Ed.), *Berceo: Milagros de Nuestra Señora,* Madrid, 1922; Goode, T. C., *El sacrificio de la misa: A Study of its Symbolism and of its Sources,* Washington, 1933; Trend, J. B., *Berceo,* Cambridge, 1952.

Bermúdez de Castro, Salvador. See under *octava italiana.*

Bernardo del Carpio. Hero and epic of the *cantares de gesta,* known only through prose versions in the chronicles of the 12th and 13th centuries. Bernardo is the only epic hero of Spain who cannot be identified with any historical character, thus leading to the assumption that his historic prototype existed in France rather than in Spain. Evidence seems to indicate that there were two different *cantares* about Bernardo, one French in spirit, and one Spanish. In the 12th century chronicles, Lucas de Tuy follows the French version, whereas Rodrigo de Toledo follows the Spanish version. The *Crónica general* attempts a fusion of these two versions, but is not entirely successful. In the French version, Bernardo is related to Charlemagne, while in the Spanish version he is the son of Jimena, sister of Alfonso II el Casto, and of the Conde Saldaña. The King, indignant at Bernardo's parents, separates the family, forcing the mother into a convent and the father into a dungeon, while Bernardo is reared at the court, ignorant of his parentage. He discovers his identity, and after heroic feats in the service of Alfonso II, and a period of rebellion against Alfonso III, he gains the freedom and custody of his father, who is delivered to him dead. The Spanish version thus assumes a nationalistic aspect, for Bernardo appears as a rebel against a weak and perfidious king. As in the case of other epic heroes, cycles developed around the figure of Bernardo del Carpio. Of the many subsequent treatments, the best known are those by Juan de la Cueva (1543-1610), Bernardo de Balbuena (1568-1627), and Lope de Vega (1562-1635). See also under *Balbuena, Bernardo de.*

Cf. Bédier, J., *Les légendes épiques,* Paris, 1908-1913; Menéndez Pidal, R., *Historia y epopeya,* Madrid, 1934.

Bernardo o la victoria de Roncesvalles. See under *Balbuena, Bernardo de.*

Bernhard de Clairvaux. See under *mysticism.*

Bibl. hisp. (Abbr. of *Bibliotheca hispanica).* See under *Foulché-Delbosc.*

Biblia políglota complutense. See under *Jiménez de Cisneros.*

Biblioteca "Andrés Bello". See under *Blanco-Fombona.*

Biblioteca Arábico-Hispana. See under *Ribera, Julián.*

Biblioteca de Autores Españoles (Abbr. *BAE*). A critical text collection of 71 volumes, published in Madrid from 1846 to 1880, under the editorship of Manuel Rivadeneyra (1805-1872). It is one of the monuments of Spanish scholarship in the 19th century. The *BAE* contains the greater part of Spanish literature up to about the middle of the 19th century, Manuel José Quintana (1772-1857) being the last author represented. Reflecting the state of literary scholarship in its day, it lacks the discoveries and reorientations of subsequent research. As a result, there are some omissions and some of the texts and prefaces are now outmoded. It is being continued at the present time by the *Nueva Biblioteca de Autores Españoles (NBAE)*, whose first editor was Menéndez y Pelayo. Since 1905 some 26 volumes of the *NBAE* have been published.

Biblioteca de las tradiciones populares. See under *Machado y Álvarez, Antonio; folklore.*

Biblioteca Nacional. The National Library of Spain, located in Madrid and containing over one million volumes. It was founded in 1712 by Philip V and was originally known as the *Biblioteca Real.* Juan Ferreras was its first chief librarian. The roster of directors, librarians and others associated with the *Biblioteca Nacional* in one capacity or another contains many illustrious names from Spanish literature, among them: Juan de Iriarte (1702-1771), García de la Huerta (1734-1787), T. A. Sánchez (1723-1802), L. F. de Moratín (1760-1828), J. E. Hartzenbusch (1806-1880), García Gutiérrez (1813-1884), and Menéndez y Pelayo (1856-1912). Among the valuable collections of the *Biblioteca Nacional* are over 2,500 incunabulae, over 25,000 rare books (*i.e.* only extant copy), and some 24,000 original manuscripts.

Cf. Ponce de León, E., *Guía del Lector en la Biblioteca Nacional,* Madrid, 1942.

Biblioteca Real. See *Biblioteca Nacional.*

Biblioteca Rivadeneyra. The same as *Biblioteca de Autores Españoles;* so-called after the name of the editor, Manuel Rivadeneyra (1805-1872). See *Biblioteca de Autores Españoles.*

Biblioteca selecta de clásicos españoles. See under *Real Academia Española.*

Bibliotheca hispanica. (Abbr. *Bibl. hisp.*). See under *Foulché-Delbosc.*

bigardo. A licentious friar or cleric. See under *pícaro.*

Bishop Golias. The imaginary personage to whom the *goliardo* poets attributed their work. See under *goliardo.*

bizantina. See *novela bizantina.*

Bizarrerías de Belisa. See under *Vega, Lope de.*

Blaine, James G. See under *Pan American Union.*

Blanco-Fombona, Rufino (1874-1944). Venezuelan literary historian and critic. As a political exile, he spent most of his life in Europe and did not return to Venezuela until 1935. The most prolific writer of his generation, he produced poems, short stories, novels, and literary essays. As the founder and editor of various publishing enterprises (Biblioteca "Andrés Bello," Editorial América), he performed a tremendous service to South American literature in disseminating the works of American authors. His poems and short stories have considerable literary merit but he is best known for his literary criticism. Although highly subjective, his *El modernismo* and *Diario de mi vida* are standard source books of the modernist movement and its writers. In politics he stood for a continuation of the Spanish cultural heritage in South America, and was opposed to the political influence of the United States. Among his chief works were: *Pequeña Opera lírica,* 1904; *Cuentos americanos,* 1904; *El hombre de hierro,* 1907; *Letras y letrados de Hispanoamérica,* 1908; *Cuentos de la prisión y del destierro,* 1911; *La evolución política y social de Hispanoamérica,* 1911; *La lámpara de Aladino,* 1915; *El hombre de oro,* 1915; *Cancionero del amor infeliz,* 1917; *Grandes escritores de América,* 1919; *El conquistador español del siglo XVI,* 1921; *El modernismo y los poetas modernistas,* 1929; *Camino de imperfección, diario de mi vida (1906-1913),* 1929.

Cf. Goldberg, I., *Studies in South American Literature,* N. Y., 1920; Picón-Salas, M., *Formación y proceso de la literatura venezolana,* Caracas, 1940; Carmona Nenclares, F., *Rufino Blanco-Fombona, Su vida y su obra,* Caracas, 1944.

Blanco White, José María. See under *Escuela sevillana.*

Blasco Ibáñez, Vicente (1867-1928). Novelist, journalist and politician. Born in Valencia; died in Mentone, France. As a youth of 16 he left home and found employment as the secretary of Manuel Fernández y González, a writer of historical novels and romantic thrillers. This experience, together with anti-royalist political activities which included the founding of a radical journal *(El pueblo)*, street brawls, duels and romantic love affairs, rounds out the first phase of his eventful career. He served seven times as a deputy of Valencia in the Cortes, but his radical activities repeatedly brought him imprisonment and exile. In 1909 he left Spain for the Argentine and Paraguay, where he achieved success as a lecturer; but certain agricultural enterprises in which he engaged resulted in failure. In 1914 he returned to Europe and became an active propagandist for the Allied cause. His last years were spent in a villa on the *Côte d'Azur,* living in comfortable circumstances on his book and film royalties. He continued his anti-royalist propaganda to the very end. The works of Blasco Ibáñez fall into three groups: (a) regional novels of Valencia; (b) social novels of Spain; and (c) South American and European novels. The first group presents Valencian types, customs and backgrounds with Zolaesque naturalistic detail *(Arroz y Tartana, La barraca,* etc.). The second group comprises novels of social protest, expressing anti-clerical ideas *(La catedral, El intruso,* etc.). The documentary style of early naturalistic socialism is particularly prominent in *La horda* (1905), dealing with the proletariat of Madrid. The third group represents a broadening of perspective, the scene of *Los argonautos* (1914) being Argentina, and that of *Los cuatro jinetes del Apocalipsis* (1916), the Europe of World War I. Blasco Ibáñez's style is frequently hurried and crude, but always virile. He was a master at creating dramatic suspense. His descriptions frequently rise above mere naturalism to heights of epic grandeur. The far too prolific output of his latter phase has tended to obscure the real genius he displayed at the period of his greatest artistry (1894-1902), when he produced his Valencian novels and short stories. Among his chief works were: *Arroz y Tartana,* 1894; *Flor de Mayo,* 1895; *Cuentos valencianos,* 1896; *La barraca,* 1898; *Entre naranjos,* 1900; *Cañas y barro,* 1902; *La catedral,* 1903; *El intruso,* 1904; *La bodega,* 1905; *La horda,* 1905; *Sangre y arena,* 1908; *Los muertos mandan,*

1909; *Los argonautos,* 1914; *Los cuatros jinetes del Apocalipsis,* 1916; *Mare nostrum,* 1917; *Los enemigos de la mujer,* 1919; *La tierra de todos,* 1922; *El paraíso de las mujeres,* 1922; *La vuelta al mundo de un novelista,* 1924; *El papa del mar,* 1926.

Cf. González-Blanco, A., *Historia de la novela en España,* Madrid, 1909; Zamacois, E., *Vicente Blasco Ibáñez,* Madrid, 1910; Pitollet, C., *Blasco Ibáñez: ses romans et le roman de sa vie,* Paris, 1922; Martínez de la Riva, R., *Vicente Blasco Ibáñez,* Madrid, 1929; Blasco Ibáñez, V., *Obras completas,* 3 vols., Madrid, 1947.

Blest Gana, Alberto (1830-1920). Chilean novelist, mathematician and statesman. Blest Gana served as Chile's ambassador to France and to England. He lived in Paris at the end of his career. Influenced by Balzac, he depicted the lives of people from all strata of the society of Santiago, seen against the background of its historical development, from the days of independence to the beginning of the 20th century. Blest Gana initiated the documentary social novel in Spanish American letters. In 1860 he was awarded a literary prize for his novel, *La aritmética en el amor.* Among his chief works were: *El jefe de la familia,* 1858; *La aritmética en el amor,* 1860; *Martín Rivas,* 1862; *Durante la reconquista,* 1897; *Los trasplantados,* 1905.

Cf. "Alone" (Hernán Díez Arrieta), *Don Alberto Blest Gana: biografía y crítica,* Chile, 1940.

bobo. The fool, simpleton or "booby". A stock character in Spanish comedies of the 16th and 17th centuries. A type in the *pasos* of Lope de Rueda. A clown or Merry Andrew.

Bocados de oro. See under *folklore.*

Bocanegra, Simón. See under *García Gutiérrez.*

Bocángel, Gabriel (1608?-1658?). See under *gongorism.*

Bodega (La). See under *Blasco Ibáñez.*

Bodet. See *Torres Bodet, Jaime.*

Boggs, Ralph Steele (1901). Hispanist and folklorist. Professor of Spanish, University of North Carolina, 1929-1950. Director, Hispanic American Institute, University of Miami, Florida, since 1950. Author of *Spanish folktales,* N. Y., 1932; *Outline History of Spanish Literature,* 1937 (in Spanish, Montevideo, Uruguay, 1945); *Bibliography of Latin American Folklore,* N. Y., 1940;

Tentative Dictionary of Medieval Spanish (in collaboration), Chapel Hill, North Carolina, 1946.

Böhl de Faber, Cecilia. See *Fernán Caballero.*

Böhl von Faber, Johann Nikolaus (1770-1863). German hispanist and folklorist. The father of Fernán Caballero (Cecilia Böhl de Faber, 1796-1877). Editor of collections of old Spanish poetry and pre-Lope de Vega drama. Translator of Schlegel's *Über dramatische Kunst und Literatur,* 1808 *(Reflexiones de Schlegel sobre el teatro,* 1814), which gave rise to the Calderonian controversy in the early days of the Spanish romantic movement. See also under *Schlegel; Fernán Caballero; folklore.*

Cf. Del Río, A., *Historia de la literatura española,* N. Y., 1948.

Bola de nieve (La). See under *Tamayo y Baus.*

Boletín de la Real Academia Española. (Abbr. *BolReAc;* or *BRAE).* See under *Real Academia Española.*

Boletín folklórico español. See under *folklore.*

Bolinger, Dwight LeMerton (1907). American hispanist and linguistic scientist. Professor, University of Southern California, since 1944. Author of many articles on Spanish linguistics, in *Hispania, Language, P.M.L.A., American Scholar, Word, etc.*

Bolívar, Simón (1783-1830). The Liberator of Venezuela was also a gifted prose writer. A keen political analyst, his letters, essays and speeches belong to the great political documents of Venezuelan literature. The most famous of his addresses is *Discurso en el Congreso de Angostura* (1819), in which he outlines a model constitution. The *Discurso* is a masterpiece of forensic eloquence and political sagacity.

Cf. Blanco-Fombona, R. (ed.), *Símón Bolívar: Discursos y proclamas,* Paris, 1933.

boliviano. A Quechua dialect. See under *Quechua.*

BolReAc. Abbr of *Boletín de la Real Academia Española.* See under *Real Academia Española.*

Bonilla y San Martín, Adolfo (1875-1926). Literary scholar, philosopher, editor, lecturer and writer. Born and died in Madrid. One of the most famous pupils of Menéndez y Pelayo, he was Professor of Law at Valencia and Professor of Philosophy at Madrid. His scholarship was extensive and profound, including such fields as the theory of law, political science, esthetics, history and philosophy. Outstanding among his philosophical works were:

Luis Vives y la filisofía del Renacimiento (1903); and *Historia de la filisofía española* (1908-1911). Among his best known literary studies were: *Don Quijote y el pensamiento español* (1905); *Las teorías estéticas de Cervantes* (1916); and *Las leyendas de Wagner en la literatura española* (1913). The most important of his many critical editions are: *Libros de caballerías* (1907-1908); and *Obras completas de Cervantes* (1914-1941), in collaboration with Rudolph Schevill, late Professor at the University of California.

Cf. Romera-Navarro, M., *Historia de la literatura española,* 2a. ed., Boston, 1949.

bordón. See under *seguidilla.*

Borges, Jorge Luis (1899). Argentine poet and essayist. Born in Buenos Aires. Lived in Geneva, Switzerland, during World War I. A member of the ultraist group in Spain (1918), he brought its theories to Buenos Aires (1921). Like other ultraist writers, Borges, as a rule, eschews description and narration in favor of imagery and metaphor. Despite the cryptic aspect of his writing, he displays true creative talent. His latter works are highly original literary and philosophic essays. Among his chief works are: *Fervor de Buenos Aires,* 1923; *Luna de enfrente,* 1925; *Inquisiciones,* 1925; *Cuaderno San Martín,* 1929; *Ficciones,* 1941; *El Aleph,* 1949; *Otras Inquisiciones (1937-1952),* 1952.

Cf. Noé, Julio, *Antología de la poesía argentina moderna,* Buenos Aires, 1932; Revol, E. L., "Aproximación a la obra de Jorge Luis Borges," *Cuadernos,* Paris, 1954.

Boscán, Juan (1493?-1542). Catalan lyric poet of the Renaissance. Full name, Juan Boscán Almogáver. Born and died in Barcelona. Of an aristocratic family, he was attached to the court of Charles V and became tutor to the Duke of Alba. In a famous letter to the Duquesa de Soma, Boscán recorded a conversation with the Venetian ambassador, Andrea Navagero, whom he met in Granada in 1526: "*. . . me dixo por qué no probaba en lengua castellana sonetos y otras artes de trovas usadas por los buenos autores de Italia; . . .*" The results of this conversation were of vast significance in the development of Spanish poetry, for Boscán introduced into Spanish literature the Italian *octava real,* octets in hendecasyllabic lines, which became the metrical form of all Spanish epic poets of the Renaissance. He also made the sonnet *(soneto)* and the *terza rima (tercetos)* into standard Spanish verse forms. His poems were published in 1543 together with those of his more gifted friend and collaborator, Garcilaso de la Vega. The author of some 40 *coplas* and over 90 *sonetos,* Boscán was a mediocre poet, more noted as the initiator of metrical reform than as a creative lyricist in his own right. However, he was an excellent prose stylist, as is shown in his admirable translation of Castiglione's *Courtier (El Cortesano,* Barcelona, 1534).

Cf. Works in *BAE,* XXXV and XLII; Knapp, W. I., (Ed.), *Las obras de Juan Boscán,* Madrid, 1875; Menéndez y Pelayo, M., *Antología de poetas líricos,* Vol. XIII, Madrid, 1919; Riquer, M. de, *Juan Boscán y su cancionero barcelonés,* Barcelona, 1945.

Bradomín, Marqués de. See under *Valle-Inclán.*

BRAE. Abbr. of *Boletín de la Real Academia Española.* See under *Real Academia Española.*

Bretón de los Herreros, Manuel (1796-1873). Satirical dramatist. A volunteer at the age of 15, he served in a clerical capacity in various army offices. Educated in Madrid, he participated in the literary and social life of the capital, frequenting fashionable salons and contributing to literary journals. In 1824 he attained success as a dramatist with his satire, *A la vejez viruelas.* From then until about 1860 he produced some 387 works, of which 175 were plays. He became a member of the *Academia Española* in 1837 and director of the *Biblioteca Nacional* in 1847. Although a poet, translator (Schiller, Racine, Voltaire) and adapter of classical plays (Lope de Vega, Calderón), he is best known for his satirical comedies, for the most part, composed in verse. Inspired by Moratín, he shunned the romantic vogue of his day except for one comedy *(Elena)* and some historical plays *(Don Fernando el Emplazado,* etc.). His subjects were the customs and types of middle-class Madrid society, satirizing the foibles of dotards, women, romanticists and foreign imitators. However, his satire was gentle and without malice, his chief purpose being to edify through entertainment. His most famous plays were *Marcela, o ¿Cuál de los tres?,* a sprightly comedy of an independent widow who sanely rejects three marriage prospects; *Muérete y verás,* showing the practical and unromantic side of a girl who, believing her lover dead, does not hesitate to choose another; and *La escuela del matrimonio,* which preaches the necessity of compatibility in age, social status and education for successful marriage. His chief works were: *A la vejez viruelas,* 1824; *A Madrid me vuelvo,* 1828; *Marcela, o ¿Cuál de los tres?,* 1831; *Elena,* 1834; *Todo se pasa en este mundo,* 1835; *Don Fernando el Emplazado,* 1837; *Muérete y verás,* 1837; *Ella es él,* 1838; *Vellido Dolfos,* 1839; *El pelo de la dehesa,* 1840; *La escuela del matrimonio,* 1852; *El abogado de pobres,* 1866.

Cf. *Obras de Bretón de los Herreros,* Madrid, 5 vols., 1883-1884; Molíns, M. de, *Bretón de los Herreros: recuerdos de su vida y de sus obras,* Madrid, 1883; Le Gentil, G., *Le poète Manuel Bretón de los Herreros et la société espagnole de 1830 à 1860,* Paris, 1909.

Brevíssima relación. See under *Casas, Bartolomé de las.*

Brocense (El). The Latinized name of Francisco Sánchez de las Brozas (1523-1601). See under *humanism.*

Bruerton, Courtney (1890). American hispanist. Various teaching posts at Dartmouth, Tufts, Simmons, Wellesley, Harvard. Lecturer in Spanish, Brown University, 1941-1951. Co-author of *The Chronology of the Comedias of Lope de Vega,* N. Y., 1940. Articles in *Hispania, Hispanic Review, Nueva Revista de Filología Hispánica, Modern Philology.*

Bulletin Hispanique. (Abbr. *Bull. Hisp.).* The quarterly journal of French hispanists. Among its founders was Alfred Morel-Fatio. Now edited by Marcel Bataillon. Published in Bordeaux. It contains articles and reviews on all the hispanic languages and literatures. See also under *Morel-Fatio; Bataillon.*

Bulletin of Hispanic Studies. A scholarly review founded in 1923 by E. Allison Peers. Published by the University Press of Liverpool, England. Editor: Albert E. Sloman, University of Liverpool.

Burlador de Sevilla (El). See under *Tirso de Molina.*

burlería. A yarn or fairy tale; a tall story.

Buscón (El). See under *Quevedo.*

Bustamante, Calixto (mid-18th century). Peruvian writer about whom little is known. His full name is Calixto Bustamante Carlos Inga, alias Concolorcorvo. Presumably the author of *El lazarillo de ciegos caminantes desde Buenos Aires hasta Lima* (1773), a realistic and satirical commentary on contemporary manners and customs, based on the travel diary of one, Alonso Carrión de la Bandera. The work is considered a classical example of the early travel narrative and represents an embryo stage in the development of the South American novel.

Cf. Moses, B., *Spanish Colonial Literature in South America, 1810-1824,* N. Y., 1922.

C

caballeresco. See under *romance: romances of chivalry.*
caballería. See under *romances of chivalry.*
Caballero Cifar (El). The oldest original Spanish romance of chivalry. It was written between 1299 and 1305. The author is unknown, although evidence indicates that he was a cleric. The first printed edition bears the date 1512 and the ornate title, *Historia del Caballero de Dios que avia por nombre Çifar, el qual por sus virtuosas obras et hazañosas cosas fue rey de Menton.* The work is a medley containing adaptations of a saint's life (Eustacius), popular tales, *exempla,* adventures of knight errantry, miraculous occurrences, etc. The knight errantry of Cifar, of his sons, Garfín and Roboan, and the episode of the Lady of the Lake, are conceived in the spirit of the Arthurian legends. The *Cifar* resembles the Milesian tale of late Greek literature in its varied content and rambling plot. El Ribaldo, Roboan's peasant squire, is a kind of forerunner of Sancho Panza. He is the outstanding character in the book, introducing the note of picaresque realism and self-mockery typical of the romances of chivalry.

Cf. *El libro del Caballero Zifar,* (Ed.) Wagner, C. P., Ann Arbor, Michigan, 1929; Wagner, C. P., "The Sources of 'El Caballero Cifar'", *Revue hispanique,* X, 1903; Menéndez y Pelayo, M., *Orígines de la novela,* Buenos Aires, 1946.

Caballero del cisne (El). See under *Gran conquista de ultramar; López Soler.*
"Caballero del milagro." See under *Rojas Villandrando.*
Caballero de Olmedo. See under *Vega, Lope de.*
Cabeza del Bautista. See under *Valle-Inclán.*
Cabeza de Vaca. See *Núñez Cabeza de Vaca.*
"cabo roto" verse. Verse with "broken" or incomplete end rhyme.

A famous example occurs in Cervantes' introduction to *Don Quijote.*

Cacharrería. See under *Palacio Valdés.*

Caciques (Los). See under *Azuela, Mariano.*

caciquismo. (Eng. *bossism*). A system of semi-feudal authority exercized by influential members of the aristocracy, landowners, church officials and political leaders, whereby administrative, military, clerical and educational posts are allocated according to birth or on the basis of political patronage. *Caciquismo* was given as one of the reasons for Spain's decadence, and hence was attacked by writers of the Generation of 1898; in particular by Joaquín Costa, in his *Oligarquía y caciquismo* (1901-1902). See under *Costa y Martínez.*

Cada cual con su razón. See under *Zorrilla y Moral.*

Cadalso, José (1741-1782). Anacreontic poet, dramatist, and prose elegist. Born in Cádiz; died in Gibraltar. His full name was José Cadalso y Vásquez de Andrade. Educated as a nobleman, widely traveled, a soldier and patriot, Cadalso was one of the most colorful figures of his time. He was characterized by Cejador y Frauca in his monumental history of Spanish literature as the man who wrote in classical style but lived a romantic life. A frequenter of various literary *tertulias* in Madrid and in Salamanca, he associated with many writers, among them, Ayala, Iriarte, and N. F. de Moratín. His romantic love for the celebrated actress, María Ignacia Ibáñez, who died quite young, inspired his prose elegy, *Noches lúgubres* (1798), suggested by Young's *Night Thoughts* (1742). The work is significant in that it reveals Cadalso as a precursor of romanticism. It inaugurated the trend toward sepulchral melancholy that became one of the hallmarks of romantic literature. Cadalso's most popular work was *Los eruditos a la violeta* (1772), a prose satire directed against sciolists, literary flops and poetasters. Among Cadalso's other writings are the verses of his youthful period, *Ocios de mi juventud* (1773), significant for its revival of anacreontic verse, echoes of which are to be found in other writers of the Salamancan group (Jovellanos, Valdés, *etc.*). His one extant attempt at classical tragedy, *Sancho García* (1771), was unsuccessful. Of especial interest to modern comparative literature is his *Cartas marruecas* (1789), in the style of Montesquieu's *Lettres persanes*

(1721). Using the device of an exchange of correspondence between two Moors, one of whom is traveling in Spain, Cadalso reveals himself as a penetrating critic of Spanish society and culture.

Cf. *Obras,* 3 vols., Madrid, 1821; "Cartas marruecas," *BAE,* XIII, and also ed. by Tamayo, J., Madrid, 1935; "Poesías de Cadalso," *BAE,* LXI; Mulertt, W., *Die Stellung der "Marrokanischen Briefe" innerhalb der Aufklärungsliteratur,* Halle, 1937; Cotton, E., "Cadalso and his Foreign Sources," *Liverpool Studies in Spanish Literature,* Liverpool, 1940.

Calavera, Ferrán Sánchez de. See under *decir.*

Calderón de la Barca, Pedro (1600-1681). With Lope de Vega, Tirso de Molina and Ruiz de Alarcón, one of the four great dramatic luminaries of the Golden Age. Born and died in Madrid. His full name was Pedro Calderón de la Barca Henao de la Barrera y Riaño. His family belonged to the lower aristocracy of La Montaña, in northern Castile, and his father was connected with the royal court in Madrid as an employee of the treasury. Calderón was educated at the Jesuit *Colegio Imperial* in Madrid, pursued ecclesiastical studies at Alcalá (1614), and studied canon law at Salamanca until 1620, shortly before his debut as a poet (1622). After a period of military service in Milan and Flanders (1623-1624), he settled in Madrid, where from 1625 to 1637 he devoted himself to playwriting and produced most of the comedies for which he is famous. The peak of his career was reached in 1635, when he was chosen to furnish the inaugural musical play at the opening of the royal palace *Buen Retiro,* with its fabulous theatrical installations. The play was *El mayor encanto, amor,* the first of his many *zarzuelas.* From 1640 to 1641 Calderón served with distinction in the Catalan War. He retired from active service in 1642, devoting the rest of his life to playwriting. After a series of personal reverses, including the death of his brother and of his sweetheart, he entered the church and was ordained a priest in 1651. From this time on he wrote only religious plays and mythological plays for the court. Toward the end of his career (1663) he was appointed Chaplain of Honor to the King, and thereafter lived in semi-religious retirement.

Calderón wrote 120 comedies, 80 *autos sacramentales* and some 20 minor compositions. His chief themes were love and honor, patriotism, religion and philosophy. The best of his tragedies dealing with honor is *El alcalde de Zalamea,* which reflects his disillusioning experiences of the Catalan War, and which is his best play of characterization. Others of this type, dealing with *puntillo* or *pundonor,* are *El médico de su honra* and *A secreto agravio secreta venganza.* He also excelled in the *comedia de capa y espada,* the comedy of intrigue, love and honor, first popularized by Lope de Vega and perfected by Calderón. Among his plays of this type are *La dama duende, Casa con dos puertas mala es de guardar,* and *Guárdete del agua mansa.* The greatest of his patriotic plays is *El príncipe constante,* which glorifies monarchy in the person of a 15th century prince, Fernando of Portugal, who gave his life for country and church. Calderón's best religious play is *El mágico prodigioso,* based on the legend of Saint Cyprian of Antioch (4th century), whose pact with the Devil is reminiscent of the Faust theme. His religious plays also include some 20 *autos sacramentales,* most of which he produced for the municipality of Madrid for public performance on Corpus Christi Day. His imaginative use of allegory and his lyrical power raise the *auto* to its highest level in his *La cena del rey Baltasar, El gran teatro del mundo, El divino Orfeo,* etc. Calderón's supreme masterpiece is his allegorical and philosophical drama, *La vida es sueño* (1635). Through its symbolic character Segismundo it explores the mysteries of human destiny, the illusory nature of mundane existence, and the conflict between predestination and free will. Calderón's solutions are essentially religious, to wit, that good works and mastery of the baser instincts will lead to salvation in the hereafter.

Calderón's style is extremely uneven, ranging from passages of great lyrical simplicity and beauty to the involved and overburdened rhetoric of gongoristic writing. He is frequently given to bizarre metaphors and artificially imposed symbolism. At his worst he revels in metaphysical conceits, lush imagery and sophisticated affectation. But at his best he is sublime, inspired, subtle, profound and, above all, natural. These odd and intemperate contrasts have led to the current view of Calderón as the Baroque dramatist par excellence, after periods of over and underestimation by critics of the 18th and 19th centuries (Schlegel–Menéndez y Pelayo). Among his chief works were: *Saber del mal y del bien,*

1628; *El príncipe constante,* 1629; *La dama duende,* 1629; *Casa con dos puertas mala es de guardar,* 1629; *Mañanas de abril y mayo,* 1632; *La devoción de la cruz,* 1633; *La cena de Baltasar,* 1634; *La vida es sueño,* 1635; *El médico de su honra,* 1635; *A secreto agravio secreta venganza,* 1635; *El mayor encanto, amor,* 1635; *El mágico prodigioso,* 1637; *El mayor monstruo los zelos,* 1637; *El alcalde de Zalamea,* 1642; *Guárdete del agua mansa,* 1649; *La hija del aire,* 1653; *El golfo de las sirenas,* 1657; *La púrpura de la rosa,* 1660; *El hijo del sol,* 1661; *Faetón,* 1661; *Eco y Narciso,* 1661; *El monstruo de los jardines,* 1667; *La estatua de Prometeo,* 1669.

Cf. Texts: *BAE,* VII, IX, XII, XIV; *La vida es sueño,* (Ed.) Buchanan, M. A., Toronto, 1909; *El alcalde de Zalamea,* (Ed.) Farnel, I., Manchester, 1921; *Autos sacramentales,* (Ed.) Valbuena Prat, A., 2 vols., Madrid, 1926-1927; *Comedias religiosas,* (Ed.) Valbuena Prat, A., Madrid, 1930; *Obras completas,* 2 vols., Madrid, 1932-1947. Criticism: Menéndez y Pelayo, M., *Calderón y su teatro,* Madrid, 1881; Cotarelo y Mori, E., *Ensayo sobre la vida y obras de don Pedro Calderón de la Barca,* Madrid, 1924 (Repr. from *Boletín de la Real Academia,* VIII, IX, X); Valbuena Prat, A., *Calderón, su personalidad, su arte dramático, su estilo y sus obras,* Madrid, 1941; Parker, A. A., *The Allegorical Dramas of Calderón,* Oxford, 1943.

Calila y Dimna. An anonymous collection of oriental fables translated from the Arabic into Castilian at the behest of Alfonso X, under the title of *Libro de Kalila et Digna* (1251). The earliest example of Spanish prose fiction, it contains many animal fables. The title derives from the chief protagonists, two lynxes, whose philosophical colloquy provides the frame of the book. In the usual manner of the animal apologue, it contains satirical comment regarding humans and their illogical behavior. The origin of the fables has been traced back through Latin, Greek and Hebrew sources to the Sanskrit *Panchatantra.*

Cf. *BAE,* LI; (Ed.) Allen, C. G., Macon, 1906; (Ed.) Alemany y Bolufer, J., Madrid, 1915; Penzol, P., *Las traducciones del "Calila e Dimna,"* Madrid, 1931.

Calisto y Melibea. See under *Celestina.*

Cambacèrés, Eugenio (1843-1888). Argentine novelist. Influenced by Zola, Cambacèrés employed the naturalistic technique in his novels which depicted the seamy side of Argentine urban society. The mushroom growth of Buenos Aires in the 80's led to social dislocations, financial speculation, exploitation, crime and prostitution. Despite great opposition, Cambacérès persisted in his naturalistic exposés of these conditions.

Cf. Torres Ríoseco, A., *La novela en la América hispana,* Berkeley, U. of Cal. Press, 1939.

Camino de perfección. See under *Teresa de Jesús.*

Camino, León Felipe. See *Felipe, León.*

Campo, Estanislao del (1834-1880). Argentine soldier, political journalist and poet. One of the foremost representatives of gaucho poetry. Following the example of his master, Ascasubi (pseud. *Aniceto el Gallo*), Campo chose the pseudonym, *Anastasio el Pollo.* He is chiefly known as the author of *Fausto* (1866), a long poetic dialogue in six episodes, relating a gaucho's impressions of a performance of Gounod's *Faust* at the Teatro Colón in Buenos Aires. Despite the artificial situation, Campo's poem is a masterpiece of "poesía gauchesca" because of its language and its sustained metrical form.

Cf. Page, F. M., "Fausto, A Gaucho Poem," *Publications of the Modern Language Association,* XI, 1896; Tiscornia, E. F., *Poetas gauchescos,* Buenos Aires, 1940.

Campoamor, Ramón de (1817-1901). Poet and epigrammatist. Born in Navia, Asturias; died in Madrid. His full name was Ramón María de los Mercedes de Campoamor y Campoosorio. He abandoned his early plan of studying for the priesthood and took up medicine; but he dropped his medical studies at the University of Madrid, took courses in law and then devoted himself to literature and politics. He was Governor of Alicante (1854) and of Valencia (1856). After a belated but brilliant literary career, he became a member of the *Academia Española* in 1861. Campoamor was an important figure in the late 19th century anti-romantic reaction. He represents a kind of middle-class sobriety and rationalism, faintly ironic, but also sentimental and didactic. Although he wrote dramas and philosophical treatises, what little fame he still possesses today is due to his shorter poems. In his *Poética* (1883) he rejected romantic emotion and form in favor of *"el arte por la idea."* He claimed to have invented new poetic forms, the *dolora* (from his *Fábulas morales y doloras,* 1846), and the *humorada* (collected subsequently in his *Humoradas,* 1886). The *humorada* is a rhymed couplet or quatrain. Despite his pretensions, the form is indistinguishable from the epigram. The *dolora* is a concise poem dramatizing a universal truth and characterized by delicacy, pathos and a moral message expressed through irony. His most famous poem of this type was *¡Quién supiera escribir!,* a ballad-like dialogue in three parts in which an illiterate peasant girl vainly attempts to dictate to a learned but obtuse cleric a letter addressed to her far-off lover. *Las dos espejos* and *Verdad de las tradiciones* are other famous examples of the type of philosophizing irony that made Campoamor famous in his day. His longer philosophical poems (*El alma en pena, Colón, El licenciado Torralba, El drama universal,* etc.) are now read only by scholars.

Cf. *Obras completas,* 8 vols., Madrid, 1901-1903; González Blanco, A., *Campoamor: biografía y estudio crítico,* Madrid, 1912; Hilton, R., *Campoamor, Spain, and the World,* Toronto, 1940.

Campos de Castilla. See under *Machado y Ruiz, Antonio.*

Camprubi, Zenobia. See under *Jiménez, Juan Ramón.*

Canción de cuna. See under *Martínez Sierra, Gregorio.*

cancionero. An anthology of songs and lyric poetry of a particular epoch, school, or of a single poet. The earliest known *cancioneros* are in the Gallego-Portuguese dialect and date from the 13th century. The oldest is the collection of King Dennis of Portugal (1259-1325), entitled *El Canzioneiro de Ajuda,* which contains poetry and songs influenced by the Provençal troubadour school. Of a more indigenous type are the *Canzioneiro portuguez da Vaticana* and the *Canzioniere portoghese Colocci-Brancuti,* both containing specimens from Gallego-Portuguese poets of the 13th and 14th centuries. In these are to be found art-versions of Galician folksongs, including the three distinct types known as *cantiga de amigo* (amatory), *cantiga de ledino* (joyous), and *cantiga de escarnio* (satirical). The earliest Castilian anthologies of this type are the *Cancionero de Baena* (1445) and the *Cancionero de Stúñiga,* the former containing courtly, the latter, popular lyrics. The largest and most important Castilian anthology is the *Cancionero General* (Valencia, 1511), compiled by Hernando del Castillo and containing almost 1,000 poems by over 100 poets who flourished during the reigns of Juan II and Henry IV. The types of poetry represented are love lyrics, ballads, didactic, religious and satirical poems. A famous Portuguese imitation of Castillo's collection was the *Cancionero General de Resende* (Lisbon, 1516). The metrical form of the early *cancioneros* is chiefly *arte mayor*. Examples of *cancioneros* containing the verse of a single poet are those of Jorge Manrique and Juan del Encina.

Cf. *Canzioneiro gallego-castelhano,* (Ed.) Lang, H. R., 1902; *Canzioneiro da Ajuda,* (Ed.) Vasconcellos, C. C. M. de, Halle, 1904; *Canzioneiro portuguez da Vaticana,* (Ed.) Braga, T., Lisbon, 1878; *Canzioniere portoghese Colocci-Brancuti,* (Ed.) Molteni, E. G., Halle, 1880; *Cancionero de Baena,* (Ed.) Pidal, P. J., Madrid, 1851; *Cancionero general de Hernando del Castillo,* (Ed.) Balenchana, J. A., Madrid, 1882; "Cancionero castillano del siglo xv," (Ed.) Foulché-Delbosc, R., *NBAE,* XIX, XXII, 1912-1915; Menéndez y Pelayo, M., *Antología de poetas líricos castellanos,* Madrid, 1890-1916; Menéndez Pidal, R., *Poesía juglaresca y juglares,* Madrid, 1924.

Cancionero sin año. See under *romance.*

Candamo, F. A. (1661?-1704). Outstanding librettist of the 17th century musical play. His full name was Francisco Antonio de Bances Candamo. See under *zarzuela.*

Canfield, Delos Lincoln (1903). American hispanist. Authority on Latin American literature and linguistics. At the University of Rochester, with minor interruptions, since 1927; Professor of Spanish and Head of Department of Foreign Languages, since 1954. Other teaching posts at Columbia University, University of Guatemala, Florida State University. Author of *Spanish Literature in Mexican Languages as a Source for the Study of Spanish Pronunciation,* N. Y., 1934. Many articles on Latin American pronunciation in *The Spanish Review, Hispania, Modern Language Journal,* etc.

cantar. A short lyric of popular origin. As a literary form, usually in verses of *arte menor,* it was revived by some romantic poets (*e.g.* Rosalía de Castro, *Cantares gallegos,* 1863) and is still encountered in modern poets (*e.g.* Manuel Machado, *Los cantares,* 1907).

cantar de gesta. The early Spanish poetic epic or *chanson de geste.* Of anonymous origin, the earliest *cantares* were probably composed as far back as the 10th or 11th century, judging from historical and internal evidence of prose versions in the *crónicas.*

The *cantares de gesta* show Greek *(Iliad)*, Latin *(Aeneid)*, Germanic *(Hildebrandslied)*, French *(Roncesvalles)*, and Moorish *(Crónica de Abenalcotía)* influences. As a result, a vast body of scholarship has sprung up regarding their origin. The chief scholars and their theories are: Menéndez Pidal (Germanic), Bédier (Classical), Paris (French), Ribera (Moorish). As an argument for the theory of Germanic origin is the fact that the earliest examples of the *cantar de gesta* were composed in verses of varying length *(versificación irregular)* and with assonance rather than rhyme, both features of the Germanic epic. This was unlike the metrical uniformity of later versions which show signs of clerical and learned adaptation in their use of the alexandrine in its Spanish form, *cuaderna vía*, i.e. four-line, single-rhymed stanzas of 14-syllable verses. The subject of the *cantares de gesta* was the exploits *(gesta)* of historical or legendary heroes: Rodrigo el Godo, Bernardo del Carpio, Fernán González, Los infantes de Salas, El Cid, Rodrigo Díaz, *et al.* The *cantares* provided a fertile source for subsequent ballads, epics, novels and dramas throughout the history of Spanish literature.

Cf. Menéndez Pidal, R., *L'Épopée castillane à travers la littérature espagnole*, Paris, 1910; *idem, Historia y epopeya*, Madrid, 1934; *idem, Poesía juglaresca y juglares*, Madrid, 1924; Bédier, J., *Les Légendes épiques*, Paris, 1908-1913; Morf, H., *Aus Dichtung und Sprache der Romanen*, Strassburg, 1903; Paris, G., *Poèmes et légendes du moyen âge*, Paris, 1900; Ribera, J., *Discurso de ingreso en la Academia de la Historia*, Madrid, 1915. For further bibliography see under the various *cantares* or under the names of the epic heroes.

Cantar de gesta de Don Sancho II. See *Cantar de Zamora.*

Cantar del Cerco de Zamora. See *Cantar de Zamora.*

Cantar del romero. See under *Zorrilla y Moral.*

Cantar de Mío Cid. The great medieval Spanish epic, of which the original manuscript has been lost, but which is preserved in a single copy of some 3,730 lines *(Poema del Cid)*, written in 1307 and signed by one, Per Abbat (Pero Abad), of whom nothing is known. The first page (lines 1-49) and two interior pages of the codex are missing. An unknown Castilian *juglar* (minstrel) is supposed to have written the original in about 1140. The reconstructed epic (done by Menéndez Pidal), is based on prose versions in the *crónicas,* comparison of other Cid poems, references to the Cid in other epics, historical sources, *etc.*, and is called the *Cantar de Mío Cid,* as distinguished from the *Poema del Cid.* The latter circulated in the 14th and 15th centuries but was not published until 1779 (Ed. by Tomás Antonio Sánchez, in *Colección de poesías castellanas anteriores al siglo xv).* The plot of the *Poema del Cid* is divided into three parts: (a) the banishment of Rodrigo Díaz (El Cid) by his sovereign, King Alfonso; (b) the Cid's victory over the Moors at Valencia, reconciliation with his sovereign, and the marriage of his daughters, Doña Elvira and Doña Sol to the Infantes de Carrión; and (c) the cruel treatment and desertion of his daughters and the trial by combat of his former sons-in-law, resulting in the vindication of the Cid's honor. The meter of the *Poema del Cid* is irregular, comprising alexandrines (14-syllable lines with middle caesura), *versos de romance* or ballad meter (16-syllable lines with middle caesura and stress at or near the end of each half-line), and irregular long and short lines. The oldest monument of Castilian literature, the *Poema del Cid* is admirable for its realism, its comparative historical fidelity, its fusion of disparate Cid themes into a unified whole, and for the spirit of Christianity and nationalism which pervades it. See also under *Cid* and *cantar de gesta.*

Cf. *Cantar de Mío Cid,* (Ed.) Menéndez Pidal, R., 3 vols., Madrid, 1906-1911; *Poema de Mío Cid, idem,* Madrid, 1913; *La España del Cid, idem,* 2 vols., Madrid, 1929; Lang, H. R., "Contributions to the Restoration of the 'Poema del Cid,'" *Revue hispanique,* LXVI; *idem,* "Notes on the Metre of the Poem of the Cid," *Romanic Review,* V; Rose, R. S., and Bacon, L., *The Lay of the Cid,* Berkeley, 1919.

Cantar de Rodrigo. See under *Rodrigo el godo; Cid.*

Cantar de Roncesvalles. See under *Roncesvalles.*

Cantar de Zamora (*ca.* 12th century). A medieval epic known only from the prose version of its plot in the *Primera crónica general* (1270 *et seq.*). The title derives from the siege of Zamora, a climactic episode of the epic, and hence it is often referred to as the *(Cantar del) Cerco de Zamora.* A reconstruction of the Zamora epic was done by Puyol y Alonso under the title of *Cantar de gesta de Don Sancho II de Castilla* (1911). The historical fact upon which the epic is based is the war of succession caused by the division of the kingdom of Fernando I (1035-1065) among his children. The heroes are Diego Ordóñez, vassal of King Sancho II of Castile, and Arias Gonzalo, vassal of King Alfonso of León. Sancho lays siege to Zamora but is treacherously slain by a Zamoran noble, Bellido Dolfos, who had gained the victim's confidence by pretending to be a deserter. Diego Ordóñez avenges his lord's murder in a trial by combat against the sons of Arias Gonzalo. The new ruler is Alfonso VI, who attempts to unite the Castilian and Leonese factions. Because the Cid figures in this epic, it is sometimes considered a part of the Cid cycle, but some scholars hold that the appearance of the Cid is a later interpolation.

Cf. Puyol y Alonso, J., "Cantar de gesta de Don Sancho II de Castilla," *Archivo de investigaciones históricas,* I, 1911; Menéndez Pidal, R., *Historia y epopeya,* Madrid, 1934; Reig, C., *El cantar de Sancho II y el cerco de Zamora,* Madrid, 1947.

cantarcillos de amores. See under *Encina, Juan del.*

Cantares gallegos. See under *Castro, Rosalía de.*

cantica de serrana. A pastoral lyric dealing with shepherdesses or cowgirls *(serranas).* See under *serranilla.*

Cántico. See under *Guillén, Jorge.*

Cántico espiritual. See under *Cruz, San Juan de la.*

cantiga. A type of song or lyric first used by Gallego-Portuguese poets of the 13th century. Among the earliest specimens are those found in the various *cancioneros* of the 13th and 14th centuries. The antecedents of the *cantiga* are to be found in *Provençal* poetry and in popular Galician songs, adapted by court poets for their lyrics. Until about the 16th century, even Castilian poets used the Galician dialect in their *cantigas,* since it was the conventional medium of expression for lyric poetry. The *cantigas* are generally classified into three or four groups, based on their themes: (1) *cantiga de amor* (a lyric in which a lover bemoans his unrequited love); (2) *cantiga de amigo* (a lyric in which a girl pines for her lover); (3) *cantiga de escarnio or maldecir* (a lyric of scurrilous satire, often obscene). There is also the *cantiga de ledino* (so called from its cheerful tone). The Middle Ages also produced the religious *cantiga,* of which Alfonso el Sabio's *Cantigas de Santa María* is a famous example.

Cf. Menéndez y Pelayo, M., *Antología de poetas líricos caste-*

llanos, 2nd ed., Madrid, 1944; Menéndez Pidal, R., *La primitiva lírica española,* Madrid, 1919; *Poesía juglaresca y juglares,* 2nd ed., Buenos Aires, 1945; Bell, A. F. G., "The 'Cantigas de Santa María' of Alfonso X," *Modern Language Review,* X, 1915; Alonso, D., *Poesía de la edad media,* 2nd ed., Buenos Aires, 1942; Le Gentil, P., *La poésie lyrique espagnole et portuguaise à la fin du moyen âge,* Rennes, 1949. See also *cancionero.*

Cantigas de Santa María. See under *Alfonso X.*

Cantos del trovador. See under *Zorilla y Moral.*

Cantos de vida y esperanza. See under *Darío.*

Cantos populares españoles. See under *folklore.*

capa y espada. "Cloak and sword." Designation for a type of comedy of elaborate intrigue, popularized by Lope de Vega (1562-1635) and brought to its highest level of perfection by Calderón (1600-1681). The term is derived from the typical street costume worn by the noblemen of Lope de Vega's era. The *comedia de capa y espada* deals with characters of the upper middle classes and of the aristocracy. It reflects their hypersensitive preoccupation with matters of honor *(pundonor),* their gallantry, elegance, and their taste for adventure. The plots are exceedingly complex, involving multiple *qui pro quo* confusion, disguises, amatory adventures, duels, etc. The chief dramatic motives are love and honor. They have happy endings, with reunions of estranged lovers, family reconciliations and, frequently, dual or triple weddings.

Cf. Schevill, R., *The Dramatic Art of Lope de Vega,* Berkeley, 1918; Menéndez y Pelayo, M., *Estudios sobre el teatro de Lope de Vega,* 1919-1927; Menéndez y Pelayo, M., *Calderón y su teatro,* Madrid, 1881; Valbuena Prat, A., *Calderón,* Barcelona, 1941.

Cárcel de amor. See under *San Pedro, Diego de.*

Carlos V. See under *Sandoval, Prudencio de.*

Carmen latino. See under *Cid.*

Caro, José Eusebio (1817-1853). Colombian poet, journalist and politician. Left school in Bogotá to become a journalist. Editor of *El granadino,* a political journal (1837). Elected to the Colombian legislature (1841). A political exile in the United States (1849-1853). Influenced by Byron, he became an outstanding figure of the South American romantic period. His poems deal with the themes of civil liberty, freedom of conscience and moral heroism.

His metrical style was of some influence on the modernists of the following century.

Cf. Beltrán, O. A., *Manual de historia de la literatura hispanoamericana,* Buenos Aires, 1938.

Carolingian Cycle. See under *Roncesvalles.*

Carrillo y Sotomayor, Luis de (1583?-1610). Soldier, classical scholar and poet. Born in Córdoba. He was the son of a councillor of Philip III. Educated at the University of Salamanca. While at the court in Naples, he frequented literary circles and read the poetry of Marino. Among his prose works are translations of Seneca and Ovid. He also wrote a *Fábula de Acis y Galatea,* which is supposed to have had some influence on Góngora. Carrillo was the chief theoretician of *culteranismo.* He expounded his literary doctrines in his *Libro de la erudición poética,* which circulated in manuscript in 1607 and was published in 1611. According to Carrillo, the poet must be erudite and must address himself only to the learned. The Spanish language should be "improved" by making it conform to Latin. Obscure allusions and profound subtlety should render the poem difficult to comprehend except for the highly-cultured élite. Clarity of expression should be considered a weakness. The application of these theories is seen in his own cryptic poems, posthumously published by his brother Alonso in 1611-1613.

Cf. García Soriano, J., "Carrillo y los orígines del culteranismo," *Boletín de la Real Academia Española,* XIII, 1926; *Poesías,* (Ed.) Alonso, D., Madrid, 1936; *Libro de la erudición poética,* (Ed.) Cardenal Iracheta, M., Madrid, 1946.

Carrión de la Bandera. See under *Bustamante.*

carro. The "chariot" or wagon carrying scenery and props and serving as a mobile stage for the presentation of *autos sacramentales.*

Cartas del pobrecito hablador. See under *Larra, Mariano José de.*

Cartas de relación. See under *Cortés, Hernán.*

Cartas eruditas y curiosas. See under *Feijóo y Montenegro.*

Cartas españolas. See under *Mesonero Romanos.*

Cartas marruecas. See under *Cadalso.*

Carvajal, Micael de. See under *Danza de la muerte.*

Casa Hispánica. See under *Hispanic Institute.*

Casal, Julián del (1863-1893). Cuban poet. A forerunner of the *modernista* movement. Influenced by Baudelaire and the Parnassian poets. A friend of Rubén Darío. A collection of Casal's verse appeared in 1916, edited by Blanco-Fombona. A chronic invalid, Casal frequently takes a morbid view of life. His moods run the gamut from a sincere though exotic lyricism to *fin-de-siècle* alienation and irony. Among his chief works were: *Hojas al viento,* 1890; *Nieve, bocetos antiguos,* 1892; *Bustos y rimas,* 1893.

Cf. Nunn, M., "Julián del Casal, First Modernista Poet," *Hispania,* XXIII, 1940; Monner Sans, J. M., *Julián del Casal y el modernismo hispanoamericano,* Mexico, 1952.

Casamiento de Laucha. See under *Payró, Roberto J.*

Casamiento engañoso (El). See under *Cervantes.*

Casares, Julio (1877). Literary critic and lexicographer. Secretary of the *Real Academia Española.* Principal works: *Crítica profana; Cosas del lenguaje; Crítica efímera; Diccionario inglés-español y español-inglés; Diccionario ideológico de la lengua española.*

Cf. *Hispania,* XXXVI, 1953.

Casas, Bartolomé de las (1475-1566). Church dignitary, humanitarian and historian. Born in Seville, Spain, he went to Santo Domingo in 1502. Revolted at the treatment of the natives by the Spaniards, he joined the Dominican order and assumed the task of protector of the Indians. His proselytizing and humanitarian efforts on their behalf earned him the name of "Apostle of the Indies." He attained the status of Bishop of Chiapa. His outstanding project was the founding of a plantation cultivated by converted Indians under a system of self rule. As a historian, "El Padre Las Casas" wrote a *Historia de las Indias* and a sequel, *Historia apologética de las Indias.* However, he is chiefly known for his *Brevíssima relación de la destruyción de las Indias* (1552), an accusation of Spanish brutality against the Indians. Dedicated to Emperor Charles V, the work led to an investigation by a royal commission which refuted the charges. Nevertheless, the work became a fertile source for anti-imperialist agitation.

Cf. Brion, M., *Bartolomé de las Casas,* N. Y., 1929; Ortiz, F., "La 'leyenda negra' contra Fray Bartolomé," *Cuadernos Americanos,* XI, 1952; Hanke, L., *Bartolomé de las Casas, Historian,* U. of Florida Press, 1952.

Castelar, Emilio. See under *krausismo.*

Castellano. See under *Spanish.*

Castellano, Juan Rodríguez (1900). Hispanist, literary scholar and editor. Born in Spain; naturalized U. S. citizen, 1934. Various teaching posts at Middlebury College, Vanderbilt University, Peabody College, Ohio State University. Associate Professor, Duke University, since 1947. Author, *Brief History of Spain,* N. Y., 1939; *En busca de oro negro,* N. Y., 1945; *Estampas sudamericanas,* N. Y., 1950. Annotated editions, Casona's *La dama del alba,* N. Y., 1947; and *Los árboles mueren de pie,* N. Y., 1953. Articles on Alejandro Casona, Cervantes, modern Spanish theater, Antonio Buero Vallejo, in *Hispania.*

casticismo. (From Sp. *castizo,* of good origin or race; pure-bred). In general, purity of style in language, customs and manners. In particular, purity of language; *i.e.* without admixture of foreign terms or idioms.

Castiglione. See under *Garcilaso de la Vega.*

Castigos e documentos. See under *Disciplina clericalis.*

Castilian. See under *Spanish.*

Castillejo, Cristóbal de (1490?-1550). Renaissance poet. Born in Ciudad Rodrigo; died in Vienna. He served at the court of Charles V as a page to the King's brother, Archduke Ferdinand. After becoming a priest, Castillejo again entered Fernando's service and was appointed to a benefice in Ardegge. In 1539 he resigned and went to Venice, where he was employed by the Spanish ambassador, Diego Hurtado de Mendoza. Later, in the service of his former patron, now King Ferdinand of Austria, he went to Vienna. Here his last years were marred by ill-fortune and ill health. His grave is in Wiener-Neustadt. Castillejo's collected works were not published until 1573. He championed traditional Spanish verse forms, the *villancico* and *romance,* against the vogue of Italian forms. His polemic verses in this traditionalist cause were entitled *Contra los que dejan los metros castellanos y siguen los italianos* (ca. 1540). His satire did not keep him from inserting a few Italian sonnets in the poem, merely to show that his objection was not due to lack of ability. He also gained some notoriety as a writer of erotic verse (*Sermón de amores,* 1542). In *Diálogo de mujeres* (1544), he resurrected a favorite medieval theme, the virtues and (chiefly) vices of women. One of the best of his occasional lyrics, in *romance* form, begins with the lines,

"Tiempo es ya, Castillejo," and is a melancholy plaint expressing his desire to retire from a world full of vanity. This note of worldly disillusionment is most strident in his satire, *Diálogo y discurso de la vida de corte*. Despite his disappointment in love, his poverty, his lack of preferment and his poor health, Castillejo's satire is not entirely devoid of humor.

Cf. *Poesías* in *BAE*, XXXII; *Obras*, (Ed.) Domínguez Bordona, J., Madrid, 1926; Nicolay, C. L., *The Life and Works of Cristóbal de Castillejo*, Philadelphia, 1910; Menéndez Pidal, J., "Datos para la biografía de Castillejo," *Boletín de la Real Academia Española*, II, 1915.

Castillo, Hernando del. See under *cancionero*.

Castillo interior (El). See under *Teresa de Jesús*.

Castillo Solórzano, Alonso de (1584-1648). Picaresque novelist. Little is known of his life except that his father was in the service of the Duke of Alva, and he himself in the service of various Spanish noblemen. His literary career began in 1619 in Madrid. He wrote many series of short stories in the style of the *Decameron*, several novels, *entremeses*, and a number of plays. However, he is chiefly remembered for his picaresque novels which were very popular in Spain and widely imitated by French writers. His novels were distinguished for their simplicity of style and for their evocation of an era through the narration of the adventurous existence of certain unsavory characters of 17th century Madrid and Seville. *Las Harpías de Madrid y coche de las estafas* (1631), for example, is the story of four female rogues who practise their frauds behind a false front of social ostentation. His other famous novels were *La niña de los embustes, Teresa del Manzanares* (1632), *Las aventuras del bachiller Trapaza* (1637), and a sequel, *La garduña de Sevilla y anzuelo de bolsas* (1642).

Cf. *Obras*, (Ed.) Cotarelo y Mori, E., Madrid, 1906-1909; *La garduña de Sevilla*, (Ed.) Ruiz Morcuende, F., Madrid, 1922; García Gómez, S., "Boccaccio y Castillo Solórzano," *Revista de filología española*, XV, 1928; Chandler, F. W., *The Picaresque Novel in Spain*, N. Y., 1899.

Castro, Américo (1885). Literary historian and critic; romance philologist; editor, professor and lecturer. Of Spanish parentage, he was born in Cantagallo, Brazil. He studied in Germany, France and Spain, where he was a pupil of Menéndez Pidal and Giner de los Ríos. He has occupied teaching and professorial posts at the *Centro de Estudios Históricos* and at the Universities of Madrid, La Plata, Santiago de Chile, Mexico, Columbia and Princeton. E. L. Ford Prof. of Spanish, Princeton U., 1940; Prof. Emeritus, 1953. An indefatigable hispanist, he has contributed to the chief philological journals in the field (Cf. "Lo hispánico y el erasmismo," *Revista de Filología Española,* II, 1940; IV, 1942); and has produced many critical editions of the Spanish classics (Lope de Vega, Rojas Zorrilla, Tirso de Molina, Quevedo, Zamora, *etc.*) His more extensive works on Spanish language and literature are: *Vida de Lope de Vega* (1919); *La enseñanza del español en España* (1922); *El nuevo Diccionario de la Academia Española* (1925); *El pensamiento de Cervantes* (1925); *Don Juan en la literatura española* (1924); *Santa Teresa y otros ensayos,* (1929); *Antonio de Guevara* (1945); and others.

Cf. Del Río, A., *Historia de la literatura española,* N. Y., 1948.

Castro, Guillén de (1569-1631). Outstanding dramatist of the Lope de Vega school. Born in Valencia; died in Madrid. His full name was Guillén de Castro y Bellvís. Of aristocratic descent, he occupied various civil and military posts, among them that of captain of cavalry in the service of Valencia. His interest in literature led him to join the Valencian *Academia de los Nocturnos* (1591-1594), and later, when it had ceased to function, he revived it under the name of *Montañeses del Parnaso* (1616). He was a friend, admirer and imitator of Lope de Vega, to whom he dedicated the first volume of his plays (1618). A second volume of his plays appeared in 1625. These volumes included historical plays, plays of the *capa y espada* type, plays of chivalry, classical and mythological plays *(Los amores de Dido y Eneas)* and religious plays, some fifty in all. Castro's importance in Spanish literature derives from the fact that he was the first to dramatize the Cid legend, using ballad material as his sources. In his *Las mocedades del Cid* (1618) he does not utilize the full range of the Cid epic but concentrates on the character of Jimena, the Cid's wife, who is a prey to conflicting emotions of love and honor. The theme was later exploited by Corneille (*Le Cid,* 1636). Castro again used a theme from the Cid epic in his *Las hazañas del Cid* (1618), which deals with Rodrigo, the siege of Zamora, and other adventures of the Cid. Castro's *El conde Alarcos* also uses epic material from ballad sources. Among his other plays are two interesting dramatizations of episodes from Cervantes' masterpieces *(Don Quijote de la Mancha* and *El curioso impertinente).* Castro's drama is extremely uneven in plot and characterization, the former marked by extreme intricacy and abrupt transitions, the latter by violent temperament. The sole dramatic motivation of his heroes is honor, exaggerated to the point where it must inevitably lead to catastrophe. Nevertheless he was one of the most successful imitators of Lope de Vega and the foremost dramatist of the Valencian school.

Cf. *Obras, BAE* XLIII; Mérimée, H., "Pour la biographie de Don Guillén de Castro," *Revue des langues romanes,* L; Green, O. H., "New Documents for the Bibliography of Guillén de Castro," *Revue hispanique,* LXXXI; Ruggieri, J., "Le 'Cid' de Corneille et 'Las Mocedades' de Guillén de Castro," *Archivum Romanicum,* XIV, 1930.

Castro, Inés de. See under *Vélez de Guevara.*

Castro, Rosalía de (1837-1885). Regional poet and novelist. Born in Santiago de Compostela; died in Padrón. A precocious child, she began to write verses at the age of eleven. Her first book of poems appeared in 1857 *(La flor).* Except for brief periods, her life was a protracted struggle to achieve status (she was of illegitimate birth) and to overcome her innate feeling of insecurity, so deep-seated as to amount to a kind of metaphysical anxiety. After coming to Madrid, she was married in 1858 to a Galician writer, Manuel Martínez Murguía; but the burden of a difficult husband and the cares of a poverty-ridden household of five children, combined with nostalgia for her native Galicia; and, in her later years, the slow torture of incurable illness, all served to confirm her natural melancholy, her withdrawal from the world, and her intense pessimism. Her difficulties, however, were also her creative motivation. The first collection of verse which brought her fame, *Cantares gallegos* (1863), was written in Galician, as was her later one, *Folhas novas* (1880). Her most celebrated book of poetry in Castilian was *En las orillas del Sar* (1884). Among her novels were: *La hija del mar* (1859); *Flavio* (1861); *Ruinas* (1864); and *El caballero de las botas azules* (1867). Rosalía de Castro was the interpreter par excellence of the spirit of Galicia, its landscape, its people and its customs. In addition to her theme of subjective despair, a note of social compassion emerges from her verse. Her work, like that of Bécquer, represents a transition from romantic poetry to the modern lyric. She derived her literary inspiration from medieval Gallego-Portuguese poetry and from Galician folk-songs, to which she added modern metrical innovations. Her influence on the school of modernist poetry was considerable.

Cf. *Obras completas, (Ed. García Martí)*, Madrid, 1944; González Besada, A., *Rosalía de Castro. Notas biográficas*, Madrid, 1916; Azorín, *Clásicos y modernos*, Madrid, 1919; Prol Blas, J. S., *Estudio bio-bibliográfico-crítico de las obras de Rosalía de Castro*, Madrid, 1917; Brenan, G., *The Literature of the Spanish People*, 2nd ed., Cambridge, 1953; Machado da Rosa, A., "Rosalía de Castro, poeta incomprendido," *Revista Hispánica Moderna*, XX, 3, 1954.

Catalan (Catalonian). See under *Spanish.*

Catedral. See under *Blasco Ibáñez.*

Catedral de Sevilla (La). López Soler's novel inspired by Hugo's *The Hunchback of Notre Dame.* See under *López Soler.*

Catholic Reformation. See under *Reformation.*

cazuela. The "stew-pan." A section of the early Spanish theater, located at the rear of the *corral*, facing the stage. It was a barred enclosure for women of the lower classes.

Cebrián, Juan C. See under *American Association of Teachers of Spanish.*

Cejador y Frauca, Julio (1864-1927). Literary historian, professor and editor. Born in Zaragoza; died in Madrid. He was Professor of Latin at the University of Madrid. In addition to his innumerable articles, monographs and studies, he published many annotated editions of Spanish classics (*Libro de buen amor, Lazarillo de Tormes, La Celestina, Guzmán de Alfarache, Los Sueños, El Criticón*, etc.). His chief works were *Tesoro de la lengua castellana* (1908-1914) and the compendious *Historia de la lengua y literatura castellana*, 14 vols., (1915-1921). Among his other important works were: *La lengua de Cervantes* (1906); *El Cantar de Mío Cid y la epopeya castellana* (1920); and *La verdadera poesía popular castellana* (1921-1924).

Cf. Romera-Navarro, M., *Historia de la literatura española*, 2a. ed., Boston, 1949.

Celestina. The title of a remarkable drama, actually a dramatized novel, considered by many critics second only to *Don Quijote* in intrinsic greatness and in literary influence. The full title of the work in its earlier editions was *(Tragi)comedia de Calisto y Melibea,* but it is generally known by the name of its most outstanding character, Celestina. Because of missing dates, discrepancies in the earliest extant manuscripts, uncertainty as to dates and authorship of subsequent interpolations and additions, a vast body of scholarship on the *Celestina* theme and problems has accumulated. The facts as established at the present time seem to be as follows: The first preserved edition was published at Burgos in 1499 and contains 16 acts; the second earliest edition (Seville, 1501) contains 21 acts (both edited by Foulché-Delbosc, 1900, 1902). An edition of 1526 contains 22 acts. In the 1501 editions are some acrostic verses stating that the author was "El Bachiller Fernando de Royas." Authorities agree that this Fernando de Rojas, a converted Jewish lawyer who died in 1541, was the author of the 16 acts of the original *Celestina.*

The plot deals with the love of Calisto for Melibea, whose initial indifference prompts him to engage the services of a go-between, Celestina, who with her devious ways, persuades the girl to respond to her lover's suit. After a meeting, however, Calisto, while leaving Melibea's window, falls from a ladder and is killed. Melibea then hurls herself from a tower to join her lover in death.

The chief literary sources of the work have been traced to the medieval Spanish writers, Juan Ruiz and Martínez de Toledo. Some researchers have also found parallels in Ovid, Petrarch, and in Plautus and Terence. Lope de Vega's *Dorotea* was a later treatment of the same theme.

The greatness of this dramatized novel lies in its realistic delineation of character. The crone, Celestina, a panderess of satanic cunning, is depicted as the incarnation of evil. Other characters such as the picaresque servants, the prostitutes, the braggart soldier, etc., give us a vivid picture of life among the common people of early 16th century Spain. Even Calisto, with his flowery diction and his abject adoration, is a faithful portrayal of the Petrarchan lover of his day. The *Celestina* had a tremendous vogue and greatly influenced the development of the novel. There were 63 editions during the 16th century in Spain alone, to say nothing of innumerable imitations and translations into French, Italian, German and English (James Mabbe, *The Spanish Bawd,* 1631).

Cf. *Comedia de Calisto y Melibea,* (Ed.) Foulché-Delbosc, R., Vol. 1, 1900, Vol. II, 1902; Hispanic Society of America (facsimile of 1499 edition), N. Y., 1909; Foulché Delbosc, R., "Observations sur la Célestine," *Revue hispanique,* VII, IX; House, R. E., "The Present Status of the Problem of the *Celestina,*" *Philological Quarterly,* II; "Notes on the Authorship of the *Celestina,*" *Philological Quarterly,* III; Valle Lersundi, F. del, "Documentos referentes a Fernando de Rojas," *Revista de filología española,* XII, XVI; Espinosa y Maeso, R., "Dos notas para 'La Celestina' " *Boletín de la Real Academia Española,* XIII; Castro Guisasola, F., *Observaciones sobre las fuentes literarias de "La Celestina,"* Madrid, 1924.

Celoso extremeño (El). See under *Cervantes.*

Cena del rey Baltasar (La). See under *Calderón.*

Centro de Estudios Históricos. See under *Giner de los Ríos; krausismo; Menéndez Pidal.*

Cepeda y Ahumada, Teresa. See *Teresa de Jesús.*

Cerco de Zamora. See *Cantar de Zamora.*

Cervantes Saavedra, Miguel de (1547-1616). Spain's greatest novelist and one of the most eminent figures in world literature. Born in Alcalá de Henares; died in Madrid. Cervantes was the son of an obscure physician. Little is known about his early education. It is believed that he attended the Jesuit school in Seville. In about 1568 he studied under the Madrid humanist, Juan López de Hoyos, and at the same time wrote his first verses, on the occasion of the funeral of Queen Isabelle of Valois. Cervantes had little formal education, but his native curiosity led him to read translations of the classics, Spanish and Italian authors, romances of chivalry, and whatever else chance threw his way. This haphazard self-schooling was rounded out by travel and by the experiences of an eventful life. In 1569 he went to Italy where he served in the household of Cardinal Acquaviva in Rome and became acquainted with Italian art and literature. His Italian sojourn was an emotionally and intellectually stimulating experience which he remembered warmly throughout his life. In Italy he also served as a soldier (1570-1575). As the result of wounds received in the battle of Lepanto (1571), his left hand was permanently crippled. Returning to Spain in 1575, he was captured by pirates and sold into slavery in Algiers. After many desperate attempts to escape, he was finally ransomed in 1580. In 1584 he married Catalina de Salazar y Palacios. In 1585 he published his first extensive work, *La Galatea,* a pastoral romance which brought him some fame but little money. After unsuccessful attempts to compete against Lope de Vega as a playwright, Cervantes took a government post as purchasing agent and tax collector. Irregularities in his accounts led to his imprisonment in 1597. It was in prison that he began to write *Don Quijote.* The publication of Part I of *Don Quijote* (1605) brought Cervantes immediate acclaim and banished his material cares. Thenceforth he was able to devote himself entirely to writing. The *Novelas ejemplares* appeared in 1613; the *Viaje del Parnaso* in 1614; Part II of *Don Quijote* appeared in 1615. The same year saw the publication of *Ocho comedias y ocho entremeses nuevos, nunca representados.* Death overtook him on the 23rd of April, 1616, shortly after he had completed his final work, *Los trabajos de Persiles y Sigismunda* (published 1617).

The full title of Cervantes' immortal masterpiece is *El ingenioso hidalgo don Quijote de la Mancha.* The first part went through 10 editions before the appearance of the second part. It was widely translated and imitated, notably by an author writing under the pseudonym of Alfonso Fernández de Avellaneda, who published a spurious sequel in 1614. The effect of this was to spur Cervantes on to his own completion of the second part. The story of *Don Quijote* is that of a naive country gentleman whose favorite pastime of reading romances of chivalry becomes an obsession to the point where he takes them literally. Deciding to become a knight errant, he dons a battered suit of armor, assumes the name of Don Quijote de la Mancha, and sets out on his noble charger, a decrepit hack whom he names Rocinante. He chooses a simple village girl as the object of his devotion, naming her Dulcinea del Toboso; and as squire, he takes an ignorant but loyal peasant, Sancho Panza. Laboring under the delusion that he is living in the age of chivalry, Don Quijote imagines the typical roadside characters whom he encounters to be knights, men-at-arms, damsels in

Cervantes

distress, giants, ogres and monsters. At one point he tilts at the sails of windmills which his disordered imagination transforms into living beings. His attempts to fight injustice and to live the ideals of chivalry lead him into ridiculous and painful situations, yet he remains a noble and dignified, though pathetic, figure. The second part continues his adventures, including a sojourn among the nobility and Sancho Panza's appointment as governor of the imaginary island of Baratraria. At the end, Don Quijote is stricken with a severe illness, and after coming to his senses, renounces the romances of chivalry, and dies a penitent.

In *Don Quijote* Cervantes originally aimed at a satire of the romances of chivalry which, although they upheld chivalric ideals, had degenerated into absurd and affected attitudinizing. The picaresque novel, which had supplanted the chivalric romance, was characterized by greater realism but had the fault of moral cynicism. By achieving a synthesis of chivalric idealism with picaresque realism, Cervantes created a new form of fiction more appropriate to the new age of gunpowder, the printing press and secularism. Idealism and realism are symbolized in the two major characters, Don Quijote and Sancho Panza, the former, despite all reverses, sublime in his faith in the nobility of human nature, the latter self-seeking, materialistic and deceitful, although contradictorily enough, loyal to his master. Don Quijote, in spite of the frequently ridiculous role which he plays, is nonetheless a dignified and tragic figure striving to maintain the ideals of a vanished past in the face of a materialistic present. By creating a serried throng of minor characters, Cervantes also provided a memorable picture of the society of 16th century Spain. Other elements which give the novel its universal appeal are its varied style, its humor, its broad humanity, and its philosophic depth, especially in the second part. Successive generations of critics have found new meanings in *Don Quijote,* some taking it as an expression of the dualism of human nature, others as an allegory of the Spanish character. The fact that it says so many things to so many different individuals is testimony of its universal greatness.

Even if he had never written his great novel, Cervantes would have been outstanding among the writers of his day by virtue of his *Novelas ejemplares* (1613), a collection of twelve short stories in the style of the Italian *novella,* but with an exemplary or ethical purpose. Some of these short stories follow the pattern of the *novela picaresca* in their realistic accounts of the adventures of a criminal hero; but Cervantes dignifies the genre by his eschewal of cynicism and by his gentle satire tempered with compassion. Notable among his stories of this type is *Rinconete y Cortadillo,* a tale of criminal life in Seville; *El celoso extremeño,* a triangle situation involving the old husband, the young wife and the gay lover; *La ilustre fregone,* a romantic escapade in which a picaresque student marries a scullery maid who, fortunately, turns out to be well born. Cervantes aimed to entertain by variety, and as a result, his *novelas* cover a wide range, from the crude realism of *El casamiento engañoso,* the delightful animal satire of *Coloquio de los perros,* the philosophical tone of *El licenciado vidriera,* to the colorfully romantic, Italianesque tales of *La gitanilla, El amante liberal, Las dos doncellas, La fuerza de la sangre* and *La señora Cornelia.*

As a poet and dramatist Cervantes was unsuccessful. His *Viaje del Parnaso* (1614), a versified critique of the writers of his day, is notable only for having preserved the names of some minor poets. In his comedies, his eclipse by Lope de Vega was inevitable, since he lacked a dramatic sense. Most memorable in his latter work are the Dedication and Preface to *Persiles y Sigismunda,* the last pages he ever wrote, in which he takes leave of his friends and looks forward to the other world with gallant optimism.

Texts: *Obras completas,* (Ed.) Schevill, R. and Bonilla, A., 19 vols., Madrid, 1914-1941; *Don Quijote, Nueva edición crítica,* (Ed.) Rodríguez Marín, F., 7 vols., Madrid, 1927-1928; (The best English translation of *Don Quijote* is by John Ormsby, *The Ingenious Gentleman, Don Quijote of La Mancha,* 4 vols., London, 1896; reprinted with critical introduction and notes by J. Fitzmaurice-Kelly, London, 1901); *Novelas ejemplares,* (Ed.) Rodríguez Marín, F., 2 vols., Madrid, 1914-1917; *Poesías sueltas,* (Ed.) Schevill, R., and Bonilla, A., Madrid, 1922; *Entremeses,* (Ed.) Herrero García, M., Madrid, 1945.

Criticism: Unamuno, M. de, *Vida de Don Quijote y Sancho,* Madrid, 1905; Fitzmaurice-Kelly, J., *Miguel de Cervantes Saavedra. A Memoir,* Oxford, 1913; Ortega y Gasset, J., *Meditaciones del Quijote,* Madrid, 1914; Icaza, F. A. de, *Las novelas ejemplares de Cervantes,* Madrid, 1915; Schevill, R., *Cervantes,*

N. Y., 1919; Castro, A., *El pensamiento de Cervantes,* Madrid, 1925; Maeztu, R. de, *Don Quijote, Don Juan y la Celestina,* Madrid, 1926; Hazard, P., *Don Quijote: étude et analyse,* Paris, 1931; Bernadete, M. J. and Flores, A., *The Anatomy of Don Quixote,* Ithaca, 1932; *Cervantes Across the Centuries,* N. Y., 1947; Madariaga, S. de, *Don Quixote,* London, 1934; Entwistle, W. J., *Cervantes,* Oxford, 1940; Grismer, R. L., *Cervantes, a Bibliography,* N. Y., 1946; Bell, A. F. G., *Cervantes,* Norman, Oklahoma, 1947; Casalduero, J., *Sentido y forma del Quijote,* Buenos Aires, 1949.

Cid (El) (1040?-1099). Spain's national epic hero of the period of the reconquest. His birthplace is thought to have been in or near Burgos in the privince of Vivar. He died in Valencia in 1099. His name was Rodrigo Díaz de Vivar. The name "El Cid" is derived from the Arabic title, *Sidi,* meaning "Lord." He was called "Mío Cid" by his Arabic followers, and "El Cid Campeador" by the unknown *juglar* who composed the epic narrative of his exploits. Although banished by his sovereign, Alfonso VI, and, in some accounts, a champion of the people (including the Moors) against the monarchy, he nevertheless remained a loyal vassal, who through his conquest of Valencia helped in the expulsion of the Saracens and in the extension of Castilian dominion. A figure of great physical prowess and moral courage, he captured the national imagination so that Spanish medieval literature is replete with his exploits. The first references to the Cid are in a clerical *Carmen latino (ca.* 1090) and in a *cronicón,* entitled *Gesta Roderici Campidocti* (1110?) variously referred to as the *Historia Roderici* or *La crónica particular del Cid.* About this national hero an epic cycle grew up, based on history and legend, and culminating in the *Cantar de Mío Cid (ca.* 1140), of which the first extant copy is dated 1307 *(Poema del Cid).* Reference to the Cid is also found in prose versions of earlier epics (e.g., *Cerco de Zamora)* and in various historical *crónicas,* especially in the *Crónica de 1344,* and in the *Crónica de Veinte Reyes (ca.* 1360). For example, the *Cantar de Rodrigo* or *Las mocedades del Cid,* although lost, is known from a prose version in the *Crónica de 1344.* It recounts the youthful exploits of the Cid, particularly his marriage to Ximena, after having killed her father in a duel. Derived from the *Rodrigo* is *La crónica rimada del Cid (ca.* 1400), an extant fragment of some 1,132 lines, in which the Cid is not the loyal vassal but a bold leader of popular revolt. The *Rodrigo* and the *Crónica rimada,* rather than the earlier *Poema del Cid,* were the sources of most of the ballads in the *Romancero del Cid (ca.* 1500), and of Guillén de Castro's *Las mocedades del Cid* (1618), which, in turn, was the source of Corneille's *Le Cid* (1636). Among Spanish authors who have treated the Cid theme are Moratín, Hartzenbusch, Manuel Machado, *et al.* Famous writers of other countries have also exploited the theme (Herder, Hugo, Heredia, Southey, *et al.).* See also under *Cantar de Mío Cid.*

Cf. Menéndez Pidal, R., *Cantar de Mío Cid,* 3 vols., Madrid, 1906-1911; *idem, Historia y epopeya,* Madrid, 1934; *idem* (Ed.), *Poema de Mío Cid,* Madrid, 1913; *idem,* "El poema del Cid y las crónicas generales," *Revue hispanique,* V; *idem; La España del Cid,* Madrid, 1939; Cejador, J., "El Cantar de mío Cid y la epopeya castellana," *Revue hispanique,* XLIX; "El Cantar de Rodrigo," (Ed.) Bourland, B. P., *Revue hispanique,* XXIV.

cielitos heroicos. See under *Hidalgo, Bartolomé.*

Ciento diez consideraciones divinas. See under *Valdés, Juan de.*

Cifar. See *Caballero Cifar.*

Cigarrales de Toledo (Los). See under *Tirso de Molina.*

Cisneros. See *Jiménez de Cisneros.*

Clarín (1852-1901). The pen name of Leopoldo Alas, literary critic, professor and creative writer. Born in Zamora; died in Oviedo. For many years a professor of law and political economy at the University of Oviedo, he advocated the liberal educational ideas of C. F. Krause. Later he abandoned the *krausista* philosophy for a subjective idealism. Clarín's greatest fame was achieved as a literary critic. For many years he contributed to the leading periodicals and reviews of Madrid, and he became a close friend of Menéndez y Pelayo, Unamuno, Galdós, Palacio Valdés, and other scholarly and literary lights of his day. He was celebrated for his trenchant and often caustic literary criticism, displaying a considerable degree of polemic ardor. All of this, however, was relieved by his wit, humor, subtlety and the serious ethical tone that pervaded his work. The titles of his collected critical essays (1879-1898) are *Solos de Clarín, Paliques, La crítica y la poesía en España.* Outstanding is his critical study entitled *Galdós* (Madrid, 1912). Clarín's most important creative work was a long

Zolaesque novel, *La Regenta* (1884-1885), depicting every stratum of the society of a cathedral city. Vetusta (actually Oviedo), in naturalistic detail. The exposure of the sham mysticism of the heroine, Ana Azores, and of the temporal ambitions of the cathedral's prebendary, Don Fermín, show Clarín's power of psychological analysis as well as the anti-clerical criticism typical of his earlier period. Clarín was also notable as a short story writer *(Cuentos morales, El gallo de Sócrates,* etc.).

Cf. Sáinz y Rodríguez, P., *Discurso sobre "Clarín,"* Universidad de Oviedo, 1921; Cabezas, J. A., *"Clarín,"* Madrid, 1935; Bull, W. E., "Clarín's Literary Internationalism," *Hispanic Review,* XVI.

Claros varones de Castilla. See under *Pulgar, Hernando del.*

Clásicos y modernos. See under *Azorín; Generation of 1898.*

Clavería, Carlos (1909). Spanish literary scholar and professor. Lecturer and Professor of Spanish and Romance Languages at the Universities of Marburg, Frankfurt, Upsala, Stockholm, University of Pennsylvania, Harvard University. *Catedrático Gramática General,* University of Murcia, 1951-1953. Author of *Cinco estudios de literatura española moderna,* Salamanca, 1945; *"Le chevalier délibéré" y sus versiones castellanas,* Zaragoza, 1950; *Estudios sobre los gitanismos del español,* Madrid, 1951; *Temas de Unamuno,* Madrid, 1952; *La caracterización de la personalidad en "Generaciones y Semblanzas,"* Murcia, 1953; *Estudios hispanosuecos,* Granada, 1954.

Clavijo y Fajardo, José. See under *Costumbrismo.*

Clemencia. See under *Altamirano.*

Cleofás. The student in *El diablo cojuelo* (1641) by Luis Vélez de Guevara. See under *Vélez de Guevara.*

clerecía poetry. See under *mester de clerecía.*

Coe, Ada May (1890). American hispanist. At Wellesley College since 1917; Professor of Spanish, since 1947. Author of *Catálogo bibliográfico y crítico de las comedias anunciadas en los periódicos de Madrid desde 1661 hasta 1819,* Baltimore, 1935; *Entertainments in the Little Theatres of Madrid 1759-1819,* N. Y., 1947; *Carteleras madrileñas* (1677-1792, 1819), Mexico, 1952.

Cojo ilustrado (El). See under *criollismo.*

Cola de paja. See under *Ocantos, Carlos María.*

Colección de romances antiguos. See under *Durán, Agustín.*

Colegio de México. See under *Reyes, Alfonso.*

Colocci-Brancuti. See under *cancionero.*

Colonne, Guido delle. See under *Historia troyana.*

coloquio. (Eng. colloquy). A type of literary composition in the form of dialogue; e.g., the *Coloquio de los perros,* by Cervantes. The form occurs frequently in early Spanish literature, especially in moral or didactic works.

Coloquio de los perros. An animal satire by Cervantes. See under *Cervantes; pícaro; picaresque novel.*

Columbus Memorial Library. See under *Pan American Union.*

Comedia de Calisto y Melibea. See *Celestina.*

comedia de capa y espada. See *capa y espada.*

comedia de figurón. A type of 16th and 17th century play in which the principal character was satirized or caricatured.

comedia de gracioso. See under *Rojas Zorrilla.*

Comedia de Rubena. See under *Vicente, Gil.*

comedia de ruido. A type of play dealing with heroic figures of early Spanish history. These plays were frequently melodramatic and sensational *(ruido.)* Chronicles and ballads were the chief source material for this type of comedy. The genre was cultivated by Tirso de Molina and reached its height in Lope de Vega and his dramatic school.

Comedia de viuvo. See under *Vicente, Gil.*

Comedia nueva (La). See under *Moratín.*

comedia palaciega. The "palace play" of the 16th and 17th centuries, developed chiefly by Lope de Vega. So-called because the chief characters were kings or noblemen. The plots were involved and the settings were usually in some remote or ancient kingdom. The themes treated in this type of play were chiefly love and honor.

comedias a fantasía. See under *Torres Naharro.*

comedias a noticia. See under *Torres Naharro.*

Comedieta de Ponza. See under *Santillana.*

compañías de título. A reference to the eight royal troupes of actors organized in 1600 during the reign of Philip III. The administration of Philip III regulated the status of actors in an attempt to overcome clerical objections to the profession.

conceptismo. Exaggerated subtlety of wit cultivated by Spanish baroque writers of the 17th century and frequently combined with the style of *culteranismo*. The distinction between *culteranismo* and *conceptismo* is that the former pertains to lexical and syntactical features of baroque style (chiefly expressed in poetry), whereas the latter pertains to the realm of ideas (chiefly expressed in prose). The term *conceptismo* derives from *concepto*, a brilliant flash of wit expressed in pithy or epigrammatic style. The initiator of *conceptismo* was Alonso de Ledesma (1552-1623), a minor poet, whose *Conceptos espirituales* (1600 *et seq.)* first introduced the word *concepto* in the meaning defined above. The great prose *conceptista* was Baltasar Gracián (1601-1658), who elaborated his theories of *conceptismo* in his *Agudeza y arte de ingenio* (1648). Acuity of wit *(agudeza)* and the terse, subtly-refined utterance are the quintessence of style according to Gracián. The other great example of *conceptismo* was Francisco de Quevedo (1580-1645), whose prose style was characterized by vivid and far-fetched conceits and whose sharp wit was reflected in sardonic caricature. Although an opponent of *culteranismo*, as shown in his literary satire, *Aguja de navegar cultos*, 1631, Quevedo's preciosity of style, sharp flashes of wit and brilliant interplay of word and idea, emphasize the intellectual subtlety of *conceptismo* as distinguished from the verbal emphasis of *culteranismo*. See also *culteranismo*.

Cf. Alonso de Ledesma, *Obras*, *BAE*, XXXV; Baltasar Gracián, *Obras completas*, (Ed.) Correa Calderón, E., Madrid, 1944; May, T. E., "An Interpretation of Gracián's 'Agudeza y arte de ingenio,'" *Hispanic Review*, XVI; Francisco de Quevedo, *Obras completas*, (Ed.) Marín, L. A., Madrid, 1932.

Conceptos del amor de Dios. See under *Teresa de Jesús.*

Conceptos espirituales. See under *conceptismo; Ledesma.*

Concolorcorvo. See *Bustamante, Calixto.*

Conde Alarcos (El). See under *Castro, Guillén de.*

Conde Fernán González. See *Fernán González.*

Conde Lucanor. See under *Juan Manuel.*

Condenado por desconfiado (El). See under *Tirso de Molina.*

Confesiones de un pequeño filósofo. See under *Azorín.*

Conjuración de Venecia (La). See under *Martínez de la Rosa, Francisco.*

Conquest of Mexico. See under *Prescott.*

Conquest of Peru. See under *Prescott.*

Conquista de la Nueva España. See under *Díaz del Castillo.*

Conquista de ultramar. See *Gran conquista de ultramar.*

Consuelo. See under *López de Ayala, Adelardo.*

Contemporáneo (El). See under *Bécquer, Gustavo Adolfo.*

contiguous assimilation. See under *assimilation.*

Contra esto y aquello. See under *Unamuno.*

Convidado de piedra. The second half of the title of Tirso de Molina's Don Juan drama, *El burlador de Sevilla.* The reference is to the statue of Don Juan's victim who invites the latter to dine with him at his tomb. See under *Don Juan; Tirso de Molina.*

copla. (1) A popular lyric. (2) A ballad of popular origin, varying in length. It has a stanza that varies from 3 to 5 lines of 8 to 12 syllables each. Rhyme or assonance generally occurs in the even lines. (3) The art-form of the *copla,* cultivated by medieval and Renaissance poets. The *copla* of Renaissance poets varies from 8 to 12 syllables each verse, with 8 or 10-line stanzas. For example, the *coplas* of Juan Boscán (1493?-1542) have 10 octosyllabic lines, rhymed ABBABCDCDC. The rhyme scheme varies somewhat, but the first five lines have an AB pattern, while the last five have CD. The verse of Jorge Manrique (1440-1479) offers an example of the elegiac *copla (Coplas por la muerte de su padre,* 1476). Manrique uses 12-line stanzas of varying length *(pie quebrado),* rhymed ABCABCDEFDEF. The late 15th century also produced anonymous popular satires bearing the title of *coplas (Coplas de ¡Ay panadera!, Coplas del Provincial).* Outstanding among these popular satires are the *Coplas de Mingo Revulgo* (1464), an allegorical dialogue between two shepherds discussing political evils during the reign of Henry IV.

Cf. *Jorge Manrique: Coplas por la muerte de su padre,* (Ed.) Foulché-Delbosc, M. R., Madrid, 1912; Salinas, P., *Jorge Manrique: o tradición y originalidad,* Buenos Aires, 1947; *Las obras de Juan Boscán,* (Ed.) Knapp, W. I., Madrid, 1875; Menéndez y Pelayo, M., *Antología de poetas líricos castellanos,* 2nd. ed., Madrid, 1944.

Coplas de ¡Ay panadera! See under *copla.*

Coplas de Mingo Revulgo. See under *copla.*

Coplas de Yoçef. See under *Poema de Yuçuf.*

Coplas por la muerte de su padre. See under *Manrique, Jorge.*

Corbacho (Corvacho) (El). See under *Arcipreste de Talavera.*

Corominas, John (1905). Romance philologist, Arabist, and lexicographer. Born in Catalonia; naturalized U. S. sitizen, 1953. Professor of Romance Linguistics, Arabic and Latin, University of Barcelona, 1927-1939. Professor of Romance Philology, Universidad Nacional de Cuyo, Argentina, 1939-1945; Professor of Romance Philology, University of Chicago, since 1946. Author of *Diccionario crítico-etimológico de la lengua castellana,* 4 vols., Bern-Madrid, 1954; *Vocabulario Aranés,* Madrid, 1931; *Mots catalans d'origens aràbic,* Barcelona, 1936; *Estudios de etimología hispánica,* Mendoza, Argentina, 1942; *Indianorománica,* Buenos Aires, 1944.

corral. "Courtyard." The earliest type of Spanish theater. The stage was erected at one end of a *corral.* The surrounding houses provided the balconies from which the aristocracy viewed the performance. There were a few benches in front of the stage. The remainder of the courtyard was "standing room" for the commoners. The present *Teatro Español,* the National Theater of Spain, located in Madrid, stands on the site of the *Corral del príncipe,* formerly called the *Corral de la Pacheca,* where theatrical performances were presented as early as 1568.

Correas, Gonzalo. See under *folklore.*

Corte de milagros. See under *Valle-Inclán.*

Cortés, Donoso. See under *Romanticism.*

Cortés, Hernán (1485-1547). Spanish adventurer, explorer and conqueror of Mexico. Born in Medellín, Extremadura. Educated at the University of Salamanca. Went to Santo Domingo (1504). Served under Diego Velásquez in the conquest of Cuba (1511). Leader of the expedition which conquered Mexico (1519). Cortés is significant in the history of Spanish literature for his *Cartas de relación* (1519-1526), five letters addressed to Emperor Charles V of Spain, giving in vivid detail the account of his own conquest. Influenced by the style of Julius Caesar, whose *Commentaries* he had studied at the University of Salamanca, Cortés created documents of literary as well as of historical value.

Cf. *Cartas de relación de la conquista de Méjico,* Madrid, 1922. MacNutt, F. A., *Letters of Cortés* (with biographical introduction), N. Y., 1908.

Cortes de la muerte. See under *Danza de la muerte.*

Cortesano (El). See under *Boscán, Juan.*

Corvacho (Corbacho) (El). See under *Arcipreste de Talavera.*

Cossante. A verse form of the early Middle Ages, frequently occurring in Galician *cantigas de amigo.* It consists of alternate *i* and *a* assonanced couplets, each ending with the same refrain. The pattern of *i* and *a* assonance followed by the refrain (R) is as follows: IIR, AAR, IIR, AAR, *etc.* The *cossante* also has an interweaving sense pattern; *i.e.* each *a* couplet repeats the sense of each *i* couplet with variations.

Cf. Brenan, G., "A Glossary of Medieval Verse Forms," *The Literature of the Spanish People,* 2nd ed., Cambridge, 1953.

Cossío, Manuel Bartolomé (1858-1935). Author of a masterly and influential biography of *El Greco* (1908). See under *krausismo.*

Costa y Martínez, Joaquín (1844-1911). One of the precursors of the "Generation of 1898." Of Aragonese peasant origin, he was a virile personality, and as a jurist, journalist, historian, scholar and lecturer in the fields of law, economics and sociology exercised a widespread influence on the younger generation of his day (Unamuno, Azorín, Ortega y Gasset). Costa championed a national renewal to be accomplished by the "De-Africanization" and "Europeanization" of Spain. He was opposed to *españolismo* and other trends of the past that had contributed to Spain's decadence. His frequently repeated slogan, "Doble llave al sepulcro del Cid," characterized his break with outworn tradition.

Chief works: *La vida del derecho,* 1876; *Teoría del hecho jurídico, individual y social,* 1880; *Poesía popular española y mitología y literatura celto-hispanas,* 1881; *Colectivismo agrario en España,* 1898; *Oligarquía y caciquismo,* 1901-1902; *Crisis política de España,* 1914; *Tutela de pueblos en la historia,* 1917.

Cf. Gambón y Plana, M., *Biografía y bibliografía de D. Joaquín Costa,* Huesca, 1911; Antón del Olmet, L., *Costa,* Madrid, 1917; Jackson, G., "Joaquín Costa," *South Atlantic Quarterly,* LIII, 1954.

costumbre criolla. See under *Payró, Roberto J.*

costumbrismo. A trend in Spanish prose fiction stressing the realistic portrayal of manners, customs and characters. It began in the late 18th century and reached its height around the middle of the 19th century. The literary media for this trend were the *artículos* or *cuadros de costumbres,* short essays or sketches in prose or verse, depicting the types and customs of a particular social or provincial milieu. Description of a social background rather than plot was the outstanding feature of these sketches. Their tone was frequently satirical or philosophical. Many of the early *costumbrista* sketches appeared in periodicals; e.g. *El Pensador* (1762-1767), edited by José Clavijo y Fajardo (1730-1806). Among the first of 19th century *costumbrista* writers was Sebastián de Miñano (1779-1845), whose *Cartas del pobrecito holgazán* (1820) combined political criticism with a general satire of Spanish customs. Collections of *costumbrista* sketches were common at the height of the trend, the most famous being one of over fifty authors, entitled *Los españoles pintados por sí mismos* (Madrid, 1851). The outstanding *costumbrista* writers were Mesonero Romanos (1803-1882), Mariano José de Larra (1809-1837) and Estébanez Calderón (1799-1867). The importance of the *costumbrista* movement was that it laid the foundations for the 19th century regional novel (Fernán Caballero, *et al.*). The movement had its repercussions in South America from 1840 on (Altamirano, *et al.*).

Cf. *Costumbristas españoles,* (Ed.) Correa Calderón, E., Madrid, 1950-1952; Montgomery, C. M., *Early Costumbrista Writers in Spain,* 1750-1830, Philadelphia, 1931; Lomba y Pedraja, J. R., *Costumbristas españoles de la primera mitad del siglo xix,* Oviedo, 1933; Pitollet, C., "Mesonero Romanos, costumbrista," *La España moderna,* Oct., 1903; Spell, J. R., "The Costumbrista Movement in Mexico," *PMLA,* L, 1935.

Cotarelo y Mori, Emilio (1857-1936). Literary historian and editor. A pupil of Menéndez y Pelayo, he became the foremost authority of his time on the history of the Spanish theater. In 1897 his book entitled *Iriarte y su época* received the prize of the *Academia Española,* and he was elected to that august body in 1898, serving later as Permanent Secretary (from 1913 on). Many of his critical contributions appeared in the *Boletín de la Real Academia Española.* He was the author of many literary biographies (Villamediana, Ramón de la Cruz, Tirso de Molina, López Zorrilla, Vélez de Guevara, Calderón, etc. His critical editions of Spanish classics include the works of Encina, Lope de Rueda, Tirso, Lope de Vega, and others. In addition to these, his more extensive works on the theater were: *Juan del Enzina y los orígines del teatro español* (1901); *Lope de Rueda y el teatro español* (1901);

and *Bibliografía de las controversias sobre la licitud del teatro en España* (1904).

Cf. Romera-Navarro, M., *Historia de la literatura española,* 2a, ed., Boston, 1949.

Council of Trent. See under *Reformation.*

Counter-Reformation. See under *Reformation.*

Courtier (The). See under *Garcilaso de la Vega.*

Covarrubias y Orozco, Sebastián de (1539-1613). A Toledan priest, later a canon at the Cathedral of Cuenca. Author of a homiletic work entitled *Emblemas morales* (1610). He is chiefly known as the compiler of the famous *Tesoro de la lengua castellana o española* (1611), the best dictionary published during the Golden Age of Spanish literature. Covarrubias included idiomatic constructions and proverbs in addition to single terms, and accompanied his definitions by quotations from the authors of his day. Thus the *Tesoro* is an indispensable tool for the interpreting and editing of the Spanish classics. A revised and enlarged edition appeared in 1673-1674, (Ed.) Remigio Noydens, B.

Cf. Mérimée, E. and Morley, S. G., *History of Spanish Literature,* N. Y., 1930.

creacionismo. A post-modernist literary and esthetic movement started in about 1916 by the Chilean poet, Vicente Huidobro (1893-1948), at that time resident in Paris and under the influence of vanguardist esthetic theories. In 1918 Huidobro propagated his theories in Spain, where the movement spread in the 1920's (Gerardo Diego, Juan Larrea). Like ultraism, surrealism and other post-modernist movements, *creacionismo* was a phase through which many contemporary poets passed. The reason for the evanescence of *creacionismo* was its rejection of tradition and its self-defeating programmatic goal. Huidobro's principle was to create rather than to write about creation. He rejected description and narration for elemental, extra-rational expression. The logical consequence of such a theory exceeds the limits of verbal communication and ultimately leads to a private idiom. The verbal experiments of creationism extended the dimensions and perspectives of poetic expression, but the movement was bound to be transitory in its very nature. See also under *Huidobro.*

Cf. Holmes, H. A., *Vicente Huidobro and Creationism,* N. Y., 1933; *idem,* "The Creationism of Vicente Huidobro," *The Spanish*

Review, I, 1934; "Alone" (Díaz Arrieta, Hernán), *Panorama de la literatura chilena durante el siglo xx*, Santiago, 1931; Gómez de la Serna, R., *Ismos*, 2nd ed., Buenos Aires, 1943; Alonso, D., *Ensayos sobre poesía española:* "La poesía de Gerardo," Madrid, 1944; Undaraga, A. de, "Huidobro y sus acusadores o la querella del creacionismo," *Cultura Universitaria*, XLII, 1954.

criollismo. A Spanish-American realistic literary trend which set in at the end of the 19th century, especially in Venezuela, where it was promoted by the periodical *El cojo ilustrado* (Caracas, 1892-1915). The term "criollismo" was popularized by the Venezuelan novelist, Vicente Romero García, in his novel *Peonía* (1890), which is a realistic portrayal of life on a country estate in Venezuela. Other writers in the same tradition were Miguel Eduardo Pardo (*Todo un pueblo*, 1899) and Gonzalo Picón-Febres (*El sargento Felipe*, 1899). The *criollismo* trend emphasized the literary treatment of native (creole) characters and background. It gave impetus to a regional literature, realistic and often naturalistic in its style, and concerned with social reform.

Cf. Ratcliff, D. F., *Venezuelan Prose Fiction*, N. Y., 1933; Picón-Salas, M., *Formación y proceso de la literatura venezolana*, Caracas, 1940.

Crisis del humanismo. See under *Maeztu, Ramiro de.*

Crispo Acosta, Osvaldo (1884). Literary critic and professor of literature at Montevideo. Principal works: *Motivos de crítica hispanoamericana; Carlos Reyles; Rubén Darío y José Enrique Rodó; Gustavo Adolfo Bécquer.*

Cf. *Hispania*, XXXVI, 1953.

Cristiado (La). See under *Hojeda, Diego de.*

Cristino y Febea. See under *Encina, Juan del.*

Cristo en los infiernos. See under *León, Ricardo.*

Criticón (El). See under *Gracián y Morales.*

crónica. The Spanish historical chronicle from the 13th through the 15th century, written in the vernacular; distinguished from the *cronicón*, written in Latin and dating from the 5th century on. The *cronicones* were generally brief, unadorned annals of important events and were recorded in convents or monasteries. Rising above the level of these were the *Chronicum mundi*, written by Bishop Lucas de Tuy (d. 1249) and covering the history of Spain from the beginnings to the conquest of Cordova (1236) by

Fernando III; and the *Historia gothica,* written by the Archbishop of Toledo, Rodrigo Jiménez de Rada (1170-1247), who ended his account with the victory of Las Navas de Tolosa (1212). Based on these is the most famous of the *crónicas,* the *Crónica general,* begun in 1260 under the sponsorship of Alfonso X. The first version of this work is known as *La primera crónica general.* The *Segunda crónica general* (also known as *La crónica de 1344)* was begun in 1289 under Sancho IV. The *Tercera crónica general* (printed by Florián Ocampo, 1541) was the only printed edition of Alfonso's chronicle until 1906, when Menéndez Pidal reconstructed it from the former work. Alfonso's *Crónica* starts with the deluge, goes through classical history, the history of the Goths, the loss of Spain to the Moors, and ends with the reconquest, *i.e.* through the reign of Fernando III, El Santo. The literary importance of the *Crónica general* is that it contains "prosifications" of many 12th century *cantares* which have been lost (e.g. *El cantar de Zamora*), thus permitting scholars to reconstruct them. Subsequent *crónicas* often subordinated fact to legend in greater measure than the *Crónica general,* thus giving rise to a literary type of chronicle (e.g. Pedro del Corral's *Crónica sarracina, ca.* 1443). Chronicles of a more artistic and scholarly type begin with the Chancellor, Pero López de Ayala (1332-1407), who wrote histories of *Don Enrique* and *Don Pedro.* Among the famous chronicles of the 15th century are the *Crónica de Don Juan II (ante* 1460) and the *Crónica de los reyes católicos (ante* 1493).

Cf. *La primera crónica general,* (Ed.) Menéndez Pidal, R., *NBAE,* V, Madrid, 1906; *idem, Crónicas generales de España,* Madrid, 1918; *Colección de grandes crónicas españolas,* (Ed.) Mata Carriazo, Madrid, 1940-1947.

Crónica abreviada. See under *Juan Manuel.*

Crónica de Abenalcotía. See under *cantar de gesta.*

Crónica de los Reyes Católicos. See under *Pulgar, Hernando del.*

Crónica del Toledano. So called because it was written by the Bishop of Toledo, Ximénez de Rada (d. 1247). It is a history of Spain, originally entitled *De rebus Hispaniae,* or *Historia Gothica.* See under *Ximénez de Rada.*

Crónica de veinte reyes. See under *Cid (El).*

Crónica general. See under *crónica.*

Crónica particular del Cid. See under *Cid (El).*

Crónica rimada de Alfonso XI. See under *Poema de Alfonso Onceno.*

Crónica rimada del Cid. See under *Cid; Rodrigo el godo.*

Crónica troyana. See under *Historia troyana.*

cronicón. See under *crónica.*

Crow, John Armstrong (1906). American hispanist. Authority on Latin American literature. Professor and Head of Department of Spanish and Portuguese, University of California, Los Angeles, since 1949. Author of *Horacio Quiroga—sus mejores cuentos,* Mexico City, 1943; *Spanish American Life,* N. Y., 1940; *The Epic of Latin America,* N. Y., 1946. Co-author of *Outline History of Spanish American Literature,* N. Y., 1941; *Anthology of Spanish American Literature,* N. Y., 1946. Editor, Latin American Literature, *Encyclopedia Americana,* 1942.

Crusades. See under *Gran conquista de ultramar.*

Cruz, Ramón de la (1731-1794). Popular writer of the one-act farce *(sainete).* Born and died in Madrid. His full name was Ramón Francisco de la Cruz Cano y Olmedilla. A minor government official and protégé of the Duchess of Benaventa, he took an active interest in the literary life of Madrid as a member of the *Academia de los árcades.* Ten volumes of his dramatic works *(Teatro)* were published in Madrid (1786-1791) during his lifetime. Subsequent editions in the 19th and 20th centuries do not seem to have exhausted his immense output, estimated at 500 plays. He began as a writer of tragedies, a translator and adapter of Italian and French plays (Metastasio, Goldoni, Molière, Racine, Ducis) before settling down to his ideal medium, the one-act comical interlude, descended from the *entremés* and known as the *sainete.* Departing from his earlier neo-classical ideals, Ramón de la Cruz cultivated the realistic and humorous portrayal of native types and customs. He was an enormous popular success to the dismay of his neo-classical rivals who carried on a futile campaign against him. His lower-class characters spoke in dialect. His middle-class characters were taken from the contemporary scene. Since he wished to instruct as well as to entertain, his realism was tinged with satire. In the introduction to his *Teatro,* he proclaims truth to be his guide: "*Yo escribo y la verdad me dicta.*" He lauds Plautus and Terence for having taken their characters from life. He claims to have painted a picture of the century. And indeed, his *sainetes* provide the best documentation that we have of the people, customs and manners of 18th century Spain. He depicts the middle classes *(El sarao, La visito de duelo)*; he satirizes the fashionable dandies *(El cortejo fastidioso)*, the foppery and shallow wit of the *à la mode* gallant *(El petimetre)*, the sham pretensions of actors *(El teatro por dentro)*, and the smug decorum of neo-classic dramatists *(Manolo)*. Like Molière, he also dramatized types; e.g. the incorrigible female *(La embarazada ridícula)*. Of interest to historians of literature is his *Hamleto, rey de Dinamarca* (1772), adapted from the French of Ducis. Also notable are his vivid pictures of public life *(El rastro por la mañana, El Prado por la noche, La Plaza Mayor por Navidad*, etc.). Ramón de la Cruz, in these colorful and realistic *sainetes*, created a type of dramatic sketch without a clearly defined plot. But his treatment of contemporary reality, his dramatic vigor, and his introduction of natural speech, provided a wholesome influence on the development of the Spanish theater.

Cf. *Sainetes de Don Ramón de la Cruz*, (Ed.) Cotarelo y Mori, E., *NBAE*, XXIII; *Don Ramón de la Cruz y sus obras*, Cotarelo y Mori, E., Madrid, 1899; Hamilton, A., "Ramón de la Cruz, Social Reformer," *Romanic Review*, XII; Kany, C. E., (Ed.) *Five Sainetes of Ramón de la Cruz*, Boston, 1926.

Cruz, San Juan de la (1542-1591). The purest lyric poet among the mystics of the classical period. Born at Fontiveros; died at Ubeda. His name was Juan de Yepes before he entered the Carmelite Order in 1563. He completed his studies at Salamanca in 1568. A friend of St. Theresa, he became an ascetic reformer, was imprisoned for his pains and spent more than eight months in a monastic cell at Toledo, undergoing privation and torture. It was here that he composed most of his mystical poetry. After escaping, he devoted himself to zealous effort on behalf of the propagation of his Order. His works were not published until 1618. He was beatified in 1674 and canonized in 1726. His great work, *La subida del Monte Carmelo* (1578-1583), consists of eight *canciones* (some of them in *lira* form) accompanied by prose commentaries. The work reveals a mystical pattern which, as far as it can be encompassed in logical terms, consists essentially of "stages" on the way to identification with the Divine; from the dark night of the soul *(Noche oscura del alma,* 1579), obscured by sense but guided by faith, to the searing, all-infusing daylight vision of the Holy Spirit *(Llama de amor viva,* 1584.) In his *Cántico espiritual* (publ. 1627), the metaphors of the "Song of Songs" are evident in the mystical union between the soul *(La Esposa)* and Christ *(El Esposo).* The poet's sensitivity to nature is here transfigured into a metaphysical absolute by love and adoration:

> Mi alma se ha empleado,
> y todo mi caudal, en su servicio,
> ya no guardo ganado
> ni ya tengo otro oficio,
> que ya solo en amar es mi ejercicio.

The bucolic simplicity of his verses conceals untold depths of significance. Although San Juan de la Cruz is frequently the ecstatic visionary, beyond the ken of ordinary mortals, it is the simple note of selfless commitment to Divine Love that makes him accessible to all and that accounts for his lyrical supremacy.

Cf. *Obras, BAE,* XXVII; *El cántico espiritual,* (Ed.) Martínez Burgos, M., Madrid, 1924; *Poesías completas,* (Ed.) Salinas P., Madrid, 1936; Menéndez y Pelayo, M., "De la poesía mística," *Estudios de crítica literaria,* Madrid, 1884; Peers, E. A., *Studies of the Spanish Mystics,* N. Y., 1927; *St. John of the Cross,* Cambridge, 1932; *Spirit of Flame,* London, 1944; Jesús Sacramentado, C. de, *San Juan de la Cruz: el hombre, el doctor, el poeta,* Barcelona, 1935; Alonso, D., *La poesía de San Juan de la Cruz,* Madrid, 1942.

Cruz, Sor Juana Inés de la (1648?-1695). Mexican intellectual prodigy, nun and poetess. The greatest lyrical poet of the colonial period. Born in San Miguel de Nepantla, Mexico, and baptized Juana Inés de Asbaje y Ramírez de Santillana, she is frequently referred to as the "Décima Musa de México." A precocious scholar and poetess, she took religious vows at the age of sixteen, devoting herself to a life of charity, meditation and literature. She wrote many lyrics, sonnets, *romances, redondillas, villancicos,* and *autos sacramentales,* mostly on religious themes and showing the influence of Góngora and Calderón. However, at her best she transcends the gongoristic excesses of her time. Her feminist spirit and lyric power are shown in the following verses from her much-anthologized poem, *Redondillas:*

> Hombres necios, que acusais
> a la mujer sin razon,
> sin ver que sois la ocasion
> de lo mismo que culpais.
> Si con ansia sin igual
> solicitais su desden,
> ¿por qué quereis que obren bien
> si las incitais al mal?

Only two of her works were published during her lifetime: *Inundación castálida* (1689) and *Segundo tomo* (1692). A third volume of her works appeared in 1700 *(Fama y Obras Póstumas del Fénix de México y Dézima Musa).* The standard critical edition of her poems is: Abreu Gómez, E., *Sor Juana Inés de la Cruz: Poesías,* (Clásicos de México, I), Mexico City, 1940.

Cf. Vossler, K., *Die Zehnte Muse von Mexico,* Munich, 1934; Rueda, J. J., *Sor Juana Inés de la Cruz en su época,* Mexico, 1951; "Homenaje a Sor Juana," *Revista Iberoamericana,* XVII, 1951.

Cruz Varela, Juan (1794-1839). Argentine patriot, humanist and poet. Educated in Spain. Began his literary career with translations of the classical Latin poets and with two neo-classical tragedies of his own: *Dido* (1836) and *Argía* (1837). He is chiefly known for his patriotic odes: *Triunfo de Ituzaingó* (1827) and *El 25 de mayo* (1838). His many occasional poems are of slight merit but reveal the civic reformer and patriot. In 1915-1916 new editions of his poems and tragedies were published in Buenos Aires.

Cf. Beltrán, O. R., *Manual de historia de la literatura hispanoamericana,* Buenos Aires, 1938.

Cruzados de la causa. See under *Valle-Inclán*

cuaderna vía. The stanza form of Spanish narrative poetry from the 13th to 15th centuries. It is also known as the Spanish alexandrine and was used by clerical poets of the *mester de clerecía* school. The form consists of stanzas of four verses, each verse having fourteen syllables, middle caesura, and the same rhyme. Although *cuaderna vía* shows the influence of Provençal poetry, it has the same origin as the French alexandrine, namely medieval Latin verse. Among the early works of poetry in *cuaderna vía* are the *Libro de Apolonio (ca.* 1235), the *Libro de Alexandre (ca.* 1240), and Gonzalo de Berceo's (1195?-1265?) lives of various saints. By the end of the 14th century, *cuaderna vía* began to be superseded by *arte mayor,* the 8-line stanza in 12-syllable meter.

Cf. Menéndez y Pelayo, M., *Antología de poetas líricos castellanos,* Madrid, 1914-1916; Menéndez Pidal, R., *Poesía juglaresca y juglares,* Madrid, 1924; Henríquez Ureña, P., *La versificación irregular en la poesía castellana,* Madrid, 1920; Trend, J. B., *Berceo,* Cambridge, 1952.

Cuadernos Americanos. See under *Larrea, Juan.*

cuadros de costumbres. See *costumbrismo.*

cuarteta. A quatrain, or stanza of four lines of varying length *(arte menor),* generally rhymed ABAB. Compare *cuarteto; redondilla.*

cuarteto. A quatrain, or stanza, or group of four lines of eleven syllables *(arte mayor),* rhymed ABBA. Compare *cuarteta; redondilla.*

Cuarto poder (El). See under *Palacio Valdés.*

cuatrisílabo. A poetic line or verse of four syllables. Also called *tetrasílabo.*

Cuatro jinetes del Apocalipsis. See under *Blasco Ibáñez.*

Cuento de abril. See under *Valle-Inclán.*

Cuervo, Rufino José. See under *Bello, Andrés.*

Cuestión de amor. An anonymous *novela sentimental* of the early 16th century *(ca.* 1510), having as its background the life, loves and intrigues of the Spanish court at Naples. Its full title is *Cuestión de amor de dos enamorados.* It is thought to be a *roman à clef,* including among its characters contemporary figures thinly disguised under a veil of fiction. The frame is a dialogue, in mixed prose and verse, between two unhappy lovers who have lost their ladies and who vie with each other as to whose grief is the greater. The *Cuestión de amor,* because of its vivid and colorful pictures of court life, is considered the best of the many imitations of Diego de San Pedro's *Cárcel de amor* (1492).

Cf. *Cuestión de amor,* (Ed.) Menéndez y Pelayo, M., *NBAE,* VII; Croce, B., *Di un antico romanzo spagnuolo relativo alla storia di Napoli: "La Questión de Amor,"* Naples, 1894; Menéndez y Pelayo, M., "Orígines de la novela," *NBAE,* I.

Cuestión palpitante (La). A critical study on the French naturalist movement, written in 1883 by Pardo Bazán. The work was enthusiastically greeted by Emile Zola. See under *naturalism; Pardo Bazán.*

Cueva, Juan de la (1543-1610). Poet and dramatist of the pre-Lope de Vega school. Born and died in Seville. Although he began as a poet, he is chiefly known for his plays and dramatic theories. He wrote fourteen plays, published in Madrid in 1583. His best known drama is *El infamador* (1581), an allegorical play which has some parallels with the Don Juan legend and is therefore considered by some critics as a precursor of Don Juan literature. It served as a model for Tirso de Molina's *Burlador de Sevilla* (1630). Cueva's place in Spanish literature is assured despite the mediocrity of his literary output, because he was the first Spanish dramatist to have conceived a truly national drama based on national history and tradition. He went to the Spanish chronicles and ballads *(romanceros)* for his lyrical dramatizations of epic themes, *Bernardo de Carpio* and *Los siete infantes de Lara* (1579). In his *Saco de Roma* and *Cerco de Zamora* he also used historical sources. Most of his plays are of little merit, for they abound with the fantastic and supernatural elements typical of the literature of his day. With little regard for verisimilitude, his characters are subject to magic spells and metamorphoses; divine and satanic intervention disrupt the action; disguises and *qui pro quo* situations are rife; violence and sensationalism rule the boards. Perhaps the most human of his dramas is *La muerte de Virginia,* which introduced into Spanish drama the theme of filicide as a point of honor. Cueva would scarcely be remembered today if he had not formulated his theories of dramaturgy in a versified *ars poetica* entitled *Ejemplar poético* (1606). Here he departed from theories of the classical drama as interpreted by critics of the Italian renaissance. He cast aside the classical unities, reduced the number of acts from five to four, and favored a variety of verse forms. Most important of all he urged the use of national themes. Thus, in theory, if not entirely in practice, Cueva laid the foundations for the national drama of the Golden Age.

Cf. *Comedias y tragedias,* (Ed.) Icaza, F. A., Madrid, 1917; *El infamador, Los siete infantes de Lara y El ejemplar poético,* (Ed.) Icaza, F. A., Madrid, 1924; Walberg, E., "Juan de la Cueva et son *Ejemplar poético*," *Acta Universitatis Lundensis*, XXXIX, 1904; Gillet, J. E., "Cueva's 'Comedia del infamador' and the Don Juan Legend," *Modern Language Notes*, XXXVI; Morby, E. S., "Notes on Juan de la Cueva: Versification and Dramatic Theory," *Hispanic Review*, VIII, 1940.

culteranismo. Affected elegance of style cultivated by Spanish baroque writers of the 16th and 17th centuries. The characteristics of *culteranismo* were an extremely esoteric and stylized diction influenced by Latin syntax. The esthetic theory of *culteranismo*, as expounded by Carrillo de Sotomayor and the Marqués de Santillana, held that only the culturally élite were fit to appreciate literature and that writers should therefore address themselves to those grounded in the classics, capable of grasping remote mythological allusions, classical neologisms, involved metaphors and periodic constructions in unconventional word order. The extreme example of *culteranismo* is Góngora's *Soledades (ca.* 1613), scarcely readable without the aid of learned commentaries. Yet, despite its elaborate obscurity, it has elements of greatness lacking in the fustian style of Góngora's lesser imitators (Paravicino, Bocángel, *et al.).* The baroque style was not only a Spanish phenomenon *(Cp.* Euphuism in England, Marinism in Italy, *etc.).* In its esotericism, *culteranismo* may be considered as still viable in certain contemporary vanguardist movements. See also *conceptismo.*

Cf. Cañete, M., "Observaciones acerca de Góngora y del culteranismo en España," *Revue hispanique*, XLVI; Buceta, E., "Algunos antecedentes del culteranismo," *Romanic Review*, XI; García Soriano, J., "Carrillo y los orígines del culteranismo," *Boletín de la Real Academia Española*, XIII, 1926; Alonso, D., *La lengua poética de Góngora*, Madrid, 1935; Díaz-Plaja, G., *El espíritu del barroco*, Barcelona, 1940.

Cumandá. See under *Mera, Juan León de; "indianista" literature.*

Curioso Parlante (El). See *Mesonero Romanos.*

Cuthbertson, Stuart (1894). American hispanist. Associated with the University of Colorado since 1925; Professor and Head of Department since 1936. Author of *The Poetry of José Mármol*, 1935. Editor and co-author of *Historia cómica de España*, 1939; *Miguel Cané's Juvenilia*, 1942. Editor, *Hispania*, 1937-1939.

cuzqueño. A *Quechua* dialect. See under *Quechua.*

CH

Chacón y Calvo, José María (1893). Cuban literary critic, historian and essayist. Dean of the *Facultad de letras, Universidad Católica,* Havana. Founder of the *Revista Cubana.* Principal works: *Nueva vida de Heredia; Ensayos de literatura cubana; Gertrudis Gómez de Avellaneda; Orígenes de la poesía en Cuba; Romances tradicionales de Cuba; Estudios heredianos.*

Cf. *Hispania,* XXXVI, 1953.

chanson de geste. See *cantar de gesta.*

Chanson de Roland. See under *Roncesvalles.*

chanzoneta. (1) A gay or festive poem or song; a ballad or *chansonnette.* (2) In early Spanish literature, a festive song or poem intended for religious holidays.

Charlemagne. See under *Roncesvalles.*

chinchaya. A *Quechua* dialect. See under *Quechua.*

chiste. (adj. *chistoso).* (1) A witty saying or anecdote; a joke or jest; mockery or fun. (2) A comical or gay story, poem or song.

chivalric novel. See under *romances of chivalry.*

chivalric romances. See *romances of chivalry.*

Chocano, José Santos. (1875-1934). Peruvian poet, teacher, editor, political propagandist, diplomat and adventurer. A friend of Pancho Villa and of President Wilson, active in various political missions as a representative of Peru and of other countries, he either visited or resided in almost every Central and South American country, at times being expelled for political intrigue. His picaresque existence was terminated by an assassin in Chile. Chocano championed the cause of South American nationalism, striving for a synthesis of South American, Spanish and Indian culture and opposing North American imperialism. Considered in his day the peer of Rubén Darío as a modernist, Chocano was an inveterate versifier and literary-political essayist throughout his hectic career. An experimenter in many forms, his lyrical background of South American life and landscapes gives an authentic national imprint to his essentially romantic poetry. Among his chief works were: *En la aldea,* 1893; *Iras santas,* 1895; *El derrumbe,* 1899; *Alma América,* 1906; *Fiat lux,* 1908; *Poesías completas,* 1910; *Interpretación sumaria del programa de la revolución mejicana,* 1915; *El carácter agrario de la revolución,* 1915; *Ayacucho y los Andes,* 1925; *Primicias de oro de las Indias,* 1934; *Poesías escogidas,* 1938.

Cf. Umphrey, G. W., "José Santos Chocano," *Hispania,* III, 1920; Sánchez, L. A., "Amanecer, ocaso y mediodía de José Santos Chocano," *Cuadernos Americanos,* Nov.-Dec., 1954.

Chronicum mundi. See under *crónica.*

churrigueresco. An extravagantly ornate style *(estilo churrigueresco)* introduced by the Spanish architect, Churriguera, at the beginning of the 18th century. This term, as well as *churriguerismo,* is also used in literary criticism to designate the over-elaborate style of writing typical of the 17th century. Compare *plateresco.*

churriguerismo. See *churrigueresco.*

D

dactílico. A variant of the eleven-syllable verse, accented on the 4th, 7th and 10th syllables. Also known as the *endecasílabo de gaita gallega.* See under *gaita gallega; endecasílabo.*

Dalmiro. The pastoral name adopted by Cadalso as a member of the *Parnaso salmantino.* See under *Escuela de Salamanca.*

Dama boba (La). See under *Vega, Lope de.*

Dama duende (La). See under *Calderón.*

Dança de la Mort. A 15th century Catalan poem dealing with the *danse macabre* theme. See under *Danza de la muerte.*

danse macabre. See under *Danza de la muerte.*

Danza de la muerte (early 15th century). An anonymous poem of 79 stanzas in *arte mayor.* It is preserved in a manuscript in the *Biblioteca Escorial.* Because the codex includes the proverbs of the Rabbi Sem Tob, it was thought that he may have been the author, but this theory is now rejected. This Spanish version of the popular medieval theme of the *danse macabre* is superior to most others because of its social satire. In it the idea of Death, the Great Leveller, is applied to the various social classes and professions of 15th century Spain (Pope, Emperor, cleric, layman, Jew, Moor, merchant, lawyer, doctor, prostitute, usurer, *et al.);* and Death appears as the pitiless, grimly humorous excoriator of all. The antiphonal alternation of the victims' pleas and Death's inexorable condemnation lends a dramatic air to the poem. A contemporary Catalan poem *(Dança de la Mort)* treats the same theme. In the following century it was again taken up by Gil Vicente in his various *Autos de barca* (1517-1519), by Juan de Pedraza in his *Farsa llamada danza de la muerte* (1551); and it also appears in *Las cortes de la muerte* (1557), begun by Micael de Carvajal and completed by Luis Hurtado de Toledo.

Cf. *Danza de la muerte,* (Ed.) Icaza, F. A. de, Madrid, 1919; Kurtz, L. P., *The Dance of Death and the Macabre Spirit in European Literature,* N. Y., 1934.

Dares. See under *Historia troyana.*

Darío, Rubén (1867-1916). Nicaraguan poet, journalist and essayist. Born in Metapa; died in León, Nicaragua. Of mestizo descent, he was baptized Félix Rubén García y Sarmiento, but later assumed his nickname "Darío" as a pen name. A precocious versifier, his poetic talents were encouraged by his aunt, with whom he lived after his parents had separated. He was educated in a Jesuit school and later worked as a librarian and as a journalist before winning acclaim with the publication of *Azul* (Chile, 1888). From 1890 until his death he was a correspondent of *La Nación* of Buenos Aires, being sent to Spain on two occasions, 1892 and 1898. He was intimately associated with the literary and intellectual life of South America, France and Spain, founded the *Revista de América* (1896) together with Freyre, and was a friend of Rafael Núñez, Martí, Rodó, Verlaine, and many other writers of his time. Spanish America's greatest poetic genius, Darío was the founder and chief exemplar of modernism, exercising a profound regenerative influence not only on New World writers (Lugones, *et al.*) but also on those of Spain (Jiménez, *et al.*). Darío's work epitomizes the entire *modernista* movement, from its beginnings in the romantic nostalgia and French formalism of *Azul* (1888), to its apogee in the ivory-tower, Parnassian estheticism of *Prosas profanas* (1896), to its final synthesis in the Hispanic nationalism of *Cantos de vida y esperanza* (1905). The supersedence of modernism at its very height is already foreshadowed in the symbolic lines from his *Sonatina,* in which the imprisoned princess longs for the far-off prince who will liberate her from the cold palace of marble in which she is stifling:

> Pobrecita princesa de los ojos azules!
> Está presa en sus oros, está presa en sus tules,
> en la jaula de mármol del palacio real; . . . .

In *Cantos de vida y esperanza* the barren estheticism of the past is satirically dismissed:

> . . . . y muy siglo diez y ocho y muy antiguo
> y muy moderno, audaz, cosmopolita;
> con Hugo fuerte y con Verlaine ambiguo,
> y una sed de ilusiones infinita.

Darío's poetry ends on a positive note. It marks a return to lyrical simplicity and a faith in the Latin heritage of South America. See also under *modernismo*. His most important works were: *Primeras notas,* 1885; *Epistolas y poemas,* 1885; *Abrojos,* 1887; *Canto épico a las glorias de Chile,* 1887; *Azul,* 1888; *Rimas,* 1888; *Los raros,* 1893; *Prosas profanas,* 1896; *Castelar,* 1899; *Peregrinaciones,* 1901; *Cantos de vida y esperanza,* 1905; *Oda a Mitre,* 1906; *El canto errante,* 1907; *España contemporáneo,* 1907; *Poema del otoño y otros poemas,* 1910; *Canto a la Argentina y otros poemas,* 1910; *Historia de mis libros,* 1912; *Caras y caretas,* 1912; *Vida de Rubén Darío, escrita por él mismo,* 1916. *Obras completas,* Madrid, 1922 (Edited by the author's son, Rubén Darío Sánchez); *Obras poéticas completas,* Madrid, 1932 (Edited by Ghiraldo, A.; new edition by Méndez Plancarte, A., Madrid, 1952).

Cf. Lugones, L., *Rubén Darío,* Buenos Aires, 1919; Blanco-Fombona, R., *El modernismo y los poetas modernistas,* Madrid, 1929; Contreras, F., *Rubén Darío: su vida y su obra,* Barcelona, 1930; Torres-Ríoseco, A., *Rubén Darío, casticismo y americanismo,* Cambridge, Mass., 1931.

Débat du corps et de l'âme. See under *Disputa del alma y el cuerpo.*

debate. A literary form common in the allegorical literature of the Middle Ages. It is essentially a controversy in verse between two or more characters or personified abstractions, with the decision referred to a judge. The *debate* is usually didactic and/or satirical, and the subject may be love, honor, religion, ethics, literature, etc. Originating in Latin, Provençal and French poetry, the *debate* became a stock device in European literature. Examples in early Spanish literature are: *Disputa del alma y el cuerpo; Razón de amor con los denuestos del agua y el vino; Elena y María;* etc.

décima. The ten-line stanza of classical Spanish verse. The meter is octosyllabic; the rhyme scheme, ABBAACCDDC. The *décima* stanza form was used in the drama by Lope de Vega (1562-1635). Subsequently it was widely adopted, *e.g.,* by Meléndez Valdés (1754-1817), López García (1840-1870), and other poets. The *décima* is also called the *espinela,* after Vicente Espinel (1551-1624), who is supposed to have been its originator.

"Décima Musa de México". See *Cruz, Sor Juana Inés de la.*

decir. Title given to certain short poems in the Middle Ages and revived at various times since then. Older spellings are: *dezyr, dezir, desir,* etc. The form appears frequently in the *Cancionero de Baena* (1445), especially in selections from Francisco Imperial, Ferrán Sánchez de Calavera, Fernán Pérez de Guzmán, the Marqués de Santillana, and others. Most cited as examples of the form are the *decires* of Micer (Messer) Francisco Imperial *(Decir a las siete virtudes, Decir a estrella Diana, pidiéndole armas,* etc.), the first imitator of Dante in Spanish letters. Imperial's *decires* have an eight-line strophe, with either eleven, twelve or nine syllables to the line. In modern times the *decir* was revived by Rubén Darío (1867-1916) in his *Dezires, layes y canciones;* but he did not use the Italian eleven-syllable verse (hendecasyllable), preferring the irregular verses of primitive medieval poetry.

Cf. Foulché-Delbosc, R., "Cancionero castellano del siglo xv," *NBAE,* XIX; Chavez, M., *Micer Francisco Imperial: apuntes bio-bibliográficos,* Seville, 1899; García Rey, V., "El arcipreste de Talavera," *Revista de archivos, bibliotecas y museos,* 1928; Santillana, M. de, *Canciones y decires,* (Ed.) García de Diego, V., Madrid, 1913.

Decir a las siete virtudes. A Dantesque, allegorical poem in sixty *coplas* by Micer Francisco Imperial, early Renaissance poet. The poem appears as number 250 in the *Cancionero de Baena.* It is important as the first imitation of Dante in Spanish literature. See under *decir; Imperial.*

Defensa de la hispanidad. See under *Maeztu, Ramiro de.*

De la verdad como fuente de belleza. . . . See under *Tamayo y Baus.*

Delicado, Francisco (early 16th century). Andalusian priest and novelist about whom little is known except the dates of his publications and certain autobiographical allusions therein. His sojourn in Rome (1523-1527) is reflected in his novel, *Retrato de la loçana andaluza* (Venice, 1528), generally referred to as *La lozana andaluza.* Diffuse in plot and with a teeming confusion of minor characters, its importance is as a document of Roman manners during the Renaissance; for its vivid prose dialogue and crude realism paint a sordid picture of the licentiousness and corruption of Rome. In the Celestina-Justina tradition, the adventures of the female "rogue", from whom the novel takes its title, make it one of the first of the picaresque genre. Delicado is also known as the editor of an *Amadís* (Venice, 1533).

Cf. *Retrato de la lozana andaluza,* (Ed.) Segovia, E. M. de, Madrid, 1916; Haan, F. de, *An Outline of the History of the "Novela Picaresca" in Spain,* N. Y., 1903; Menéndez y Pelayo, M., *Orígines de la novela,* Buenos Aires, 1946; Suárez, M., *La novela picaresca y el pícaro en la literatura española,* Madrid, 1926.

Delio. The pastoral name adopted by Diego González, leader of the *Parnaso salmantino.* See under *Escuela de Salamanca.*

De los nombres de Cristo. See under *León, Luis de.*

Del rey abajo ninguno. See under *Rojas Zorrilla.*

del Río, Ángel. See *Río, Ángel del.*

Del sentimiento trágico de la vida. See under *Unamuno.*

Denuestos del agua y el vino (Los). A medieval *debate* which is appended to the manuscript of *Razón de amor* (13th century). See under *Razón de amor.*

De rebus Hispaniae. See under *Ximénez de Rada.*

De rege et regis institutione. See under *Mariana, Juan de.*

desafricanización. See under *europeización.*

Desdén con el desdén (El). See under *Moreto, Agustín.*

Desheredada (La). See under *Pérez Galdós.*

Deshumanización del arte (La). See under *Ortega y Gasset.*

desir. See *decir.*

Desolación. See under *Mistral, Gabriela.*

dezir. See *decir.*

dezyr. See *decir.*

Diable boiteux (Le). Le Sage's novel (1707) based on *El diablo cojuelo* (1641) by Luis Vélez de Guevara. See under *Vélez de Guevara.*

Diablo cojuelo (El). See under *Vélez de Guevara.*

Diálogo de Lactancio. See under *Valdés, Alfonso de.*

Diálogo de la doctrina cristiana. See under *Valdés, Juan de.*

Diálogo de la lengua. See under *Valdés, Juan de.*

Diálogo de Mercurio y Carón. See under *Valdés, Alfonso de.*

Diálogo de mujeres. See under *Castillejo.*

Diálogos. See under *Vives, Juan Luis.*

Diálogos de amor. See under *Hebreo, León.*

Diana. See under *Montemayor, Jorge de.*

Diana enamorada. A pastoral romance by Gaspar Gil Polo, written in 1564, and superior in its poetry to its model, the *Diana* of Jorge de Montemayor. See also under *Montemayor, Jorge de.*

Diario de los Literatos. A literary review of the 18th century. A quasi-official publication, it appeared from 1737 to 1742 and was edited by Juan Martínez Salafranca and Leopoldo Jerónimo Puig. Among its contributors was Iriarte.

Díaz del Castillo, Bernal (1492-1581). Soldier and historian. Member of an influential family in Medina del Campo, Spain, he came to America in 1514 and participated in several expeditions and battles of the conquest. He served with Dávila in Darien, with Velásquez in Cuba, with Grijalva in Yucatan, and with Cortés in Mexico. Taking issue with the learned humanist, López de Gómara, who had written a *Crónica de la conquista de la Nueva España* (1552), Bernal Díaz composed his *Verdadera historia de los sucesos de la conquista de Nueva España,* which, however, was not published until 1632. Although his style is not as polished as that of his predecessor, Bernal Díaz gives a much more balanced account of the conquest, written from the viewpoint of a professional soldier.

Cf. Cunninghame Graham, R. B., *Bernal Díaz del Castillo,* London, 1915.

Díaz Mirón, Salvador (1853-1928). Mexican poet. Influenced by Byron and Hugo in his early work *(Poesías,* 1886), he developed into a forerunner of the modernists. He was greatly admired by Darío and Chocano, but his work also contained the elements that were to supersede modernism. His fame rests on a single volume of his later poems, *(Lascas,* 1901), in which the frequently vague and cryptic content is overshadowed by an exquisite perfection of form.

Cf. Blanco-Fombona, R., *El modernismo y los poetas modernistas,* Madrid, 1929; Meza Fuentes, R., *De Díaz Mirón a Rubén Darío,* Santiago, 1940; *Poesías completas,* Ed. by Castro Leal, A., Mexico, 1941.

Díaz-Plaja, Guillermo (1909). Literary historian, critic and poet. Born in Barcelona. In 1931 he took his doctorate in philosophy and literature at the University of Madrid. In 1936 his work on Spanish romanticism, *Introducción al estudio del romanticismo español,* was awarded the National Prize for Literature. Among his other studies, much quoted in histories of Spanish literature, are: *Rubén Darío* (1930); *La poesía lírica española* (1937); *El espíritu del barroco,* (1941); and *Federico García Lorca* (1948). Among his poetic works is *Vencedor de mi muerte* (1952).

Díaz Rodríguez, Manuel (1868-1927). Venezuelan poet, essayist and novelist. Outstanding "modernista" writer. Many of his works are considered classical examples of modernist style. His influence, notably on the work of Rodó, was considerable. His work was a combination of realism with psychological insight and esthetic subtlety. Díaz Rodríguez had one essential theme, romantic alienation and frustration. His chief works were: *Cuentos de color,* 1898; *Ídolos rotos,* 1901; *Sangre patricia,* 1902; *Camino de perfección,* 1907; *Peregrina o el pozo encantado,* 1922.

Cf. *Obras completas,* Caracas, 1955; Ratcliff, D. F., *Venezuelan Prose Fiction,* N. Y., 1933.

Diccionario de autoridades. The popular name of the *Diccionario de la lengua castellana;* derived from the fact that the dictionary is based on the authoritative usage of the great Spanish writers. See under *Real Academia Española.*

Diccionario de la lengua castellana. See under *Real Academia Española.*

Diccionario de la Real Academia Española. (Abbr. *DRAE).* See under *Real Academia Española.*

Dictys. See under *Historia troyana.*

Diego, Gerardo (1896). Lyric poet. Born in Santander. Studied at Salamanca and at Madrid. A gifted teacher, lecturer and musician, he began his writing career in 1918 when he won a prize in a literary contest sponsored by *La Revista General.* In 1925, on the basis of a collection of his verse entitled *Versos humanos,* he was awarded the National Prize for Literature (jointly with Alberti). Since 1947 he has been a member of the *Academia Española.* His early poems revealed the influence of the theories of *ultraísmo* and *creacionismo (Imagen,* 1922; *Manual de espumas,* 1924). A similar doctrinaire influence, that of neogongorism, is evident in his *Fábula de Equis y Zeda.* Diego is at his best when his poetic emotions transcend his vanguardist theories *(Romancero de la novia; Soria; Versos humanos).* The personal religious note of his later period seems to point to a synthesis of his previous styles *(Ángeles de Compostela).* Diego has also com-

Durán, Agustín (1793-1862). Bibliographer, librarian, folklorist, editor of ballad collections, historian and theoretician of the Spanish theatre. Director of the *Biblioteca Nacional.* A friend of Quintana and of Böhl de Faber, he was one of the theoreticians of Romanticism, opposing the strait jacket of Neoclassicism (Cf. his "Discurso sobre el influjo de la crítica moderna en la decadencia del teatro antiguo español . . . ," *Memorias de la Real Academia Española,* I, Madrid, 1828). From 1828 to 1832 Durán compiled and edited a *Colección de romances antiguos* and *Colección de romances castellanas anteriores al siglo* XVIII, popularly known as the *Romancero general,* or *Romancero de Durán.*

E

Echegaray, José (1832-1916). Spain's outstanding dramatist in the last third of the 19th century. A man of great energy and intellectual endowment, he was successively a professor of mathematics, an engineer, an economist and a minister in various governments from 1868 on. As Minister of Finance (1874), he was instrumental in the founding of the Bank of Spain. Not until he was past 40 did he turn to the theater, his first effort being *El libro talonario* (1874), a thesis play proving that the punishment fits the crime. From this time on until shortly after the turn of the century, he produced some 64 dramas, comedies and one-act plays, both in prose and in verse, becoming a favorite of public and critics alike. He was elected to the *Academia Española* in 1894, and received the Nobel prize for literature (jointly with Frédéric Mistral) in 1904. Until about 1885 Echegaray's plays were chiefly romantic (*La esposa vengador, En el seno de la muerte,* etc.). But with the increasing vogue of the European thesis or problem plays of Ibsen, Strindberg and Sudermann, by whom he was strongly influenced, he also turned to this medium. Echegaray frequently conveyed his message of moral and social conflicts by a satirical reversal of popular notions of morality. Thus, he demonstrated that honesty is not the best policy, since the world considers the truly honest man to be insane *(O locura o santidad);* or that virtue is not its own reward, because society with its cynical calumny drives the virtuous into sin *(El gran galeoto).* The satirical reversal is also evident in *A fuerza de arrastrarse* (success can be achieved by crawling through life), and in *El poder de la impotencia* (those who lack the moral strength to do good can still be strong enough to prevent others from doing so), etc. Although deft in craftsmanship, much of Echegaray's dramatic art is fantastic and contrived. Like Sudermann, he was overestimated in his time and has now gone into an eclipse. The undisputed monarch of the boards in his day is now scarcely revived in the modern theater. The titles of his more important plays are: *El libro talonario,* 1874; *La esposa vengador,* 1874; *O locura o santidad,* 1877; *En el seno de la muerte,* 1879; *La muerte en los labios,* 1880; *El gran galeoto,* 1881; *Lo sublime en lo vulgar,* 1890; *Un crítico incipiente,* 1891; *Malas herencias,* 1892; *Mariana,* 1892; *El hijo de don Juan,* 1892; *El estigma,* 1895; *Mancha que limpia,* 1895; *La duda,* 1898; *El loco dios,* 1900; *A fuerza de arrastrarse,* 1905; *Recuerdos,* 1917.

Cf. *Obras dramáticas,* 9 vols., Madrid, 1874-1898; Goldberg, I., *Don José Echegaray: A study in Modern Spanish Drama* (Diss.), Harvard, 1912; Courzon, H., *Le théâtre de José Echegaray,* Paris, 1913; Mérimée, H., "José Echegaray et son oeuvre dramatique," *Bulletin hispanique,* XVIII, 1916; González Blanco, A., *Los dramaturgos españoles,* Valencia, 1917; Eguía Ruiz, C., *Crítica patriótica,* Madrid, 1921; Quintero, A., "Echegaray, dramaturgo," *Boletín de la Real Academia Española,* XIX, 1932; Bell, A. F. G., *Contemporary Spanish Literature,* N. Y., 1933.

Echeverría, Esteban (1805-1851). Argentine poet. Born in Buenos Aires. Educated at the *Colegio de Ciencias Morales* (1820-1823). Lived in Paris (1826-1830), where he read Schiller and Byron and came under the influence of Hugo and De Musset, developing into a full-fledged romanticist in his own right. An opponent of the dictator Rosas, he was exiled in 1839 and lived in Uruguay until his death in Montevideo. Echeverría was the conscious innovator and theoretician of the romantic school in Spanish American literature, formulating its program, ideology and esthetics in his essay, *Fondo y forma de las obras de imaginación.* He envisioned an American epic, independent of classical influence, and glorified the poet as the supreme creative being subject to nothing but his own untrammeled imagination. He himself did not quite achieve the goals of his program, never exceeding the work of his French masters. His most famous poem, *La cautiva,* is a typical romantic product with its aura of vague melancholy emanating from the Argentine landscape. The titles of his chief works are: *Elvira o la novia del Plata,* 1832; *Los consuelos,* 1834; *Rimas* (including *La cautiva*), 1837; *El matadero,* 1838; *Obras completas* (Edited by Gutiérrez, J. M., 1870-1874).

Cf. Rojas, R., *La literatura argentina,* Buenos Aires, 1924-1925.

Eckehard. See under *mysticism.*

eclogue. See *égloga.*

Ecos de las montañas. See under *Zorrilla y Moral.*

Eco y Narciso. One of Calderón's musical plays. See under *zarzuela.*

Edad de Oro. See *Siglo de Oro.*

Edipo. See under *Martínez de la Rosa.*

Editorial América. See under *Blanco-Fombona.*

Edwards Bello, Joaquín (1888). Chilean journalist and novelist. Editor of *La Nación* in Santiago. Awarded the National Literary Prize in 1943. Of aristocratic origin, he is democratic in spirit, advocating the welfare of the lower and middle classes. His style is journalistic but raised to a high level by his social compassion. Among his chief works are: *El inútil,* 1910; *El roto,* 1920; *El chileno en Madrid,* 1928; *En el viejo almendral,* 1943.

Cf. Torres Ríoseco, A., *Novelistas contemporáneos de América,* Santiago, 1940.

égloga. (Eng. *eclogue*). A bucolic or pastoral poem. Modeled after Virgil's bucolics, the type was cultivated in the Middle Ages and continued into the Renaissance. Juan del Encina (1468?-1529) was the first to use the term in Spanish literature (in reference to his pastoral plays). Later the name was used by Garcilaso de la Vega (1503-1536) for lyric poetry. Garcilaso's *églogas* were written in a variety of meters, thus showing that it was the pastoral aspect rather than the poetic form which was distinctive of the eclogue. See also under *Encina, Juan del.*

Ejemplar poético. See under *Cueva.*

ejemplo. Older spellings, *enxemplo, enxiemplo.* Derived from Latin, *exemplum* (pl. *exempla*). Sometimes called *apólogo* (apologue) or *fábula* (fable), although the latter terms also have specialized meanings. The *ejemplo* is the didactic or moral tale of the 13th through the 15th centuries. The earlier specimens are contained in anonymous collections and are generally a series of stories within a story, known as the "frame." The origin of these tales is oriental. They have been traced back to Sanskrit, Persian, Arabic, Greek and Latin sources. Chronologically arranged, the chief works containing *ejemplos* are Pero Alfonso's *Disciplina Clericalis* (early 12th century), *Calila et Digna* (1251), *Libro de los engaños y asayamientos de las mujeres* (1253), *Barlaam y Josaphat* (13th century), Juan Manuel's *Libro de los* *enxiemplos del Conde Lucanor et de Patronio* (1330-1335), *Castigos y documentos* (mid-14th century) by García de Castrojeriz, *Libro de los gatos* (early 15th century), and *Libro de los enxemplos* or *Suma de enxemplos por A.B.C.* by Clemente Sánchez de Vercial (d. 1426). The latter was fashioned after the Latin *Alphabeta exemplorum* or *Alphabeta narrationum* (13th century), and is the most extensive collection of *ejemplos* (476 tales). The moral of each tale is given in a rhymed couplet under the Latin inscription at the beginning. This feature and the alphabetical arrangement facilitated its use by preachers in preparing their sermons.

Cf. Hilka and Söderhjelm, (Ed.) *Die disciplina clericalis des Petrus Alfonsi,* Heidelberg, 1911; Alemany, J., (Ed.) *Calila et Digna,* Madrid, 1915; Bonilla y San Martín, (Ed.) "Libro de los engannos et los assayamientos de las mugeres," *Bibliotheca hispanica,* XIV; Lauchert, (Ed.) "Barlaam et Josaphat," *Romanische Forschungen,* VII, 1893; Knust, H., (Ed.) *El libro de los enxiemplos del conde Lucanor et de Patronio,* Leipzig, 1900; Gayangos, P., (Ed.) "Castigos e documentos," *BAE,* LI; Northup, G. T., (Ed.) "El libro de los gatos," *Modern Philology,* V, 1908; Morel-Fatio, A., (Ed.) "Libro de los enxemplos de Clemente Sánchez de Vercial," *Romania* VII, 1878.

"El Divino." See *Herrera, Fernando de.*

El Europeo. Influential Romantic periodical published in Barcelona (1823-1824). See under *Romanticism.*

Elena, La ingeniosa. See under *Salas Barbadillo.*

Elena y María. An anonymous *juglaría* poem written in the 13th century in Leonese dialect. The manuscript copy, dating from the 14th century, consists of 402 lines, irregular in length and rhyming in couplets. Assonance occasionally occurs instead of rhyme. The poem is an example of popular rather than courtly *mester de clerecía.* It is also known under the title of *Disputa del clérigo y del caballero.* In a popular, realistic tone, two ladies debate the respective merits of their lovers, one an abbot, the other a knight. In a spirited interchange of argument and counter-argument, the dispute waxes acrimonious and satirical. Both the contemplative life and the vocation of knighthood are alternatively praised and damned. The topic was a favorite one in medieval Latin and French literature. Inconsistencies in the manuscript lead to the assumption that there were earlier prototypes, now lost.

Cf. Menéndez Pidal, R., (Ed.), "Elena y María, o Disputa del clérigo y del caballero," *Revista de filología española,* I, 1914.

El Inca. See *Garcilaso de la Vega (El Inca).*

El Sabio. See *Alfonso X.*

El sí de las niñas. See under *Moratín.*

"El Solitario." See Estébanez Calderón, Serafín.

emigrado. A term referring to a political exile. In particular, one of the romanticists exiled during the absolute monarchy of Fernando VII (1808-1833). Many of these *emigrados* returned to Spain after 1833 and became potent influences in the renewal of Spanish letters: *e.g.* Martínez de la Rosa (1787-1862), Duque de Rivas (1791-1865), José de Espronceda (1808-1842), *et al.* More recently the term is understood as applicable to one of the literary or intellectual exiles following the Spanish Civil War (1936 *et seq.*); *e.g.* Juan Larrea (b. 1895), León Felipe (b. 1884), Juan Ramón Jiménez (b. 1881), Tomás Navarro Tomás (b. 1884), Américo Castro (b. 1885), Pedro Salinas (1892-1951), Jorge Guillén (b. 1893), *et al.* See also under *Romanticism.*

Cf. Peers, E. A., *A History of the Romantic Movement in Spain,* 2 vols., Cambridge, 1940; Díaz-Plaja, G., *Introducción al estudio del romanticismo español,* 2a ed., Madrid, 1942; Río, A. del, "La guerra civil y sus consecuencias," *Historia de la literatura española,* vol. 2, pp. 267-271, N. Y., 1948.

Empresas políticas. See under *Saavedra Fajardo.*

encabalgamiento. In metrics, the running over of a thought or sentence from one verse or line into the next. The opposite phenomenon is called *esticomitia;* i.e. the ending of a sentence at the exact end of a metrical line. In *encabalgamiento* the syntactical exceeds the metrical unit; in *esticomitia* the syntactical and metrical units are identical. The French term *enjambement* is frequently used with the same meaning as *encabalgamiento.* Compare *esticomitia.*

encadenamiento. The linking of stanzas through continuation of a rhyme. For example, *tercetos en cadena* are rhymed ABA, BCB, *etc.* See also under *terceto.*

Encina, Juan del (1468?-1529?). Musician, poet and playwright. The earliest dramatic writer of importance in the history of the

Spanish theater, he is referred to as the "patriarco del teatro español". The exact place of his birth is not known, but it is thought to have been Encinas, near Salamanca. He probably died in León. Educated at the University of Salamanca, he became a musical composer, and in 1492 was attached to the household of the second Duke of Alva. His first *églogas* (pastoral-religious plays) were performed in the ducal palace at Alba de Tormes (1492 *et seq.*). He served as cantor in the Chapel of Pope Leo X at Rome, where he spent many years from 1502 on, and where one of his plays, *Égloga de Plácida y Vitoriano,* was performed in 1512. Although he took minor orders at an early age, he was not ordained as a priest until 1519, after which he undertook a pilgrimage to Jerusalem, where he celebrated his first mass. He spent his closing years as a canon at León. Encina's *Cancionero* (1496) contains eight plays, several lyrics and, as an introduction, his *Arte de la poesía castellana.* The *Cancionero* editions of 1507 and of 1509 contain two further plays each. In addition, some 68 of his musical compositions have been preserved. Although a fine lyricist, as shown by the *villancicos* at the end of his plays, Encina is now remembered as a dramatist, particularly for his adaptations of Virgil's *Eclogues,* which in his *églogas* became a truly Spanish genre, with peasants as shepherds, speaking their racy *sayagués* dialect of the region around Salamanca. Encina's earlier efforts were religious plays *(representaciones)* presented before the nobility at Christmas, Good Friday and Easter, forerunners of the *autos sacramentales* of the Golden Age. His first *églogas* combined secular and religious elements *(Égloga de las grandes lluvias, Égloga de tres pastores,* 1498-1507). In their final development his *églogas* were almost completely secularized, or else dealt with themes from classical mythology *(Égloga de Plácida y Vitoriano, Égloga de Cristino y Febea,* 1513-1514). All of Encina's work was in verse (octosyllabic meter and varied stanza forms). He himself composed the lyrics and music *(villancicos, cantarcillos de amores)* which, accompanied by dances, terminated almost all of his plays. Thus he can also be considered as having introduced the germinal idea of the *zarzuela* of succeeding centuries. His importance in the history of the Spanish theater is that he began almost all of the genres that were to be developed by later dramatists. In his own day he was responsible for giving the previous liturgical drama its secular transformation under the influence of the Renaissance pastoral.

Cf. *Teatro completo de Juan del Encina,* (facsimile ed. with intro. by Cotarelo y Mori, E.), Real Academia Española, Madrid, 1893; *Teatro completo,* (Ed.) Cañete, M. and Barbieri, F. A., Madrid, 1913; Barbieri, F. A., *Cancionero musical de los siglos XV y XVI,* Madrid, 1890-1904; Wickersham Crawford, J. P., *Spanish Drama Before Lope de Vega,* 2nd ed., Philadelphia, 1937; *idem, The Spanish Pastoral Drama,* 2nd ed., Philadelphia, 1938.

endecasílabo. A verse of eleven syllables, variously accented. Of Italian origin, the form was introduced into Spanish poetry by Santillana and then rendered indigenous by Boscán and Garcilaso. The type of *endecasílabo* used by the latter is also known as the *yámbico* or *heroico,* which is accented on the 6th and 10th syllables. Other variants of the *endecasílabo* are the *sáfico,* accented on the 4th and 8th syllables; and the *anapéstico,* accented on the 4th, 7th and 10th syllables. This latter form, cultivated in the Middle Ages, is also known as the *endecasílabo de gaita gallega or dactílico.* See also under *gaita gallega.*

endecha. A short lyric, sad or plaintive in tone. Its usual form is the rhymed quatrain, with verses of six or seven syllables. A variation of this form is the *endecha real,* which combines two such quatrains, except that the last line of each quatrain has eleven syllables.

endecha real. See under *endecha.*

eneasílabo. A verse of nine syllables.

Engaños y asayamientos de las mujeres. See *Libro de los engaños, etc.*

Englekirk, John Eugene (1905). Professor and Chairman of Department of Spanish and Portuguese, Tulane University, since 1939. Visiting Professor, Columbia University and universities of Pennsylvania, Wisconsin, Chicago and Texas. President, A.A.T.S., 1949. Author of *Edgar Allen Poe in Hispanic Literature,* N. Y., 1934; *Bibliografía de obras norteamericanas en traducción española,* Mexico, 1944; *La novela colombiana* (with Wade, G. E.), Mexico, 1952; Co-author of *An Outline History of Spanish American Literature,* N. Y., 1941; and *An Anthology of Spanish*

American Literature, N. Y., 1946. Co-editor of *Los de abajo,* N. Y., 1939.

enjambement. (Sp. *encabalgamiento).* The running over of the thought of one metrical line into the next. The term is French but is used internationally. Compare *encabalgamiento; esticomitia.*

En las orillas del Sar. See under *Castro, Rosalía de.*

Ennio español (El). See under *Mena, Juan de.*

Ensayos sobre la poesía española. See under *Alonso, Dámaso.*

En torno al casticismo. See under *Unamuno.*

entrega. A fascicle of a publication. *La literatura por entregas* is a reference to a popular 19th century type of serialized novel printed in fascicles as supplements to newspapers and magazines. These works were of French inspiration (Eugene Sue, Victor Hugo, *etc.).* They were a minor example of the romantic historical novel, careless in style, vague and rambling in plot. The chief representatives of this type were Manuel Fernández y González (1821-1888), and Wenceslao Ayguals de Izco (1801-1873).

entremés. A one-act, humorous or satirical play, skit or character sketch, generally with songs and dances, presented between the acts of a longer play. It corresponds to the English "interlude" and the French *entr'acte.* The term is derived from the French word *entremets* ("between courses"), and originally referred to musical entertainment between courses at sumptuous banquets. The first mention of the term occurs in a collection of plays entitled *Turiana,* compiled by Juan de Timoneda (d. 1583) and published in Valencia in 1565. The *entremés* represents a Spanish dramatic tradition that begins with the *pasos* (short dramatic sketches) of Lope de Rueda (d. 1565), was cultivated as the *entremés* in the 17th century (Cervantes, Quiñones de Benavente, Calderón), developed into the *sainete* from the 18th century on (Ramón de la Cruz), and continued as the *género chico* in the 19th century. In modern times the form was adopted by the Quintero brothers. The *entremeses* of Cervantes *(El Rufián viudo, El juez de los divorcios, La cueva de Salamanca,* etc.) are considered the best of the type. They lasted about a half hour at most, and ended with songs and dances. The most prolific *entremesista* (generally ranked after Cervantes in this genre) was

Luis Quiñones de Benavente (1589?-1651), who devoted himself entirely to the *entremés* and is supposed to have written some 900 of them (*El murmurado, Los coches, El marido flemático, El borracho,* etc.). See also *género chico; paso.*

Cf. Cotarelo y Mori, E., (Ed.) "Colección de entremeses . . . ," *NBAE,* XVII-XVIII, Madrid, 1911; Herrero García, M., (Ed.) *Cervantes: Entremeses,* Madrid, 1945; Cayetano Rosell, (Ed.), "Entremeses . . . de Quiñones de Benavente," *Libros de antaño,* I-II; "Calderón: Entremeses," *BAE,* XIV; Rouanet, L., *Intermèdes espagnoles du XVIIe siècle,* Paris, 1897.

entremesista. See under *entremés.*

Entre Nosotros. Official publication of *Sigma Delta Pi,* U. S. national honorary Spanish society.

Entwistle, William J. (1896-1952). British hispanist. Professor at Oxford University. Author of *The Arthurian Legend in the Literatures of the Spanish Peninsula* (1925); *The Spanish Language* (1936); *European Balladry* (1939); and *Cervantes* (1940).

enxemplo. see *ejemplo.*

enxiemplo. See *ejemplo.*

epenthesis. (Sp. *epéntesis*). The insertion of a sound or letter in a word or sound group. The inserted element is called an "anaptyctic" or "excrescent" sound or letter (*sonido epentético*). The cause of such a phenomenon is often phonetic rather than etymological (*i.e.* to facilitate a difficult transition between two other adjacent sounds, or to promote euphony). Examples: venire habeo > *ven're* > *vendré;* tua > *tuya;* tonu > *trueno.*

Cf. Pei, M. A. and Gaynor, F., *A Dictionary of Linguistics,* N. Y., 1954; Lázaro Carreter, F., *Diccionario de términos filológicos,* Madrid, 1953.

Episodios nacionales. See under *Pérez Galdós.*

Epitome de Gramática. See under *Real Academia Española.*

equívoco. A figure of speech or stylistic device involving word play or equivocation; a quibble or pun. The *equívoco* was a type of deliberate ambiguity allowing the possibility of more than one interpretation of the same word or expression. This type of word play with double meanings was in vogue during the baroque period. See also under *gongorismo.*

Erasmus. See under *humanism; mysticism; Reformation.*

Ercilla, Alonso de (1533-1594). Spanish courtier, soldier and poet. Born in Madrid. A favorite of Philip II., Ercilla spent seven years in South America (1556-1563), during which time he served as a captain under García Hurtado de Mendoza in the conquest of Chile. The experiences of this campaign against the brave and stubborn resistance of the Araucanian Indians provided the inspiration for his *La Araucana,* an epic poem in royal octaves, divided into three parts and 37 cantos. The three parts were published separately in Madrid (1569, 1578, 1589). *La Araucana* is the best example of the Golden Age epic. It introduced the Indian theme to Spanish literature. Ercilla treats the Indians with great sympathy. His descriptions of characters, action and background are vivid and authentic, rising at time to heights of true poetic emotion. Because of its subject matter and locale, *La Araucana* belongs as much to South American as to Spanish literature. (Text in BAE, XVII; facsimile edition by Huntington, A. M., Hispanic Society of America, N. Y., 1902.)

Cf. Ducamin, J., *L'Araucana,* Paris, 1900; Lillo, S. A., "Ercilla y La Araucana," *Anales de la Universidad de Chile,* VI, 1928; Solar Correa, E., *Semblanzas literarias de la colonia,* Santiago, 1933.

Eruditos a la violeta (Los). See under *Cadalso.*

Escenas andaluzas. See under *Estébanez Calderón.*

Escenas matritenses. See under *Mesonero Romanos.*

Escenas montañesas. See under *Pereda, José María de.*

Escuela del matrimonio (La). See under *Bretón de los Herreros.*

Escuela de Salamanca. There are two Salamancan schools referred to by historians of Spanish literature, one in the 16th and one in the 18th century. The chief poet of the earlier Salamancan school was the humanist and mystic, Fray Luis de Léon (1527-1591). Among his followers were Pedro Malón de Chaide (1530?-1581) and Francisco de la Torre (1534?-?). Unlike the poets of the Sevillan school, this group emphasized content over form. Their language was more sober, their orientation more spiritual and subjective. Mysticism, humanism and "Erasmism" were the hallmarks of the 16th century Salamancan school. In the second half of the 18th century, a poetic renaissance began at Salamanca under the leadership of Fray Diego González (1732-1794), who was the central figure of the so-called *Parnaso salmantino.* In imitation of the custom of the Italian Renaissance literary academies, the members of the 18th century Salamancan school adopted pastoral names. Thus, Diego González was known as *Delio;* Juan Fernández de Rojas (1750?-1819) as *Liseno;* José Iglesias de la Casa (1748-1791) as *Arcadio,* etc. Others associated with this later Salamancan school were José Cadalso (1741-1782) –*Dalmiro*–; Juan Pablo Forner (1756-1797)–*Aminta*–; Gaspar Melchor de Jovellanos (1744-1811)–*Jovino*–; and the greatest poet of them all, Juan Meléndez Valdéz (1754-1817)–*Batilo*–. At first addicted to neoclassic forms (bucolics, anacreontics, eclogues, etc.), the younger members of the group broke away from the pastoral tradition and began to occupy themselves with moral and philosophical poetry, especially under the inspiration of Jovellanos. Also known as *Escuela salmantina.*

Cf. Del Río, A., *Historia de la literatura española,* N. Y., 1948.

Escuela de traductores de Toledo. The group of medieval scholars assembled by Don Raimundo, Archbishop of Toledo (d. 1150), for the purpose of translating Arabic works into Latin. Their translations, preceding the work of Alfonso X, were an important source of Arabic, Hebrew and Greco-Roman culture for Spanish writers of the Middle Ages.

Cf. González Palencia, A., *Don Raimundo y los traductores de Toledo,* Madrid, 1942.

Escuela modernista. See *modernismo.*

Escuela salmantina. See *Escuela de Salamanca.*

Escuela sevillana. Of the two different schools identified by this name, the 16th century group consisted mainly of poets and humanists. Their leaders were the poet, Fernando de Herrera (1534?-1597), and the humanist educator, Juan de Mal Lara (1524-1571). Herrera's chief theoretical work was his *Anotaciones a las obras de Garcilaso de la Vega* (1580). Mal Lara was the head of the *Escuela de Humanidades y Gramática,* at which many of the 16th century Sevillan poets studied. Among the other poets identified with the 16th century *Escuela sevillana* were Francisco de Medrano (1570-1607), Francisco Pacheco (1540?-1599), Baltasar del Alcázar (1530-1606), Francisco de Medina (d. 1615?), and Juan de la Cueva (1543-1610). This earlier Sevillan school was neoclassic, *culto* and aristocratic in its orientation. Its emphasis was on form and language. It represented the transition between the first stage of Renaissance, Italianate classicism (Garcilaso) and its final decadent stage (Góngora). At the end of the 18th century a group of writers and poets also began a movement of literary reform in Seville. They represented the transition between neoclassicism and romanticism. The leaders of the Sevillan school were: Alberto Lista (1775-1848), Félix José Reinoso (1772-1841), Manuel María Arjona (1771-1820), and José María Blanco White (1775-1841). These men formed the *Academia de letras humanas* (1793) to spread their ideas and to raise the level of literary appreciation. In general, however, they preached neoclassicism and their failure was a foregone conclusion in the face of the emergent romanticism of the 19th century. Thus, Alberto Lista, as a literary critic, schooled the taste of Espronceda and Ventura de la Vega according to his neoclassic standards, but they developed in a contrary direction. Lacking originality and inspiration as poets, nonetheless the writers of the 18th century Sevillan school made a few positive contributions which found rapport with the younger romantic generation. They admitted Biblical and religious subjects, a distinct departure from classical precepts; and they encouraged patriotic and humanitarian themes.

Cf. Del Río, A., *Historia de la literatura española,* N. Y., 1948.

"Es de Lope". A phrase used in Lope de Vega's time to denote excellence in regard to anything. It was a reflection of the universal acknowledgment of his genius.

España del Cid (La). See under *Menéndez Pidal.*

España invertebrada. See under *Ortega y Gasset.*

España Sagrada. See under *Flórez, Enrique.*

Español. See *Spanish.*

españolismo. (1) Extreme cultural isolationism as a Spanish national trait. It is expressed chiefly in resistance to foreign influences and accounts for much of the parochialism of Spanish literature.

(2) Patriotic concern for the revival and preservation of the permanent cultural values in the Spanish heritage, land and people. It is expressed in regionalism, folklore, adaptation of foreign influences to the Spanish character *(europeización de España),* insistence on *voluntad* as an antidote to *abulia,* and is typical of the *regeneracionismo* of the Generation of 1898.

The term is most commonly used in critical literature in the first of the two meanings above. In this sense, *españolismo* reached its height during the period of Spain's greatness (15th and 16th centuries), when national glorification, with its corollary disdain for other cultures, was the general attitude of Spanish intellectuals. It has been variously explained as the result of geographical, historical, racial, social and religious factors ("peninsularity", separatism, *casticismo, caciquismo, catolocismo).* A weak counter-current to this trait set in with the Renaissance (Italian, humanist influence), and again appeared during the 18th century Enlightenment (French, rationalist influence); but these movements never flourished in Spain as they did in other European countries. In the 19th century the Spanish romanticists, especially the *emigrados* who returned in 1833, introduced a leavening of cosmopolitanism into Spanish letters (Hugo, Byron, *etc.).* However, the romantic revival of interest in medieval literature, popular folksongs and ballads, the regional landscape, customs and manners foreshadowed an *españolismo* in the second meaning given above. In this sense, we find a patriotic and enlightened concern for those elements in the national culture that can be a source of strength in overcoming Spain's decadence. This was the major theme of Costa *(Oligarquía y caciquismo,* 1901), Unamuno *(Ensayos,* 1890 *et seq.)* and Ganivet *(Idearium español,* 1897, who, in spite of their wide background in many languages and cultures and their general cosmopolitan outlook, were obsessed with the destiny of Spain above all.

Cf. Northup, G. T., *An Introduction to Spanish Literature,* 2nd ed., Chicago, 1936. García Mercadal, J., *Ideario español: Costa,* Madrid, 1919; Espina, A., *Ganivet: el hombre y la obra,* Buenos Aires, 1942; Marías, J., *Miguel de Unamuno,* Madrid, 1943.

esperpento. Valle-Inclán's designation for a type of novel combining the satirical with the grotesque. The best of his novels of this type was *Los cuernos de Don Friolera* (1921). See under *Valle-Inclán.*

Espina, Concha (1879-1955). Contemporary novelist. Born in Santander; died in Madrid. Her first book was a collection of verse, *Mis flores* (1903). She is principally known for her novels depicting the Santander area in northern Spain. Some of her works were cited by the *Academia Española,* among them the novel, *La esfinge maragata* (1914). Her first novel of international repute was *El metal de los muertos* (1921), a story of the hardships of Spanish miners in the English-owned mines at Río Tinto. It was widely translated and was especially acclaimed in Germany for its anti-British implications. Her novel, *Altar mayor* (1926), received the *Premio Nacional de Literatura* in 1927. From 1925 on, she was an honorary member of the Hispanic Society of America. Stricken with blindness in 1937, she nevertheless continued her writing, one of her later novels being *Retaguardia* (1937), a story of war and revolution. Her last novel was *Una novela de amor* (1953). Concha Espina was noted for her sentimental realism, her descriptive powers and her delicate style.

Cf. Rosenberg, M., *Concha Espina,* Los Angeles, 1927; Lagoni, F., *Concha Espina y sus críticos,* Toulouse, 1929.

Espinel, Vicente (1550-1624). Novelist, poet, musician, soldier and priest. Born in Ronda; died in Madrid. Educated at Salamanca, he led an adventurous and dissolute life in his youth, to judge from his partly autobiographical picaresque novel, *Relaciones de la vida del escudero Marcos de Obregón* (1618). Interspersed with humor, lively episodes and anecdotes, the novel differs from the usual picaresque type in that it treats of a higher level of society and is more refined in its appreciation of natural beauty and of music. However, it does include the typical picaresque feature of digressive moralizing. Espinel's novel is important in comparative literature because Le Sage borrowed several episodes from it for his *Gil Blas.* As a poet, Espinel's fame is due to his popularization of a previously little-used stanza form, the *décima* (10 octosyllabic verses), sometimes called the *espinela,* because its invention was erroneously ascribed to him. His collected poems, *Diversas rimas,* were published in 1591. See also *décima.*

Cf. *La vida del escudero Marcos de Obregón,* (Ed.) Guzmán, J. P., *BAE,* XVIII, Barcelona, 1881; *idem,* (Ed.) Gili y Gaya, S., Madrid, 1922-1923; Brunetière, F., "La question de Gil Blas," "*Histoire et littérature,* vol. 2, Paris, 1891.

espinela. See under *Espinel, Vicente; décima.*

Espinosa, Aurelio. See under *American Association of Teachers of Spanish.*

Espinosa, Pedro. See under *Quevedo.*

Espronceda y Delgado, José de (1808-1842). Romantic poet and revolutionary. Born near Badajoz; died in Madrid. The son of a cavalry officer, he was educated at the Colegio de San Mateo in Madrid. Here, inspired by his tutor, Lista y Hermosilla, he wrote his first poems in a neo-classic style (e.g. *Himno al sol*). As a student he engaged in radical activities, was imprisoned, amnestied, and began a romantic Odyssey in 1826, traveling from Gibraltar to Lisbon, where he met Teresa Mancha, whose fatal attraction was to hold him in thrall until her tragic death (*Canto a Teresa*) in 1839. He followed her to London (1827), but his urge for revolutionary glory drove him on to further travels. Some years later, after she had married another, he induced her to leave her husband and to run off with him as his mistress. Before this romantic episode, however, he spent some time in Holland and then in Paris, where he fought on the barricades in the revolutionary uprising of July, 1830. Like other émigrés, he returned to Spain in 1833, but his radical journalistic diatribes proved too much for the newly established liberal regime, again resulting in his exile. In the final years of his stormy existence, he seems to have attained a measure of stability, serving in the Spanish Embassy at the Hague, and later as a deputy in the Cortes. His *Poesías líricas* were published in 1840, affording him a brief interval of renown before his demise. Espronceda was a Byronic figure both in his life and in his poetry. He was the insatiable and yet sad lover, the permanent revolutionary, and the romantic pessimist. Although he wrote a historical novel influenced by Scott (*Sancho Saldaña*, 1834), some journalistic pieces, and an excellent verse legend on the Don Juan theme (*El estudiante de Salamanca*), he is chiefly remembered for his lyric poetry of social criticism and romantic nostalgia (*Canción del pirata, El mendigo, El verdugo, A Jarifa en una orgía, Canto a Teresa*, etc.). Also of interest is his unfinished poem of philosophical despair and ironic disillusionment, *El diablo mundo* (1841). Espronceda's technical virtuosity and emotional power make him the most representative of the Spanish romantic poets. However, his cynicism, irony and emotional pyrotechnics are frequently so flamboyant as to lead many critics to speculate about his essential sincerity.

Cf. *Obras poéticas*, (Ed.) Moreno Villa, J., 2 vols., Madrid,

1923; Cascales y Muñoz, J., *Don José de Espronceda: su época, su vida y sus obras,* Madrid, 1914; Churchman, P. H., "Byron and Espronceda," *Revue hispanique,* XX; Mazzei, P., *La poesia di Espronceda,* Florence, 1935; Alonso Cortés, N., *Espronceda: ilustraciones biográficas y críticas,* Valladolid, 1942.

estancia. Strophe or stanza. In Spanish metrics, a combination of metrical lines, generally of eleven syllables *(endecasílabos)* or seven syllables *(heptasílabos)* in length. The number of lines in an *estancia* may vary, but the same number given in the first *estancia* is continued in the succeeding ones.

estanza. The same as *estancia.*

Estébanez Calderón, Serafín (1799-1867). Andalusian local-colorist, scholar and statesman. Born in Malaga; died in Madrid. His interest in *belles lettres* waned as he turned to a political career, in the course of which he became a Councillor of State and a Senator. His scholarly hobbies included the collecting of old books and manuscripts and items pertaining to Moorish lore. A contributor to the literary journal, *Cartas españolas,* he adopted the pseudonym, *El Solitario.* Although he published a collection of *Poesías* (1831) and a historical novel, *Cristianos y moriscos* (1838), he is chiefly known for his collection of *costumbrista* sketches, *Escenas andaluzas* (1847), which previously appeared in *Cartas españolas* (1831-1832). Estébanez Calderón exploited the picturesque background and colorful types of his native province of Andalusia. As a result of his antiquarian interests and his self-conscious striving for perfection of style, his prose is labored and abounds with archaic expressions and local idiom. Nevertheless, his mastery of local color makes him a significant contributor to *costumbrismo* and a forerunner of the Andalusian regional novels of Fernán Caballero and Juan Valera.

Cf. Cánovas del Castillo, A., *"El Solitario" y su tiempo,* Madrid, 1883; Montgomery, C. M., *Early Costumbrista Writers in Spain, 1750-1830,* Philadelphia, 1931; Lomba y Pedraja, J. R., *Costumbristas españoles de la primera mitad del siglo xix,* Oviedo, 1933.

esticomitia. In metrics, the distribution of sentences in a stanza so that each sentence forms a single line of verse. It is essentially the coincidence of a single thought and a single metrical line. *Esticomitia* is the opposite of *encabalgamiento* or *enjambement;* i.e. the running over of a thought or sentence from one metrical line into the next. In *esticomitia* there is identity of the syntactical and the metrical unit. In *encabalgamiento,* the syntactical unit goes beyond the metrical unit. The term *esticomitia* is derived from the Greek *stichomuthia,* meaning "dialogue" (Eng. *stichomythia).* Its original reference was to verse dialogue in which each person speaks one line at a time. Compare *encabalgamiento.*

estilo churrigueresco. See *churrigueresco.*

estilo plateresco. See *plateresco.*

estrambote. A lyrical after-thought consisting of cynical or humorous commentary on a poem just concluded. The *estrambote* adopts a rhyme from the preceding poem, but does not necessarily continue the same metrical length. It is frequently employed after a sonnet.

Estrella de Sevilla. See under *Vega, Lope de.*

estribillo. The opening theme-line, or lines, or stanza of a song or lyric poem, repeated or developed as a sort of refrain at the end of each succeeding stanza. The repetition may be purely phonic, as in popular songs, or it may develop or comment upon the central theme of a poem. The development or commentary is referred to as the *glosa* (gloss), and lines so developed are said to be *glosados* (glossed). The *estribillo* is an integral feature of the *villancico,* a form of popular dance-song which repeats and develops a theme-line or stanza; and of the *letrilla,* a short lyric which repeats the same thought at the end of each stanza. Some authorities use the term *villancico* for the *estribillo* alone. The *estribillo* is also encountered in popular forms such as the *seguidilla.* Examples of the *estribillo* as a part of various verse forms *(villancicos, letrillas,* etc.) may be found in the poetry of Montesino, Encina, Góngora, Quevedo, etc. See also *villancico.*

estribote. An obsolete name for the *villancico.*

estrofa sáfica. A stanza of four verses, of which the first three have eleven syllables and the fourth has only five. See under *sáfico.*

Études sur l'Espagne. See under *Morel-Fatio.*

Eucharist plays. See under *auto sacramental.*

europeización. A term used by Costa (1844-1911) in his campaign to regenerate Spanish life and culture *(regeneracionismo).* It was an exhortation to cast aside provincialism and intellectual aloofness and to adapt European ideas to the Spanish situation and character. It meant turning away from the Moorish past *(desafricanización)* and Spanish peninsular isolation to cross the barrier of the Pyrenees in an identification with European destiny.

Eustacius. See under *Caballero Cifar.*

excrescent sound. (Sp. *sonido epentético).* See under *epenthesis.*

Exemplar poético. See under *Cueva, Juan de la.*

exemplum. See *ejemplo.*

F

fabla. Conventional imitation of archaic Spanish as a literary device.

fabliella. A medieval term for a short story or narrative. Also a proverb conveying a moral.

fábula. A fable. A fictional, allegorical or mythological work designed to entertain or to point a moral. Frequently used in the same sense as *apólogo,* or apologue. See also under *apólogo; ejemplo.*

Fábula de Faetón. See under *Villamediana.*

Fábula de Píramo y Tisbe. See under *Góngora y Argote.*

Fábula de Polifemo y Galatea. See under *Góngora y Argote.*

fábula milesia. Milesian tale. In modern usage, an immoral story. In its early meaning, a tale of romantic adventures. For a definition of *Milesian tale,* see under *novela bizantina.*

Fábulas literarias. See under *Iriarte, Tomás de.*

Fábulas morales. See under *Samaniego, Félix María.*

Fábulas morales y doloras. See under *Campoamor.*

fanfarrón. Braggart. A type character in the *pasos* of Lope de Rueda. See under *Rueda, Lope de.*

farsa. A term used in early Spanish literature to denote a comedy. A short, comic dramatic composition. A vulgar and grotesque play.

Farsa llamada danza de la muerte. A treatment of the *danse macabre* theme, written by Juan de Pedraza in 1551. See under *Danza de la muerte.*

Fastenrath. See under *Premio Fastenrath.*

Fausto. See under *Campo, Estanislao de.*

Feijóo y Montenegro, Benito Jerónimo (1676-1764). Benedictine monk, professor of theology and encyclopedic scholar. Born in Casdemiro, Galicia; died in Oviedo. Educated at Salamanca. Professor of philosophy and theology at the University of Oviedo.

A controversial figure in his day because of his unswerving integrity in opposing provincial obscurantism *(españolismo),* he led a life of indefatigable intellectual endeavor. Very aptly he referred to himself as a "dauntless citizen of the republic of letters" *("atrevido ciudadano de la república literaria"),* for his mission was to expose superstition and error in all spheres of Spanish life. The results of his encyclopedic scholarship are contained in his *Teatro crítico universal* (8 vols., 1726-1739, plus a supplementary volume, 1741), and in his *Cartas eruditas y curiosas* (5 vols., 1742-1760). Thoroughly conversant with the intellectual currents in other European countries, his range of subjects included science, mathematics, medicine, philosophy, religion, law, political economy, education, literature and popular superstitions. In the form of miscellaneous essays and in a sober, logical style, he advocated temperance and sanity in matters intellectual and literary. His opposition to Gongorism was inevitable. As an opponent of extremes, he attacked not only provincialism but also gallomania. In literature, he favored formal rules but accorded due recognition to the claims of genius, transcending all rules. Feijóo represented the trend of the 18th century Enlightenment in Spain.

Cf. *Obras escogidas de Feijóo, BAE,* LVI; *Teatro crítico universal,* (Ed.) Millares, C. A., Madrid, 1923-1926; Entrambasaguas, J. de, *Antología (de Feijóo),* Madrid, 1942; Morayta, M., *El Padre Feijóo y sus obras,* Valencia, 1913; Marañon, G., *Las ideas biológicas del Padre Feijóo,* Madrid, 1934; Delpy, G., *Feijóo et l'esprit européen,* Paris, 1936.

Felipe V. See under *Real Academia Española.*

Felipe, León (b. 1884). Post-modernist poet. Born in Salamanca. His full name is León Felipe Camino. A restless spirit, searching for new horizons and new avenues of expression, he led an unsettled existence as an actor in Spain and as a pharmacist in Africa. Disillusioned by the outcome of the Spanish Civil War, he left for South America in 1939, and there continued his career as a writer, poet and professor. He first attracted favorable critical notice in Spain with his *Versos y oraciones del caminante* (1920). Since then he has published several volumes *(Libro II, Drop a Star, El hacha, El español de éxodo y del llanto, Ganarás la luz,* etc.). A wide selection of his works appeared in Buenos

Aires in 1947 *(Antología rota, 1920-1947)*. León's work shows the influence of the Spanish mystics, the Bible, Cervantes, Machado and Unamuno. He was also attracted by Walt Whitman, whose poems he translated. Unhappy in exile and pessimistic regarding the future of his native land *(El español de éxodo y del llanto)*, León finds surcease from man's metaphysical and temporal tragedies by placing his art in the service of freedom.

Cf. Del Río, Ángel, *Historia de la literatura española,* Vol. II, N. Y., 1948; Wolfe, B. D., "León Felipe, Poet of Spain's Tragedy," *American Scholar,* XII, 1943; Torre, G. de, "León Felipe, poeta del tiempo agónico," *La aventura y el orden,* Buenos Aires, 1943.

Felix y Felismena. See under *Montemayor, Jorge de.*

Féminas. See under *Valle-Inclán.*

"Fénix de México". See *Cruz, Sor Juana Inés de la.*

Ferdinand and Isabella. See under *Prescott.*

Fernán Caballero (1796-1877). The pen name of Cecilia Böhl de Faber. Born in Switzerland; died in Seville. The daughter of a Spanish mother (Francisca Larrea) and of a German father (Johann Nikolaus Böhl von Faber). She was educated in a French boarding school in Hamburg, and then lived in Andalusia from the age of 17. She was married and widowed three times. Both her parents were interested in literature and folklore; her father, in particular, was the compiler of collections of Spanish poetry and drama. Inspired by her parents, she became interested in Andalusian peasant folklore, collecting and publishing songs, ballads and folk tales *(Cuentos y poesías populares andaluces)*. She wrote her first novel *(La gaviota,* 1849) in French and then translated it into Spanish. It was a romantic story of a peasant girl who marries a German surgeon, becomes an opera singer, falls in love with a bull-fighter and, after the demise of both husband and lover, ends by marrying a village barber. As far as plot and style go, the literary merit of the novel is negligible. However, its folkloristic elements began the trend toward the *costumbrista* or regional novel. Among her chief works were: (novels) *La gaviota,* 1849; *Clemencia,* 1852; *La familia de Alvareda,* 1856; *Un servilón y un liberalito,* 1857; *Un verano en Bornos,* 1858; (folklore and tales) *Cuentos y poesías andaluces,* 1859; *Cuadros de costumbres populares andaluzas,* 1852; *Relaciones,* 1857. See also under *Böhl von Faber.*

Cf. *Obras completas*, Ed. by Asensio, J. M., Madrid, 1893-1910; Coloma, P. L., *Recuerdos de Fernán Caballero*, Bilbao, 1920; Palma, A., *Fernán Caballero, la novelista novelable*, Madrid, 1931; Hespelt, E. H., *Fernán Caballero, A Study of her Life and Works*, (Diss.), Cornell U., 1925.

Fernández de Avellaneda, Alonso. The pseudonym of an unknown author who, in 1614, published a spurious sequel to the first part of Cervantes' *Don Quijote*. See under *Cervantes*.

Fernández de Lizardi, José Joaquín (1776-1827). Mexican novelist, dramatist, editor and political agitator. He was the founder of a radical journal, *El pensador mexicano* (1812), a title which he used as a pen name. His inflammatory articles against royal and papal authority led to imprisonment and excommunication. Influenced by the French political writers of the 18th century, and also by Cervantes, he combined the picaresque form with a trenchant criticism of society and manners in his *El periquillo sarniento*, generally considered the first South American novel. Among his chief works were: *El periquillo sarniento*, 1816; *La Quijotita y su prima*, 1819; *Noches tristes y día alegre*, 1823; *Vida y hechos del famoso caballero Don Catrín de la Fachenda*, 1825.

Cf. Spell, J. R., *The Life and Works of José Fernández de Lizardi*, Philadelphia, 1931; González Obregón, L., *Novelistas mexicanos: Don José Fernández de Lizardi*, Mexico City, 1938.

Fernández de Moratín. See *Moratín*.

Fernández de Rojas, Juan. See under *Escuela de Salamanca*.

Fernández Pacheco. See under *Real Academia Española*.

Fernández y González, Manuel (1821-1888). Historical novelist, poet and dramatist. Born in Seville; died in Madrid. Educated at Granada, he led a literary-bohemian existence for most of his life. Although his literary earnings were considerable, he died in poverty. Among his works are some verse legends *(La Alhambra*, etc.) and some dramas *(Deudas de la honra, La muerte de Cisneros*, etc.). However, it was as the most prolific of romantic novelists that he gained his popularity. Devoting himself almost entirely to the historical genre, and modeling himself after Eugene Sue and Victor Hugo, he composed over 200 novels. Of particular interest are those dealing with recurrent themes in Spanish literature: *Los siete infantes de Lara, Bernardo del*

Carpio, etc. Also significant as examples of *costumbrismo* are *Los desheredados, Los hijos perdidos,* etc. Fernández y González was among the first of modern polygraphs aiming at popular success and financial returns. He ground out his novels at a rapid rate with the aid of secretaries (Blasco Ibáñez once worked for him). As may be expected, the quality of his writing was very uneven. His works are diffuse, poor in motivation and character development, and frequently in bad taste. Nevertheless, his fertile imagination, dynamic action and techincal skill in maintaining reader interest make some of his novels still readable (e.g., *Men Rodríguez de Sanabria, El cocinero de Su Majestad,* etc.). The titles of his chief works are: *El condestable don Álvaro de Luna,* 1851; *Los siete infantes de Lara,* 1853; *Men Rodríguez de Sanabria,* 1853; *El cocinero de Su Majestad,* 1857; *Bernardo del Carpio,* 1858; *El pasterelo de Madrigal,* 1862; *Los desheredados,* 1865; *Los hijos perdidos,* 1866; *María,* 1868; *El conde-duque de Olivares,* 1870; *El príncipe de los ingenios Miguel de Cervantes Saavedra,* 1876.

Cf. Sánchez Moguel, A., *Manuel Fernández y González,* Madrid, 1888; Blanco García, F., *La literatura española en el siglo xix,* Madrid, 1891-1894; González Blanco, A., *Historia de la novela en España. . . ,* Madrid, 1909; Peers, E. A., *A History of the Romantic Movement in Spain,* Cambridge, 1940.

Fernando VII. See under *Romanticism.*

Fernán González. The title of a medieval folk-epic, the original of which is lost but which is known from prose versions in the *Crónica general* and in the *Crónica de 1344.* The earliest extant poetic version is in erudite *mester de clerecía* style and is entitled *El poema de Fernán González (ca.* 1250.) It was probably composed by a monk of the Monastery of San Pedro de Arlanza and is the only *mester de clerecía* poem on an epic theme. It recounts the deeds of Count Fernán González (d. 970), who liberated Castile from Leonese rule and thus became a national hero. The theme occurs in many ancient ballads *(e.g.* in the *Romancero general)* and was treated by subsequent writers *(e.g.* Lope de Vega, Rojas Zorrilla, *etc.).* According to legend the liberation of Castile occurred as a result of royal frivolity, for Sancho, King of León, practically traded Castile for a horse and a hawk. In his desire to acquire these medieval luxuries from their owner, Fernán González, Sancho contracted a debt with the stipulation that it was to be doubled for each day of deferred payment, the result being that he was finally obliged to settle by granting the independent rule of Castile to Fernán González. Among the interesting episodes in the poem are Fernán's heroic feats against the Moors, his defiance of the Kings of León, and his dramatic escape from prison in Navarra with the connivance of his custodian's daughter, Princess Sancha, who later became his wife.

Cf. *Poema de Fernán González,* (Ed.) Marden, C. C., Baltimore, 1904, and also (Ed.) Serrano, L., Madrid, 1943; Menéndez Pidal, R., "Notas para el romancero del Conde Fernán González," in *Homenaje a Menéndez y Pelayo,* vol. I, Madrid, 1899; *idem, L'épopée castillane à travers la littérature espagnole,* Paris, 1910.

Ferreras, Juan. The first chief librarian of the *Biblioteca Real (ca.* 1712). See under *Biblioteca Nacional.*

Fichter, William L., (1892). American hispanist. Professor of Spanish, Brown University, since 1938. Visiting lecturer on Spanish Literature, Harvard University, 1951. Chief publications: Lope de Vega's *El castigo del discreto,* N. Y., 1925; and *El sembrar en buena tierra, A Critical and Annotated Edition of the Autograph Manuscript,* N. Y., 1944; *Publicaciones periodísticas de don Ramón del Valle-Inclán, Edición, estudio preliminar y notas,* Mexico, 1952.

Fígaro. See *Larra, Mariano José de.*

figurón. See *comedia de figurón.*

Filis. See under *Vega, Lope de.*

fin de fiesta. The grand finale of the classical comedy, comprising songs, dances and general revelry.

Fitzgerald, John D. See under *American Association of Teachers of Spanish.*

Fitzmaurice-Kelly, James (1857-1923). The dean of British hispanists at the turn of the century. Professor of Spanish at the Universities of Cambridge, Liverpool, and London. Author and editor of innumerable articles, monographs, critical editions and extended works on Spanish authors, history of Spanish literature, bibliographies of Spanish literature, etc. Most of his extended works have appeared in Spanish translations. Chief works: *A History of Spanish Literature, London,* 1898; *Lope de Vega and*

Spanish Drama, London, 1902; *Cervantes in England*, London, 1905; *Chapters on Spanish Literature*, London, 1908; *Miguel de Cervantes. A Memoir*, Oxford, 1913; (Ed.) *The Oxford Book of Spanish Verse*, 1913 (rev. by J. B. Trend, 1949); *Miguel de Cervantes Saavedra*, London, 1917 (Sp. trsl. Madrid, 1917); *A Primer of Spanish Literature*, London, 1921; *Fray Luis de León, A Biographical Fragment*, Oxford, 1921; *Spanish Bibliography*, Oxford, 1925; *A History of Spanish Literature*, Oxford, 1926.

Flor de los recuerdos. See under *Zorrilla y Moral.*

Flor de Santidad. See under *Valle-Inclán.*

Flores, Ángel (1900). American hispanist. Born in Puerto Rico. Professor of Spanish, Queens College, Flushing, N. Y. Literary historian, critic, translator and anthologist. Author of *The Anatomy of Don Quijote*, Ithaca, 1932 (in collaboration); *Cervantes Across the Centuries*, N. Y., 1947 (in collaboration); *Great Spanish Novels and Tales*, N. Y., 1956; *El cuento y la novela en Hispanoamérica*, Universidad de Guadalajara, Mexico, 1956.

Flores, Juan de (15th century). Renaissance writer of the *novela sentimental.* He is chiefly known for two novels, both Italian in inspiration. *Grimalte y Gradisa* (ca. 1495) is a continuation of Boccaccio's *Fiammetta*, according to its introduction. It narrates Grimalte's rambling peregrinations in quest of Fiammetta on behalf of his lady love, Gradisa. The *Historia de Grisel y Mirabella (ca.* 1495) is a tragic love story in the style of the medieval *disputa.* In their day, these novels had a vogue almost as great as that of the *Amadís*, and they were widely translated and read in Italy, France and England. The theme of *Grisel y Mirabella* is re-echoed in Lope de Vega's *La ley ejecutada.*

Cf. Matulka, B., *The Novels of Juan de Flores and Their European Diffusion*, N. Y., 1931.

Flores de poetas ilustres de España. See under *Quevedo.*

floresta. A literary anthology.

Floresta de rimas antiguas castellanas. See under *folklore.*

Flores y Blancaflor. An anonymous chivalric romance belonging to the Graeco-Oriental cycle of medieval European literature. It relates the love story of a Moorish knight, Flores, who is converted to Christianity by his lady fair, Blancaflor, who later becomes his wife. Subsequently, the noble pair convert all of Spain to Christianity. References to this fanciful tale occur in Spanish sources as early as the 13th century; however, the first known Spanish version dates from the 16th century. Its immediate Spanish origin is thought to be either Italian or French.

Flórez, Enrique (1702-1773). Augustine monk and ecclesiastical historian. Professor at the University of Alcalá. Author of one of the great achievements of Spanish historical scholarship, the *España Sagrada* (52 vols., 1747-1918), of which he himself wrote the first 29 volumes. It is a detailed history of the Church in Spain. An index to this monumental series was published in 1918 by Ángel González Palencia. Containing reproductions of many ancient manuscripts and chronicles, and the histories of convents and monasteries, the work is still indispensable for literary and historical research, particularly in the medieval period.

Cf. Salvador y Barrera, J. M., *El P. Flórez y su "España Sagrada"*, Madrid, 1914.

florilegio. A literary anthology.

folklore. The English term is used in Spanish with the same meaning, *i.e.* the study of popular wisdom and customs as revealed in folksongs, ballads, legends, idioms, proverbs, rhymes, riddles, epitaphs, etc. Research in folklore generally corresponds to a need for national perspective. In Spain the first significant collections of popular legend began with the *Crónicas.* The 13th century produced proverb collections *(Bocados de oro, Libro de los buenos proverbios,* etc.). The next important book of proverbs, attributed to Santillana, appeared in the 15th century *(Refranes que dicen las viejas tras el fuego).* The *Diálogo de la lengua (ca.* 1535), by Juan de Valdés is a contribution to linguistic aspects of folklore in the 16th century. Although not published until 1906, the *Vocabulario de refranes of Gonzalo Correas* (d. 1631) is also an important source of folklore material of the same period. During the 14th and 15th centuries we find important collections of folksongs and ballads in the various *cancioneros* and *romanceros,* culminating in the 16th century with the *Silva de varios romances.* However, it was not until the 19th century, during the period of romanticism and under the influence of Herder, Grimm and Schlegel, that folklore began to flourish in Spain. Fernán Caballero, inspired by her father Nikolaus Böhl de Faber (author of *Floresta de rimas antiguas castellanas,* 1821-1825), compiled her *Cuentos, oraciones, advinas, y refranes* *populares e infantiles* (1877). The two-volume ballad collection (*Romancero general* or *Romancero de Durán*) appeared from 1828 to 1832, edited by Agustín Durán (1793-1862). The 1880's witnessed the organization of folklore societies and periodicals: *El folklore andaluz* (1882-1883), *Boletín folklórico español* (1885). The eleven-volume *Biblioteca de las tradiciones populares españolas*, edited by Antonio Machado y Álvarez (1848-1892), appeared from 1883 to 1886. Notable contributions to proverb folklore (*Refranero español*, 10 vols., 1874) were also made at this time by José María Sbarbi y Osuna (1834-1910). One of the greatest of contemporary scholars in the field of the folksong (*Cantos populares españoles*, 1882-1883) was Francisco Rodríguez Marín (1855-1943). The foremost contemporary authority in the field of the popular legend is Ramón Menéndez Pidal (b. 1869).

Cf. Picazo, J., *El folklore español*, London, 1953.

Folklore andaluz (El). See under *folklore*.

folla. A theatrical divertissement composed of alternate comical and musical episodes.

folletín. Diminutive of *folleto*. A printed insert or special supplement to a magazine or newspaper.

folletinesco. A reference to popular fiction, especially serialized novels, printed as inserted supplements to newspapers and magazines. See also under *entrega*.

folleto. Printed matter of less than one hundred pages.

Fombona. See *Blanco-Fombona*.

Ford, Jeremiah D. M. (1873). American hispanist and Romance philologist. On the Harvard University teaching staff since 1895. Smith Professor of the French and Spanish languages, Harvard University, since 1907. Emeritus, since 1943. Foreign member of the *Academia Española* since 1909. An authority on Spanish medieval literature and editor of many medieval texts. Author of *Main Currents in Spanish Literature*, N. Y., 1919. Author or editor of some 60 books and innumerable articles and book reviews in American and European learned journals. See also under *Smith Professorship*.

Forner, Juan Pablo. See under *Escuela de Salamanca*.

Fortunata y Jacinta. See under *Pérez Galdós*.

Forza del destina (La). See under *Saavedra*.

Foulché-Delbosc, Raymond (1864-1929). The most prominent French hispanist at the turn of the century. Professor of Spanish at the University of Paris. Founder and editor of the *Revue hispanique* (80 vols., 1894-1933), in which literally hundreds of his articles on Spanish literature and bibliography appeared. His major interests were in the Spanish literature of the 15th through 17th centuries. He was also editor of the *Bibliotheca hispanica* series of critical editions (22 vols., Barcelona, Madrid, N. Y., 1900-1921), an associated enterprise of the *Revue hispanique.* Besides the introductions to his critical editions, he also wrote an *Essai sur les origines du romancero, Prélude* (Paris, 1914), and, in collaboration with Barrau-Dihigo, compiled a bibliography for hispanists, *Manuel de l'hispanisant* (N. Y., 2 vols., 1920-1925). Among his more famous critical editions are: *Cárcel de amor (Bibl. hisp.,* XV); *Vida de Lazarillo de Tormes (Bibl. hisp.,* III); *Comedia de Calisto y Melibea (Bibl. hisp.,* I, XII); *Danza de la muerte* (Barcelona, 1907); *Obras poéticas de D. Luis de Góngora (Bibl. hisp.,* XVI, XVII); and *Cancionero castellano del siglo xv (NBAE,* XIX, 1912-1915), which includes the poems of Santillana, Mena and Manrique.

Francesilla (La). A play written *ca.* 1599 by Lope de Vega, notable because it introduced the type character of the *donaire,* or *gracioso.*

Fray Gerundio. See under *Isla, José Francisco de.*

Freyre. See *Jaimes Freyre, Ricardo.*

fronterizos. See under *romance.*

Fuente Ovejuna. See under *Vega, Lope de.*

G

Gaceta Literaria (La). A journal of modern literature founded in 1927 by Guillermo de Torre and Ernesto Giménez Caballero. See under *Torre, Guillermo de.*

gaita gallega. A type of meter originally used in popular Galician verse and then adopted by early Castilian poets. The *gaita gallega* verse may vary from nine to twelve syllables. It is accented on the 4th and 7th (and 10th) syllables. See under *endecasílabo.*

Galatea (La). See under *Cervantes.*

Galba, Martí Johán de. See under *Tirant lo Blanch.*

Galdós. See *Pérez Galdós.*

Galeotes (Los). See under *Álvarez Quintero.*

Galician-Portuguese. See *gallego-portugués.*

Gallardo, Bartolomé José (1776-1852). Scholar, poet, and bibliographer. He was a pioneer in establishing the science of literary research. His bibliographical papers, published after his death, are still a basic source for research in Spanish literature: *Ensayo de una biblioteca española de libros raros y curiosos* (1863-1889).

Cf. Buchanan, M. A., "Notes on the Life and Works of Bartolomé José Gallardo," *Revue hispanique,* LVII.

gallego-portugués. Generic term for a dialect group from which modern Portuguese evolved. It comprises *gallego,* the romance language of Galicia, several dialect variants of *gallego* spoken in León and Asturias, and the old Portuguese of northern Duero. In about the 12th through 14th centuries, *gallego* was almost identical with the Portuguese language of that time. As a result of Provençal influence and the cultivation of poetry at the court of King Denis (Diniz) of Portugal (1259-1325), the troubador lyric flourished in Galicia, giving great prestige to *gallego* and raising it to the level of a more or less standardized common language for Castilian as well as for Portuguese poets. For almost two centuries, it was the conventional medium of lyric expression for cultured Spanish poets. Alfonso X's *Cantigas de Santa María* (late 13th century) and all the poems of the earlier *Cancioneros* (13th and 14th centuries) were written in *gallego-portugués.* Not until the 15th and 16th centuries did the Castilian language supersede this tradition. See also under *cancionero.*

Cf. Bell, A. F. G., *Portuguese Literature,* Oxford, 1922; Menéndez Pidal, R., *Poesía juglaresca y juglares,* 2nd ed., Buenos Aires, 1945; Rodrigues Lapa, M., *Das origens da poesia lírica em Portugal na idade média,* Coimbra, 1942.

Gallegos, Rómulo (1884). Venezuelan educator, politician, short-story writer and novelist. Born in Caracas. Director of various schools in Venezuela (1912-1922). A political exile in Spain (1932-1936). Venezuelan Minister of Education (1936). President of Venezuela for one year (1947), but was deposed by a military Junta. His masterpiece is *Doña Bárbara* (1929), a symbolic novel about a "femme fatale," pictured against the background of the Venezuelan *llanos.* The names of the hero (Santos) and of the heroine (Bárbara) suggest the central conflict between good and evil, civilization and barbarism. The work was widely translated and has gone through more than twenty editions. A master of poetic style, Gallegos excels in his descriptions of the *llanos* and of *llanero* life. The titles of his chief works are: *Reinaldo Solar,* 1920; *La trepadora,* 1925; *Doña Bárbara,* 1929; *Cantaclaro,* 1931; *Canaima,* 1935; *Pobre negro,* 1937; *La rebelión y otros cuentos,* 1947.

Cf. Spell, J. R., *Contemporary Spanish-American Fiction,* Chapel Hill, N. C., 1944; Arciniegas, G., "Novela y verdad en Rómulo Gallegos," *Cuadernos Americanos,* July-August, 1954; Vila Selma, J., *Procedimientos y técnicas en Rómulo Gallegos,* Seville, 1954; Crow, J. A., "The Essays of Rómulo Gallegos," *Hispania,* XXXVIII, I, 1955; "Homenaje a Rómulo Gallegos," *Cuadernos Americanos,* Sept.-Oct., 1954; *Humanismo,* Mexico, Aug. 1954.

Gálvez, Manuel (1882). Argentine novelist, short-story writer, essayist and biographer. Born in Paraná. Graduate of the School of Law, University of Buenos Aires (1904). Inspector of Secondary Schools (since 1906). After beginning with poetry, literary criticism and the socio-cultural essay, he won acclaim with his first novel, *La maestra normal* (1914). A prolific and gifted writer, he was awarded the National Prize for Literature in 1932. Gálvez feels a strong affinity for the culture of Spain and believes in its wholesome influence on Spanish America *(El solar de la raza,* 1910-1911). His work ranges through contrasting high and low strata of Argentine society, from the provincial town to the capital city. A truly national writer, he has used his country's history as background for many of his novels and fictionalized biographies. Perhaps his greatest achievement is the trilogy, *Escenas de la guerra del Paraguay* (1928-1929), and the two volumes of *Escenas de la época de Rosas* (1932-1933). Among his other important works are: *La maestra normal,* 1914; *La sombra del convento,* 1917; *Nacha Regules,* 1919; *La tragedia de un hombre fuerte,* 1922; *Historia de Arrebal,* 1923; *El cántico espiritual,* 1923; *Escenas de la guerra del Paraguay,* 1928-1929; *Escenas de la época de Rosas,* 1932-1933; *Vida de Fray Mamerto Esquiú,* 1933; *La noche toca a su fin,* 1935; *Cautiverio,* 1935; *Hombres en soledad,* 1938; *Hipólito Yrigoyen,* 1939; *Don Francisco de Miranda,* 1948.

Cf. Coester, A., "Manuel Gálvez, Argentine Novelist", *Hispania,* V, 1922; Spell, J. R., *Contemporary Spanish-American Fiction,* Chapel Hill, N. C., 1944.

Gamboa, Federico (1864-1939). Mexican novelist, dramatist, professor and diplomat. Professor of Mexican literature at the University of Mexico and President of the Mexican Academy of Letters. Influenced by Zola and the Goncourts, Gamboa wrote in the naturalistic style. Although frequently lapsing into discursive sermonizing, he displayed keen psychological observation of human conflict, both social and religious. Some of his chief works were: *Del natural,* 1888; *Impresiones y recuerdos,* 1893; *Suprema ley,* 1896; *Metamorfosis,* 1899; *Santa,* 1908; *Reconquista,* 1908; *La llaga,* 1912; *Entre hermanos,* 1928; *Mi diario,* 1907-1938.

Cf. Moore, E., "Bibliografía de obras y crítica de Federico Gamboa," *Revista Iberoamericana,* II, 1940; Hooker, A. C., Jr., *La novela de Federico Gamboa,* (Diss.), Middlebury, Vt., 1954.

Ganar perdiendo. See under *Zorrilla y Moral.*

gangarilla. In the early Spanish theater, a theatrical company composed of three or four men and a boy for the female roles. Compare *garnacha.*

Ganivet, Ángel (1865-1898). Philosopher, diplomat and critic. A precursor of the Generation of 1898. Born in Granada; died in Riga. He received his doctorate in philosophy at the University of Madrid, and then embarked upon a diplomatic career, serving in various Baltic countries. His suicide at the age of 33, while a consul in Riga, cut short a brilliant career. Although versed in Greek, Romance and Germanic philology, and thoroughly cosmopolitan in spirit, he was intensely patriotic and, like his friend Unamuno, preoccupied with the destiny of his decadent country. His *Idearium español* (1897) was a profound analysis of the Spanish character and exerted considerable influence on the writers of the Generation of 1898. According to Ganivet, the chief defect in the Spanish character is a paralysis of the will *(abulia).* To counteract this trait, he preached the doctrine of *voluntad.* In his volume of correspondence with Unamuno, *El porvenir de España* (1912), he urged the adaptation of modern foreign thought, politics and social forms to the Spanish tradition. Ganivet also wrote two novels and a drama, using these literary forms chiefly as vehicles for his ideas. His novel, *Los trabajos del infatigable creador Pío Cid* (1898), is interesting as a spiritual autobiography. Although frequently vague (his predilection was for the Spanish mystics) and self-contradictory, Ganivet was a seminal writer of great influence. See also *abulia; españolismo; Generation of 1898; voluntad.*

Cf. *Obras completas,* 2 vols., (Ed.) Fernández Almagro, M., Madrid, 1943; *idem, Vida y obra de Ángel Ganivet,* Valencia, 1925; Burin, G., *Ganivet,* Granada, 1921; Jeschke, H., "Ángel Ganivet, seine Persönlichkeit und Hauptwerk," *Revue hispanique,* LXXII, 1928; Espina, A., *Ganivet: el hombre y la obra,* Buenos Aires, 1942.

García Calderón, Francisco (1883). Peruvian critic, sociologist, diplomat and cultural historian. Son of a former President of Peru and brother of the famous writer, Ventura García Calderón. Served with the Peruvian legation in France for the greater part of his career. A life-long student and interpreter of Latin American culture. Many of his works were written in French. His cultural study on Peru was awarded a French Academy Prize in 1908. Chief works: *Litteris,* 1904; *Hombres y ideas de nuestro tiempo,* 1907; *El Perú contemporáneo,* 1908; *Profesores de* *idealismo,* 1910; *Les démocraties latines de l'Amérique,* 1912; *La creación de un continente,* 1914; *Testimonios y comentarios,* 1934.

Cf. García Godoy, F., *Americanismo literario,* Madrid, 1917; "Homenaje a Francisco García Calderón," *Mercurio Peruano,* XXXIV, 1953.

García de Castañar. See under *Rojas Zorrilla.*

García de Castrojeris. See under *Disciplina clericalis.*

García de la Huerta, Vicente (1734-1787). Poet and dramatist. One of the early directors of the *Biblioteca Real* (now the *Biblioteca Nacional).* Author of a collection of Spanish classical dramatists, entitled *Teatro español* (16 vols., 1785-1786). A defender of the Calderonian tradition against the Spanish imitators of the French classical drama, he produced in his *Raquel* (1778) the outstanding Spanish tragedy of the 18th century. Its theme of the tragic end of the beautiful Jewess who had captured the heart of King Alfonso VIII (1158-1214) had already been treated by Lope de Vega *(Judía de Toledo)* and other Spanish dramatists.

García de Resende. See under *cancionero.*

García Gutiérrez, Antonio (1813-1884). Dramatist of the late Romantic period. Born near Cádiz; died in Madrid. In the military and diplomatic service, he traveled extensively in England, France, Switzerland, Cuba and Mexico. In 1862 he became a member of the *Academia Española.* His first play, written while he was a soldier, was *El trovador* (1836). It was an immediate success and later inspired the libretto for Verdi's *Il trovatore* (1853). In all, he composed some 56 dramas, comedies and *zarzuelas,* some of the dramas superior to *El trovador* but never as popular; although his *Simón Bocanegra* (1843) inspired another Verdi opera, and his *Venganza catalana* (1864) had an extended run in Madrid. His dramatic technique was conventional, following the tradition of the French *pièce bien faite* school of Scribe and Dumas, some of whose plays he translated and adapted for the Spanish stage. One of his dramatic devices was the last-minute revelation of previously concealed identities; *e.g.* in *El trovador,* after Count De Artal has had Manrique executed, the Count discovers that Manrique is his own brother who had been kidnapped in childhood by the vindictive gypsy, Azucena. Also notable are his *zarzuelas,* to which Arrieta supplied the music: *El grumete* (1846) and *La vuelta del corsario* (1865).

Cf. Funes, E., *García Gutiérrez: estudio crítico de su obra dramática,* Cádiz, 1900; Adams, N. B., *The Romantic Dramas of García Gutiérrez,* N. Y., 1922.

García Lorca, Federico (1898-1936). Andalusian poet and dramatist. He was executed in Granada by a Falangist firing squad in the opening days of the Spanish Civil War. Having completed his university studies in philosophy and literature (1923), he embarked upon a literary career. His trip to the United States (1930) is reflected in his *Poeta en Nueva York.* In 1931 he founded the experimental theater *La Barraca* in collaboration with Eduardo Ugarte. In 1933-1934 he traveled in the Argentine. Although he began writing in early adolescence, his first significant poetry appeared in 1927 *(Canciones).* His most mature and unified poetry is represented by the *Romancero gitano* (1928), which reflects the spirit of his native Andalusia in dramatic and often surrealist style. Among his other poetic works are the *Poema del cante jondo* (1931) and *Llanto por Ignacio Sánchez Mejías* (1935). In addition, García Lorca wrote a number of experimental plays, among them the tragedy, *Bodas de sangre* (1933), the poetic comedy, *Doña Rosita la soltera* (1935), and the dramatic caprice, *Amor de don Perlimplín con Belisa en su jardín* (1931). García Lorca's poetry contains musical and dramatic elements in a rich profusion of forms, themes and styles. It is often complex, using simple, childlike language veiled in a cryptic aura. Ranging through classical, romantic and surrealist phases, García Lorca's versatility is amazing. Few modern poets have equaled his bravura abandon over so wide a gamut of Spanish lyrical tradition, transfigured by the modern spirit.

Cf. *Obras completas,* 6 vols., Buenos Aires, 1940; Río A. del and Onís F. de, *Federico García Lorca (1899-1936): Vida y obra,* N. Y., 1941; Berenguer Carísomo, A., *Las máscaras de Federico García Lorca,* Buenos Aires, 1941; Honig, E., *García Lorca,* Norwalk, Conn., 1944; Días-Plaja, G., *Federico García Lorca,* Buenos Aires, 1948; Río, A. del, *Vida y obras de Federico García Lorca,* Zaragoza, 1952; Guardia, A. de la, *García Lorca, Persona y Creación,* 3a ed., Buenos Aires, 1952.

García Monge, Joaquín (1881). Literary critic and editor. Former Director of the *Biblioteca Nacional de Costa Rica.* Publisher and Editor of *Repertorio Americano,* one of the most influential literary reviews of Latin America since 1919.

Cf. *Hispania,* XXXVI, 1953.

Garcilaso de la Vega (1501?-1536). Renaissance poet, courtier and soldier. Born in Toledo; died in Nice. Older spellings of his name are *Garci-Lasso* and *Garcilasso.* Of aristocratic lineage, he received a nobleman's education in music, classical and modern literature, horsemanship, fencing, and in the arts of courtesy and war. Garcilaso was a perfect specimen of the Renaissance gentleman, modeled after Castiglione's *Courtier,* a work which he induced his friend, Boscán, to translate. At an early age he was attached to the household of Emperor Charles V. Save for a brief period of disfavor (he was interned for three months on Grosse-Schütt, a Danubian island), he stood high in the Emperor's graces. He served with distinction in various campaigns in Austria, Africa and France. For a while he was at the court in Naples, in the service of the viceroy, the Marqués de Villafranca. In 1536, while campaigning in Southern France, he was mortally wounded during a rash assault on an unimportant fortified position. Shortly thereafter he died at Nice. Two years later his remains were re-interred at Toledo. Garcilaso's poems were first published together with Boscán's poetry by the latter's widow (*Las obras de Boscán y algunas de Garcilasso de la Vega. . . ,* Barcelona, 1543). Garcilaso encouraged Boscán to adapt Italian meters to Spanish verse. However, unlike Boscán, who was a better theoretician than poet, Garcilaso was a consummate artist, polishing and re-polishing his poems until they were models of form and beauty. This conscientious regard for perfection accounts for his limited but choice output and his great influence on later poets. In all he wrote 38 sonnets, 5 *canciones,* 3 eclogues, 2 elegies, an epistle, and 8 *coplas.* Of these, his eclogues, *canciones* and sonnets are most memorable. More than Boscán he was responsible for the naturalization of the Italian hendecasyllable in Spanish verse. In addition, he introduced a metrical form which he called the *lira,* a five-verse stanza with verses of seven and eleven syllables, rhymed ABABB. Garcilaso's forte was not originality. The influence of Virgil and Petrarch is evident in his work. His major theme is love, expressed with the conventional melancholy and frustrated Platonism of his Italian masters; but with such perfection of form and rhythmic grace as to make him the most representative Spanish lyricist of the Golden Age.

Cf. Keniston, H., *Garcilaso de la Vega: A Critical Study of his Life and Works,* N. Y., 1922; *idem,* (Ed.), *Garcilaso de la Vega: Works. A Critical Text with a Bibliography,* N. Y., 1925; Navarro Tomás, T., (Ed.), *Garcilaso: Obras,* Madrid, 1911 *et seq.;* Arce, M., *Garcilaso, contribución al estudio de la lírica española del siglo XVI,* Madrid, 1930; Lapesa, R., *La trayectoria poética de Garcilaso,* Madrid, 1948.

Garcilaso de la Vega (El Inca) (1539-1616). Soldier, translator and historian. Born in Cuzco, Peru, of a Spanish father and an Incan princess. He was related to the great Spanish poet of the same name. He went to Spain in 1560 and there became a soldier in 1564, eventually attaining the rank of captain. His burial place is in Córdova, Spain. Having received a liberal education in the humanities, he began his literary career with an admirable translation of León Hebreo's *Diálogos de amor.* His historical works were: *Historia de la Florida y jornada que a ella hizo el gobernador Hernando de Soto* (1605); *Los comentarios reales que tratan del origin de los Incas* (1609); and *Historia general del Perú* (1616). Familiar with the native language, Garcilaso had the advantage of using original sources. However, his vivid imagination frequently places his work in the realm of creative writing rather than of sober historical narrative.

Cf. Fitzmaurice-Kelly, J., *El Inca Garcilasso de la Vega,* London, 1921.

Garduña de Sevilla (La). See under *Castillo Solórzano.*

Garfín. One of the sons of the *Caballero Cifar.*

garnacha. In the early Spanish theater, a company of strolling players composed of five or seven men, and two boys for the major and minor female roles. Compare *gangarilla.*

Gatomaquia. A satire of the Italian epic, recounting the loves of the beautiful feline, Zapaquilda. It was written by Lope de Vega in 1634. See under *Vega, Lope de.*

Gato Negro. See under *tertulia.*

gatos. A word which appears in the title of the 14th century Spanish translation of a Latin work, *Narrationes,* by Odo de Cheriton.

The Spanish title is *Libro de los gatos*. Although most of the tales in this collection are animal apologues, it has been suggested that the word "*gatos*", as here used, is a variant of *quentos (cuentos)*. See under *Libro de los gatos*.

gauchismo. See *gaucho literature*.

gaucho literature. The most indigenous type of Spanish-American literature in that it deals directly with regional types and background, in this case, the La Plata region of Argentina and Uruguay. It sprang originally from the minstrel songs *(payadas)* of anonymous gaucho minstrels *(payadores)* who, like medieval troubadours, wandered from place to place, improvising lyrics to their own guitar accompaniment. This early *poesía gauchesca* had a folk-song quality, being composed in simple, popular language and singing of the cowboy's life, love and adventures in his native setting, the *llanuras* or plains of the River Plata region. The most common of the verse forms employed by the *payador* were the *cielito*, the *vidalita* and the *triste*, all derived from the Spanish *copla*. Gradually, the primitive, romantic stage of gaucho poetry developed into a ballad or epic form, treating historical, social and political themes: the national hero, the outlaw, the revolutionary hero, etc. Early gaucho works of this type were Hidalgo's *Diálogo patriótico* (1822), Ascasubi's *Santos Vega* (1851), Del Campo's *Fausto* (1866) and José Fernández's *Martín Fierro* 1872). This more consciously literary and stylistic phase of gaucho literature continued into the 20th century with Payró's *Historias de Pago Chico* (1908) and Reyles' *El gaucho Florido* (1932). Among the better-known of contemporary gaucho writers are Rafael Obligado (1851-1920), the poet of Argentine folk legends, Benito Lynch (b. 1885), the master of gaucho dialect, and Ricardo Güiraldes (1886-1927), the great stylist of gaucho literature.

Cf. Rojas, R., "Los gauchescos," in *La literatura argentina*, Buenos Aires, 1924-1925; Tiscornia, E. F., (Ed.), *Poetas gauchescos: Hidalgo, Ascasubi, Del Campo*, Buenos Aires, 1940; *Poesía gauchesca*, (Ed. Borges, J. L., and Casares, A. B.), Mexico, 1955.

Gayangos, Pascual de (1809-1897). Professor, bibliographer and historian. Born in Seville; died in London. Known to American hispanists chiefly as the translator of Ticknor's *History of Spanish Literature* (1849 *et seq.*) *(Historia de la literatura española,*

Madrid, 1851-1856). Gayangos was a noted Arabic scholar as well as an authority on Spanish history and literature. He also edited two volumes of the *Biblioteca de Autores Españoles (Escritores en prosa anteriores al siglo XV; Libros de caballerías).* See also under *Ticknor.*

Cf. Romera-Navarro, M., *Historia de la literatura española,* 2a. ed., Boston, 1949.

Gelves, La Condesa de. See under *Herrera, Fernando de.*

Generaciones y semblanzas. See under *Pérez de Guzmán.*

General estoria. See under *Alfonso X.*

Generation of 1898. In its broadest sense, the group of Spanish writers (most of them born in the 1860's and 1870's) who were actively creating at the time of the Spanish débacle of 1898, and who joined in promoting the patriotic and literary revival following that date. Although the term had been used loosely at the turn of the century, the first unitary notion of a *generación del noventa y ocho* was elaborated by Azorín in various critical essays that appeared in literary periodicals and were collected in his *Clásicos y modernos* (1913). Joaquín Costa (1844-1911), Ángel Ganivet (1865-1898) and Miguel de Unamuno (1864-1936) are usually considered the immediate precursors of the group, although many literary historians consider Ganivet, and in most instances, Unamuno, as belonging within the group proper. The writers of the Generation of 1898, in addition to Unamuno, were: the critic Azorín (Martínez Ruiz), the journalist Ramiro Maeztu, the historian Rafael Altamira, the philologist Ramón Menéndez Pidal, the poets Antonio and Manuel Machado, Pérez de Ayala, Ramón Jiménez and Rubén Darío, the novelists Valle-Inclán, Pío Baroja and Blasco Ibáñez, and the dramatists Benavente, Linares Rivas, the Quintero brothers and Villaespesa. The disastrous outcome of the War of 1898, in which Spain lost the last of her colonies, provided these writers with the stimulus for national rehabilitation. In their works they rediscovered the beauties of the Spanish landscape and of old Spanish cities; they revived the poets of Spain's glorious past (Berceo, Juan Ruiz, Santillana, Góngora); they brought about a renaissance in Spanish scholarship and literary criticism; and they opened their spirits to the leavening influence of literary and intellectual influences from abroad.

Cf. Azorín, "La generación del 98," in his *Clásicos y modernos,* Madrid, 1913; Jeschke, H., *Die Generation von 1898 in Spanien,* Halle, 1934; Armani, C., *Angel Ganivet e la rinascenza spagnola del 98,* Napoli, 1934; Reding, K. P., *The Generation of 1898 Seen Through its Fictional Hero,* Northampton, Mass., 1935; Seeleman, R., "The Treatment of Landscape in the Novelists of the Generation of 1898," *Hispanic Review,* IV, 1936; Laín Entralgo, *La generación del noventa y ocho,* Madrid, 1945; Díaz-Plaja, G., *Modernismo frente a noventa y ocho,* Barcelona, 1951.

género chico. The "petit genre." A term used in reference to short, popular dramatic or dramatico-musical playlets, skits or operettas, generally one act in length; *e.g.* the one-act *sainete,* the *zarzuela menor* (as distinguished from the *zarzuela grande,* or full length operetta or musical comedy). The term *género chico* is used in contradistinction to the *género grande,* or major dramatic genre; *e.g.* tragedy, comedy, grand opera. Historically derived from the *paso* or *entremés* (interlude), the *género chico* developed in the latter part of the 19th century *(Teatro de la Zarzuela,* 1856; *Teatro del Recreo,* 1868). Although there are some regional examples, the *género chico* was mainly a development of the Madrid theater. The factors accounting for its vogue were its comical, satirical and burlesque features, its depiction of types and customs of the lower classes of Madrid society, its sentimentality, homely philosophy and racy, vernacular idiom. The lyrical and linguistic innovations of the *género chico* had a definite influence on certain modern Spanish poets. Among the outstanding representatives of this genre were Ricardo de la Vega (1839-1910), Tomás Luceño (1844-1931) and Carlos Arniches 1866-1943). See also *entremés; paso; sainete; zarzuela.*

Cf. Zurita, M., *Historia anecdótica del género chico,* Madrid, 1920; Deleito y Piñuela, J., *Origen y apogeo del género chico,* Madrid, 1949.

género grande. See under *género chico.*

Gente conocida. See under *Benavente.*

Gerifaltes de antaño. See under *Valle-Inclán.*

gerigonza. Jargon; gibberish. A derogatory term for *gongorismo* or *culteranismo.* Also spelled *jerigonza.*

germanía. (1) A jargon spoken by gypsies, thieves and rogues *(pícaros).* (2) A brotherhood or guild of rogues.

gesta. A collection of memorable deeds and exploits performed by a real or mythical character. The *cantar de gesta* is an epic poem which celebrates the deeds or exploits of a legendary or national hero. See *cantar de gesta.*

Gesta Roderici Campidocti. See under *Cid (El).*

Gil Blas. See under *picaresque novel.*

Gili y Gaya, Samuel (1892). Professor of literature in the *Instituto-Escuela de Madrid.* Linguist, grammarian, lexicographer and literary historian. Principal works: *Curso superior de sintaxis española; Tesoro lexicográfico.* Critical editions of Alemán, Espinel, Moncado, Diego de San Pedro.

Cf. *Hispania,* XXXVI, 1953.

Gil y Carrasco, Enrique (1815-1846). Romantic poet, critic, and novelist. A close friend and collaborator of Espronceda, he was the author of regional sketches, verse legends and critical essays on Rivas, Espronceda, Hartzenbusch and other romantic writers. He died at the age of thirty-one while with the foreign service in Berlin. His most enduring work is a historical novel, *El señor de Bembibre* (1844), notable for its elegiac mood and poetic descriptions of nature.

Cf. Samuels, D. G., *Enrique Gil y Carrasco: a Study in Spanish Romanticism,* N. Y., 1939.

Gillet, Joseph Eugene (1888). American hispanist. Born in Belgium; naturalized U. S. citizen, 1918. Various teaching posts at University of Edinburgh, University of Wisconsin, University of Illinois, Princeton. At Bryn Mawr College from 1924; Professor of Spanish and Head, Spanish Department, 1929-1949. Professor of Romance Languages, University of Pennsylvania, since 1949. Editor, *Hispanic Review,* since 1949. Critical editions: *Micael de Carvajal, Tragedia Josephina,* Princeton & Paris, 1932; *Bartolomé de Torres Naharro, Propalladia and other works,* Bryn Mawr, 1942-1951.

Giménez Caballero, Ernesto. See under *Torre, Guillermo de.*

Giner de los Ríos, Francisco (1839-1915). Philosopher, educator and literary critic. Born in Málaga; died in Madrid. An adherent of the *krausista* school of philosophy, he was professor of the philosophy of law at the University of Madrid. After losing his post at the university as the result of political agitation, he founded the famous *Institución Libre de Enseñanza* (1876), an educational institution completely independent of state and church. Giner de los Ríos exercised an immense influence on his pupils and on Spanish intellectual and cultural life in general. Most important among his publications were: *Estudios de literatura y arte* (1876); *Estudios sobre educación* (1886); *Filosofía y sociología* (1904); and *Filosofía del derecho* (1912).

Cf. Altamira, R., *Giner de los Ríos, educador,* Valencia, 1915.

Gitanilla (La). See under *Cervantes.*

Gloria de las artes. *See under Meléndez Valdés.*

Gloria de Niquea. See under *Villamediana.*

glosa. (Eng. *gloss).* (1) An explanation of or commentary on a difficult text. (2) A poetic composition at the end of which one or more lines, previously introduced, are repeated and developed. The repetition and development of an opening theme line or lines at the end of each stanza of a poem. Verses so repeated and developed are said to be *glosados,* or glossed. See also under *estribillo.*

glosado. Said of verses which repeat and develop an introductory theme verse at the end of a stanza. See under *glosa; estribillo.*

gnómica. A literary type which emphasizes ethical teaching in concentrated, aphoristic form. An example is the *Proverbios morales* (bet. 1350 and 1369) by the medieval poet, Sem Tob. See also under *poesía gnómica; Sem Tob.*

Godoy Alcayaga, Lucila. See *Mistral, Gabriela.*

Golden Age. See *Siglo de Oro.*

Golfo de las sirenas (El). See under *Calderón.*

goliardesco. Referring to the style of *goliardo,* or ribald and satirical verse. See *goliardo.*

goliardo. (1) Addicted to gluttony and licentiousness. (2) A medieval student or cleric given to a life of vagabondage and licentiousness. Among such wandering students and clerics were *juglares,* who wrote ribald and satirical verse. They sometimes attributed their work to an imaginary Bishop Golias.

Gómez de Avellaneda, Gertrudis (1814-1873). Cuban poetess, novelist and dramatist. Born in Cuba but lived in Spain from 1836 on, except for a return visit to Cuba (1859-1863). During this time she founded the literary review, *Album Cubano,* and engaged in many literary and cultural activities. She belongs both to Cuban and to Spanish literature as one of the most celebrated writers of 19th century romanticism. Famous in her day for her dramas, comedies and historical novels, she was widely feted, receiving literary prizes and enthusiastic popular and critical acclaim. However, her most permanent creative achievement was her poetry, in which she treats the themes of love, religion and esthetic emotion with exquisite lyrical sensitivity and in a rich variety of metrical forms. Her chief works were: *Poesías,* 1841; (novels) *Sab,* 1839; *Espatolino,* 1844; *Guatimozín,* 1845; (dramas) *Alfonso Munio,* 1844; *El príncipe de Viana,* 1844; *Egilona,* 1845; *Saúl,* 1849; *Recaredo,* 1850; *Baltasar,* 1858; (comedies) *Errores del corazón,* 1852; *La hija de las Flores o Todos están locos,* 1852; *Obras completas,* 1869 *et seq.*

Cf. Williams, E. B., *The Life and Dramatic Works of Gertrudis Gómez de Avellaneda,* Philadelphia, 1924; Cotarelo y Mori, E., *La Avellaneda y sus obras,* Madrid, 1930.

Gómez de la Serna, Ramón (1888). Vanguardist literary critic, novelist, dramatist and biographer. Born in Madrid. Educated as a lawyer, he never practised, but instead devoted his entire life to writing and lecturing. Possessing one of the most stimulating and fertile imaginations among contemporary Spanish writers, his reputation is such that he is referred to by critics simply as Ramón; and his original system of interpreting art and nature is known as *ramonismo.* Intimately associated with the literary and esthetic world of Madrid, where he founded the famous *tertulia* at the *Café Pombo,* he has lived in Buenos Aires since the Spanish Civil War. His works exceed the hundred mark, including novels *(El doctor inverosímil, El torero Caracho, El caballero del hongo gris,* etc.); biographies *(El Greco, Goya, Azorín, Valle-Inclán,* etc.); plays *(El drama de palacio deshabitado, Los medios seres,* etc.); and criticism *(La hiperestética, Ismos,* etc.). Ramón is noted as the inventor of the *greguería,* an almost indefinable literary genre which is a hybrid between the poetic metaphor and the prose aphorism. Since 1910 he has published a series of these *greguerías (Tapices, El rastro, El circo, Pombo,* etc.). Highly original, humorous, facile, inventive and sometimes eccentric and flippant, Ramón anticipated surrealism in literature. He deals with the indefinable, attempting to show the interconnection or logic behind the apparent confusion of things. His method is what might be called the attainment of insight through the incongruous metaphor. See also under *greguería*.

Cf. Pérez Ferrero, M., *Vida de Ramón*, Madrid, 1935; Del Río, A., *Historia de la literature española*, N. Y., 1948.

Gómez de Quevedo. See *Quevedo, Francisco de.*

Góngora y Argote, Luis de (1561-1627). The greatest and most complex poet of the late Golden Age. Born and died in Córdoba. Of a cultured family, he studied canon law at the University of Salamanca, but neglected his studies in favor of riotous living and poetry. His dissolute propensities were still in evidence even after he had taken deacon's orders and had been appointed prebendary of the Córdoba Cathedral (1577), for he was reprimanded by his bishop in 1589 for frequenting bullfights and associating with actors. Góngora's poetic genius was first recognized by Cervantes (in *Galatea*, 1585). With the appearance of his poems in the *Romancero general* (1600), his fame became widespread. He came to Madrid in 1612 and was appointed chaplain to the king, occupying this honorary post until 1626. His latter days were spent in the shadow of physical and mental illness. Góngora's works were not published during his lifetime, although several of his *romances* appeared anonymously in the *Flor de varios romances nuevos* (1589), and his *Fábula de Polifemo y Galatea* as well as the first part of his *Soledades* were circulated in manuscript in the literary academies of Madrid in 1613. His collected poems were first published in 1627 by Juan López de Vicuña. Góngora's poetic production from 1580 to 1612 was chiefly lyrical. He wrote *romances* (ballads) and *letrillas* (popular lyrics with an ironical or satirical refrain or *estribillo*). He also excelled in the sonnet form, in which he is one of the great Spanish masters. This lyrical period shows us Góngora at his best, his verse distinguished by grace, charm, wit, vitality, melancholy and cynicism. However, from 1609 on, there are already signs of increasing complexity and stylization in his work. Góngora's *Panegírico al duque de Lerma* (1609) marks his adoption of Carrillo y Sotomayor's theory of *culteranismo* and the beginning of his baroque phase. In his *Fábula de Polifemo y Galatea* (1613) and *Fábula de Píramo y Tisbe* (1618) he relates mythological love stories with esoteric allusions and violent conceits *(conceptismo)* comprehensible only to the learned *élite* *(culteranismo)*. The culmination of Góngora's baroque style is his *Soledades* (1613), an unfinished poem in two parts comprising some 2,000 verses in an irregular hendecasyllable meter known as the *silva*. Although a pastoral idyll in praise of the simple life, its lexical, syntactical and figurative complexity is in odd contrast with its theme. The *Soledades* touched off a literary controversy that continued for three centuries. Not until the 20th century did it find critical understanding and acceptance as one of the greatest and most ambitious poems ever written in the Spanish language. See also *gongorismo; culteranismo; conceptismo*.

Cf. *Obras poéticas*, (Ed.) Foulché-Delbosc, R., 3 vols., N. Y., 1921; *Soledades de Góngora*, (Ed.) Alonso, D., Madrid, 1927; *Romances de Góngora*, (Ed.) Cossío, J. M. de, Madrid, 1927; Artigas, M., *Don Luis de Góngora: biografía y estudio crítico*, Madrid, 1925; Kane, E. K., *Gongorism and the Golden Age*, Chapel Hill, N. C., 1928; Thomas, L. P., *Don Luis de Góngora*, Paris, 1932; Alonso, D., *La lengua poética de Góngora*, Madrid, 1935; *idem*, *Ensayos sobre poesía española*, Buenos Aires, 1944.

gongorismo. The 17th century baroque style in Spanish literature, named after its most distinguished exemplar, Luis de Góngora y Argote (1561-1627). The meaning of *gongorismo* is commonly equated with that of *culteranismo (e.g.* in the *DRAE)* because of its appeal to the learned élite with its obscure classical and mythological allusions. In this sense it is generally the lexical and syntactical features of gongorism that are emphasized (extreme latinization of vocabulary, classical neologisms, unconventional word order, *etc.)*. However, the gongoristic style also includes many traits of *conceptismo* (the striking conceit–*concepto*–, metaphysical subtlety, the complex metaphor, wordplay–*equívoco*–, *etc.)*. In the objective meaning of the term, gongorism is the artistic, literary reflection of an era (the decadent late Golden Age). As such it has its correlates in other countries (marinism or *secentismo* in Italy, *préciosité* in France, *etc.)*. However, gongorism also has emotive connotations. The controversy begun at its inception (the appearance of Góngora's *Soledades*, 1613) still lives on in the limitation of its meaning to cultivated affectation and obscurity of style. The theoretician of gongorism (in the meaning of *culteranismo)* was Luis de Carrillo y Sotomayor (*Libro de la erudición poética,* 1607). In addition to Góngora, the great writers exemplifying the style (in the meaning of *conceptismo*) were Baltasar Gracián (*Agudeza y arte de ingenio,* 1648), Francisco de Quevedo (*El Parnaso español,* 1648), and Calderón de la Barca (1600-1681). Among the admirers and imitators of Góngora were the Conde de Villamediana (1582-1622), Gabriel Bocángel (1608?-1658?) and Juana Inés de la Cruz (1651?-1695). Lope de Vega and Quevedo were among the outstanding opponents of gongorism. Quevedo, in particular, although his *conceptismo* also resulted in verbal and figurative complexity, wrote the most scathing satire of gongorism (*Aguja de navegar cultos con la receta para hacer Soledades en un día,* 1631). See also *conceptismo; culteranismo; Góngora y Argote.*

Cf. Thomas, L. P., *Gongora et le gongorisme considérés dans leurs rapports avec le marinisme,* Paris, 1911; Reyes, A., *Cuestiones gongorinas,* Madrid, 1927; Kane, E. K., *Gongorism and the Golden Age,* Chapel Hill, N. C., 1928; Alonso, D., *La lengua poética de Góngora,* Madrid, 1935; Díaz-Plaja, G., *El espíritu del barroco,* Barcelona, 1940.

González, Diego. See under *Escuela de Salamanca; Meléndez Valdés.*

González de Eslava, Fernán (1534?-1601?). Early Mexican dramatist. Born in Spain, he came to Mexico in 1559. Several of his religious "coloquios" were posthumously published in 1610. His work contains the allegorical and homiletic elements, as well as the comic interludes, typical of early religious drama. Naturalness of characterization and plot, and simplicity of language constitute his chief merit.

Cf. Alonso, A., "Biografía de Fernán González de Eslava," *Revista de filología hispánica,* II, 1940.

González Martínez, Enrique (1871-1952). Mexican poet, physician, professor and diplomat. He practiced medicine until 1911 and then went to Mexico City to embark on a university and diplomatic career. At various stages in his career he was his country's ambassador to Spain, Argentina, and Chile. He received the Avila Camacho award for his poetry in 1946. Of a sober and logical temperament, he decried the superficial estheticism of the modernistic trend, symbolized as a swan in his *La muerte del cisne* (1915). Having wrung the neck of the swan, he sets up his own symbol, the owl. This metaphor, exhorting poets to less preening and more sense, marks the beginning of the reaction against modernist excesses. Chief works: *Preludios,* 1903; *Los senderos ocultos,* 1911; *La muerte del cisne,* 1915; *El romero alucinado,* 1923; *Poemas truncos,* 1935; *El diluvio de fuego,* 1938; *Vilano al viento,* 1948; *Babel,* 1949; (memoirs) *El hombre del buho,* 1951; *La apacible locura,* 1951.

Cf. Díez-Canedo, E., "Enrique González Martínez en su plenitud," *Revista iberoamericana,* II, 1940; Topete, J. M., "La muerte del cisne(?)," *Hispania,* XXXVI, 1953.

González Palencia, Ángel (1889-1949). Authority on Arabic and Spanish literature and folklore. Professor at the University of Madrid. Author of innumerable articles, monographs, research studies and critical editions in the field of Mozarabic and Spanish literature. Among his chief extensive works are: *Historias y leyendas (*1942), *Vida y obras de don Hurtado de Mendoza* (1941-1943), in collaboration with Eugene Mele; and *Historia de la literatura española* (5th ed., 1943), in collaboration with Juan Hurtado. See also under *Flórez, Enrique.*

González Prada, Manuel (1844-1918). Peruvian reformer, journalist and poet. As much a political and social reformer as he was a writer, he was ardently nationalistic, pro-Indian, anti-Spanish and anti-clerical. He founded many periodicals and political parties to propagandize his socialistic views. In his youth he was influenced by poets of romantic revolt (Schiller, Heine), whose works he translated; and, in turn, he himself exercised a decisive influence on Haya de la Torre, the founder of *Aprismo.* González Prada was a virtuoso in the vocabulary of invective, combining a romantic intensity of emotion with a pervasive sense of form. His metrical improvisations and revival of ancient and exotic verse forms were of great influence on the development of Spanish American poetry. Much of his work has been posthumously edited and published by his son, Alfredo González Prada. Among his chief works were: *Páginas libres,* 1894; *Minúsculas,* 1901; *Horas de lucha,* 1908; *Presbiterianas,* 1909; *Exóticas,,* 1911; *Bajo el oprobio,* 1933; *Baladas peruanas,* 1935; *Grafitos,* 1937; *Antología poética de Manuel González Prada,* 1940; *El tonel de Diógenes,* 1945.

Cf. Sánchez, L. A., *Don Manuel,* Santiago de Chile, 1930;

Mead, R. G., "Manuel González Prada y la prosa española," *Revista Iberoamericana,* XVII, 1952; Sánchez, L. A., "González Prada y el modernismo," *Cuadernos Americanos,* 1953.

Gonzalo de Ulloa. See under *Don Juan.*

Gonzalo González. See under *Infantes de Lara.*

Gonzalo Gustios. See under *Infantes de Lara.*

gozo. A poetic composition in praise of the Virgin or the saints.

Gracián y Morales, Baltasar (1601-1658). Moral philosopher and great prose stylist of *conceptismo.* Born in Aragon, at Belmonte de Calatayud; died in Tarazona. Educated by the Jesuits at Calatayud and at Huesca, he entered the Jesuit Order in 1619, taking his final vows in 1635. Most of his life was spent as a teacher at various Jesuit schools. His literary production extended from 1637 almost until his death, embittered by the cruel opposition of his superiors. His chief works were several treatises on principles of conduct for leaders, a book on literary criticism and a long allegorical novel. In *El héroe* (1637), *El político Fernando* (1640), *El discreto* (1646), and *Oráculo manual y arte de prudencia* (1647) he discusses the ethical principles that should govern the hero, the politician and the courtier. The last mentioned work contains maxims that were of great influence on La Rochefoucauld and La Bruyère. In his *Arte de ingenio* (1642) and the sequel that incorporates it, *Agudeza y arte de ingenio* (1648), Gracián provides the literary theory of *conceptismo* together with examples from *conceptista* writers. *Agudeza* (subtlety) is his chief critical canon. Gracián's most notable work was a philosophical novel, *El criticón* (Pt. I, 1651; II, 1653; II, 1657). The three parts of this allegorical work are divided according to the ages of man: youth, maturity and old age. Two attitudes towards life are contrasted in the form of the two chief characters: Critilo, the rational, introspective man of civilization; and Andrenio, the instinctive, extrovertive man of nature. Gracián's pessimism is shown in his idyllic portrayal of the primitive life as contrasted to the evils of civilization. The novel was to come into its own two centuries later when Schopenhauer recognized in it a kindred philosophy. Gracián's style is epigrammatic. In his attempt to compress the maximum number of ideas into the minimum number of words, he achieved a kind of ellipsis and understatement that makes it necessary to ponder and interpret each of his phrases. In the opinion of some critics his style suffers from the same obscurity characteristic of gongorism. See also *conceptismo; gongorismo.*

Cf. *Obras completas,* (Ed.) Correa Calderón, E., Madrid, 1944; *El criticón,* (Ed.) Romera-Navarro, M., Philadelphia, 1938-1940; Morel-Fatio, A., "Gracián interpreté par Schopenhauer," *Bulletin hispanique,* XII; Bell, A. F. G., *Baltasar Gracián,* Oxford, 1921.

gracioso. The buffoon or comic character of the Spanish classical drama. The *gracioso* was first developed as an integral character in Lope de Vega's *La Francesilla (ca.* 1599), where he is referred to as "la figura del donaire". The *gracioso* supplied the comic relief, somewhat similarly to the Merry Andrew, clown or fool of Elizabethan drama. With Lope de Vega, he became a traditional figure on the Spanish stage, appearing in the comedies of Tirso de Molina, Ruiz de Alarcón, and Calderón. Usually a servant or squire, he served as a kind of parody of the principal character, often accompanied by the *graciosa,* the chambermaid or soubrette. At his best he was gay, witty and even tragicomical, supplying the realistic or cynical counterpoint that enhanced the theme of the major character. The term also has a broader connotation in reference to any literary, musical or artistic creation; *e.g.* "Chistoso, agudo, lleno de donaire y gracia." (DRAE).

Gráfico (El). See under *Guzmán, Martín.*

Gramática castellana. See under *Nebrija; Bello.*

Granada. See under *Zorrilla y Moral.*

Granada, Luis de (1504-1588). Ascetic writer, mystic and celebrated preacher of the Renaissance. Born in Granada; died in Lisbon. His name was Luis Sarria before he entered the Dominican Order in 1525. Although of extremely humble origin, he was able to pursue his studies at the College of San Gregorio in Valladolid thanks to the patronage of the Count of Tendilla. Having gained extraordinary fame as a devotional writer and preacher, he finally attained the status of Dominican Provincial in Portugal (1557). He wrote many works in Latin, Portuguese and Spanish. Of interest is his translation of Thomas à Kempis' *Imitation of Christ,* which for a time was the standard translation in Spain until superseded by that of Juan Eusebio Nieremberg. Granada's most popular work was his *Guía de pecadores* (1567), a treatise on the attainment of virtue. Another of his contributions to devotional literature was his *Libro de la oración y meditación* (1554), a book of prayers, meditation and ascetic virtues. His greatest work was his *Introducción del símbolo de la fe* (1583), a masterpiece of Catholic apologetics designed for the layman. Granada's inspiration was derived chiefly from the Church Fathers and from Cicero. This accounts for his religious asceticism and his oratorical style. Yet his astonishing sensitivity to the beauties of nature is at times in contrast with his asceticism.

Cf. *Obras,* 14 vols., (Ed.) Cuervo, J., Madrid, 1906 *et seq.;* Cuervo, J., *Biografía de Fray Luis de Granada,* Madrid, 1896; Peers, A., *Studies of the Spanish Mystics,* I, N. Y., 1927; Brentano, Sister M. B., *Nature in the Works of Fray Luis de Granada,* Washington, D. C., 1935.

Granadino (El). See under *Caro.*

Gran conquista de ultramar (La). One of the early chivalric romances, probably written at the beginning of the 14th century and relating the story of the Crusades up to 1271. It was first published in 1503 in Salamanca, and is a long, rambling prose account of 1100 chapters combining fact and fiction. The work is a translation of a lost Old-French original which in turn had been adapted from William of Tyre's (d. 1184) *Historia rerum in partibus transmarinis gestarum.* Since it incorporates many prose versions of Old French epics, *La gran conquista de ultramar* is an important research source in comparative literature. It introduced many themes of the cycle of the Crusades into Spanish literature. Most important of these themes are that of the Swan Knight, Lohengrin, *(El caballero del cisne),* the prototype of Wagner's hero; and that of *Mainet* (Sp. *Maynete),* the story of Charlemagne's youthful exploits.

Cf. "La gran conquista de ultramar," (Ed.) Gayangos, P., *BAE,* XLIV; Mazorriaga, E., *La leyenda del cauallero del cisne,* Madrid, 1914; Northup, G. T., "*La gran conquista de Ultramar* and its Problems," *Hispanic Review,* II, 1934.

Gran teatro del mundo (El). See under *Calderón.*

Grases, Pedro (1909). Venezuelan literary scholar, philologist and bibliographer. Professor at the *Universidad Central,* Caracas. Editor of the definitive edition of the works of Andrés Bello (in progress). Principal works: *Antología de Andrés Bello; Doce* *estudios sobre Andrés Bello; Andrés Bello: el primer humanista de América.*

Cf. *Hispania,* XXXVI, 1953.

Grecia. One of the most important literary reviews associated with the ultraist movement. It was published in Seville from 1919 to 1920. One of its collaborators was Guillermo de Torre (b. 1900). See also under *ultraísmo.*

Green, Otis Howard (1898). American hispanist. Authority on Spanish Renaissance literature. Studied at the *Centro de Estudios Históricos,* 1922. On the staff of the University of Pennsylvania since 1923; Professor since 1939; Chairman of Department, 1938-1945. Visiting Professor, University of Colorado Summer Session, since 1934. Co-editor, *Hispanic Review.* Chief publications: *The Life and Works of Lupercio Leonardo de Argensola,* 1927; "A Critical Survey of Scholarship in the Field of Spanish Renaissance Literature, 1914-1944," *Studies in Philology,* XLIV, 1947; "Courtly Love in the Spanish Cancioneros," *Publications of the Modern Language Association,* LXIV, 1949; "Ni es Cielo ni es Azul," *Revista de Filología Española,* XXXIV, 1950; *Estudios dedicados a Menéndez Pidal,* 1950; etc.

greguería. An almost indefinable literary genre invented by Gómez de la Serna (b. 1888). It is a sort of hybrid between the poetic metaphor and the prose aphorism. The word *greguería* means "outcry"; and presumably the idea is to denote an instinctive or primitive utterance of an everyday or prosaic nature, yet calculated to divulge a new insight into the relationship of things. Example: "See in the typewriter the smile of the alphabet's false teeth!" It is essentially a method of attaining awareness through the incongruous metaphor. See also under *Gómez de la Serna.*

Cf. Brenan, G., *The Literature of the Spanish People,* 2nd ed., Cambridge, 1953.

Grimalte y Gradisa. See under *Flores, Juan de.*

Grisel y Mirabella. See under *Flores, Juan de.*

Grismer, Raymond Leonard (1895). American hispanist, literary scholar and bibliographer. Professor of Spanish, University of Minnesota since 1931. Author of *A Reference Index to 12,000 Spanish American Authors,* 1939; *A New Bibliography of the Literature of Spain and Spanish America,* 7 vols., 1941; *The*

Influence of Plautus in Spain Before Lope de Vega, 1944; *Cervantes—A Bibliography,* 1946.

Gritos del combate. See under *Núñez de Arce.*

Grosseteste, Robert. See under *Santa María Egipciaca.*

Guerra de Granada. See under *Hurtado de Mendoza.*

Guerras civiles de Granada. See under *Pérez de Hita.*

Guevara, Antonio de (1480?-1545). Courtier, writer and priest. At the death of his royal patroness, Queen Isabella, he entered the Franciscan Order, rising eventually to the status of Bishop. Guevara's real vocation was literary rather than priestly. His works were very popular in Spain and throughout Europe and England. His most notable achievement was *Reloj de príncipes o Libro áureo del emperador Marco Aurelio* (1529), a didactic novel containing imaginary letters of the Roman Emperor, and preaching the virtues of the perfect prince. The style is extremely ornate and the book is supposed to have had some influence on the development of euphuism in England. Guevara's classical scholarship was rather weak and the many errors of fact in his writings occasioned critical comment even in his own day.

Cf. Costes, R., *Antonio de Guevara: sa vie; son oeuvre,* Bordeaux-Paris, 1925-1926; Thomas, H., "The English Translators of Guevara's Works," *Homenaje a Bonilla,* II, Madrid, 1930.

Guía del lector del Quijote. See under *Madariaga.*

Guía de pecadores. See under *Granada.*

Guillén, Jorge (1893). Poet and scholar. Born at Valladolid. A professor at the Universities of Murcia and of Seville, he has also lectured at the Sorbonne and at Oxford. He left his post at the University of Seville in 1938 and came to the United States, where he has been Professor of Spanish at Wellesley College. Guillén is one of the most gifted of contemporary Spanish poets. Although he has only published a single volume of poetry *(Cántico),* the four successively augmented editions (1928, 1936, 1945, 1950) of this work are evidence of a high degree of continuous creative productivity, the latest edition containing well over 300 poems. Critics have pointed out the influence of Valéry on Guillén, referring to him as a representative of "pure poetry". The designation seems apt in view of his preference for classical forms and his almost austere yet deceptive simplicity. According to Del Río, Guillén belongs to "the grand tradition of Castilian poets in whose poetry there is an indissoluble fusion of reality and spirit, of immanence and transcendence" *(Historia de la literatura española,* II, 256, N. Y., 1948.

Cf. *Cántico, Fe de Vida,* Buenos Aires, 1950; Pleak, F. A., *The Poetry of Jorge Guillén* (Introduction by Castro, A.), Princeton, 1943; Casalduero, J., *Jorge Guillén: Cántico,* Santiago de Chile, 1946.

Guillén, Nicolás (1904). Cuban "nativist" poet. An outstanding composer of Negro poetry in the Spanish language. His style is sensuous, full of colorful imagery and onomatopoeic rhythms. His themes are rooted in native folklore and racial atmosphere. His chief works are: *Motivos de son,* 1930; *Sóngoro cosongo,* 1931; *West Indies Limited,* 1934; *Cantos para soldados y sones para turistas,* 1937; *El son entero,* 1946.

Cf. Marinello, J., *Literatura hispanoamericana,* Mexico, 1937.

Guillermo de Tiro. William of Tyre. See under *Gran conquista de ultramar.*

Güiraldes, Ricardo (1886-1927). Argentine poet and short-story writer. Born in Buenos Aires and died in Paris. He was the co-founder of *Proa,* a vanguardist review. One of the most significant of contemporary Argentine writers, his fame rests on his masterful blending of the gaucho tale with modernistic technique. He lived and loved the life of the *estanciero,* and is at his best in describing it, as in *Don Segundo Sombra,* a classical tale of the pampas. The titles of his chief works were: *El cencerro de cristal,* 1915; *Cuentos de muerte y de sangre,* 1915; *Xaimaca,* 1923; *Don Segundo Sombra,* 1926; *Seis relatos porteños,* 1929.

Cf. Flores, A., "Latin American Writers: Ricardo Güiraldes," *Panorama,* Washington, D. C., Dec., 1940.

Gutiérrez Nájera, Manuel (1859-1895). Mexican poet, editor, and short-story writer. A pioneer of the "modernista" movement, he founded its first literary organ, the *Revista azul* (1894). Influenced by Bécquer, DeMusset, and Verlaine, his poetry reflects his development from romanticism to modernism. A collection of his poems, edited by Justo Sierra, appeared in 1896. Among his modernist prose tales were *Cuentos frágiles* (1883). His favorite among the many pseudonyms he adopted was "El duque Job", taken from the title of one of his most famous poems. This romantic metaphor of the sufferer ennobled by his pain is a revealing self-portrait of an unhappy individual whose conflicts were sublimated into pure lyricism.

Cf. Walker, N., *The Life and Works of Manuel Gutiérrez Nájera,* Columbia, Mo., 1927.

Guzmán, Martín Luis (1887). Mexican novelist, journalist and soldier. He was a colonel in the revolutionary army under Pancho Villa in 1914. A political exile from 1914 to 1934, he was editor of *El Gráfico* in New York and a journalist in Madrid. Guzmán is generally classed with Mariano Azuela as one of the foremost Mexican novelists deriving their inspiration from the experiences of the Mexican Revolution. Chief works: *El áquila y la serpiente,* 1928; *La sombra del caudillo,* 1929; *Mina el Mozo, héroe de Navarra,* 1932; *Memorias de Pancho Villa,* 1938-1939.

Cf. Houck, H. P., "Las obras novelescas de Martín Luis Guzmán," *Revista iberoamericana,* III, 1941.

Guzmán de Alfarache. See under *Alemán, Mateo; picaresque novel.*

Guzmán el Bueno. See under *Vélez de Guevara.*

H

Hacia otra España. See under *Maeztu.*

Hamlet. See under *Ramón de la Cruz; Moratín.*

Harpías de Madrid (Las). See under *Castillo Solórzano.*

Hartzenbusch, Juan Eugenio (1806-1880). Scholar, editor, critic and dramatist of the Romantic period. Born and died in Madrid. The son of a German father (d. 1808) and of a Spanish mother, his studies at the Jesuit College of San Isidro were interrupted by financial straits. Although obliged to work as a cabinet-maker, he managed by dint of self-instruction to become one of the eminent literary scholars of his day, finally attaining the position of Director of the *Biblioteca Nacional* (1862). He edited several volumes of the Golden Age drama for the *Biblioteca de Autores Españoles,* and the *Teatro escogido* (12 vols., 1839-1842) of Tirso de Molina (Fray Gabriel Téllez). In addition he wrote various critical introductions to the works of Lope de Vega, Rojas, Calderón, Molière, Voltaire, Dumas, *etc.* His poetry was negligible (*Ensayos poéticos,* 1843). His *Fábulas* (1848 and 1861) were an engaging blend of satire and humor. However, it was as a critic and creator of drama that Hartzenbusch excelled. He achieved popular success with his comedy, *La redoma encantada* (1839), and wrote various other comedies in the tradition of Moratín (*Los polvos de la madre Celestina,* 1840; *La coja y el encogido,* 1843; *etc.*). Outstanding among his serious dramas were *Los amantes de Teruel* (1837) and *La jura de Santa Gadea* (1845), the former being his great masterpiece, based on a legend that had already been treated in the classical theater by Tirso de Molina and Pérez de Montalbán; and the latter dramatizing a legend of the Cid. Written in prose and verse, *Los amantes de Teruel* is a beautiful and touching legend of two lovers, Diego Marsilla and Isabel de Segura, separated by circumstance and intrigue, to be united only in death. The version by Hartzenbusch was a contribution not only to the drama of romanticism but to the permanent Spanish drama.

Cf. *Obras de Hartzenbusch,* 4 vols., Madrid, 1888-1892; Gil Albacete, A., (Ed.) *Los amantes de Teruel y La jura de Santa Gadea,* Madrid, 1935; Hartzenbusch, D. E., *Bibliografía de Hartzenbusch,* Madrid, 1900; Cotarelo y Mori, E., "Sobre el origen y desarrollo de la leyenda de 'Los amantes de Teruel'", *Revista de Archivos,* VIII, Madrid, 1907; Corbière, A. S., *Juan Eugenio Hartzenbusch and the French Theater,* Philadelphia, 1927.

Hatzfeld, Helmut A. (1892). German hispanist and Romance philologist. Naturalized U. S. citizen, 1945. Professor at Frankfurt (1929), Heidelberg (1932), Louvain (1938), and Catholic University of America (since 1940). Noted as a Cervantes scholar, his outstanding work in this field is *Don Quijote als Wortkunstwerk,* Leipzig, 1927 *(El Quijote como obra del lenguaje,* Madrid, 1949). He has contributed articles on Spanish literature to the *Dictionary of World Literature,* N. Y., 1943; and the *Encyclopedia of World Literature,* N. Y., 1946. A specialist in the field of stylistics, his articles on Cervantes, Mysticism, *etc.,* have appeared in *Anales Cervantinos, Nueva Revista de Filología Hispánica, Clavileño, Hispania,* etc. Among his important contributions to research in stylistics is *A Critical Bibliography of the New Stylistics Applied to the Romance Literatures, 1900-1952,* Chapel Hill, North Carolina, 1953.

Haya de la Torre, Víctor Raúl. See under *Aprismo.*

Hazañas del Cid (Las). See under *Castro, Guillén de.*

Haz de leña (El). See under *Núñez de Arce.*

Hebreo, León (1460?-1521?). Jewish poet of Spanish origin. His real name was Judas Abravanel. After the expulsion of the Jews from Spain, he found refuge in Naples. His famous work, *Diálogos de amor,* first appeared in Italian *(Dialoghi d'amore;* Rome, 1535). Although placed on the *Index,* the *Diálogos de amor* found a wide audience throughout Europe, being translated into Latin, Spanish and French. The first translation into Castilian was by Carlos Montesa (Zaragoza, 1582). Its most famous Spanish translation (1590) was by El Inca, Garcilaso de la Vega (available in *NBAE,* XXI). The *Diálogos de amor* preached the platonic doctrines of ideal beauty and spiritual love. Its influence on Spanish writers of the Renaissance was considerable (Boscán, Garcilaso, Cervantes, *etc.).* It was in a large measure responsible for the diffusion of neoplatonic ideas in Spain during the Renaissance.

Cf. Carvalho, J., *León Hebreo, filósofo,* Coimbra, 1918; Pflaum, H., *Die Idee der Liebe. León Hebreo.,* Tübingen, 1926.

Heliodorus. See under *novela bizantina.*

Helios. A literary review. See under *Martínez Sierra.*

Helman, Edith F. (1905). American hispanist. Studied at the *Centro de Estudios Históricos* (1930, 1934, 1936). Professor of Spanish, Simmons College, since 1947. Chief publications: *Noches lúgubres de Cadalso,* Madrid, 1950; textbooks, articles *(Hispanic Review),* etc., on Valera, García Lorca, Jovellanos, and on 18th century Spanish literature.

hemistiquio. (Eng. *hemistich).* Half of a metrical line or verse. Either part of a verse divided by a caesura, or pause. Occasionally, a short line in a stanza.

Henríquez Ureña, Pedro (1884-1946). Literary scholar and professor. Born in the Dominican Republic; died in La Plata, Argentina. Professor at the University of Mexico and at the University of Buenos Aires. Occupied important public posts as director and superintendent of education in Mexico and in the Dominican Republic. Associated with the *Revista de Filología Española* in Madrid. Lectured at North American universities. Chief publications: *Ensayos críticos,* 1905; *La enseñanza de la literatura,* 1913; *Tablas cronológicas de la literatura española,* 1913; *Don Juan Ruiz de Alarcón,* 1915; *Literatura dominicana,* 1917; *La versificación irregular en la poesía castellana,* 1933; *Corrientes literarias en la América hispana,* (Eng. 1945; Span. 1949).

Cf. Leguizamón, J. A., *Historia de la literatura hispanoamericana,* Buenos Aires, 1945; "Pedro Henríquez Ureña," *Repertorio Americano,* May, June, 1953.

heptasílabo. A metrical line or verse of seven syllables, variously stressed.

Heredia, José María (1803-1839). Cuban poet. Born in Santiago, Cuba, and died in Mexico. A political exile most of his life, he lived in Venezuela, Mexico, and the United States. Although he wrote essays, dramas and translations from the French and the Italian, his greatest achievement was his poetry. Among the foremost of Spanish American poets, his work has been widely translated. Heredia's style combines classical form with romantic elements. His romantic feeling is evidenced in his nature poems *(En una tempestad, Niágara),* in which the abiding grandeur of natural phenomena is contrasted with the temporal insignificance of man.

Cf. Chacón y Calvo, J. M., *Ensayos de literatura cubana,* Madrid, 1922; *Poesías, discursos, cartas,* Havana, 1939.

Hermana San Sulpicio (La). See under *Palacio Valdés.*

Hermosa fea (La). See under *Vega, Lope de.*

Hermosura de Angélica. See under *Vega, Lope de.*

Hernández, José (1834-1886). Argentine poet. He received very little formal education, spending his youth on the *estancias,* where he became intimately familiar with gaucho life. At various stages in his career he was a soldier in the Argentine civil wars, editor of the newspaper, *Río de la Plata,* and a minor functionary in the government. In creating his octosyllabic verse epic, *Martín Fierro* (1872), and its sequel, *La vuelta de Martín Fierro* (1879), he emerged as the chief poet of gaucho literature. *Martín Fierro* is the first truly indigenous South American epic. With it Hernández achieved a rare combination of great literary art and national popularity. His depiction of the gaucho speech and manners of his time preserves a memorable chapter in the history of Argentine national development.

Cf. Holmes, H. A., *Martín Fierro, an Epic of the Argentine,* N. Y., 1923; Rojas, R., *La literatura argentina,* Buenos Aires, 1924-1925.

Héroe (El). See under *Gracián y Morales.*

heroico. The type of eleven-syllable verse *(endecasílabo)* adapted to Castilian meters by Boscán and Garcilaso. It is accented on the 6th and 10th syllables. Also known as the *endecasílabo yámbico.* See under *endecasílabo.*

heroida. A poetic composition dealing with a celebrated personage or hero.

Herrera, Fernando de (1534-1597). Renaissance poet of the Sevillan school. Born and died in Seville. After taking minor orders, he was appointed to a benefice connected with the Church of San Andrés (St. Andrew) in Seville. The income from this benefice was sufficient to allow him to lead a life of study and writing, and he was never ordained. His poems appeared in 1582 under the title of *Algunas obras.* In addition he wrote a history *(Relación de la guerra de Chipre y batalla naval de Lepanto,* 1572) and a biography *(Elogio de la vida y muerte de Tomás Moro,* 1592). A great admirer of Garcilaso (Cf. his *Anotaciones a las obras de Garcilasso de la Vega,* 1580), he developed a more elaborate and exuberant style than his master, in many ways anticipating *culteranismo.* Herrera was greatly admired in his day for his love lyrics and sonnets (he was called "El Divino"); but these poems, despite their metrical deftness and transfigured emotionalism, merely reflect the conventional Petrarchan neoplatonism of the Renaissance. The platonic love of his poems was, in real life, Leonor de Millán, the wife of the Count of Gelves, a grandson of Columbus. Herrera's most abiding contribution to the poetry of the Renaissance was his patriotic odes. In them he achieved a noble, vigorous, elevated style, inspired by the lofty and solemn cadences of the Book of Psalms. Among the more famous of his odes are *Canción por la victoria de Lepanto* and *Canción por la pérdida del rey Don Sebastián,* the former celebrating the triumph of the Christian forces under Don Juan of Austria over the Turks in the naval battle of the Gulf of Lepanto (1571), and the latter elegizing the heroic death of King Sebastian of Portugal, whose forces were routed by the Moors at Alcazarquivir (1578). See also under *Escuela sevillana.*

Cf. *Poesías,* (Ed.) García de Diego, V., Madrid, 1914; Coster, A., *Fernando de Herrera (El Divino),* Paris, 1908; Rodríguez Marín, F., *El Divino Herrera y la Condesa de Gelves,* Madrid, 1911.

Herrera y Reissig, Julio (1875-1910). Uruguayan poet. Founder of a literary coterie known as the "Torre de los Panoramas." Beginning under the influence of the French symbolists, he first wrote comparatively simple lyrics on pastoral themes. His work grew more complex when, under the influence of Darío and Lugones, he became an important figure in the *modernista* group, perhaps its most outstanding symbolist. Later, his poetry assumed an experimental phase, showing the crypticism and syntactical license characteristic of the *ultraísta* school. His most important works were: *Los maitines de la noche,* 1903; *Los éxtasis de la montaña,*

1905-1909; *Los parques abandonados,* 1909; *Obras completas* (5 vols., Montevideo, 1913).

Cf. Blanco-Fombona, R., *El modernismo y los poetas modernistas,* Madrid, 1929; Torre, G. de, *La aventura y el orden,* Buenos Aires, 1943; Bula Píriz, R., *Herrera y Reissig,* Hispanic Institute, N. Y., 1952.

Herreros. See *Bretón de los Herreros.*

Hespelt, Ernest Herman (1886). American hispanist and authority on Spanish American literature. On the staff of New York University since 1926. Professor of Spanish, New York University, since 1942. Emeritus, 1952. General Editor of Publications, *Instituto de las Españas,* 1927-1928; Editor, *Revista de Estudios Hispánicos,* 1938. Associate Editor, *Hispania,* 1927-1938, 1942-. Associate Editor, *Revista Iberoamericana,* 1943-1952. President, American Association of Teachers of Spanish and Portuguese, 1938. Editor of school editions of works by Eduardo Marquina, Hugo Wast, Fernán Caballero, Gregorio López y Fuentes, and Mariano José de Larra. Co-author of *An Outline History of Spanish American Literature,* N. Y., 1941; *An anthology of Spanish American Literature,* N. Y., 1946. Author of the article on "Spanish American Literature," *Encyclopedia Britannica,* 14th ed., 1929; and of articles on Pedro Antonio de Alarcón, Concha Espina, and Ricardo León, *Columbia Dictionary of Modern European Literature,* N. Y., 1947.

hexámetro. Hexameter. A poetic line or verse of six metrical feet, variously stressed. In particular, the dactylic hexameter of Greek and Latin verse, used especially in the epic.

hexasílabo. A verse of six syllables, variously stressed. Common types are stressed either on the first and fifth, or on the second and fifth syllables.

Hidalgo, Bartolomé (1788-1822). Uruguayan soldier and poet. Hidalgo adapted the "poesía gauchesca" style to patriotic verse in his *Diálogos patrióticos.* He also wrote a number of poems termed "cielitos heroicos." Together with Ascasubi, he is considered one of the best gaucho poets of the early 19th century.

Cf. Rojas, R., *La literatura argentina,* Buenos Aires, 1924-1925; Tiscornia, E. F., *Poetas gauchescos,* Buenos Aires, 1940.

Hija de Celestina (La). See under *Salas Barbadillo.*

Hija del aire (La). See under *Calderón.*

Hijas del Cid (Las). See under *Marquina, Eduardo.*

Hijo del sol (El). See under *Calderón.*

Hilton, Ronald (1911). American hispanist. Born in England. Naturalized U. S. citizen, 1946. Editor, *Who's Who in Latin America* (7 vols.); *Handbook of Hispanic American Source Materials in the United States.* Author, *Campoamor, Spain and the World,* University of Toronto Press, 1940.

Himenea. See under *Torres Naharro; pundonor.*

Himno de sangre. See under *Acevedo Díaz.*

hipérbaton. (Eng. *hyperbaton*). A departure from regular word order or syntax. Transposition of words to create a special effect.

hipotiposis. (Eng. *hypotyposis*). The effective use of language for purposes of vivid description. In particular, the use of sensory terms to give the impression of the actual presence of what is being described.

Hispania. The official literary and philological organ of The American Association of Teachers of Spanish and Portuguese; founded in 1917. First Editor, Aurelio Espinosa. See under *American Association of Teachers of Spanish.*

Hispanic Foundation. A special section (capacity 100,000 volumes) of the Library of Congress, established in 1927 for the purchase of books and other publications in the Spanish and Portuguese languages. Made possible by a gift of $100,000 from Archer M. Huntington. In 1928 another gift of $50,000 from Mr. Huntington provided for a permanent consultant in Hispanic literature. The Hispanic Foundation provides a reference service on Hispanic culture and publishes various bibliographical aids.

Hispanic Institute. The "Hispanic Institute in the United States" has its library and headquarters at the *Casa Hispánica,* Columbia University. The Institute was founded in 1920 at Columbia University by the Institute of International Education, the American Association of Teachers of Spanish, the *Junta para Ampliación de Estudios,* the *Junta de Relaciones Culturales,* and several Spanish and American universities. The purpose was to create a center for the study of Hispanic culture, to promote interest in the Spanish and Portuguese civilizations, and to foster cultural relations between the United States and all Hispanic nations. Among other activities, the Institute promotes international exchange of professors and students, foreign educational tours, lectures, social and club activities, and the publication of books and periodicals on Hispanic subjects. Of especial interest to the student of Spanish literature are the Institute's periodicals, *Revista hispánica moderna* and *Revista de filología hispánica.* The Institute's publications include critical editions of Hispanic authors, literary studies, textbooks, works on Hispanic philology, culture, folklore, comparative literature, Sephardic literature, and Hispanic bibliography. The present Director of the Hispanic Institute is Federico de Onís; the Director of Publications is Tomás Navarro; both of Columbia University.

Hispanic Review. (Abbr. *Hisp. Rev.*). A quarterly journal devoted to research in the hispanic languages and literatures. Founded by J. P. Wickersham Crawford. Published by the University of Pennsylvania Press, Philadelphia. Editors: Otis H. Green and Joseph E. Gillet.

Hispanic Society of America. A cultural foundation established 1904 in New York City by Archer M. Huntington, American Hispanist, art collector, bibliophile and philanthropist. The object of the Society is the advancement of the study of the Spanish and Portuguese languages, literature and history. Its Trustees and Corresponding Members include prominent Hispanists of all countries. The Hispanic Society maintains a free public library of over 100,000 volumes on Spanish and Portuguese culture, as well as a museum of Spanish and Portuguese painting, arts and crafts. In addition to ancient manuscripts, the library collections include some 250 Hispanic incunabula as well as over 8,000 volumes of first and early editions of the important Spanish authors. The Society has published more than 650 volumes on Spanish art, history and literature. Of especial value to the Hispanist bibliographer are the following publications of the Hispanic Society: Penny, C. L., *List of Books Printed Before 1601,* N. Y., 1929; *List of Books Printed 1601-1700,* N. Y., 1938; *Catalogue of Publications,* N. Y., 1943.

hispanidad. (1) The generic character of all communities of Spanish language and culture. (2) The kinship and community of all hispanic peoples.

hispanismo. (1) A term or idiomatic expression peculiar to or characteristic of the Spanish language. (2) A Spanish word or expression used in another language. (3) The idiomatic use of Spanish words or expressions. (4) An affection or inclination, on the part of a non-Spanish person or group, for the study of Spanish culture; in particular, for the study of Spanish language and literature; and in general, for the study of Spanish art, music, history, folkways, and all matters pertaining to Spain and the Spanish peoples.

hispanista. Hispanist. A person versed in Spanish culture; in particular, a scholar or student of Spanish language and literature.

Hisp. Rev. Abbr. of *Hispanic Review.*

Historia de Barlaam y Josafat. See *Barlaam y Josafat.*

Historia de Grisel y Mirabella. See under *Flores, Juan de.*

Historia de la conquista de México. See under *Solís, Antonio de.*

Historia de las ideas estéticas en España. See under *Menéndez y Pelayo.*

Historia de las Indias. See under *Casas, Bartolomé de las.*

Historia del caballero Cifar. See *Caballero Cifar.*

Historia de los heterodoxos en España. See under *Menéndez y Pelayo.*

Historia de Pago Chico. See under *Payró.*

Historiae de rebus hispaniae. See under *Mariana, Juan de.*

Historia Gothica. See under *Ximénez de Rada; crónica.*

Historia Roderici. See under *Cid (El).*

Historia troyana *(ca.* 1270). One of the sources for the cycle of classical themes in the medieval chivalric romances. It dealt with the siege and destruction of Troy, not according to Homer but in the fanciful Latin versions of the 4th century chroniclers, Dares and Dictys. The motif appears in the *Libro de Alexandre* (13th century), for example. The peninsular versions of the history of Troy were based on the French *Roman de Troie (ca.* 1164) by Benoît de Sainte-More, and on an Italian version by Guido delle Colonne entitled *Historia troyana* (1287). These works inspired many Galician and Castilian versions. Various extant fragments dealing with the theme were collected and edited by Menéndez Pidal and Varón Vallejo under the title of *Historia troyana polimétrica.* The best of the latter versions of the *Historia troyana* is that of El Canciller López de Ayala (1332-1407), entitled *Crónica troyana.*

Cf. Menéndez y Pelayo, M., *Orígines de la novela,* Madrid,

1905-1910; Buenos Aires, 1946; Menéndez Pidal, R., *Poesía juglaresca y juglares,* Madrid, 1924; Buenos Aires, 1945.

History of the Seven Wise Masters. See under *Libro de los engaños, etc.*

Hojeda, Diego de (1570?-1615). Peruvian priest and poet. Born in Seville, Spain, and came to Peru as a young man. Joined the Dominican Order in 1591 and became prior of a monastery in Cuzco. Relieved of his post in 1612 owing to difficulties with his superiors, he spent the rest of his life as a simple monk. His fame rests on a single work, *La Cristiada* (Seville, 1611), a sacred poem in 12 cantos, each having an introductory octave summarizing the argument. The theme is the Passion of Christ, encompassing the period between the Last Supper and the Interment. *La Cristiada* has some shining moments of lyrical beauty but falls short of true epic quality on account of its theological digressions.

Cf. Corcoran, M. H. P., *La Cristiada,* Catholic U. of America, Washington, 1935.

Hombre de estado (Un). See under *López de Ayala, Adelardo.*

Hombres de bien (Los). See under *Tamayo y Baus.*

Homero romanceado. See under *Mena, Juan de.*

Horacio en España. See under *Menéndez y Pelayo.*

Horda (La). See under *Blasco Ibáñez.*

Horozco, Sebastián de. See under *refranero.*

Hostos, Eugenio María. (1839-1903). Puerto Rican sociologist, educator, journalist and novelist. Born in Puerto Rico and educated in Spain. Expelled from that country for his radical activities, he lived in New York and in several South American countries. Professor of international law in Chile. Dean of the *Escuela Normal* in Santo Domingo. Hostos was a life-long fighter for the freedom and confederation of the Antilles. His most important work is based on that theme *(Moral social).* Among his other works were: *La peregrinación de Bayoán,* 1863; *Biografía de Plácido,* 1872; *Moral social,* 1888; *Tratados de sociología,* 1901; *Obras completas* (20 vols., Havana, 1939).

Cf. Sánchez, L. A., *Historia de la literatura americana,* Santiago, 1940.

HR. Abbr. of *Hispanic Review.* See under *Hispanic Review; Romera-Navarro.*

huancayo. A *Quechua* dialect. See under *Quechua.*

Huasipungo. See under *Icaza, Jorge.*

Huerta, Vicente García de la. See *García de la Huerta.*

Huidobro, Vicente (1893-1948). Chilean poet. Huidobro wrote in French *(Horizon Carré,* 1917) as well as in Spanish. He was the founder of the vanguardist movement known as *creacionismo* (1916-1920). Huidobro proposed a radical departure from traditional descriptive and narrative poetry in favor of elemental creation of a new poetic reality, engendered in, but independent of, nature. An art-for-art's-sake theory, creationism, like ultraism and surrealism, had its brief moment of influence on a small, élite group of Spanish and Latin-American writers shortly after World War I. See also *creacionismo.* Chief works: *Ecos del alma,* 1910; *Poemas árticos,* 1918; *Cagliostro,* 1926; *Vientos contrarios,* 1926, *Mío Cid Campeador,* 1929; *Temblor de cielo,* 1931; *Altazor,* 1931.

Cf. Holmes, H. A., *Vicente Huidobro and Creationism,* N. Y., 1933; Undarraga, A. de, "Huidobro y sus acusadores o la querella del creacionismo," *Cultura Universitaria,* Universidad Central de Venezuela, XLII, 1954.

Humanism. Humanism in Spain emerges as one of the accompanying trends of the Renaissance (in Spain, *ca.* 1450-1550). In other European countries, the movement resulted in a relaxation of dogma, but in Spain humanism developed, for the most part, within orthodox limits. Unorthodox humanists, *e.g.* Juan de Valdés (d. 1541) and Luis Vives (1492-1540) did most of their work abroad. The effect of the Inquisition (1478) was decisive. Although scholarly and scientific investigation were carried on, the limitations on inquiry were later typically expressed by Francisco Sánchez, el Brocense (1523-1599?) in the preface to his *Paradoxa* (1581), where he stated that everything might be freely examined except the orthodox faith. Thus, the humanists of Spain were mainly eminent in religious and classical scholarship (Nebrija, Cisneros). The creative writers (Santillana, Mena, Boscán, Garcilaso) were humanists in the sense that they were influenced by Italian and classical models. The movement reached Spain through the influx of humanists from Italy during the reign of Ferdinand and Isabella (1474-1504). Among them were such Latin scholars as Pedro Mártir (1459-1526), author of *Decades de orbe novo* (1511), the first history of discoveries in the

New World. The greatest of Spanish humanists were Antonio de Nebrija (Lebrija?) (1441?-1522), noted for his classical scholarship and his work in normalizing Spanish grammar and orthography (*Gramática castellana,* 1492); and Cardinal Jiménez de Cisneros (1436-1517), founder of the University of Alcalá (1508), which became a center of humanist studies. Cisneros sponsored the greatest monument of Spanish humanist scholarship, the Polyglot Bible (*Biblia poliglota complutense,* 1514-1517). Although the Cardinal personally adhered to the official Latin Vulgate, the mere inclusion of the earlier Hebrew and Greek versions invited comparison and, in a sense, was an act of critical inquiry. Other noted humanists were Juan de Valdés (*Diálogo de la lengua, ca.* 1535), and Luis Vives (*Introductio ad sapientiam,* 1524; *De anima et vita,* 1538), a philosopher who in his inductive approach was a precursor of Bacon. Probably the most pervasive humanist influence exercised in Spain was that of Erasmus of Rotterdam (1466-1536), whose *Enquiridión o Manual del caballero cristiano* was translated into Spanish in 1521. Among the followers of *erasmismo* were the Valdés brothers, Alfonso and Juan. Alfonso de Valdés (1490-1532), in particular, as secretary to the chancellor of Charles V, influenced royal policy indirectly. Criticism of the clergy and of the temporal policies of the Pope (Clement VII), and a desire for a political accord with the Protestant countries prevailed for a time. However, with the founding of the Jesuit Order (1534) and with the onset of the Counter-Reformation (Council of Trent, 1545-1563), the words of Erasmus were placed on the Index in 1559. Traces of Erasmist influence (a personal relationship to the Deity and religious reform) continued in the mystical writers, especially in the works of Fray Luis de León (1527?-1591).

Cf. Unamuno, M. de, "De mística y humanismo," Chap. IV of *En torno al casticismo,* Madrid, 1902; Bonilla y San Martín, A., *Luis Vives y la filosofía del Renacimiento,* Madrid, 1903; Heep, J., *Juan de Valdés in seinem Verhältnis zu Erasmus und dem Humanismus,* Leipzig, 1909; Fernández de Retana, L., *Cisneros y su siglo,* Madrid, 1929-1930; Bataillon, M., *Erasme et l'Espagne,* Paris, 1937; Bell, A. F. G., *Luis de León: A Study of the Spanish Renaissance,* Oxford, 1925.

humorada. A verse form devised by Campoamor and used in his book *Humoradas* (1886). See under *Campoamor.*

Huntington, Archer Milton (1870-1955). American hispanist, bibliophile, art collector, poet and philanthropist. Established the *Hispanic Society of America* (1904) with its library and museum of Spanish and Portuguese literature and culture. Honorary President of the American Association of Teachers of Spanish, since 1915. Donor of funds to the Library of Congress for the establishment of the *Hispanic Foundation* (1927). *Doctor honoris causa,* University of Madrid. Chief works: Editor, *El Cid campeador,* reprinted from the unique manuscript at Madrid; with translation and notes; 3 vols., N. Y., 1907-1908 (one-volume edition, N. Y., 1942). *Collected Verse,* N. Y., 1953. See also under *Hispanic Society of America; Hispanic Foundation; American Association of Teachers of Spanish.*

Cf. "Homenaje a Archer M. Huntington," *Estudios Hispánicos,* Wellesley, Mass., 1952.

Hurtado de Mendoza, Diego (1503-1575). Renaissance diplomat, poet and historian. Born in Granada; died in Madrid. The son of the Marqués de Mondéjar, he served in the army and later became one of the foremost of Spain's ambassadors and diplomats, serving Charles V and Philip II in London, Venice and other European capitals. His accomplishments in letters were as great as those in diplomacy. A disciple of Boscán and Garcilaso, he played a prominent part in the literary life of his time as a distinguished humanist writer and poet. Castillejo attacked him for his addiction to Italian meters, and Lope de Vega adored him for his *redondillas.* For a long time he was considered the author of *Lazarillo de Tormes,* but modern scholarship has not discovered any but presumptive evidence of this claim. Although he wrote some distinguished Petrarchan sonnets, he is chiefly remembered as the author of one of the most artistic of Spanish historical works, the *Guerra de Granada* (publ. 1627). It is the history of the Moorish uprising in the Alpujarras (Granada) and the wars which the troops of Philip II waged (1568-1571) to suppress it. Based on first-hand observations and the accounts of participants, the history is notable for its vivid descriptions of local background, its portraits of the protagonists, and interpretations of their motives and actions. As the first instance of a truly pragmatic Spanish history, it is objective and fair in its treatment of the enemy. Stylistically, the work measures up to the classical historians, Sallust and Tacitus, whom the author had selected as his models.

Cf. *Obras poéticas,* (Ed.) Knapp, W. I., Madrid, 1877; *Guerra de Granada,* in *BAE,* XXI; also editions by Hämel, A., Leipzig, 1923; and Gómez Moreno, M., Madrid, 1948; Mele, E. and González Palencia, A., *Don Diego Hurtado de Mendoza: estudio biográfico y crítico,* Madrid, 1940.

Hurtado de Toledo, Luis. See under *Danza de la muerte; Palmerín cycle.*

I

Ibarbourou, Juana de (1895). Uruguayan poetess and short-story writer. A favorite throughout South America, she is frequently referred to as "Juana de América." In 1950 she was elected President of the *Sociedad Uruguaya de Escritores*. Her poetry is simple in structure and rich in imagery, treating the themes of love and nature with delicate feminine sensitivity. Chief works: *Lenguas de diamante,* 1918; *Raíz salvaje,* 1922; *La rosa de los vientos,* 1930; *Cuentos,* 1944.

Cf. Blanco-Fombona, R., (Ed.), *Juana Ibarbourou: sus mejores poemas,* Madrid, 1930; *Obras completas,* (Ed. García Calderón, V. and Russell, D. I.), Madrid, 1953.

Iberian. See under *Spanish.*

Icaza, Jorge (1906). Ecuadorian novelist and playwright. He first achieved fame for his starkly realistic picture of Indian life, *Huasipungo* (1934), a masterpiece of its type, which has gone into several editions. He was awarded the National Prize of Ecuador for his novel, *En las calles* (1935). His work expresses intense indignation at the injustices perpetrated on native Indian as well as on poor white workers.

Chief works: (novels) *Barro de la sierra,* 1933; *Huasipungo,* 1934; *En la calles,* 1935; *Cholos,* 1937; *Media vida deslumbrados,* 1942; *Huatrapamushcas,* 1948; (plays) *El intruso,* 1929; *Flagelo,* 1936.

Cf. Torres Ríoseco, A., "Nuevas tendencies en la novela," *Revista iberoamericana,* I, 1939.

Idea de un príncipe político-cristiano. See under *Saavedra Fajardo.*

Idearium español. See under *Ganivet, Ángel.*

idilio. Idyll. A pastoral love poem. A poetic work dealing with shepherds and their loves, amid bucolic surroundings. The characters are generally allegorical.

Ifigenia. See under *Parra, Teresa de la.*

Iglesias de la Casa, José. See under *Escuela de Salamanca.*

Ignacio de Loyola. See under *Reformation.*

iluminismo. The name given by adherents of the Counter-Reformation to the Erasmian movement among Spanish humanists and mystics in the 15th and 16th centuries. The term was a derogatory epithet linked with Protestant heresy. See also under *Reformation.*

iluminista. A derogatory name given by adherents of the Counter-Reformation to the followers of Erasmus. The same as *alumbrado.* See also under *iluminismo; Reformation.*

Ilusiones del doctor Faustino (Las). See under *Valera, Juan.*

Ilustración de Madrid (La). See under *Bécquer.*

Ilustre fregone (La). See under *Cervantes.*

Imitation of Christ. See under *Granada.*

Imperial, Micer Francisco. Early Renaissance poet. He was born in the second half of the 14th and died in the first half of the 15th century. His father was a Genoese jeweler who lived in Seville. Francisco Imperial was a man of broad culture, conversant with Latin, Greek, Italian, French, English and Arabic literature. A predecessor of Boscán, he was the first to introduce the Italian *endecasílabo* into Castilian verse. Imperial was also the first to imitate Dante in Spanish literature. This is seen in his most important work, entitled *Dezyr a las syete virtudes,* an allegorical poem in sixty *coplas,* clearly showing the influence of Dante's *Purgatorio* and *Paradiso.* The poem appears as number 250 in the *Cancionero de Baena.* See also under *decir.*

Cf. Chavez, M., *Micer Francisco Imperial: apuntes bio-bibliográficos,* Seville, 1899.

impresionismo. An artistic or literary theory or technique whereby reality is reproduced not objectively but as viewed through subjective impressions.

Inca (El). See *Garcilaso de la Vega (El Inca).*

incontiguous assimilation. See under *assimilation.*

Index Librorum Prohibitorum. See under *Reformation.*

"indianista" literature. A literary reflection of the realistic trend toward native themes in Spanish-American literature, beginning at the end of the 19th century and continuing to the present. It has its social roots in the Indian problem, especially prominent in those South American countries where the Indian population exceeds the white (Peru, Bolivia and Ecuador). The injustices suffered by the Indians aroused the social conscience of many writers who, rejecting the hitherto romantic and sentimental portrayal of indigenous life and characters (as for example in Mera's *Cumandá,* 1871), inveighed against the subjection of the native masses. Early representatives of the *indianista* trend were the Peruvian writers, Clorinda Matto de Turner (1854-1909), Manuel González Prada (1844-1918), Enrique López Albújar (b. 1872), and José Santos Chocano (1875-1934). Later, an extensive pro-Indian literature developed as the result of the *Aprista* movement, which originated in Peru in the 1920's. Its literary organ was the periodical *Amauta* (Lima, 1926-1930). Most prominent among contemporary *indianista* writers are the Peruvian, Ciro Alegría (b. 1909), the Bolivian, Alcides Arguedas (b. 1879), the Ecuadorian, Jorge Icaza (b. 1906), and the Mexican, Gregorio López y Fuentes (b. 1895).

Cf. Meléndez, C., *La novela indianista en Hispanoamérica,* Madrid, 1934; Cometta Manzoni, A., *El indio en la poesía de América española,* Buenos Aires, 1939; Sánchez, L. A., *La literatura del Perú,* Buenos Aires, 1939; Spell, J. R., "Jorge Icaza, Defender of the Ecuadorian Indian," in *Contemporary Spanish-American Fiction,* Chapel Hill, N. C., 1944.

Inés de Castro. See under *Vélez de Guevara.*

Infamador (El). See under *Cueva.*

Infantes de Lara. A lost medieval epic, or *cantar de gesta,* preserved only in 13th and 14th century prose versions (in the *Crónica general,* 1270, and in the *Crónica de 1344*). It is based on the legend of the seven sons of Gonzalo Gustios, Lord of Salas, and was originally referred to as *Los infantes de Salas.* In later versions the name Lara appears instead of Salas. A reconstruction of this legend, based on fragments of old *cantares,* was made by Menéndez Pidal in 1896 *(Leyenda de los infantes de Lara).* The hero of the epic is Gonzalo González, the youngest of the above-mentioned seven sons. He incurs the enmity of his aunt, Doña Lambra, by killing her cousin, Álvar Sánchez, in a tournament celebrating her marriage to Ruy Velásquez. This sets the stage for a medieval family feud. Doña Lambra and her husband plot the death of Gonzalo Gustios and his sons by betraying them to the Moors. The father is held captive by Almanzor, the magnanimous military governor of Córdoba, but the sons and their old tutor, Nuño Salido, are all killed, fighting heroically against the Moors. They are later avenged by their half-brother, Mudarra, the offspring of their father's union with a noble Moorish lady, Zeula. Mudarra kills Ruy Velásquez and has Doña Lambra sentenced to the stake. The theme recurs throughout Spanish literature in many ballads and plays (Juan de la Cueva, 1579; Lope de Vega, *El bastardo Mudarra,* 1612; Duque de Rivas, *El moro expósito,* 1834; Manuel Fernández y González, 1853).

Cf. Menéndez Pidal, R., *Leyenda de los infantes de Lara,* Madrid, 1896 *et seq.;* idem, *L'Épopée castillane à travers la littérature espagnole,* Paris, 1910; idem, *Historia y epopeya,* Madrid, 1934.

Infantes de Salas. See *Infantes de Lara.*

Infierno de los enamorados. See under *Santillana.*

infijo. See *infix.*

infix. (Sp. *infijo*). A sound or syllable inserted within a word to form a new word or change its meaning or function. The change is often merely euphonic. Examples: *correr-corretear;* homine > *hombre.*

ingenio. (1) Creative talent or inventive faculty. (2) A person gifted with such talent or faculty. (3) A gifted writer. The court poets and dramatists of the Spanish Renaissance were frequently called *ingenios.*

Ingeniosa Elena (La). See under *Salas Barbadillo.*

Institución Libre de Enseñanza. Founded in 1876 by Giner de los Ríos after the loss of his post at the University of Madrid. It is famous as an educational institution completely independent of state and church. See under *Giner de los Ríos.*

Institute of Latin American Studies. Established in 1941 by the Board of Regents of the University of Texas "to correlate and develop facilities at the University of Texas for the advanced study of Latin American culture." The institute fosters exchange of students and professors between Mexico and Texas. It offers a program in Latin American studies leading to the degrees of Master of Arts and Doctor of Philosophy. Available to those studying at the Institute is the extensive collection of books, manuscripts, newspapers, periodicals, archives, etc., of the University of Texas. The present Director of the Institute is Lewis U. Hanke.

Cf. Castañeda, C. E., and Dabbs, J. A., *Guide to the Latin American Manuscripts in the University of Texas Library,* Harvard U. Press, Cambridge, Mass., 1939.

Instituto de Filología. See under *Alonso, Amado.*

Instituto de Humanidades. See under *Ortega y Gasset.*

Instituto Francés de Madrid. See under *Mérimée, Ernest.*

Inter-American Review of Bibliography. See *Revista Interamericana de Bibliografía.*

Intereses creados (Los). See under *Benavente.*

Introducción del símbolo de la fe. See under *Granada.*

Introductiones latinae. See under *Nebrija.*

introito. The name given to the prologue of a play in the pre-Lope de Vega drama of the 16th century. The *introito* served chiefly to explain the argument of the play. The term was replaced by the word *loa.* See also *loa.*

Cf. Meredith, J. A., *"Introito" and "loa" in the Spanish Drama of the 16th Century,* U. of Pennsylvania, 1925.

Intruso (El). See under *Blasco Ibáñez.*

Inventario. See under *Abencerraje.*

Iriarte, Juan de. See under *Iriarte, Tomás de.*

Iriarte, Tomás de (1750-1791). Fabulist, translator, poet, and dramatist. Born in the Canaries Islands; died in Madrid. His full name was Tomás de Iriarte y Oropesa. He was a nephew of the noted humanist, Juan de Iriarte (1702-1771), librarian at the *Biblioteca Real* and official translator at the Ministry of State. Tomás succeeded his uncle in the latter post. He took an active part in the literary life of Madrid and was involved in a number of literary controversies. In 1777 he published a translation of Horace's *Ars poetica,* the principles of which furnished his own critical canons. His neoclassic poem, *La música* (1779), was widely admired at the time, particularly in France, but has now lapsed into oblivion. He also wrote some plays *(La señorita malcriada, El señorito mimado,* 1788) in an attempt at the comedy of manners, but not too successfully. Iriarte was not much as a poet and dramatist, but he did make a lasting contribution to Spanish letters through his *Fábulas literarias* (1782), a collection of some 76 fables in verse. Influenced by La Fontaine, Iriarte, however, was not a slavish imitator. He invented his fables, using literary criticism and satire of contemporary writers as his themes.

Cf. *Poesías y fábulas literarias,* in *BAE,* LXIII; *Fábulas literarias,* (Ed.), Fitzmaurice-Kelly, J., Oxford, 1917; Cotarelo y Mori, E., *Iriarte y su época,* Madrid, 1897.

Irving, Washington (1783-1859). Essayist, novelist, historian and literary ambassador of the United States to the Old World. Irving first went to Madrid in 1826 to join the staff of the American legation. Here he wrote his *History of the Life and Voyages of Christopher Columbus* (1828). He traveled widely in Spain, visiting the Alhambra in 1828 and residing there for a time in 1829, when his *Chronicle of the Conquest of Granada* was published. In 1832 appeared his collection of tales and essays, *The Alhambra* (revised edition, 1851). Irving was appointed American Minister to Spain in 1841, assuming the post in 1842. As a Hispanist, Washington Irving was the forerunner of the New England Hispanist historians, Prescott and Motley.

Cf. Irving, Washington, *Diary, Spain 1828-1829,* ed. by Penney, C. L., Hispanic Society of America, N. Y., 1930; Williams, S. T., *The Life of Washington Irving,* N. Y., 1936; Brooks, Van Wyck, *The World of Washington Irving,* N. Y., 1944.

Isaacs, Jorge (1837-1895). Colombian novelist. Born in Cali. Of mixed Jewish and Spanish descent. Educated in Bogotá. Of a wealthy family reduced in circumstances, he was at various stages of his career a journalist, businessman, officeholder, and Consul to Chile. He first attracted the attention of the literary world by his *Poesías* in 1864. However, he owes his secure place in Spanish American literature to the influence of a single novel, *María* (1867). Partly autobiographical and inspired by Chateaubriand, *María* is a sad, romantic tale notable for its idyllic descriptions of nature. It has been the most widely imitated romantic novel of Spanish American literature.

Cf. Carvajal, M., *Vida y pasión de Jorge Isaacs,* Santiago, Chile, 1937.

Isla, José Francisco de (1703-1781). Satirical novelist and translator. Born in a small town in the province of León; died in Bologna, Italy. His full name was José Francisco de Isla de la Torre y Rojo. A Jesuit priest, he taught in Valladolid and became known for his sermons and satirical writing. The first volume of his novel, *Historia del famoso predicador Fray Gerundio de Campazas, alias Zotes* (1758), parodied the bombastic preaching of his day and created an immediate sensation, but it was banned shortly after its appearance. From 1767 on, he lived in exile in Italy, where a second volume of the novel appeared in 1768. Although its continuity is frequently interrupted by sermonizing digressions, the novel is generally considered the best one of the 18th century, a period singularly poor in this genre. Isla's own sermons (*Sermones,* 1792-1793) often suffer from the same fault that he satirized, but they show a degree of ability that motivates his impatience with lesser practitioners of the art. Spanish criticism is indebted to Isla for *Fray Gerundio,* a name typifying the bombastic sermonizer. Isla is also known for his masterly translation of Le Sage's *Gil Blas* (1787), long considered a Spanish work because of his ambiguous statement in the introduction that he was restoring the book to its original language. His *Cartas familiares* (1789-1794) are among the best of 18th century epistolary literature.

Cf. *Obras escogidas,* (Ed.) Monlau, P. F., *BAE,* XV; *Fray Gerundio de Campazas,* (Ed.) Lidforss, E., 2 vols., Leipzig, 1885; Cortés, A., "Datos genealógicos del P. de Isla," *Boletín de la Real Academia Española,* XXIII; Boggs, R. S., "Folklore Elements in *Fray Gerundio," Hispanic Review,* IV.

Ismos. See under *Gómez de la Serna.*

isosilábico. Referring to verses or lines of poetry, words or linguistic forms which have the same number of syllables.

J

jácara. (1) A light or gay ballad. (2) Music for dancing and singing. (3) A company of nocturnal revelers, singing songs. (4) A short musical play, such as those written by Quiñones de Benavente. The *Jácara* belongs to the *género chico* and was originally conceived as a between-the-acts divertissement. See also under *género chico; Quiñones.*

Jaimes Freyre, Ricardo (1870-1933). Poet, editor, professor and statesman. Born in Bolivia but resided most of his life in Argentina, where he acquired citizenship in 1916. Bolivian minister to the United States. Professor of Spanish literature, history and philosophy at the University of Tucumán. A candidate for the Argentine presidency in 1926. Together with Rubén Darío, he founded the *Revista de América* (1896) in Buenos Aires. He is significant as a forerunner of the modernist school. His work is highly original, evoking an aura of unreality in an imaginary world suggestive of Nordic mythology. Chief works: (poems) *Castalia bárbara,* 1899; *Los sueños son vida,* 1917; *Poemas completos,* 1944; *Leyes de la versificación castellana,* 1912; *El Tucumán del siglo XVI,* 1914.

Cf. Torres Ríoseco, A., "Ricardo Jaimes Freyre," *Hispania,* XVI, 1933.

jarcha. The Arabic term for the final verse or stanza (generally three or four lines) of a *muwassaha,* an Arabic or Hebrew verse form. The *jarcha* differs from the classical Arabic or Hebrew of the first part of the *muwassaha,* in that it is composed in the vernacular (Arabic, Hebrew, Mozarabic, as the case may be). The *jarcha* is the acute or explosive culminating point of the poem, its function being somewhat like that of the *estribillo.* Another name for the *jarcha* is the *markaz.* The importance of the discovery of the *jarcha* is that it indicates a much earlier date for the beginnings of

Spanish lyrical poetry, namely the 11th century. The discovery of these Mozarabic *jarchas* was made by a Hebrew and Arabic scholar, S. M. Stern, who published twenty of them in 1948. See also *aljamiada literature; muwassaha.*

Cf. Stern, S. M., "Les vers finaux en espagnol dans les muwassahas hispano-hébraïques," *Al-Andalus,* XIII, Fascicle 2, December, 1948.

Jarifa. See under *Abencerraje.*

jerigonza. Jargon: gibberish. A derogatory term for *gongorismo* or *culteranismo.* Also spelled *gerigonza.*

Jerusalén conquistada. See under *Vega, Lope de.*

Jesuit Order. See under *Reformation.*

Jiménez, Juan Ramón (1881). Ranked with Antonio Machado as the foremost lyric poet of contemporary Spanish literature. Born in the Andalusian town of Moguer in the province of Huelva. Of delicate health and morbid sensitivity, he has always preferred a secluded existence. From 1900 on he lived in Madrid, where he became a close friend of Francisco Villaespesa and of Rubén Darío, who encouraged him in publishing his first two volumes of poetry, *Almas de violeta* and *Ninfeas* (both in 1900). After a period of illness and mental depression, during which he nevertheless continued to write and publish (*Arias tristes,* 1903; *Jardines lejanos,* 1905; *Elegías,* 1908), he returned to Madrid in 1912, living at the *Residencia de Estudiantes* and editing the publications of that famous intellectual and cultural center. In 1916, he married Zenobia Camprubi Aymar, the translator of Rabindranath Tagore. His poetic creation has continued unabated for over half a century. Many of his poems appeared in Madrid literary reviews (*Helios, Indice, España, El Sol, La Gaceta Literaria,* etc.). In 1936, as the result of the Spanish Civil War, Jiménez left Spain for Puerto Rico, Cuba, and the United States, which became his permanent residence, interrupted by a lecture tour of South America in 1948. The poetry of Jiménez reflects his esthetic temperament, his love of nature, music, art and solitude. His sombre moods are frequently expressed through the poetic evocation of moonlit gardens and melancholy landscapes. A more spirited note emerges from his *Baladas de primavera* (1910), which echo the influence of 16th century folk music and children's rhymes. His *La soledad sonora* (1911), written in alexandrines, reveals a more involved and ornate style, in the classical tradition. In about 1916-1917, Jiménez developed the theory and practice of what he called "la poesía desnuda," which meant the sloughing off of all extraneous trappings (*i.e.* rhyme and formal metres) to achieve the quintessence of poetry, expressed in free verse. This new style first emerges in the verse of *Diario de un poeta recién casado* and in the poetic prose of *Platero y yo* (both published in 1917), and is later continued in his selected poems, *Poesía en prosa y verso* (1932). The result of this *depuración* has been to make Jiménez a truer but also a more subtle poet. His influence on modern Spanish poetry, particularly on that of García Lorca, has been enormous.

Cf. *Antología poética,* Buenos Aires, 1944; *Fifty Spanish Poems of Juan Ramón Jiménez,* (transl, and ed.) Trend, J. B., Oxford, 1950; Henríquez Ureña, P., "La obra de Juan Ramón Jiménez," *Cursos y Conferencias,* XIX, Buenos Aires, 1919; Nedderman, E., *Die symbolistischen Stilelemente im Werke von Juan Ramón Jiménez,* Hamburg, 1935; Díez Canedo, E., *Juan Ramón Jiménez y su obra,* Mexico, 1944.

Jiménez de Cisneros, Francisco (1436-1517). Cardinal Jiménez de Cisneros was one of Spain's illustrious cultural figures of the Renaissance. Responsible for ecclesiastical, civil and educational reforms, he contributed greatly to raise Spain to the height of her glory during the reign of Ferdinand and Isabella. In 1508 he founded the University of Alcalá de Henares. In 1513 he sponsored Alonso de Herrera's *Agricultura general,* which he distributed at his own expense among peasant farmers. In preparing the first critical edition of the Bible, he engaged the services of the great scholars of his time (among them, Nebrija). The result was a monumental polyglot Bible with Hebrew, Chaldaic, Greek and Latin texts, vocabularies, and a Hebrew grammar (*Biblia políglota complutense,* 6 vols., Alcalá, 1514-1517).

Cf. Fernández de Retana, L., *Cisneros y su siglo,* Madrid, 1929-1930; Sáinz de Robles, F. C., *Esquema de una historia de las universidades españolas,* Madrid, 1944.

Jiménez de Rada. See under *Ximénez de Rada; crónica.*

Jiménez Rueda, Julio (1896). Mexican literary scholar and historian. *Director literario* of the *Revista Iberoamericana.* Member of the *Academia Mexicana de la Lengua.* Principal works: *Historia de* *la literatura mexicana; Juan Ruiz de Alarcón y su tiempo; Antología de la prosa en México; Letras mexicanas del siglo XIX; Herejías y supersticiones en la Nueva España.*

Cf. *Hispania,* XXXVI, 1953.

Johnson, Marjorie Cecil (1904). American hispanist. Various teaching posts, University of Texas, Stephens College, Texas State College for Women, George Washington University, and others. Associated with the U. S. Office of Education and Professor of Spanish in various U. S. Government schools. Co-author, *Los otros americanos,* N. Y., 1933; *Handbook on the Teaching of Spanish and Portuguese,* Boston, 1945. Author of many Spanish textbooks and articles on Latin American literature. President, A.A.T.S., 1951. Associate Editor, *Hispania,* 1943-1951.

Jones, Willis Knapp (1895). American hispanist. Authority on Latin American literature. Studied at the *Centro de Estudios Históricos,* 1922. Professor of Spanish, Miami University, Oxford, Ohio, since 1923. President, American Association of Teachers of Spanish, 1941. Author of many articles in *Hispania, Books Abroad, Poet Lore,* etc. Has written extensively on the Latin American theater, particularly, the article on that subject in the *Encyclopedia Americana.*

jornada. Literally, "The duration of a day." In the Spanish drama of the 16th century, *jornada* was the word for "act." The term *auto* was confined to religious plays. Bartolomé de Torres Naharro (d. 1524?), the earliest dramaturgical theoretician of the Spanish theater, seems to have been the first to introduce the term *jornada* as a translation of the Latin word *actus* (in the introduction to his *Propalladia,* 1517). In practice he adhered to the five acts of the classical Latin drama. Juan de la Cueva (d. 1610) later claimed priority in the use of the term as well as in the use of four and three acts instead of the classical five (*Exemplar poético,* 1606). The introduction of the term *jornada* as well as the reduction in the number of acts reflects the development of the Spanish drama as it gradually cast off the shackles of the Aristotelian unity of time.

Cf. Gillet, J. E., (Ed.) *Propalladia and Other Works of Bartolomé de Torres Naharro,* 3 vols., Bryn Mawr, Pa., 1943-1952; Morby, E. S., "Notes on Juan de la Cueva: Versification and Dramatic Theory," *Hispanic Review,* VIII, 1940.

Josaphat (Josafat). The name of Buddha in the medieval legend of *Barlaam y Josafat,* treated by Juan de Arce, Juan Manuel, Lope de Vega and Calderón. See under *Barlaam y Josafat.*

José. See under *Palacio Valdés.*

Jovellanos, Gaspar Melchor de (1744-1811). Statesman, reformer, humanitarian, poet, prose stylist and dramatist. Born in Gijón; died in Vega, Asturias. Inspired by the ideas of the French Enlightenment (he had read Condillac, Rousseau and Diderot in his youth), Jovellanos was nevertheless a neo-classicist in letters and a nationalist in politics. He was opposed to freedom of the press, to the rule of the untutored masses, and hence also to the French Revolution; but he believed in a monarchy limited by a bicameral legislature. His prose comedy in the manner of Diderot, *El delicuente honrado* (1774), was a melodramatic plea for judicial and penal reform. Similarly, his *Informe sobre la ley agraria* (1795) was a prose masterpiece on the necessity of reform in agricultural economy and law. Although he lost favor at court and was imprisoned because of his presumed connection with the Spanish edition of Rousseau's *Contrat Social,* he was a staunch defender of his country at the time of the Napoleonic invasion in 1808 *(Memoria en defensa de la Junta Central).* His neo-classic style as a poet is best exemplified in his serene and philosophic epistle to the Duke of Veragua, written at the monastery of El Paular *(Epístola de Fabio a Anfriso).* His diary, covering the years 1790-1801, gives us an intimate picture of his inner life and of the society of his time.

Cf. *Obras completas,* (Ed.) Nocedal, C., *BAE,* XLVI, L, 1858; *Diarios (Memorias íntimas),* Madrid, 1905; *Obras escogidas,* (Ed.) Río, A. D., Madrid, 1935-1946; González-Blanco, A., *Jovellanos: su vida y obra,* Madrid, 1911; Juderías, J., *Gaspar Melchor de Jovellanos: su vida, su tiempo, sus obras, su influencia social,* Madrid, 1913; Santullano, L., *Jovellanos,* Madrid, 1936.

Jovino. The pastoral name adopted by Jovellanos as a member of the *Parnaso salmantino.* See under *Escuela de Salamanca.*

Juana de América. See *Ibarbourou, Juana de.*

Juan de Arce. See under *Barlaam y Josafat.*

Juan de la Cruz. See *Cruz, San Juan de la.*

Juan Manuel (1282-1349?). The Infante Don Juan Manuel was an illustrious nobleman and man of letters. Born in Toledo, the grandson of Fernando III and the nephew of Alfonso X, in his youth he fought against the Moors. During the minority of his nephews, Fernando IV and Alfonso XI, he served as Regent of Castile, became involved in court intrigue and rebelled against Alfonso XI, even to the extent of allying himself with the Moors. In the end, however, he submitted to royal authority. In the intervals between wars and political strife, he devoted himself to literature and became the most artistic prose writer of his time. Many of his works have been lost, among them several prose treatises: *Libro de la caballería* (on chivalry), *Libro de engeños* (on military engineering), and *Reglas de como se debe trobar* (on poetics). His poems *(Libro de los cantares)* have also been lost. Among his minor extant works are the *Libro de la caza* (on falconry), the *Crónica abreviada* (a compendium of his uncle's *Crónica general*), *Libro del caballero y del escudero* (on chivalry), and *Libro de los estados* (an adaptation of *Barlaam y Josafat*). Several of these were inspired by the works of Raimundo Lulio (1235-1315), the great Catalan scholar of the late Middle Ages. Don Juan Manuel's great masterpiece, however, is his *Libro del Conde Lucanor* (1323-1335), a collection of fifty moral tales or exempla in the manner of Boccaccio's *Decameron,* but anticipating it by more than a decade. The frame is provided by Count Lucanor's problems and his counselor Patronio's solutions, each in the form of a tale ending with a rhymed moral. These moral fables are composed in a lucid, informal and spirited style that set the standard for the future development of Spanish prose.

Cf. *El libro de los enxiemplos del Conde Lucanor et de Patronio,* (Ed.) Knust, H., Leipzig, 1900; (Ed.) Juliá, E., *El Conde Lucanor: edición, observaciones preliminares y ensayo biográfico,* Madrid, 1933; Giménez Soler, A., *Don Juan Manuel: biografía y estudio crítico,* Zaragoza, 1932.

Juan Ruiz. "El Arcipreste de Hita." See *Ruiz, Juan.*

Juanita la Larga. See under *Valera, Juan.*

Judía de Toledo. See under *Vega, Lope de.*

juegos de escarnio. Medieval plays containing profane and sacrilegious mummery; *e.g.* mockery of religious observances, vulgarity of language and action in regard to sacred matters. In the *Siete partidas,* the codification of laws done at the behest of Alfonso X in about 1255, the clergy are forbidden to participate in *juegos de escarnio*. The reference points to the existence of a secular drama which has been lost. The *farsas* of Diego Sánchez de Badajoz (early 16th century) are a later example of the mingling of sacred and profane elements in the drama.

juegos escolares. Scholastic plays. In Spanish literature, plays written in Latin by students and clerics, generally on religious themes, similar to those of medieval liturgical drama.

juglar. A juggler, mountebank or buffoon. In literature, the Spanish equivalent of the French *jongleur,* or minstrel. Originally strolling entertainers, they also amused the nobility at court. The first reference to *juglares* occurs in early 12th century archives of the court at León. In the 13th century there are also references to them in the *Crónica general* and in the *Siete partidas* of Alfonso X. The first *juglares* were not poets but merely recited or sang the poetry of the *trovadores.* Later specialization produced the *juglar lírico,* the reciter or chanter of lyric poetry, and the *juglar narrativo* or *juglar de gesta,* who recited the *cantares de gesta,* or popular epic narratives. The highest stage of development of the *juglar* is the combined minstrel-poet, creator of the *mester de juglaría* lyric and narrative poetry of the 12th and 13th centuries. All of the *juglares* were anonymous lay poets. Although Gonzalo de Berceo (1195?-1264?), the earliest Spanish poet known by name, referred to himself as both a *juglar* and a *trobador,* he was actually not a *juglar* but a clerical poet of *mester de clerecía* verse. See also *mester de juglaría.*

Cf. Menéndez Pidal, R., *Poesía juglaresca y juglares,* Madrid, 1924.

juglarescos. See under *romance.*

juglaría poetry. See under *mester de juglaría.*

juguete. Literally, a toy, plaything, jest or carol. More specifically, in the theater, a short dramatic skit in a light vein. *Juguetes* interspersed with lyrics or songs belong to the *género chico,* or minor dramatic type, such as musical comedy, operetta, etc. In this sense, the full term is *juguete cómico* or *juguete lírico.* Originally referring to a one-act comedietta, the term is occasionally extended to include any musical comedy or review of indeterminate length.

Juguetes de Talía. See under *Torres Villarroel.*

Junta de Relaciones Culturales. See under *Hispanic Institute.*

Junta para Ampliación de Estudios. See under *Hispanic Institute; krausismo.*

Justina, La pícara. A picaresque novel dealing with the adventures of a female rogue. Its full title is *El libro de entretenimiento de la pícara Justina.* It was written in about 1582 and was published in Medina del Campo in 1605. The work is attributed to Francisco López de Ubeda, a Toledan physician about whom very little is known except that he was a real personage and that the name is not merely a pseudonym, as some authorities contend. The novel consists of three prologues and four books. An *Arte poética* prefaces the whole. The four books are entitled respectively: (1) *Pícara montañesa* (the origins and rise of Justina); (2) *Pícara romera* (Justina's adventures on a pilgrimage); (3) *Pícara pleitista* (in which Justina leaves her home); (4) *Pícara novia* (in which Justina, after tricking several lovers, finally marries a soldier named Lozano). Every episode begins with a verse summary and ends with a moral. A second part, in which Justina was to marry Guzmán de Alfarache, was never published. The novel was popular in its day and went through many editions and translations, but it is of minor literary value. Its plot is diffuse and its characterizations poor. However, its picaresque vocabulary and original style are interesting to students of the picaresque novel.

Cf. Editions by Valbuena Prat, A., in *La novela picaresca española,* Madrid, 1944-1946; by Puyol Alonso, J., Madrid, 1912; and in *BAE,* XXXIII; Chandler, F. W., *Romances of Roguery,* N. Y., 1899; Haan, F. de, *An Outline of the History of the "Novela picaresca" in Spain,* The Hague, 1903.

K

Kalila et Digna. See *Calila y Dimna.*

Kany, Charles Emil (1895). Professor of Spanish, University of California, since 1922. Author of *Life and Manners in Madrid, 1750-1800,* Berkeley, 1932; *The Beginnings of the Epistolary Novel in France, Italy and Spain,* Berkeley, 1937; *American-Spanish Syntax,* Chicago, 1945, 2nd ed., 1951. Contributing Editor, *Handbook of Latin American Studies,* Washington, D. C., 1945-1952.

Kempis, Thomas à. See under *Granada; mysticism.*

Kennedy, Ruth Lee (1895). American hispanist. Professor of Spanish, Smith College. Authority on Golden Age literature. Author of *The Dramatic Art of Moreto,* 1931-1932.

kharja. See *jarcha.*

Kiddle, Lawrence Bayard (1907). American hispanist. Professor of Spanish, University of Michigan. Author of many articles in hispanic journals. Editor of Mariana Azuelo's *Los de abajo* (in collaboration with Englekirk, J. E.), N. Y., 1939.

Krause, Karl Christian Friedrich (1781-1832). German philosopher whose ideas influenced the Spanish *krausistas* and the philosophical movement known as *krausismo* at the end of the 19th century. Krause was a younger contemporary of Kant. His philosophy was an attempt "to formulate a speculative reconciliation of theism and pantheism." He called his system "panentheism." His main works were: *Grundlehre des Naturrechts* (1803)—"Basic Theory of Natural Law"—; *System der Sittenlehre* (1810)—"System of Ethics"—; *Das Urbild der Menschheit* (1811)—"The Ideal of Humanity"—; *Vorlesungen über die Grundwahrheiten der Wissenschaften* (1829)—"Lectures on the Basic Truths of the Sciences." See also *krausismo.*

Cf. *The Dictionary of Philosophy,* (Ed. Runes, D. D.), 2nd ed., N. Y., 1942.

krausismo. A liberal philosophical and educational movement initiated at the University of Madrid by Julián Sanz del Río (1814-1869). Having studied at Heidelberg, Sanz del Río returned to Madrid, a convert to the neokantian doctrines of Karl Friedrich Krause (1781-1832). Krause's philosophical system, known as "panentheism," was an attempt to reconcile theism and pantheism. It emphasized the development of the individual as a part of the universal divine essence. Sanz del Río's lectures on the metaphysics of "panentheism" were of less importance than their results in the field of education. The *krausistas,* as his pupils were called, became the educators of modern Spain. Foremost among them was Francisco Giner de los Ríos, founder of the *Institución Libre de Enseñanza.* Among other educational institutions inspired by *krausismo* were the *Junta para Ampliación de Estudios* and the *Centro de Estudios Históricos,* commonly known as the *Residencia de Estudiantes.* Among the Spanish scholars who were influenced directly or indirectly by *krausismo* were Manuel Bartolomé Cossío (1858-1935), Francisco Pi y Margall (1824-1901), Emilio Castelar (1832-1899), Joaquín Costa (1844-1911), and others. Among the creative writers were Azorín, Machado and Jiménez. The opposition to *krausismo* was led by Menéndez y Pelayo and Unamuno. See also under *Krause.*

Cf. Jobit, P., *Les éducateurs de l'Espagne contemporaine: I. Les Krausistes,* Paris, 1936; Xirau, J., "Julián Sanz del Río y el krausismo español," *Cuadernos Americanos,* IV, 1944; Del Río, A., *Historia de la literatura española,* N. Y., 1948; López-Morillas, J., *El Krausismo español,* Mexico, 1955.

krausista. An adherent of the doctrines of Karl Friedrich Krause. In particular, a pupil or follower of Sanz del Río. See under *Krause; krausismo.*

L

La Barraca. An experimental theater. See under *García Lorca.*

Laberinto de Fortuna (El). See under *Mena, Juan de.*

Lalita Vistara. See under *Barlaam y Josafat.*

lamaño. A *Quechua* dialect. See under *Quechua.*

La Nación (Buenos Aires). See under *Mitre, Bartolomé.*

Lances de honor. See under *Tamayo y Baus.*

Lanzarote. See under *romances of chivalry.*

Lapidario. See under *Alfonso X.*

Larra, Mariano José de (1809-1837). The outstanding journalist, critic and *costumbrista* writer of the Romantic period. Born and died in Madrid. His full name was Mariano José de Larra y Sánchez de Castro. He wrote under various pseudonyms, of which the best known is "Fígaro." Larra's father had served as an army doctor in the French army under Joseph Bonaparte and, when Spain gained her independence in 1814, he went into exile with his family. Thus, when in 1817 he sent his son back to Spain to live with relatives and to be educated, the child could speak only French. Educated at various schools conducted by the Escolapians and the Jesuits, Larra also studied at the Universities of Valladolid and Valencia. After working in a government office, he embarked on a career as a journalist. His marriage at the age of twenty was a tragic failure and he sought consolation in a liaison with another woman. When she left him, he committed suicide at the age of twenty-eight. Larra lived his romanticism, even to the Werther-like conclusion. His genius as a journalist and critic was first evidenced in his own periodical, for which he wrote all the articles himself under the pen name, "El pobrecito hablador" (*Cartas del pobrecito hablador,* 1832-1833). His satirical wit is particularly mordant in a famous article from this collection: *Vuelva Vd. mañana,* which ridicules the Spanish penchant for lethargy and procrastination *(abulia)*. He is also known as the author of a romantic novel based on the tragic love of a 15th century *gallego* poet named Macías el enamorado (*El doncel de don Enrique el doliente,* 1834). In the same year he wrote a dramatization of the identical theme *(Macías)*. Larra's later criticism, collected from various periodicals, appeared in *Colección de artículos* (1835-1837). He was pre-eminent in the writing of *artículos de costumbres,* folkloristic pictures of Spanish society and manners, a genre which he enriched with trenchant satire and criticism. His subjects ranged from literature and the drama through political and social problems. His style was witty, terse and incisive. He displayed a disillusionment and pessimism which were not merely a romantic pose but the direct result of his personal and public experiences. Thus his criticism attained a depth and penetration rare among his contemporaries. So modern and cosmopolitan was he in spirit, that the Generation of 1898 hailed him as one of their precursors.

Cf. *Obras completas,* Barcelona, 1886; *Artículos completos,* (Ed.) San Martín, A., Madrid, 1944; Azorín, *Rivas y Larra, razón social del romanticismo en España,* Madrid, 1916; McGuire, E., *A Study of the Writings of Don Mariano José de Larra,* Berkeley, Cal., 1918; Burgos, C. de, *Fígaro,* Madrid, 1919; Sánchez Esteban, A., *Mariano José de Larra, "Fígaro,"* Madrid, 1934.

Larrea, Juan (1895). Post-modernist lyric poet. An experimenter and seeker, he passed successively through ultraism, creationism and surrealism. As a vanguardist poet, he influenced García Lorca, Gerardo Diego, Alberti and others. One of the most active of the Spanish expatriates, he was instrumental in founding the literary review, *Cuadernos americanos,* published in Mexico.

Cf. Poems in *Poesía española (1915-1931),* Diego, G., Madrid, 1932; Río, A. del, *Historia de la literatura española,* vol. 2, N. Y., 1948.

Larreta, Enrique Rodríguez (1875). Argentine novelist and diplomat. Served as Minister to France (1910-1911). A member of the Argentine Academy of Letters. He has been a resident of Madrid since 1948. Deeply imbued with the ideals of the Hispanic tradition, Larreta has interpreted them in critical and philosophical essays. However, he is chiefly noted for his historical novel, *La gloria de don Ramiro,* a story of Spain in the days of Philip II, considered a modern classic of its type. Chief works: *La gloria de don Ramiro,* 1908; *Zogoibi,* 1926; *La naranja,* 1947; *Orillas del Ebro,* 1949.

Cf. Torres Ríoseco, A., *La novela en la América hispana,* Berkeley, U. of Cal. Press, 1939.

Látigo (El). See under *Alarcón y Ariza.*

latiniparla. Spanish as used by speakers and writers who have a fondness for interlarding their discourse with Latin terms and expressions or Spanish words derived from Latin.

latinismo. A word or expression borrowed from Latin, unchanged in form. Example: *maximum.*

Latorre, Mariano (1886). Chilean professor, critic and short-story writer. Professor of Spanish Literature at the Pedagogical Institute. Awarded the National Literary Prize in 1943. Latorre is a descriptive regionalist whose collections of short stories are devoted to almost every contour of Chilean topography, from the Andean peaks, to the coastal highlands, to the sea. His forte is the creative evocation of natural background. Chief works: *Cuentos del Maule,* 1912; *Cuna de cóndores,* 1918; *Zurzulita,* 1920; *Chilenos del mar,* 1929; *Hombres y zorros,* 1937.

Cf. Amunátegui Solar, D., *Las letras chilenas,* Santiago, 1934; Castillo, H., "Mariano Latorre," *Hispania,* XXXVII, 1954.

Laurel de Apolo. One of Calderón's musical plays. See under *zarzuela.*

Laureola. See under *San Pedro, Diego de.*

Lazarillo castigado (El). See under *Lazarillo de Tormes.*

Lazarillo de ciegos. See under *Bustamante.*

Lazarillo de Tormes. Among the first and the best of the picaresque novels. An anonymous work, its full title is *La vida de Lazarillo de Tormes y de sus fortunas y adversidades.* Three editions of the *Lazarillo* appeared in 1554 (Alcalá, Burgos, Antwerp). Although the authorship was attributed to Diego Hurtado de Mendoza in reprints as late as the 17th century, modern scholarship rejects this notion. Attempts to ascertain the authorship have proved fruitless. Modern editions *(e.g.* by Cejador y Frauca, 1914, and by Bonilla y San Martín, 1915) are based on a critical comparison of the three editions of 1554. Internal evidence seems to indicate that the author was a Toledan and that a previous version dating as far back as 1539 may have existed. An anonymous sequel

(Segunda parte del Lazarillo), full of fantastic episodes, appeared in Antwerp in 1555. Because of its anti-clerical satire, *Lazarillo* was placed on the Index; however, an expurgated edition *(El Lazarillo castigado)* was allowed to circulate in 1573. Another sequel, by Juan de Luna (Paris, 1620), a teacher of Spanish at the French court, is marked by an even more outspoken anti-clerical tone than the original. Aside from these editions and sequels, the universal popularity of the work is evidenced by its many translations (French, 1561; English, 1576; Dutch, 1579; German, 1617; Italian, 1622; *etc.*). Lazarillo was a folklore character whose name appears in early proverbs and anecdotes. Reference to him is already found in *La lozana andaluza* (1528). The story of *Lazarillo de Tormes* is divided into seven *tratados* (treatises), each of which relates Lazarillo's adventures in the services of a different master: 1. a blind beggar; 2. a priest; 3. a nobleman; 4. a friar; 5. A seller of indulgences; 6. a chaplain; 7. a constable. In the beginning Lazarillo tells about his unsavory ancestry, the effect being a parody on the chivalric romances which generally began with an account of the illustrious descent of an aristocratic hero. *Tratados* 2, 4, 5 are satires of clerical venality; *Tratado* 3 portrays the indigent nobleman whose inflated sense of honor is nevertheless compatible with his parasitic existence at the expense of an unpaid squire. Lazarillo finally makes good as a wine merchant in Toledo, comfortably married to a canon's mistress. *Lazarillo de Tormes* ranks with the *Celestina* and *Don Quijote* as a realistic masterpiece. It provides a fascinating and unvarnished account of life in 16th century Spain. Its bold realism in regard to the clergy is wholly Erasmist in spirit.

Cf. *Vida de Lazarillo de Tormes,* in *BAE,* III; (Ed.) Morel-Fatio, A., Paris, 1886; (Ed.) Foulché-Delbosc, R., *Bibliotheca hispanica,* III; (Ed.) Cejador y Frauca, J., Madrid, 1914; (Ed.) Bonilla y San Martín, A., Madrid, 1915; Morel-Fatio, A., "Recherches sur Lazarille de Tormes," *Études sur l'Espagne,* I, Paris, 1895; *The Life of Lazarillo de Tormes,* trsl. by How, L., New York, 1917; *Lazarillo de Tormes,* trsl. by Rowland, D., 1576, republished Oxford, 1924; Luna, J. de, *La segunda parte de la vida de Lazarillo de Tormes,* trsl. by Sims, E. R., with intro. and notes by Wagner, C. P., Austin, Texas, 1928; Macaya Lahmann, E., *Bibliografía del Lazarillo de Tormes,* San José, Costa Rica, 1935; Keller

D. S., "Lazarillo de Tormes, 1554-1954. An Analytical Bibliography of Twelve Recent Studies," *Hispania,* XXXVII, 4, 1954.

Leavitt, Sturgis Elleno (1888). American hispanist, literary scholar and bibliographer. An authority on Latin American literature. With the University of North Carolina since 1917. Kenan Professor of Spanish since 1945. Director, *Institute of Latin American Studies,* since 1940. President, American Association of Teachers of Spanish and Portuguese, 1946. Author of *The Estrella de Sevilla and Claramonte,* 1931; *Hispano-American Literature in the United States,* 1932. Compiler of bibliographies of the literature of Argentina, Bolivia, Chile, Colombia, Peru and Uruguay.

Lebrija. See *Nebrija.*

Ledesma, Alonso de (1562-1623). The precursor of *conceptismo* in Spanish literature. His masterpiece was an allegorical poem in three parts, entitled *Conceptos espirituales* (1600-1612). See under *conceptismo.*

Leguizamón, Martiniano P. (1858-1935). Argentine professor, short-story writer and critic. Professor of literature and history at Buenos Aires. An exemplar, as well as a historian and critic of gaucho writing, he had a seminal effect on Argentine literature, emphasizing the national and regionalist element in his short stories. Among his chief works were: *Calandria,* 1896; *Recuerdos de la tierra,* 1896; *Alma nativa,* 1906; *De cepa criolla,* 1908; *Páginas argentinas: crítica literaria y histórica,* 1911; *Montaraz,* 1911.

Cf. Torre Revello, J., *Martiniano Leguizamón: el hombre y su obra,* Paraná, 1939.

Lejárraga, María de la O. See under *Martínez Sierra.*

Lengua poética de Góngora. See under *Alonso, Dámaso.*

León, Luis de (1527-1591). Augustinian monk, mystic poet and theologian. Born at Belmonte de Cuenca; died in Madrigal, Avila. The son of a well-to-do judge, he was educated at the University of Salamanca, where he entered the Augustinian Order in 1544. A brilliant classical and Hebrew scholar, his rise at the University of Salamanca was rapid, and in 1561 he was appointed to a professorship. However, he was denounced to the Inquisition by rival professors, and in 1572 was incarcerated at Valladolid, the charges being that he had criticized the accuracy of the Vulgate and had translated the *Song of Songs* into Spanish, the latter a grave charge since the Church had forbidden the reading of the

Holy Scriptures in the vernacular. The allegation that his great-grandmother had been a Jewess also weighed against him. After spending almost five years in a private cell, he was released in 1576 with a reprimand. According to legend, his first words on resuming his lectures at Salamanca were, "As we were saying yesterday . . ." In his later years he was entrusted with the editing of Saint Theresa's works and, shortly before his death, he was elected Provincial of his Order in Castile. Luis de León's works circulated in manuscript and did not appear until 1631, when Quevedo published them in his desire to counteract Gongorism. León's best known prose work was *De los nombres de Cristo* (1583), in which three monks carry on an inquiry into the nature of Christ by means of a kind of Platonic dialogue, discussing the significance of the various names given to Him in the New Testament *(e.g.*, Shepherd, Son of God, Prince of Peace, etc.). His *La perfecta casada* (1583) is a fusion of the ascetic side of Christianity (strictures against women) and the spirit of Renaissance humanism (the model housewife). Fray Luis de León's enduring fame, however, rests on his verse, a handful of lyric poems, some 30 in all, of impeccable style and beauty. His *Vida retirada* (1557) and *Noche serena* (1571) are a glorification of the pastoral, spiritual and contemplative life. His thoughts of God, eternity and immortality are mirrored in nature and love. The mystical element in León's poetry is frequently more of an impassioned yearning than an attainment *(Morada del cielo).*

Cf. *Obras poéticas,* (Ed.) Llovera, P., Cuenca, 1931-1933; *De los nombres de Cristo,* (Ed.) Onís, F. de, Madrid, 1914-1921; *La perfecta casada,* (Ed.) Bonilla y San Martín, A., Madrid, 1917; Blanco García, F., *Fray Luis de León,* Madrid, 1904; Alonso Getino, P. L. G., *Vida y procesos del Maestro Fr. Luis de León,* Salamanca, 1907; Fitzmaurice-Kelly, J., *Fray Luis de León: A Biographical Fragment,* Oxford, 1921; Bell, A. T. G., *Luis de León,* Oxford, 1925.

León, Ricardo (1877-1943). Poet, novelist and member of the *Academia Española.* Born in Barcelona; died in Madrid. Unlike most writers of his generation he turned his back on the contemporary scene and sought to resurrect both the style and the traditions of the old Spanish literature of chivalry and of religious mysticism. Although he wrote two volumes of verse *(Lira de* *bronce,* 1901; *Alivio de caminantes,* 1911), his major field was the novel. His *Casta de hidalgos* (1908) is an archaic re-creation of life in the historical town of Santillana del Mar. In *Alcalá de los Zegríes* (1909) the setting is the Andalusian town of Ronda against a background of political rivalries and romantic love affairs. *El amor de los amores* (1910) is a study in mysticism, using the theme of a modern St. Francis to hymn the triumph of spiritual over human love. The work was hailed as a "religious Don Quijote" and received the award of the *Real Academia.* A departure from his earlier manner, *Los centauros* (1912) is a realistic portrayal of the political, social and intellectual life of a contemporary provincial capital. Ricardo León also wrote philisophical dialogues (*La escuela de los sofistas,* 1910), historical tales (*Europa trágica,* 1918) and political novels (*Bajo el yugo de los bárbaros,* 1932). His last and reputedly best novel was *Cristo en los infiernos* (1943), a portrayal of Spanish life on the brink of the Civil War.

Cf. Menéndez-Reigada, I. G., "Ricardo León," *La Ciencia Tomista,* VIII; Asín Palacios, M., "Necrología," *Boletín de la Real Academia Española,* XXIV.

León Felipe. See *Felipe, León.*

León Hebreo. See *Hebreo.*

Leonard, Irving Albert (1896). American hispanist, literary scholar and authority on Latin American literature. Professor of Spanish, University of California, 1923-1937. Professor of Hispanic Culture, Brown University, 1940-1942. Professor of Spanish American Literature, University of Michigan, 1942; Chairman, Department of Romance Languages, 1945-1951. Visiting Professor of Spanish American Literature, Oxford University, 1952. Corresponding member of the *Acad. Esp.* Author or editor of *Poemas de Don Carlos de Sigüenza,* Madrid, 1931; *Romances of Chivalry in the Spanish Indies,* Berkeley, 1933; *Obras dramáticas de Peralta Barnuevo,* Santiago de Chile, 1937.

Leonese. See under Spanish.

L'épopée castillane, etc. See under *Menéndez Pidal.*

Leriano. See under *San Pedro, Diego de.*

Lerma, El Duque de. See under *Góngora.*

letrilla. A type of lyric poem having an *estribillo* at the end of each stanza. Occasionally the thought of the *estribillo* may begin the stanza and be repeated at the end as a sort of refrain. The *letrilla* is a short and graceful lyric dealing with religious, amorous or satirical themes. The form was used by Góngora and other poets. See also *estribillo.*

Leyenda del caballero del cisne. See under *Gran conquista de ultramar.*

Leyenda del Cid. See under *Zorrilla y Moral.*

Leyenda de los infantes de Lara. See *Infantes de Lara.*

leyenda negra. A phrase used in reference to derogatory notions regarding Spain and Spanish culture.

Cf. Juderías, J., *La leyenda negra,* Madrid, 1917.

Libre de amor. See under *Rodríguez de la Cámara.*

libriello. One of the cantos into which Gonzalo de Berceo (1195?-1264?) divided his lengthy verse narratives.

Libro de Alexandre. An anonymous late 12th or early 13th century *clerecía* poem consisting of over 10,000 lines in *cuaderna vía.* Of the two extant manuscripts, one (Madrid) ascribes the authorship to a Leonese cleric, Juan Lorenzo Segura de Astorga; the other (Paris) names Berceo; but internal evidence makes the latter unlikely. The chief sources of the work are the *Alexandreis* of Gautier de Chatillon and the *Roman d'Alexandre* by Lambert le Tort and Alexandre de Bernai. The theme deals with the adventures and deeds of Alexander the Great, who is conceived as a medieval paragon, combining the knightly virtues of skill at arms and magnanimity of soul with the vast and profound knowledge of a philosopher. Alexander is depicted as the eternally restless seeker of knowledge, fame and glory in remote lands and among esoteric peoples. Typical of its medieval origin, the narrative contains miraculous events (encounters with the Amazons and the Sirens) and anachronisms (the mother of Achilles dwelling in a convent) intermingled with historical fact. Greatly superior to the *Libro de Apolonio,* the *Libro de Alexandre* is considered the best medieval Spanish romance and the foremost example of *clerecía* poetry. The unknown author displays unusual powers of description, wide erudition, and is master of a brisk narrative style.

Cf. *El Libro de Alixandre,* (Ed.) Morel-Fatio, A., Dresden, 1906; *El Libro de Alexandre,* (Ed.) Willis, R. S., Jr., Princeton, 1934; Menéndez Pidal, R., "Sobre El Libro de Alixandre," *Cultura*

Española, VI, 1907; Macías, M., *Juan Lorenzo Segura y el Poema de Alexandre,* Orense, 1913.

Libro de Apolonio. A 13th century anonymous *clerecía* poem consisting of 2,624 lines in *cuaderna vía.* The exact date of its composition is unknown, although it is thought to pre-date the works of Berceo. It was probably translated from some lost Provençal or Latin original, which in turn had been inspired by an ancient Greek Milesian tale or romance of adventure based on the story of Apollonius, King of Tyre. The theme occurs in Shakespeare's *Pericles, Prince of Tyre.* Although the title features Apolonio, most of the plot deals with the adventures of his queen, Luciana, and their daughter, Tarsiana. The former falls into a death-like swoon, is buried in a casket at sea, floats ashore, is revived and becomes a priestess of Diana; the latter is kidnapped by pirates, sold into slavery, survives various perilous adventures, becomes a public entertainer and is finally reunited with her parents. Tarsiana, whose gypsy-like singing and dancing enthrals her audiences, is the most memorable character of the story and is supposed to have inspired Cervantes' Preciosa. The story follows the typical Milesian or Byzantine pattern of shipwrecks, pirates, strange and perilous adventures and miraculous reunions.

Cf. *Libro de Apolonio* (Ed.) Marden, C. C., Part I (Text and Intro.), Baltimore, 1917, Part II (Gram., Notes and Vocab.), Princeton, 1922; García Blanco, M., *La originalidad del "Libro de Apolonio,"* Madrid, 1945.

Libro de buen amor. See under *Ruiz, Juan.*

Libro de Kalila et Dimna. See *Calila y Dimna.*

Libro de la erudición poética. See under *Carrillo y Sotomayor.*

Libro . . . de la pícara Justina. See *Justina.*

Libro de las fundaciones. See under *Teresa de Jesús.*

Libro del Caballero Zifar. See *Caballero Cifar.*

Libro del Conde Lucanor. See under *Juan Manuel.*

Libro de los buenos proverbios. See under *folklore.*

Libro de los claros varones de Castilla. See under *Pulgar.*

Libro de los engaños y asayamientos de las mujeres. The Spanish version of an anonymous collection of oriental tales regarding the deceits and wiles of women. It was translated from the Arabic into Castilian in 1253 at the behest of the Infante Fadrique, the younger brother of Alfonso X. In ancient literature the work was known under various titles: *Dolopathos, Syntipas, Sindibad.* In early English literature it bore the title of the *History of the Seven Wise Masters.* The frame of the collection is an unwarranted charge of attempted seduction levied by a vindictive queen against her stepson, who had spurned her advances. At his trial seven wise masters speak in his defense, each relating stories illustrating the perfidy of women. These stories, totaling 24, constitute the major part of the book. The tales are frequently licentious as they elaborate on the vices of women. The oriental disdain of women coincided with the ascetic views of medieval Christianity to make these tales popular throughout Europe. The same theme of the scorn of women recurs in the *Corvacho* of the Arcipreste de Talavera. See also under *ejemplo.*

Cf. *Libro de los engannos et los assayamientos de las mugeres,* (Ed.) Bonilla y San Martín, A., *Bibliotheca hispanica,* XIV; (Ed.) Keller, J. E., Chapel Hill, North Carolina, 1953.

Libro de los enxemplos. See under *ejemplo.*

Libro de los estados. See under *Barlaam y Josafat; Juan Manuel.*

Libro de los gatos. The 14th century Spanish translation of a Latin work, the *Narrationes* of Odo de Cheriton, an Anglo-Norman monk. The work is a collection of moral tales *(exempla)* similar to the medieval *Disciplina clericalis.* Most of the tales in the *Libro de los gatos* are animal apologues, or moral fables. The tone of the work is satirical, criticism being leveled at the nobility and the clergy who are depicted as the despoilers and oppressors of the common people. Northup has suggested that the word "gatos" of the title is a variant of the word "quentos" *(cuentos).*

Cf. "El libro de los gatos," (Ed.) Northup, G. T., *Modern Philology,* V, 1908; Northup, G. T., *An Introduction to Spanish Literature,* 2nd ed., Chicago, 1936.

Libro de los tres reyes de Oriente. A *juglaría* narrative poem, probably of Provençal origin, dating from the end of the 12th or the beginning of the 13th century. The early spelling of the title was *Libre dels tres reys d'Orient.* The poem consists of some 250 lines of irregular length, but with the nine-syllable line predominating. It narrates the adoration of Jesus by the Magi, and the flight into Egypt. The work is one of the rare examples of *juglaría* poetry on a religious theme. See also *juglaría poetry.*

Cf. Menéndez Pidal, R., *Poesía juglaresca y juglares*, 2nd ed., Buenos Aires, 1945.

Libro de Patronio. See under *Juan Manuel.*

Libro de su vida. See under *Teresa de Jesús.*

Libro de Yusuf. See *Poema de Yuçuf.*

libros de caballerías. See under *romances of chivalry.*

Libros del saber de astronomía. See under *Alfonso X.*

Licenciado vidriera (El). See under *Cervantes.*

Lillo, Baldomero (1867-1923). Chilean short-story writer. Employed in the Chilean mining industry. Later, he served on the staff of the University of Chile division of publications. Influenced by Zola's *Germinal,* he devoted himself to literature, using the medium of the *cuento* to express his social message. Describing the injustices suffered by unorganized miners and city workers, Lillo was a pioneer in introducing the proletarian theme to the Chilean short story. Among his chief works were: *Sub terra,* 1904; *Sub sole,* 1907.

Cf. Silva Castro, R., *Los cuentistas chilenos,* Santiago, 1937.

Lima fundada. See under *Peralta Barnuevo.*

Linares Rivas, Manuel (1867-1938). Galician playwright. Prominent in political life and a member of the *Academia Española.* One of the Generation of 1898, he advocated "Europeanization" of Spanish life and letters. He was a master of dramatic technique and dialogue and attempted almost all the dramatic genres: musical review *(La fragua de Vulcano);* comedy playlet *(Lo posible);* one-act play *(Lo que engaña la verdad);* verse drama *(Lady Godiva);* animal allegory *(El caballero lobo);* thesis play *(La fuerza del mal);* political satire *(El ídolo);* etc. His thesis plays on the seamy side of family life satirized middle-class illusions and foibles: false pride of aristocracy *(El abolengo);* the problem of divorce *(La garra);* etc. As in Benavente's work, a vein of sophisticated satire runs through his plays; unlike Benavente, however, Linares Rivas was not a pessimist since he believed in the reform of manners.

Cf. Bueno, M., *Teatro español contemporáneo,* Madrid, 1909; González Blanco, A., *Los dramaturgos españoles contemporáneos,* Valencia, 1917.

Lindo don Diego (El). See under *Moreto.*

lira. A metrical form consisting of a five-line stanza with lines of seven and eleven syllables. The rhyme scheme is ABABB. It was introduced into Spanish literature by Garcilaso de la Vega (1501?-1536). See also under *Garcilaso de la Vega.*

Lista y Aragón, Alberto (1775-1848). Professor, poet and critic. A cleric and a scholar of broad culture, he was a professor at the Universities of Seville (1804) and Madrid (1820). Among the pupils whom he inspired, but who grew away from him in poetic practice, were Espronceda and Ventura de la Vega. Lista's *Poesías* (1822, 1837) are for the most part in classic style but already show traces of Romanticism in their descriptions of nature and in their religious emotion. Among his Spanish adaptations of foreign masterpieces is his *Imperio de la estupidez* (1798), suggested by Pope's *Dunciad.* His famous series of lectures on Spanish literature, delivered at the University of Madrid in 1822, were published in 1836 under the title of *Lecciones de literatura española.* His critical work is collected in his *Ensayos literarios y críticos* (1844). His literary idols were Rioja and Calderón, who symbolize his critical canon of sensuousness and emotion expressed in classical form. Lista represents the last phase of neo-classicism as it gave way to Romanticism.

Cf. *Poesías,* in *BAE,* LXVII; Chaves, M., *Don Alberto Rodríguez de Lista,* Seville, 1912; Metford, J. C. J., "Alberto Lista and the Romantic Movement in Spain," *Liverpool Studies,* I, 1940.

literatura aljamiada. See *aljamiada literature.*

literatura gnómica. Gnomic literature. Writings which convey an ethical message in terse, concentrated form, such as maxims, aphorisms, proverbs and fables. An example is the medieval *Proverbios morales* (bet. 1350 and 1369) by Sem Tob. See also under *Sem Tob.*

literatura indianista. See *indianista literature.*

literatura por entregas. See under *entrega.*

literatura regional. See under *costumbrismo; regional novel.*

litote. (Eng. *litotes).* A figure of speech whereby an affirmative notion is expressed by denial of its contrary. Example: "*No soy tan feo; en esto no os alabo.*" *(DRAE).*

loa. Literally, "praise". In general, any brief dramatic panegyric. According to the *DRAE,* a "short dramatic composition presented prior to the dramatic poem and serving as an introduction". In the 16th and 17th century Spanish theater, the *loa* was the prologue to a play. It developed from the pre-Lope de Vega *introito,* a dramatic prologue presenting the argument and attempting to win the favor of the audience. See also *introito.*

Cf. Meredith, J. A., *"Introito" and "loa" in the Spanish Drama of the 16th Century,* U. of Pennsylvania, 1925.

Locura de amor (La). See under *Tamayo y Baus.*

Locuras de Europa. See under *Saavedra Fajardo.*

Lohengrin. See under *Gran conquista de ultramar; romances of chivalry.*

Longfellow, Henry Wadsworth (1807-1882). As poet, scholar, traveler, professor and translator, Longfellow introduced European literature and metrical forms to the writers of America. Four years of travel and study in France, Spain, Italy and Germany (1826-29) prepared him for his duties as Professor of Modern Languages at Bowdoin College, where he lectured from 1830 to 1835 and produced seven textbooks in French, Italian and Spanish, among them a Spanish reader. In 1836 he left Bowdoin to become Ticknor's successor at Harvard, holding the Smith Professorship until 1854. As a Hispanist he is chiefly noted for his teaching of Spanish language and literature, and for his translations of Spanish poets. Represented in his *The Poets and Poetry of Europe,* (Philadelphia, 1845) are translations of Gonzalo de Berceo, Juan Ruiz, Jorge Manrique, Lope de Vega and Tomás de Iriarte.

Cf. Longfellow, Samuel (Editor), *Life of Henry Wadsworth Longfellow,* 2 vols., Boston, 1886. Long, Orie William, *Literary Pioneers,* Cambridge, Mass., 1935. Johnson, Carl L., *Professor Longfellow of Harvard,* University of Oregon Press, 1944. Doyle, Henry Grattan, "Longfellow as Professor at Harvard," *Hispania,* XXVII, October, 1944.

Lope de Moros. See under *Razón de amor.*

Lope de Vega. See *Vega, Lope de.*

López, Luis Carlos (1883). Latin-American regionalist writer, born in Cartagena, Colombia. Ignored because of his opposition to modernist tendencies, he subsequently achieved recognition as a gifted literary observer, depicting with poetic insight people, manners and customs against the social background of his native city. Some of his chief works are: *De mi villorio,* 1908; *Posturas difíciles,* 1909; *Por el atajo,* 1928.

Cf. Llorente Arroyo, A., "Luis Carlos López," *Hispania,* VII, 1924.

López Albújar, Enrique (1872). Peruvian jurist and short-story writer. Together with Turner and Valdelomar, a forerunner of the regionalist trend in Peruvian literature. His tales reflect the wild majesty of the Andean sierras and the tragedy of Indian life. Influenced by the *modernista* movement, he achieved great beauty of style despite his sombre and pessimistic outlook. His best known works are: *Cuentos andinos,* 1920; *Nuevos cuentos andinos,* 1937.

Cf. Rubio, D., "Nuevos cuentos andinos," *Revista iberoamericana,* II, 1940.

López de Ayala, Adelardo (1828-1879). Poet and dramatist. Born in Guadalcanal, Seville; died in Madrid. His full name was Adelardo López de Ayala y Herrera. He studied law but never took his degree, a meeting with García Gutiérrez having influenced him to become a playwright. After writing several plays, he went to Madrid in 1849 and took a prominent part in the literary and political life of his time. In 1870 he became a member of the *Academia Española.* López de Ayala began with historical dramas. His *Un hombre de estado* (1851) is the tragic story of a royal favorite, don Rodrigo Calderón, who is destroyed by court intrigue and his own overweening ambition. Also based on a historical theme was *Rioja* (1854), the story of a poet whose love is transfigured by heroic renunciation. López de Ayala is best known for his realistic plays of modern life: *El tejado de vidrio* (1856), a morality play in which the cynical seducer is overtaken by retribution in the form of his own wife's unfaithfulness; *El tanto por ciento* (1861) and *Consuelo* (1878), which both excoriate avarice and materialism. His *El nuevo don Juan* (1863) is a satire of the perennial seducer. In these realistic plays, López de Ayala, together with Tamayo y Baus, set up the counter-current to romanticism in the theater. A master of technique and dialogue, as well as a deft versifier he lent a note of high moral seriousness to the comedy of his time.

Cf. *Obras,* (Ed.) Tamayo y Baus, M., 7 vols., Madrid, 1881-1885;

Octavio Picón, J., *Ayala, estudio biográfico,* Madrid, 1892; González Blanco, A., *Los dramaturgos españoles,* Valencia, 1917.

López de Ayala, Pero (1332-1407). Court chronicler, poet and translator. One of the most significant literary figures of the late Middle Ages. In the service of Pedro I *(El Cruel),* Enrique II, Juan I and Enrique III, he finally rose to the position of royal chancellor of Castile (1399). As an adviser to kings and a participant in the turbulent events of his time, he was ideally suited as a chronicler. His *Crónicas* extend through the reigns of the above monarchs, from 1350 to 1406. They are written in lucid prose and, unlike most of the early chronicles, are free from legendary interpolations and are based on first-hand knowledge of the characters and events of the period. Ayala's historical accounts are extremely modern in their analysis of characters and motives. The "Great Chancellor" was also active as a translator and a poet. Among his translations are works of Livy, Boethius *(De consolatione philosophiae),* Saint Gregory the Great, Saint Isidore *(De summo bono),* and Boccaccio *(The Fall of Princes),* the latter beginning the trend of Italian influence on Spanish letters. His chief poetic work was the *Rimado de palacio (ca.* 1400), a lyrical miscellany of some 8,200 lines, the last great Spanish work in *cuaderna vía,* although it contains some parts in the new meter of *arte mayor.* The *Rimado de palacio* is a courtier's autobiography dealing with sin and repentance and satirizing the life of the palace. Ayala was a true patriot, an apostle of morality in conduct, probity in government, and peace in foreign affairs. His satire is tinged with pessimism as he contemplates the corrupt and venal environment of the court.

Cf. *Rimado de palacio, BAE,* LVII; *Crónicas, BAE,* LXVI, LXVIII, LXX; Kuersteiner, A. F., (Ed.), *Poesías del Canciller Pero López de Ayala,* Hispanic Society of America, N. Y., 1920; Díaz de Arcaya, V. M., *El Gran Canciller D. Pero López de Ayala,* Vitoria, 1900; Entwistle, W. J., "The 'Romancero del Rey Don Pedro,' in Ayala," *Modern Language Review,* XXV, 1930.

López de Gómara. See under *Díaz del Castillo.*

López de Mendoza. See *Santillana, Marqués de.*

López de Ubeda, Francisco. See under *Justina.*

López de Vicuña, Juan. See under *Góngora.*

López-Morillas, Juan (1913). Hispanist. Born in Spain; naturalized U. S. citizen, 1942. Teaching posts at University of Iowa, Harvard University. Professor of Spanish, Brown University, since 1951. Articles on Rubén Darío, Antonio Machado, Unamuno, García Lorca, Ortega y Gasset, *etc.*, in *Revista Hispánica Moderna, Cuadernos Americanos, etc.* Author, *El Krausismo español,* Mexico, 1955.

López Portillo y Rojas, José (1850-1923). Mexican jurist, statesman and novelist. A student and professor of law in Mexico City. Former Governor of Jalisco. Widely traveled and deeply versed in French, English and Spanish literature, he wrote travel sketches and literary criticism. As a novelist he belongs to the regionalist school, notably in his *La parcela* (1898), which has Jalisco as its background. His most important works were: *La parcela,* 1898; *Novelas cortas,* 1900; *Los precursores,* 1909; *Fuertes y débiles,* 1919.

Cf. Carreño, A. M., *El licenciado José López Portillo y Rojas,* Mexico, 1923.

López Soler, Ramón (1806-1836). Historical novelist of the Romantic period. Born in Barcelona; died in Madrid. His most famous historical novel was inspired by Scott's *Ivanhoe* and was entitled *Los bandos de Castilla, o el caballero del cisne* (1830). His imitation of Hugo's *Notre Dame de Paris* was entitled *La catedral de Sevilla* (1834) and was published under the pseudonym of Gregorio Pérez de Miranda. López Soler inaugurated the vogue of Sir Walter Scott and Victor Hugo imitations among the Spanish Romanticists (Larra, Espronceda, Gil, Fernández y González, *etc.).*

Cf. Churchman, P. H. & Peers, E. A., "A Survey of the Influence of Sir Walter Scott in Spain," *Revue hispanique,* LV; Martinenche, E., *L'Espagne et le romantisme français,* Paris, 1922; Zellers, G., *La novela histórica en España, 1828-1850,* N. Y., 1938.

López Velarde, Ramón (1888-1921). Mexican teacher, journalist and poet. A regionalist of great subjective originality, he was far in advance of his times, leaving modernism behind to become the founder of a vanguardist school of poetry. An early death did not end his influence. Several of his works appeared posthumously. His most important works were: *La sangre devota,* 1916; *Zozobra,* 1919; *El minutero,* 1932; *El son del corazón,* 1932.

Cf. Villaurrutia, Xavier, (Introduction) *Poemas escogidos de Ramón López Velarde,* Mexico, 1940.

López y Fuentes, Gregorio (1895). Mexican teacher, journalist, poet and novelist. Taught among the Indians in Veracruz. Awarded the National Prize in 1935 for his novel, *El indio,* in which he portrays the problems of the indigenous population. Together with Azuela and Guzmán, one of the foremost novelists of the Mexican Revolution. Chief works: *Campamento,* 1931; *Tierra,* 1933; *¡Mi General!,* 1934; *El indio,* 1935.

Cf. Moore, E. R., "Gregorio López y Fuentes," *Mexican Life,* XVI, 1940.

López y Planes, Vicente (1784-1856). Argentine soldier, statesman and poet. Chiefly noted as the author of the Argentine national anthem, *Himno nacional* (1813). His martial ballad, *Triunfo argentino,* celebrates a glorious episode in Argentine history, the repulse of a British invasion (1810).

Cf. Rojas, R., *La literatura argentina,* Buenos Aires, 1924-1925.

Lo positivo. See under *Tamayo y Baus.*

Los de abajo. See under *Azuela, Mariano.*

Loveira, Carlos (1882-1928). Cuban novelist and political propagandist. Brought to New York as a child, he returned to Cuba in 1898 to engage in revolutionary activity. Thereafter he fought against political and social injustice in many Caribbean countries. Based on the personal experiences of a hectic revolutionary career, his novels express his radical political and social views in a virile style. His most important works were: *Los ciegos,* 1922; *Juan Criollo,* 1927.

Cf. González, M. P., "Carlos Loveira," *Revista de estudios hispánicos,* II, 1929.

Lowell, James Russell (1819-1891). The genial American poet, essayist, editor, professor and statesman is significant in Romance scholarship as the successor of Ticknor and Longfellow to the Smith Professorship at Harvard (1854-91), the last five years as professor emeritus. Not as distinguished a Spanish scholar as his two predecessors, Lowell nevertheless was a cultural mediator between Spain and the United States through his lectures on Spanish literature and in his capacity as United States Ambassador to Spain (1877-1880).

Cf. Lowell, James Russell, "Address," *Publications of the Mod-*

ern Language Association of America, V, January-March, 1890. Doyle, Henry Grattan, "Spanish Studies in the United States," *Bulletin of the Pan American Union,* LX, March, 1926.

Loyola. See under *Reformation.*

Lozana andaluza (La). See under *Delicado; picaresque novel.*

Lozano. See under *Justina.*

Luca, Esteban de (1786-1824). Argentine engineer and poet. A follower of San Martín. One of the noted hymnists of the Argentine revolutionary movement.

Cf. Rojas, R., *La literatura argentina,* Buenos Aires, 1924-1925.

Lucas de Tuy. See under *Bernardo del Carpio; crónica.*

Luceño, Tomás. See under *género chico.*

Luces de Bohemia. See under *Valle-Inclán.*

Lucha por la vida. See under *Baroja.*

Lugones, Leopoldo (1874-1938). Argentine poet. An outstanding national figure, he was Director of the Argentine Council of Education and representative of his country in the Committee on Intellectual Co-operation of the League of Nations. Ranked with his close friend Darío as the greatest of modernist writers, Lugones was a protean genius whose work and ideas constantly changed as he developed. In literature he ran the gamut from romantic irony, to realism, to the complex subjectivity and symbolism of his modernistic phase. In politics he deserted his earlier social-democratic leanings to embrace an extreme nationalism with anti-democratic overtones. From the time his first book of poetry *(Las montañas de oro,* 1897) was enthusiastically greeted by Darío in a preface, Lugones exercised a profound influence on the spiritual and intellectual character of Spanish-American letters. Chief works: *Las montañas de oro,* 1897; *Los crepúsculos del jardín,* 1905; *La guerra gaucha,* 1905; *Odas seculares,* 1910; *Historia de Sarmiento,* 1911; *El payador,* 1911; *Rubén Darío,* 1919; *Las horas doradas,* 1922; *Cuentos fatales,* 1924; *Romancero,* 1924; *Poemas solariegos,* 1928; *Romances de Río Seco,* 1930.

Cf. Uriarte, G., "The Intellectual Work of Leopoldo Lugones," *Inter-América,* II, 6, 1919; Blanco-Fombona, R., *El modernismo y los poetas modernistas,* Madrid, 1929; Onís, F., *Antología de la poesía española e hispanoamericana,* Madrid, 1934; "Numero extraordinario dedicado a Lugones," *Nosotros,* VII, 1938; McMahon,

D., "Leopoldo Lugones: A Man in Search of Roots," *Modern Philology,* 1954.

Lulio, Raimundo. See under *Juan Manuel.*

Lull, Raymond (Raimundo Lulio). See under *Juan Manuel.*

Luna, Juan de. See under *Lazarillo de Tormes.*

Luna de miel. See under *Pérez de Ayala.*

Luzán Claramunt de Suelves, Ignacio (1702-1754). Poet and chief theoretician of Neoclassicism. Born in Zaragoza; died in Madrid. Of a noble family (his full name was Ignacio Luzán y Claramunt de Suelves y Gurrea), he was educated in Italy, where he lived until 1733. He occupied a number of posts in the royal government (Ministry of Commerce, Finance, Royal Library, etc.). As secretary of the Spanish Embassy in Paris (1749-1750), he came under the influence of the great French writers (Boileau, Corneille, Racine, Voltaire). Beginning as a baroque poet, he soon deserted gongorism in favor of rational, Aristotelian precepts, taking as his models the Italian Renaissance interpreters of Aristotle's *Poetics* (Muratori, Crescimbeni, Montsignani). Luzán's great contribution to Neoclassic theory was his *Poética, o reglas de la poesía en general et de sus principales especies* (Zaragoza, 1737; Madrid, 1789). The second edition, revised by his heirs, incorporates the deceased author's additions and corrections. In poetry and drama Luzán advocated the three unities, decorum, the imitation of nature, and verisimilitude. He views the purpose of literature as morally didactic, combined with beauty and entertainment *("utile dulci").* In the epic form he took Homer as his model but condemned the paganism of classical mythology, recommending Christian themes instead. Despite his theories, Luzán was a great admirer of Lope de Vega, Calderón, Moreto and Rojas. See also under *Montiano y Luyando.*

Cf. *Poética,* 2 vols., Madrid, 1937; Cano, J., *La Poética de Luzán,* Toronto, 1928; Pellisier, R. E., *The Neoclassic Movement in Spain. . . ,* Stanford, 1918.

Lynch, Benito (1885). Argentine novelist of Irish descent. The outstanding regionalist of Argentine letters, Lynch excels in his descriptions of gaucho types and scenes, written in an unaffected, straightforward style. His realism extends to the language of his characters, his novel *El romance de un gaucho* being written entirely in gaucho jargon. His important works are: *Plata dorada,* 1909; *Los caranchos de la Florida,* 1916; *El inglés de los güesos,* 1924; *El romance de un gaucho,* 1930.

Cf. Torres Ríoseco, A., *Grandes novelistas de la América hispana,* Berkeley, U. of Cal. Press, 1941.

LL

Llama de amor viva. See under *Cruz, San Juan de la.*

Llanos y Torriglia, Félix de (1868-1949). Conservative historian and essayist. A member of the *Academia Española* and a correspondent of the *Hispanic Society.* Noted for his historical works on the period of the Catholic Kings.

Llorente, Teodoro (1826-1911). Regional lyric poet from Valencia. His best poems were written in Catalán. However, he is best known for his masterly Castilian translations of the poetry of Goethe, Heine, Byron and Hugo.

Llull, Ramón. (Lulio, Raimundo). See under *Juan Manuel.*

M

Machado y Álvarez, Antonio (1848-1892). Pioneer folklorist. Born in Santiago de Compostela; died in Seville. The father of the poets, Antonio and Manuel Machado y Ruiz. He was the founder of modern folklore studies in Spain. He edited *El folklore andaluz* (1882-1883) and the *Biblioteca de las tradiciones populares españoles* (11 vols., Seville, 1883-1886). His own work is represented in Volume 5, entitled *Estudios sobre la literatura popular* (1884). See also under *folklore.*

Cf. Faura, J., "Antonio Machado Álvarez," *Boletín de la Institución Libre de Enseñanza,* Madrid, 1893.

Machado y Ruiz, Antonio (1875-1939). The most eminent lyric poet of the Generation of 1898. Born in Seville; died in Collioure, France. The son of the famous folklorist, Antonio Machado Álvarez, and brother of the poet, dramatist and critic, Manuel Machado, he was educated in Madrid at the *Institución Libre de Enseñanza.* His life was the outwardly uneventful one of a teacher of French. From 1907 to 1936 he taught at various *institutos* (secondary schools) in Spain: Soria (1907), Baeza (1912), Segovia (1919), and Madrid (1931). He was married in 1909. In 1911 he spent a year in Paris, attending the lectures of Bédier and Bergson, and reading the French symbolists, especially Verlaine. In 1927 he was elected a member of the *Academia Española.* The two great tragedies of his life were the death of his wife, Leonor, in 1912, and the outbreak of the Spanish Civil War in 1936. Machado espoused the Republican cause, gave up his post in Madrid and went to Valencia. In 1939 he fled as a refugee to France, where he died, broken in spirit. Antonio Machado was an extremely retiring and modest person. A lover of solitude and reflection, his output was sparse but of exquisite quality. His subjectivity was already evident in his first poems: *Soledades* (1903);

Soledades, galerías y otros poemas (1907), almost austere in their directness of statement without the embellishments of rhyme and rhetoric. His *Campos de Castilla* (1912) reflects his love of the Castilian landscape and tradition, engendered during his sojourn in the ancient town of Soria. His moods and reflections are objectified in pictures of a sombre and barren landscape. A note of patriotic indignation at Spain's lethargy echoes from several of the poems in this volume, showing Machado as a true disciple of Unamuno and a product of the Generation of 1898. The volume also includes an important autobiographical poem, *Retrato,* on the death of his wife, *Una noche de verano,* and his best ballad, *La tierra de Alvar-González.* Also memorable are his lyrics to Francisco Giner de los Ríos and to Juan Ramón Jiménez. From 1917 on, various editions of Machado's work appeared under the title of *Poesías completas.* The latest of these contains his *Nuevas canciones* (1925), a critical essay entitled *Juan de Mairena* (1936), and his last poems, *La guerra* (1938). He also wrote various plays in collaboration with his brother Manuel, among them a four-act tragicomedy in verse, entitled *Desdichas de la fortuna* (1926). Although he began as a modernist under the influence of Darío, Machado later opposed the new trend toward esoteric poetry as expressed in the revival of interest in Góngora. He was too profound a thinker to yield to the general admiration of rhetorical sensuousness at the expense of spiritual essences.

Cf. *Obras completas,* 4 vols., Buenos Aires, 1942-1943; Monserrat, S., *Antonio Machado, poeta y filósofo,* Buenos Aires, 1940; Peers, E. A., *Antonio Machado,* Oxford, 1940; Pérez Ferrero, M., *Vida de Antonio Machado y Manuel,* Madrid, 1947; Trend, J. B., *Antonio Machado,* Oxford, 1953; Bula Piriz, R., *Antonio Machado 1875-1939,* Montevideo, 1954.

Machado y Ruiz, Manuel (1874-1947). Poet, dramatist and critic. Born in Seville; died in Madrid. The son of the famous folklorist, Antonio Machado y Ruiz. His early life paralleled that of his brother. After an extended sojourn in France, he returned to Madrid in 1912 and devoted himself to literature. He was a librarian, dramatic critic (for *La Libertad* of Madrid), poet and dramatist. He, too, was elected a member of the *Academia Española* (in 1938). His first collection of poems, *Alma* (1902), revealed him as a disciple of Darío and modernism. In 1907 he published his collected poems to that date with an introduction by Unamuno *(Alma, Museo, Los cantares;* Madrid). Outstanding among his other volumes of poetry are *El mal poema* (1909); *Apolo* (1911); *Ars moriendi* (1922), etc. Most important of his critical essays were *La guerra literaria* (1913) and *Un año de teatro* (1918). He wrote many plays in verse, of which the best known is *Desdichas de fortuna o Julianillo Valcárcel* (1926), done in collaboration with his brother, Antonio. Unlike his brother, Manuel was more permanently identified with the modernist movement. His poetry was frequently gay, popular and superficial. Whereas Antonio derived his inspiration from nature and achieved a personal style of profound and elemental simplicity, Manuel's poetry was essentially descriptive.

Cf. *Poesías completas,* Madrid, 1940-1942; González-Ruiz, N., "Manuel Machado y el lirismo polifónico," *Cuadernos de literatura,* Madrid, 1942; Pérez Ferrero, M., *Vida de Antonio Machado y Manuel,* Madrid, 1947.

Macías. See under *Larra.*

Madariaga, Salvador de (1886). Essayist, historian and diplomat. Born at La Coruña, Galicia. After a brief career as an engineer (1911-1916), he turned to political journalism. In 1916 he went to England, where he devoted himself to literary research and writing. His first book was published in 1920 *(Shelley and Calderon,* Oxford). From 1921 to 1927 he served as Head of the Disarmament Section of the League of Nations, thereafter taking an active part in the League's affairs. After World War II, he was associated with UNESCO, from which he resigned when Spain was admitted. He was appointed to an Oxford professorship in Spanish literature in 1927. His lectures and research at Oxford have alternated through the years with lecture tours in both North and South America and with diplomatic service for Spain (Ambassador to the U. S., 1931; to France, 1932). After the outbreak of the Spanish Civil War (1936), he returned to Oxford, where he devoted himself to research and writing in the field of Spanish-American history. An indefatigable worker on behalf of international co-operation, he has been honored by universities and governments throughout the world. In 1954-1955 he was Visiting Professor of Spanish at Princeton University. Although Madariaga has excelled in diverse genres (novels, plays, poems), historians of Spanish literature consider his most significant contribution to be his critical essays. As an accomplished stylist in Spanish, English and French, he has been the ideal interpreter of Spanish culture to the outside world. Because of his cosmopolitanism and his efforts on behalf of the "europeanization" of Spain, some critics see in him a disciple of Unamuno.

Chief works: *Ensayos angloespañoles,* Madrid, 1922 *(Shelley and Calderon,* Oxford, 1922); *The Genius of Spain,* Oxford, 1923 *(Semblanzas literarias contemporáneas,* Barcelona, 1924); *Guía del lector del Quijote,* Madrid, 1926 *(Don Quixote: An Introductory Essay in Psychology,* London, 1934); *El Hamlet de Shakespeare,* Buenos Aires, 1940; *Christopher Columbus,* London, 1939; *Hernán Cortés,* Buenos Aires, 1941; *Cuadro histórico de las Indias,* Buenos Aires, 1945; *Bolívar,* Mexico, 1951.

Cf. Aíta, A., "Un espíritu europeo: Salvador de Madariaga," *Nosotros,* LXXX, 1933; Barja, C., *Libros y autores contemporáneos,* Madrid, 1935.

Madre naturaleza (La). See under *Pardo Bazán.*

madrileñismo. See under *Mesonero Romanos.*

Maeztu, María de. See under *Maeztu, Ramiro de.*

Maeztu, Ramiro de (1875-1936). Journalist, critic and essayist of the Generation of 1898. Born in Vitoria; died in Madrid. His mother's British origin is shown in his full name, Ramiro de Maeztu y Whitney. A younger brother, María de Maeztu (1882-1947), later achieved eminence as a professor of literature in Madrid and in Buenos Aires. A lengthy sojourn abroad (1905-1919) as correspondent in England for various Spanish newspapers, and in France and Italy as Allied war correspondent, made him a thorough cosmopolitan. He was Spanish Ambassador to Argentina in 1928, and was elected to the *Academia Española* in 1934. Maeztu, together with Azorín and Baroja, was one of the leading spirits of the Generation of 1898. Beginning as a Nietzschean radical and an apostle of the "Europeanization" of Spain in his first book, *Hacia otra España* (1899), he became increasingly conservative in his views. In his *La crisis del humanismo* (1920) he explored the alternatives between authoritarianism and liberty in the modern state. Towards the end of his career he became a confirmed monarchist. His *Defensa de la hispanidad* (1934) is an apologia of monarchy, Catholicism and hispanic tradition. Active in conservative politics, he founded the *Acción Española* group and edited its periodical of the same name. After the outbreak of the Spanish Civil War (1936), he incurred the extreme disfavor of the Republican Government. Of particular interest in Spanish literary criticism is his penetrating study, *Don Quijote, Don Juan y La Celestina: ensayos de simpatía* (1926).

Cf. Azorín, "La generación del 98," *Clásicos y modernos,* Madrid, 1919; Laín Entralgo, P., *La generación del noventa y ocho,* Madrid, 1945.

Magallanes Moure, Manuel (1878-1924). Chilean artist, critic and poet. A member of the literary group known as *Los diez.* Influenced by the French symbolists and by Heine, his poetic style combines *modernista* elements with lyrical simplicity. His influence on the younger generation of Chilean poets was considerable. After his death, a collection of his poems was edited by Pedro Prado (Santiago, 1926). Chief works: *Facetas,* 1902; *Matices,* 1904; *La casa junto al mar,* 1909; *La jornada,* 1910; *¿Qué es amor?,* 1914; *Florilegio,* 1921.

Cf. "Alone" (Díaz Arrieta, Hernán), *Panorama de la literatura chilena durante el siglo XX,* Santiago, 1931.

Mágico prodigioso (El). See under *Calderón.*

Mainet. See under *Gran conquista de ultramar.*

Mairena, Juan de. See under *Machado y Ruiz, Antonio.*

malagueña. (1) A popular song or melody originating in the province of Málaga. (2) A dance to this song. (3) Verses consisting of four-line octosyllabic stanzas *(coplas)* originally sung to this melody.

Mala hierba. See under *Baroja.*

Mala yerba. See under *Azuela, Mariano.*

Malkiel, María-Rosa Lida (1910). Argentine literary scholar. Teaching posts at Buenos Aires, University of California, Ohio State University and Harvard University. Research assistant, *Revista de Filología Hispánica,* 1939-1947; Associate Editor, *Nueva Revista de Filología Hispánica,* 1948; Associate Editor, *Hispanic Review,* 1950; Member of the Royal Academy of Cordova, 1953. Author: *Juan de Mena, poeta del prerenacimiento español,* Mexico, 1950; *La idea de la fama en la Edad Media castellana,* Mexico, 1952; and of many articles in *Revista de Filología Hispánica, Romance Philology, etc.*

Mal Lara, Juan de. See under *Escuela sevillana.*

Malón de Chaide, Pedro. See under *Escuela de Salamanca.*

manchega. (1) A song or dance originating in the province of La Mancha. (2) The words to such a song. The *manchega* has the form of the *seguidilla;* i.e. four-line stanzas in which the first and third have seven syllables, and the second and fourth have five syllables. See also under *seguidilla.*

Manifiesto vertical ultraísta. The program of the ultraist movement, published in Madrid (1920) by Guillermo de Torre. See also under *ultraísmo; Torre, Guillermo de.*

Manrique, Gómez. See under *Manrique, Jorge.*

Manrique, Jorge (1440-1479). Lyric poet of the late Middle Ages. Born at Paredes de Nava; died at Garci-Muñoz, Cuenca. The son of the Count of Paredes, Rodrigo Manrique, Grand Master of the Military Order of Santiago, and a general of legendary fame. Of illustrious Castilian lineage, Jorge Manrique's great-uncle was the Marqués de Santillana, and his uncle was Gómez Manrique (1412?-1490?), as distinguished although not as famous a lyric poet as his nephew. Like his father, Jorge adopted the profession of arms and was killed in action fighting for Ferdinand and Isabella. Although he wrote many conventional lyrics *(El cancionero de Jorge Manrique,* Ed. by Foulché-Delbosc, R., *NBAE,* XXII) and is well represented in the *Cancionero general* (1511), Manrique is chiefly known for his elegy, *Coplas por la muerte de su padre don Rodrigo* (1476). Written immediately after his father's death, the *Coplas* express filial grief as well as *memento mori* thoughts on the vanity of life. Picturesque examples from history lend a nostalgic sadness to the theme of death and universalize the poet's personal sorrow. The poem consists of 43 12-line stanzas in *pie quebrado,* that is, with both 8 and 4-syllable lines. The rhyme scheme is ABCABCDEFDEF, with C and F representing the 4-syllable lines. One of the many famous translations of the *Coplas* is by Longfellow (1833). Although not original, Manrique gave perfect and enduring form to one of the major themes of his day. The implied contradiction in singing the vanity of mundane life while at the same time exalting mundane fame and glory shows Manrique as a transitional figure between the Middle Ages and the Renaissance.

Cf. *Coplas por la muerte de su padre,* (Ed) Foulché-Delbosc, R., Madrid, 1912; *Cancionero de Jorge Manrique,* (Ed.) Foulché-

Delbosc, R., *NBAE,* XXII; Krause, A., *Jorge Manrique and the Cult of Death,* Berkeley, Cal., 1937; Salinas, P., *Jorge Manrique o tradición y originalidad,* Buenos Aires, 1947.

Manual de Madrid. See under *Mesonero Romanos.*

Manuel, Don Juan. See *Juan Manuel.*

Manzanares, Teresa del. The heroine of Castillo Solórzano's picaresque novel, *La niña de los embustes* (1632).

Marcela. See under *Bretón de los Herreros.*

Marco Bruto. See under *Quevedo.*

Marcos de Obregón. See under *Espinel, Vicente.*

Mar de historias. See under *Pérez de Guzmán.*

Mare nostrum. See under *Blasco Ibáñez.*

María. See under *Isaacs, Jorge; Zorrilla y Moral.*

Mariana, Juan de (1536-1624). Historian and political economist. Born in Talavera de la Reina; died in Toledo. The natural son of Juan Martínez de Mariana, Dean of the Collegiate Church of Talavera, he was educated at Alcalá. He entered the Jesuit Order in 1554 and was ordained in 1561. From 1561 to 1574 he traveled to Rome, Paris and Flanders, preaching and lecturing. The rest of his life was spent in Toledo. He is best known for his own Spanish translation of his monumental *Historia de España* (1601), done after his previous Latin version, *Historiae de rebus hispaniae libri XXX* (1592-1605). The *Historia* extends from the earliest history of Spain to the death of Ferdinand the Catholic (1516). Taking Livy as his model, Mariana interspersed his account with legendary and anecdotal material, lending artistic variety to his historical narration. He made up for the loss of strict scientific accuracy by his admirable style and unfailing interest. The work went into several editions, was widely translated in Europe, and became a fertile source book for subsequent historical research. An independent and original thinker, Mariana anticipated Rousseau in his *De rege et regis institutione* (1598), holding that no government can be legitimate which is not based on justice and popular consent. He even went so far as to admit the justification of regicide under certain extreme circumstances. Far in advance of his time, Mariana was a defender of liberal principles. He believed in the power of reason and was opposed to violence and religious intolerance.

Cf. *Obras del Padre Mariana,* in *BAE,* XXX, XXXI; Girot, G.,

Mariana, historien, Bordeaux, 1905; Laures, J., *The Political Economy of Juan de Mariana,* N. Y., 1928; Köhler, G., *Juan de Mariana als politischer Denker,* Leipzig, 1938.

marianas. Legends or literary works dealing with the miracles or the cult of the Virgin Mary.

marinism. See *gongorismo.*

markaz. See *jarcha.*

Mármol, José (1817-1871). Argentine novelist, dramatist and poet. Born in Buenos Aires. An implacable opponent of the dictator Rosas, he was a political prisoner (1839) and exile (until 1852). After the overthrow of Rosas, Mármol returned to Argentina, where he was appointed Director of the Argentine National Library (1858-1871). His chief poem *(Rosas: El 25 de mayo de 1850)* and novel *(Amalia)* are both in the romantic-historical tradition, inspired by a virulent hatred of Rosas and of tyranny in general. With *Amalia* he introduced the genre of the historical novel in Argentine literature. Chief works: *El poeta,* 1842; *El peregrino,* 1847; *El cruzado,* 1851; *Amalia,* 1851-1855; *Poesías escogidas,* Buenos Aires, 1922.

Cf. Rojas, R., *La literatura argentina,* Buenos Aires, 1924-1925; Cuthbertson, S., *The Poetry of José Mármol,* Boulder, Colorado, 1935.

Marqués de Bradomín. The Don Juan type of hero in Valle-Inclán's tetralogy of *Sonatas.* See under *Valle-Inclán.*

Marqués de Santillana. See *Santillana.*

Marquina, Eduardo (1879-1946). Poet and dramatist. Born in Barcelona; died in New York. One of the early modernist poets, he began with several volumes of poems: *Odas* (1900); *Églogas* (1902); etc., from which echoed the notion of a universal love of all created things. In his second stage of development as a poet, he reflected the spirit of the Generation of 1898, treating social and political problems: *Canciones del momento* (1910); *Tierras de España* (1914); etc. He reached his peak in his verse plays on historic themes: *Las hijas del Cid* (1908); *En Flandes se ha puesto el sol* (1910); *El gran capitán* (1916); etc., dealing respectively with the Cid epic, the wars in Flanders under Philip II, and the career of Gonzalo Fernández de Córdova at the time of Fernando and Isabel. For these historical plays he received the award of the *Academia Española.* Outstanding among his plays in prose was his sentimental comedy, *Cuando florezcan los rosales* (1913). Although he also wrote some novels, Marquina was essentially a lyric poet in the national tradition. His poetic style was a blend of modernism and classicism. His national spirit was expressed not only in his choice of themes but also in his attempt to revive the classical form of the *teatro poético*.

Cf. *Obras completas,* 7 vols., Madrid, 1946; Sánchez, J. R., *El teatro poético,* Madrid, 1914; Juliá, E., "Eduardo Marquina, poeta lírico y dramático," *Cuadernos de literatura contemporánea,* III, IV, Madrid, 1942.

Marta y María. See under *Palacio Valdés.*

Martel, José (1883). Hispanist. Born in Spain; naturalized U. S. citizen, 1917. Various teaching posts at U. S. Naval Academy, Middlebury College, Columbia University, Rutgers University. Professor of Romance Languages, College of the City of New York; Emeritus, 1953. Knighted by the King of Spain, 1929 *(Caballero de la Orden de Isabel la Católica).* Annotated editions of *Valdés' La novela de un novelista,* Boston, 1932; *Alarcón's El Capitán Veneno,* Richmond, 1933; *Diez comedias del Siglo de Oro,* N. Y., 1939; and others.

Martí, José (1853-1895). Cuba's national hero. Born in Havana and died in action at Boca de Dos Ríos, fighting for his country's freedom. A journalist, editor, and poet, he was the outstanding figure of Cuba's struggle for independence, to which he devoted his entire career. Exiled for his revolutionary activities, he lived at various times in Mexico, Guatemala, Spain, France, New York and Venezuela, constantly writing, lecturing and engaging in political agitation in the cause of Cuban freedom. During his second residence in New York (1881-1895), he was on the Argentine consular staff and contributed his famous articles to *La Nación* in Buenos Aires. His *Versos sencillos* belong to this second New York period (1891). At this time he also met Rubén Darío, who, many years later, edited a selection of his verse *(Versos,* Buenos Aires, 1919). Although not a modernist in style, Martí is considered a precursor of the modernist movement through the inspiration of his life and the originality of his language. However, his style is so intensely personal as to defy identification with any literary school.

Cf. *Obras completas,* Havana, 1936 *et seq.;* Goldberg, I.,

Studies in Spanish American Literature, 1920; Torres-Ríoseco, A., *Precursores del modernismo,* Madrid, 1925; Meza Fuentes, R., *De Díaz Mirón a Rubén Darío,* Santiago, 1940; Lizaso, F., *Martí, místico del deber,* Buenos Aires, 1940; González, M. P., "Semblanza de José Martí," *Hispania,* XXXVI, 1953; "Homenaje a José Martí," *Revista Cubana,* 1953; *América* (La Habana), Feb., 1953; Peraza Sarausa, F., *Bibliografía martiana, 1853-1953,* Havana, 1954.

Martín Fierro. See under *Hernández, José.*

Martín Rívas. See under *Blest Gana.*

Martinenche, Ernest (1868-1939). French hispanist. Professor at the Sorbonne and at the University of Paris. Cited by the *Académie Française* for his chief works on Franco-Spanish literary relations: *La comédie espagnole en France* (1900); and *Molière et le théâtre espagnol* (1906).

Martínez de Cala. See under *Nebrija.*

Martínez de Jarabe. See under *Nebrija.*

Martínez de la Rosa, Francisco (1787-1862). Statesman and dramatist of the Romantic period. Born in Granada; died in Madrid. His full name was Francisco de Paula Martínez de la Rosa Berdejo Gómez y Arroyo. He was educated at the University of Granada, and later taught philosophy at Cádiz (1805). One of the most prominent statesmen of his time, he was diplomatic representative to England (1808); Deputy in the Cortes (1814); lived in exile in France (1823-1831); and served at various times as Minister of State (1820; 1834; 1845); Ambassador to France (1844) and to Italy (1848). In 1839 he became Director of the *Academia Española.* As a dramatist he began in the neoclassic tradition with the verse tragedies, *La viuda de Padilla* (1814) and *Edipo* (1829). The influence of Moratín is evident in his comedies, *Lo que puede un empleo* (1820) and *La niña en la casa y la madre en la máscara* (1821). During his exile in Paris he came under the influence of French Romanticism and developed new theories of the drama (*Apuntes sobre el drama histórico,* 1830), discarding verse and the unities. He successfully applied these theories to his historical, prose dramas, *Abén Humeya* (in French, 1830; in Spanish, 1836) and *La conjuración de Venecia* (written in Paris; staged in Madrid, 1834); the former based on the revolt of the Moors (1568) under Philip II; the latter based on an abortive revolt in Venice (1310). Both plays are characterized by exotic local color, romantic love, intrigue, and historical parallels to the contemporary political scene. Anticipating Larra and Rivas, Martínez de la Rosa introduced the Romantic drama to Spain.

Cf. *Obras dramáticas,* (Ed.) Sarrailh, J., Madrid, 1933; Sosa, L. de, *Martínez de la Rosa,* Madrid, 1931; Shearer, J. F., *The "Poética" and "Apéndices" of Martínez de la Rosa,* Princeton, 1941.

Martínez de Toledo. See *Arcipreste de Talavera.*

Martínez Ruiz, José. See *Azorín.*

Martínez Sierra, Gregorio (1881-1948). Poet and dramatist. Born and died in Madrid. At 17 his first volume of poetry, *El poema del trabajo* (1898), was hailed by Benavente. Modernist influence was evident in his verse, *Flores de escarcha* (1900), his short stories, *Pascua florida* (1901), novels, *Tú eres la paz* (1906), etc.; and in the symbolism of his first play, *Teatro de ensueño* (1905). Also allied to the modernist trend were the literary reviews he founded (*Helios, Vida Moderna, Renacimiento,* etc.). Himself the translator of Shakespeare and of Maeterlinck, he published translations of Barrie, Shaw, Molnar, Pirandello, etc., as Editor of the *Renacimiento* publishing house. He introduced the art theater to Spain as Director of the *Teatro Eslava* in Madrid. His dance suite, *El amor brujo,* became world famous through the music of Manuel de Falla. Like Benavente and the Álvarez Quintero brothers, he ushered in the revival of the modern Spanish theater. Among his popular successes were: *La sombra del padre* (1909); *Lirio entre espinas* (1911); *Canción de cuna* (1911); *Mamá* (1912); *Don Juan de España* (1921); *Mary lo insoportable* (1926); etc. His first theatrical triumph, *Canción de cuna,* remained his most famous play. In its New York performance as "Cradle Song," acknowledgment was made to Martínez Sierra's wife as the co-author. The play depicts the pathetic love which the nuns in a convent lavish on a foundling girl as she grows to womanhood under their maternal care. Martínez Sierra's style is full of delicate nuances. His psychological insight with regard to his female characters undoubtedly owed much to the collaboration of his wife, María de la O Lejárraga.

Cf. *Obras selectas,* 3 vols., Ed. with intro. by Sáinz de Robles, F. C., Madrid, 1948; *Plays of G. Martínez Sierra* (in English),

(Ed.) Underhill, J. G. and Granville-Barker, H., N. Y., 1915-1923; González Blanco, A., *Los dramaturgos españoles contemporáneos,* Valencia, 1917.

Martínez Zuviría, Gustavo. See *Wast, Hugo.*

Mártir, Pedro. See under *humanism.*

Martorell, Johanot. See under *Tirant lo Blanch.*

Más pesa el rey que la sangre. See under *Vélez de Guevara.*

Más vale llegar a tiempo. See under *Zorrilla y Moral.*

matla. The theme verse or stanza of the *zéjel* verse form, repeated and developed in subsequent stanzas. See under *zéjel.*

Matto de Turner, Clorinda (1854-1909). Peruvian novelist. Wife of an English doctor. Matto de Turner was a pioneer in the field of the social thesis novel dealing with the Indian problem. A militant crusader for social reform, she is chiefly known for her "indianista" novel, *Aves sin nido* (1889), which indignantly exposes the injustices perpetrated on the Indians by the landowning classes of Peru.

Cf. Meléndez, C., *La novela indianista en Hispanoamérica,* Madrid, 1934.

Maynete. See under *Gran conquista de ultramar.*

Mayor encanto, amor (El). See under *Calderón.*

Mead, Robert G. Jr. (1913). American hispanist, literary scholar and authority on Spanish American literature. Associate Professor, University of Connecticut. Author of "Cronología de la obra en prosa de Manuel González Prada," *Revista Hispánica Moderna,* XII, 1947; "El moderno pensamiento hispanoamericano," *Revista Hispánica Moderna,* XVI, 1950; "Manuel González Prada y la prosa española," *Revista Iberoamericana,* XVII, 1952; and many other articles on Latin American subjects.

Médico de su honra (El). See under *Calderón.*

Medina, Francisco de. See under *Escuela sevillana.*

Meditaciones del Quijote. See under *Ortega y Gasset.*

Medrano, Francisco de. See under *Escuela sevillana.*

Mejor alcalde, el rey (El). See under *Vega, Lope de.*

Meléndez Valdés, Juan (1754-1817). Neoclassic poet, professor and jurist. Born in Ribera del Fresno, near Badajoz; died in Montpellier, France. He studied law at the University of Salamanca, where he later became professor of the humanities (1781). Active in the literary life of his time, he took part in the *concursos* of the

Academia Española and was the friend of Fray Diego González, Jovellanos, Cadalso, Quintana, and others. He served as a magistrate in Zaragoza and in Valladolid, and occupied a number of public offices, achieving a reputation as a forensic speaker. However, he vacillated in his politics between Spain and France during the crisis of 1808, narrowly escaping execution by the Nationalists; and after Spain had gained her independence, was obliged to flee to France, where he spent the last few years of his life. In his early period he wrote anacreontics and eclogues (cf. his eclogue, *Batilo,* awarded the prize of the *Academia Española* in 1780); and he also cultivated the *romance (La mañana de San Juan; Doña Elvira; Rosana en los fuegos;* etc.). In this period he was influenced by the Greek and Latin poets, by Luis de León, Herrera, Garcilaso, and by the English poets, Thomson and Young. In his second period, he turned to the didactic and philosophic ode *(La gloria de las artes; La noche y la soledad; La presencia de Dios; El fanatismo;* etc.), influenced by his friend and mentor, Jovellanos, by Alexander Pope, and by his wide reading in moral philosophy (Locke, Rousseau, etc.). Meléndez Valdés has been called the only true Spanish poet of the 18th century. His form was polished and his style balanced, lucid and harmonious. He is remembered more for the delicacy and sentimentality of his early bucolic poetry, forming a transition between neoclassicism and romanticism, rather than for his philosophical odes. In the poetically barren 18th century, he stands forth as the only link between the great poets of the Golden Age and the lyricists of the 19th and 20th centuries.

Cf. *Poesías* in *BAE,* LXIII; *idem,* (Ed. Salinas, P.), Madrid, 1925; Colford, W. E., *Juan Meléndez Valdés: A Study in the Transition from Neo-Classicism to Romanticism in Spanish Poetry,* N. Y., 1942.

Melibea. See under *Celestina.*

Memorias de un setentón. See under *Mesonero Romanos.*

Mena, Juan de (1411-1456). Renaissance poet and classical scholar. Born in Córdoba; died in Torrelaguna. Little is known of his life except through a few scattered references by editors of his works. The son of a minor Cordovan jurist, he was educated at Cordova, Salamanca and Rome. Unlike his friend Santillana, Mena lived a quiet life dedicated entirely to literature. His Italian sojourn subjected him to the influence of classical and Italian authors (Lucan, Virgil, Dante). He was the first translator of the *Iliad* into Spanish *(Homero romanceado).* Because of his popularization of the *arte mayor* meter, he was called *"El Ennio español"* (after Quintus Ennius, who introduced the hexameter to Latin poetry); and the great Nebrija linked his name with Vergil in his *Gramática castellana.* Mena's classical scholarship gained him the post of Latin secretary to Juan II, to whom he later dedicated his masterpiece, *El laberinto.* His early poems were typical of the erudite versifying of his time and, although of slight merit, were included in the various *Cancioneros* of the 14th and 15th centuries (Baena, Stúñiga, Castillo, etc.). Mena's best work was a long poem in *arte mayor,* entitled *El laberinto de fortuna* (1444), called by subsequent editors *Las trescientas* because it consisted of about that number of 8-line stanzas *(coplas).* (Ed. by Hernán Nuñez, Seville, 1499; by Brocense, Seville, 1582; etc.). Inspired by Vergil and by Dante, the poem is an allegory of the three wheels of Fortune, each of which has seven circles representing chastity (Diana), sin (Mercury), sensuality (Venus), wisdom (Phoebus), military glory (Mars), royalty (Jupiter), and statesmanship (Saturn). Transported by Providence into these circles, the poet meets illustrious men of past and present. Both the artificial framework and the repetitious meter are tedious, despite some interesting passages. Nevertheless, Mena's achievement was the establishment of *arte mayor* as the standard erudite meter and the development of a special poetic language, enriched by Latinisms. In this, his influence extended to the erudite poets and the humanists of the entire following century. See also *arte mayor.*

Cf. *Poesías* in *Cancionero castellano del siglo XV,* (Ed.) Foulché-Delbosc, R., *NBAE,* XIX; Post, C. R., "The Sources of Juan de Mena," *Romanic Review, III; El laberinto de fortuna o las trescientas,* (Ed.) Blecua, J. M., Madrid, 1943; Lida de Malkiel, R., *Juan de Mena, poeta del prerenacimiento español,* Mexico, 1950.

Mendoza. See under *Hurtado de Mendoza.*

Menéndez Pidal, Ramón (1869). The dean of Spanish literary scholars and the most eminent of all contemporary Romance philologists. He was born in La Coruña. A pupil of the great Menéndez y Pelayo, he studied at the Universities of Madrid and Toulouse.

His exemplary philological studies on the *Cid* and on the *Infantes de Lara* received special citations from the *Academia Española* in 1893 and 1896 respectively. He was Professor of Romance Philology at the University of Madrid from 1899 to 1939. In 1902 he was elected to the *Academia Española,* and he became its Director in 1925. He was named Director of the *Centro de Estudios Históricos* in 1910. In 1914 he founded and edited the *Revista de filología española.* For his extraordinary achievements in Romance philology he has received honorary degrees from the Universities of Toulouse, Oxford, Tübingen, Paris, Louvain, Brussels, etc., and decorations from many foreign governments. Among his famous pupils have been Américo Castro, Federico de Onís, Navarro Tomás, A. G. Solalinde, Alfonso Reyes, etc. Menéndez Pidal's great achievement has been to introduce scientific method into Spanish philological, linguistic and historical research. Most outstanding has been his work in reconstructing and in editing medieval folk-epics, ballads, dramas and poems, and in tracing the development of the Spanish language from its origins to the 11th century. The vast scope of his contributions can be seen from the partial bibliography below.

Chief works: *La leyenda de los Infantes de Lara,* 1896; *Gramática histórica española,* 1904; *Cantar de Mío Cid: texto, gramática y vocabulario,* 1908-1912; *L'Épopée castillane à travers la littérature espagnole* (tr. by H. Mérimée), 1910; *El romancero español,* 1910; *Primera crónica general,* 1916; *Poesía juglaresca y juglares,* 1924; *Orígenes del español,* 1926; *Flor nueva de romances viejos,* 1928; *La España del Cid,* 1929; *Romancero Hispánico (Hispano-Portugués, Americano y Sefardí),* 2 vols., Madrid, 1953.

Cf. *Homenaje a Menéndez Pidal,* 3 vols., Madrid, 1925; Serís, H., *Bibliografía de Menéndez Pidal,* Madrid, 1931.

Menéndez y Pelayo, Marcelino (1856-1912). Spain's greatest historian and critic of literature. Born and died in Santander. Inspired at the University of Barcelona by Lloréns and Milá y Fontanals, he completed his studies in philosophy and literature at the University of Madrid. Gifted with a prodigious memory, critical acumen and esthetic sensitivity, intimately conversant with the major European languages (Greek, Latin, French, Italian, English, German) and their literatures, indefatigable in research, lecturing and writing, he dominated Spanish scholarship in the 19th century. From 1878 to 1898 he was Professor of Spanish literature at the University of Madrid. In 1881 he was elected to the *Academia Española.* He became Director of the *Biblioteca Nacional* in 1898. He was Librarian (1892) and Director (1910) of the *Academia de la Historia.* Twice he served as a Deputy in the Cortes (1884; 1891). His vast library, a gift to the City of Santander, is preserved in his memory. Despite his cosmopolitan learning, Menéndez y Pelayo was profoundly nationalistic and religious, his devotion to country and Church limiting his universality as a critic (*La ciencia español,* 1880; *Historia de los heterodoxos en España,* 1880). However, he provided Spanish scholarship with a sense of the unity of Spanish culture and with a high standard of scientific research and esthetic criticism (*Historia de las ideas estéticas en España,* 1883-1891). He provided critical editions of the great Spanish masters (*Calderón y su teatro,* 1881; *Teatro de Lope de Vega,* 1890-1902, etc.), and laid the foundations for the history of Spanish-American literature (*Historia de la poesía hispanoamericana,* 1911-1912). His interests included classical influences in Spain (*Horacio en España,* 1877) and the poetry of the Middle Ages (*Historia de la poesía castellana en la edad media,* 1911). Among his other great works are: *Estudios de crítica literaria* (1884-1908); *Antología de poetas líricos castellanos* (1890-1908); and *Orígenes de la novela* (1905-1910).

Cf. *Obras completas,* (Ed. by Sánchez Reyes, Artigas, González Palencia), Madrid, 1940-1950; Bonilla y San Martín, A., "Menéndez y Pelayo: bibliografía," in *NBAE,* XXI; Artigas, M., *La vida y la obra de Menéndez y Pelayo,* Zaragoza, 1939; Torre, G. de, *Menéndez Pelayo y las dos Españas,* Buenos Aires, 1943; Laín Entralgo, P., *Menéndez Pelayo, historia de sus problemas intelectuales,* Madrid, 1944; Cayuela, A. M., *Menéndez Pelayo, orientador de la cultura española,* Madrid, 1954.

menestril. The musician as distinguished from the poet in medieval verse and song. The term *menestril* replaced the term *juglar* in the 14th century. Compare *juglar.*

Mera, Juan León de (1832-1894). Ecuadorean poet and novelist. A specialist in Indian folklore. Influenced by Chateaubriand and Cooper, he wrote one of Ecuador's outstanding Indian novels of the romantic period, *Cumandá* (1871). It has a rambling plot and its Indian characters are stereotyped models of the "noble savage," but the background is authentic.

Cf. Barrera, I. J., *Literatura ecuatoriana,* Quito, 1939.

Mérimée, Ernest (1846-1924). French hispanist. Professor at the University of Toulouse. Founder of the *Instituto Francés de Madrid.* His first important work was a study of Quevedo (*Essai sur la vie et les oeuvres de Francisco de Quevedo,* Paris, 1885). The introduction and notes to his critical edition of Guillén de Castro's *Las mocedades del Cid* provide an important source for the influence on Corneille's *Cid* (*Première partie des mocedades del Cid,* Toulouse, 1890). Mérimée was a constant contributor to the *Revue hispanique* and other Romance journals, his studies ranging through such diverse authors as Jovellanos, Meléndez Valdés, Blasco Ibáñez, etc. Valuable for its detailed bibliographical notes is his *Précis d'histoire de la littérature espagnole,* Paris, 1908; 1922 (Engl. trsl. by Morley, *A History of Spanish Literature,* N. Y., 1930). His son, Henri Mérimée (1878-1926), was also a distinguished Spanish scholar (Cf. his *L'art dramatique à Valencia,* Toulouse, 1913).

Cf. Martinenche, E., *Les études hispaniques,* Paris, 1915.

Mérimée, Henri. See under *Mérimée, Ernest.*

Mesonero Romanos, Ramón de (1803-1882). *Costumbrista* writer, editor and historian of the Spanish theater. His pen-name was "*El Curioso Parlante.*" Born and died in Madrid. The son of a wealthy landowner, he was educated at the *Instituto de San Isidro.* At his father's death in 1820, Mesonero Romanos inherited an estate sufficient to make him independent for life. He devoted himself thenceforth to his major interest, the City of Madrid. Except for a few years of travel in Spain and in Europe (1822; 1833; 1840), his life was spent in his native city, exploring its physical and cultural features, its people, history and institutions. He wrote about little else, from his guide book, *Manual de Madrid* (1831) and its later revision, *El antiguo Madrid* (1861), to his collections of *cuadros de costumbres* (sketches of customs, types and manners), *Panorama matritense* (1832-1835), *Escenas matritenses* (1836-1842), *and Tipos y caracteres: bocetos de cuadros de costumbres, por El Curioso Parlante* (1843-1862), culled from a periodical which he had founded in 1836, *Semanario* *pintoresco español,* and from the famous journal, *Cartas españolas.* Through these genial and animated sketches of early 19th century Madrid life, he created what may be called the "cult of Madrid" *(madrileñismo).* For his scholarly work in the early Spanish drama of the Lope de Vega era, he was elected to the *Academia Española* in 1847. His editions of these playwrights appeared in *BAE,* XLIII, XLV, XLVII, XLIX (1857-1859). In 1864 he was named official Historian of the City of Madrid. He presented his library to the City in 1876; and in gratitude, the municipal fathers named after him the street where he was born. After Larra, Mesonero Romanos ranks with Estébanez Calderón as the best of the *costumbrista* writers of the 19th century. His *Memorias de un setentón, natural y vecino de Madrid* (1880), have been a rich source for subsequent writers, both Spanish and European.

Cf. Cotarelo, E., "Elogio biográfico de don Ramón de Mesonero Romanos," *Boletín de la Real Academia Española,* XII, 1925; Correa Calderón, E., *Los costumbristas españoles,* Madrid, 1948.

mester de clerecía. A school of erudite poets who wrote from the early 13th through the beginning of the 14th century. The term *mester* is derived from Latin *ministerium,* "office" or "function"; hence the full term means "the function of the cleric," in which "cleric" has the meaning of "scholar" or "learned man." The term was used for the first time in the *Libro de Alexandre* (13th century). Among the great *clerecía* poets and their works were: Gonzalo de Berceo (early 13th century), *Milagros de nuestra Señora;* Juan Ruiz, Archpriest of Hita (1283?-1350?), *Libro de buen amor;* and Pedro López de Ayala (1332-1407), *Rimado de Palacio.* Famous anonymous works of the *mester de clerecía* school were a number of 13th century poems: *Libro de Apolonio; Libro de Alexandre; Historia troyana;* and *Poema de Fernán González,* the only *clerecía* poem on an epic theme. Another anonymous *clerecía* poem is the *Poema de Yuçuf,* written in the early 14th century in the Spanish language but using the Arabic alphabet (*aljamiada* literature). The *clerecía* poets imitated the alexandrines of the French *chansons de geste,* but the form they developed was *cuaderna vía,* monorhymed quatrains of regular 14-syllable verses with middle caesura. The poets of this school found their inspiration in religious themes or in sources of classical antiquity. See also *cuaderna vía.*

Cf. Menéndez y Pelayo, M., *Antología de poetas líricos castellanos,* 2nd ed., Madrid, 1944; Fits-Gerald, J. D., *Versification of the Cuaderna Vía,* N. Y., 1905; Henríquez Ureña, P., *La versificación irregular en la poesía castellana,* Madrid, 1920; Trend, J. B., *Berceo,* Cambridge, 1952.

mester de gauchería. See under *gaucho literature.*

mester de juglaría. A school of poet minstrels *(juglares)* in the 12th and 13th centuries, preceding the *mester de clerecía* school. The *juglares* were anonymous popular poets. Their songs include most of the early folk-epics and ballads of Spanish literature. The form used by the *juglares* is also called *mester de clerecía,* verses of irregular length, averaging 16 syllables, with assonant rhyme and middle caesura. In addition to the various *cantares de gesta* (*Poema de mío Cid, Bernardo del Carpio, Fernán González,* etc.), *juglaría* poetry includes the popular medieval dispute or debate (*Disputa del alma y el cuerpo, Razón de amor, Elena y María,* etc.), and profane and pious biographies (*Santa María Egipcíaca, Libro de los tres reyes de oriente,* etc.). See also under *juglar; cantar de gesta.*

Cf. Menéndez Pidal, R., *La primitiva poesía lírica española,* Madrid, 1909; *idem, L'Épopée castillane,* Paris, 1910; *idem, Poesía juglaresca y juglares,* Madrid, 1924.

Metal de los muertos (El). See under *Espina, Concha.*

metátesis. (Eng. *metathesis*). (1) In rhetoric, a change of word order. (2) In linguistics, a change of the sequence of sounds or letters either within one word or between two words. It is a phenomenon of linguistic change. Examples: parabola > *palabra;* periculum > *periglo* > *peligro.*

metonimia. (Eng. *metonymy*). A rhetorical figure in which one name is used with the intention that another be understood. Example: Cervantes (for his works).

Micer Francisco Imperial. See under *decir; Imperial.*

Milagros de Nuestra Señora. See under *Berceo.*

Milá y Fontanals, Manuel (1818-1884). Romance philologist, literary critic, historian and folklorist. From 1846 on, he was professor of esthetics and of the history of literature at the University of Barcelona. Among his pupils was Menéndez y Pelayo, who later edited his works (*Obras completas,* 8 vols., Barcelona, 1888-1896). Milá y Fontanals was the originator of modern Spanish studies in comparative literature and a pioneer in the use of scientific method in literary research. His major works were: *De los trovadores en España* (1861); *De la poesía heroico-popular castellana* (1874); and *Romancerillo catalán* (1884)

Cf. Romera-Navarro, M., *Historia de la literatura española,* 2a. ed., Boston, 1949.

Milesian tale. See *novela bizantina.*

Millán, Leonor de. See under *Herrera, Fernando de.*

Mingo Revulgo. See under *copla.*

Miñano, Sebastián de. See under *costumbrismo.*

Miró, Gabriel (1879-1930). Impressionistic novelist and short-story writer. Born in Alicante; died in Madrid. He studied law at the University of Granada, and during his literary career, occupied various minor posts in the municipal and state governments. His first full length novel, *Del vivir,* appeared in 1904. One of the most consummate prose artists among the postmodernist writers, Miró expressed an innate pessimism in a symbolistic and impressionistic style. His forte was not narrative but rather descriptive. Impressions, memories, persons, landscapes and intimate confessions round out the contemplative atmosphere of his novels and short stories. Miró's plastic descriptive powers emerge especially in his religious novels, in which children, saints and lepers form a bas-relief pageant reminiscent of medieval art. The titles of his best known novels are: *Figuras de la Pasión del Señor,* 1916; *Libro de Sigüenza,* 1917; *Nuestro Padre San Daniel,* 1921; *El obispo leproso,* 1926.

Cf. *Obras completas,* Madrid, 1943; Diego, G., "Gabriel Miró," *Cuadernos de Literatura Contemporánea,* Madrid, 1942.

Misericordia. See under *Pérez Galdós.*

misterio. (1) A medieval religious play or drama. (2) Any of the passages or episodes in medieval drama dealing with the life, passion and death of Christ.

Misterio de los Reyes Magos. See *Auto de los Reyes Magos.*

mística. See *mysticism.*

Mistral, Gabriela (1889). Pseudonym of Lucila Godoy Alcayaga. Chilean poetess, born in Vicuña, Chile. A teacher, lecturer, diplomatic and cultural representative of her country, she first attracted literary acclaim with her *Sonetos de muerte* (1915). At various stages in her career she was Headmistress of the *Liceo de Niñas* in Punta Arenas, Professor of Spanish at the University of Chile, Professor of Spanish at Barnard College in New York City, and in the consular service of her country in Spain, Portugal, and Brazil. In 1922 she visited New York, where her best-known collection of poems appeared (*Desolación,* published by the "Instituto de las Españas"). Indisputably one of the great lyrical geniuses of Spanish letters, she was awarded the Nobel Prize for Literature in 1945. As great a personality as she is a poetess, Gabriela Mistral expresses in her poetry a boundless love for children, a lyrical glorification of the holy state of motherhood, and a vibrant compassion for the frustrated and the downtrodden. As the result of the tragic death of her fiancé (1907), she never married but directed her thwarted love and maternal instincts to the education and welfare of children. Her poetry is distinctive for its musical quality and great emotional depth, verging at times on mysticism.

Cf. Blackwell, A. S., *Some Spanish-American Poets,* Philadelphia, 1927; Onís, F. de, *Antología de la poesía española e hispanoamericano,* Madrid, 1934; Pinilla, N., *Biografía de Gabriela Mistral,* Santiago, 1946; Iglesias, A., *Gabriela Mistral y el modernismo en Chile,* Santiago, 1949.

Mitre, Bartolomé (1821-1906). Argentine soldier, statesman, historian and poet. Born and died in Buenos Aires. Served in the Bolivian and Uruguayan armies, participated in the siege of Montevideo (1842-1851), and fought against Rosas (1852) and Urquiza (1861). After national union had been achieved, he was elected the first president of Argentina in 1862, serving till 1868. Founded *La Nación* in 1869. Like Sarmiento, who succeeded him in office, Mitre was a poet and scholar. He wrote political verses and gaucho ballads *(Rimas),* published philological works on Indian languages and literature (*Ollantay,* etc.), and histories of South American independence *(Historia de Belgrano, de San Martín).* Chief works: *Rimas,* 1846; *Soledad,* 1847; *Historia de Belgrano y de la independencia argentina,* 1858; *Historia de San Martín y de la emancipación americana,* 1871; *Ollantay, estudio sobre el drama quechua,* 1881.

Cf. Rowe, L. S., *Bartolomé Mitre, 1821-1921,* Washington, 1921; Rojas, R., *La literatura argentina,* Buenos Aires, 1924-1925.

Mocedades del Cid (Las). See under *Cid; Castro, Guillén de.*

Mocedades de Rodrigo (Las). See under *Rodrigo el godo.*

modernismo. The literary movement which, at the end of the 19th century, initiated the contemporary period in Spanish literature. The intellectual godfathers of *modernismo* were Ángel Ganivet (*Idearium español,* 1897) and Miguel de Unamuno (*En torno al casticismo,* 1902). *Modernismo* overlapped the movement known as the *Generación del 98.* The latter was primarily a spiritual and historical phenomenon resulting from the Spanish *débâcle* of 1898. *Modernismo,* on the other hand, was predominantly a literary movement reflecting the new spirit in poetry emanating from the French symbolists and Parnassians (Baudelaire, Verlaine, *etc.*) and from South America (Rubén Darío, Gutiérrez Nájera, José Martí, *etc.*). The immediate impetus was provided by Rubén Darío *(Cantos de vida y esperanza,* 1905), who influenced Spanish poets and who propagated *modernista* theories, especially during his second visit to Spain in 1898. The poets who, in a strict sense, belonged to the *escuela modernista* were Antonio Machado (1875-1939), Juan Ramón Jiménez (b. 1881), and Francisco Villaespesa (1877-1936). In addition there were the novelist Ramón del Valle Inclán (1866-1936), and the dramatists Jacinto Benavente (1866-1955) and Martínez Sierra (1881-1947). *Modernismo* was a reaction against naturalism in literature, against bourgeois conformity and against fossilized standards. It strove for new values and for a renewed spirituality. Creativity, individualism and subjectivity were its hallmarks. Free verse and internal rhythms were its poetic media. Beginning under French influence with an ivory-tower esthetics of art for art's sake, it developed into a mature awareness of hispanic tradition. Its final stage was marked by a return to earlier Spanish verse forms. See also under *Darío.*

Cf. Blanco-Fombona, R., *El modernismo y los poetas modernistas,* Madrid, 1929; Del Río, A., *Historia de la literatura española,* N. Y., 1948; Onís, F. de, "Sobre el concepto del modernismo," *Panorama,* IX, 1954; Henríquez Ureña, M., *Breve historia del modernismo,* Mexico, 1954.

modismo. An idiom. An expression peculiar to or characteristic of a certain language.

mojiganga. A short dramatic sketch of a hilarious nature. It was one of the minor dramatic genres cultivated by Moreto and others during the classical period. The term is derived from the name of a public festival featuring animal masks and burlesque mummery.

Molinero de Arcos (El). See under *Alarcón y Ariza.*

molinosismo. The mystical doctrine of *quietismo,* as expounded by Miguel de Molinos (1628-1696). See under *quietismo.*

"monstruo de la naturaleza". "Prodigy of nature". Cervantes' epithet for Lope de Vega. The phrase occurs in the prologue to Cervantes' *Ocho comedias y ocho entremeses* (1615).

Monstruo de los jardines (El). See under *Calderón.*

Montalvo, Juan (1832-1889). Ecuadorian political journalist. Born in Ambato, Ecuador, and died in Paris. As a young man he was employed in his country's foreign service in Rome. At odds with Ecuador's dictator, García Moreno, he assailed him, his successors, and the notion of dictatorship in general in a series of impassioned essays printed in various journals which he edited *(El Cosmopolita, El Regenerador).* A political exile, he lived in Panama and in Paris, where he was editor and sole contributor of *El Espectador* (1886-1888). He also wrote an interesting imitation of *Don Quixote.* Chief works: *Catilinarias,* 1880; *Siete tratados,* 1882; *Capítulos que se le olvidaron a Cervantes* (posthumously published, 1895).

Cf. Marrera, I. J., *Literatura ecuatoriana,* Quito, 1939.

Montañeses del Parnaso. An academy founded in Valencia in 1616 by Guillén de Castro. It was the successor to the *Academia de los Nocturnos.*

Monteagudo, Bernardo de (1785-1825). Argentine political journalist. Active in the revolutionary movements of Argentina, Peru and Chile. Associated at various times with San Martín and Bolívar. As editor of various revolutionary journals, he championed the idea of an independent South American confederation. His articles and essays are in the best tradition of political journalism, distinctive for their logical argument supported by fact and inspired by the ideals of freedom. His *Obras políticas* were edited by Ricardo Rojas (Buenos Aires, 1916).

Cf. Rojas, R., *La literatura argentina,* Buenos Aires, 1924-1925.

Montemayor, Jorge de (1520?-1561). Poet and musician. Founder of the pastoral novel in Spain. Born in Portugal; died in Italy. The exact date of his birth and information as to his antecedents are not known. He was a Portuguese of humble origin, but well versed in Italian and Spanish literature. By profession a musician, he served in that capacity in the entourage of the Infanta Juana, the Spanish wife of Prince John of Portugal. After Prince John's death, Montemayor accompanied his patroness to Spain in 1554. That same year he visited the Netherlands, supposedly in the service of Philip II. He was killed in a duel in Italy. Montemayor is noted as the author of the first pastoral romance in Spain. Entitled *Diana* (Valencia, *ca.* 1559), it was an enormous success in court circles both in Spain and abroad. It is a rambling story of the frustrated loves of various shepherds and shepherdesses, their wanderings and adventures, nymphs and necromancers, magic love potions, miraculous encounters, and a final festive reunion of the chief characters, Sireno and Diana, amid the wondrous surroundings of the Temple of Diana. The romance is written in narrative prose interspersed with charming lyrics. Of its seven chapters *(libros),* the fourth *(Abindarráez y Jarifa)* was included by an editor after Montemayor's death and does not belong to the novel. Itself inspired by the Italian poet Sannazaro's *Arcadia* (1481; Spanish trsl., 1547), Montemayor's *Diana* influenced Sir Philip Sidney's *Arcadia* (1590) and Honoré d'Urfée's *Astrée* (1610-1619). It was also the source of the story of Felix and Felismena in Shakespeare's *Two Gentlemen of Verona* (1595). The most famous among its many sequels and imitations were the *Segunda parte de la Diana* by Alonzo Pérez, and the *Diana enamorada* by Gaspar Gil Polo (both 1564).

Cf. "Los siete libros de la Diana," (Ed. Menéndez y Pelayo), *NBAE,* VII; (Ed. López Estrada), Madrid, 1946; Menéndez y Pelayo, M., *Orígenes de la novela,* vol. 4, Buenos Aires, 1946; Rennert, H. A., *The Spanish Pastoral Romances,* Phila., 1912.

Monterde, Francisco (1894). Mexican literary critic and anthologist. Professor of Literature and Chief of the Bureau of Publications, *Universidad Nacional de México.* Director Técnico of the *Revista Iberoamericana.* Principal works: *Manuel Gutiérrez Nájera; Bibliografía del teatro en México; Cuentos mexicanos; Algunos* *novelistas mexicanos; Antología de poetas y prosistas hispano-americanos modernos.*

Cf. *Hispania,* XXXVI, 1953.

Montiano y Luyando, Agustín (1697-1764). Neoclassical critic and dramatist. Born in Valladolid; died in Madrid. He studied at Zaragoza. Shortly after his election to the *Academia Española,* he founded the *Real Academia de la Historia* (1737), and became its first director. He was secretary of the *Academia del buen gusto* (1749-1751) and played a leading role in championing the principles of Luzán (French neoclassicism) against Cervantes and Lope de Vega. He expounded his neoclassic theories in *Discurso sobre las tragedias españolas* (2 vols., 1750; 1753). In addition to the sacrosanct three unities, he insisted on a fourth, the unity of character; *i.e.* there should be only one predominant trait to a character. To exemplify his theories, he appended two formal and undistinguished tragedies to his *Discursos (Virginia,* 1750; *Ataulfo,* 1753).

Cf. Menéndez y Pelayo, M., *Historia de las ideas estéticas en España,* Madrid, 1883; Alonso Cortés, N., "Don Agustín de Montiano," *Revista Crítica,* 1915.

Morada del cielo. See under *León, Luis de.*

Moradas (Las). See under *Teresa de Jesús.*

Moraes, Francisco de. See under *Palmerín cycle.*

moralidad. (Eng. *morality).* A term for medieval drama, generally dealing with a debate between allegorical characters representing virtues and vices.

Moratín, Leandro Fernández de (1760-1828). Neoclassical dramatist, critic and translator of Molière and Shakespeare. Born in Madrid; died in Paris. He was the son of Nicolás Fernández de Moratín (1737-1780), a greater poet but lesser dramatist. Because of his artistic talents, Leandro was apprenticed to a jeweler, but he soon turned to literary pursuits when his early efforts were cited by the *Real Academia Española* and he received financial aid from various ecclesiastical and noble patrons. From 1790 to 1796 he traveled to France, England and Italy. Back in Spain, he was appointed Chief Librarian of the *Biblioteca Real* (later, the *Biblioteca Nacional)* by King José. Later, Moratín made the political error of siding with Joseph Bonaparte, and at the latter's fall, was obliged to flee to France, where he spent the remainder of his life in exile. As a critic, he is noted for his *La derrota de los pedantes* (1789), a prose satire directed against literary affectation. His *Orígenes del teatro español,* a fragment not published until 1830, was a pioneer attempt to trace the development of the early Spanish drama. He was the first Spanish translator of *Hamlet* (1795)—an earlier version by Ramón de la Cruz in 1772 was only an adaptation. Moratín also wrote some excellent adaptations of Molière's plays *(École des maris; Le médecin malgré lui;* etc.). In all Moratín wrote five original plays, many of them not produced or published until after his death: *El viejo y la niña* (1790), *El barón* (1803), *La mojigata* (1804), all in verse; and *La comedia nueva o El café* (1792), and *El sí de las niñas* (1806), in prose; the latter his masterpiece. One of the first of modern thesis plays, its argument is that marriages arranged by parents are doomed without the consent of their children. Although greatly influenced by Molière, Moratín created genuine Spanish types. His dialogue is natural and his humor in good taste. His choice of the three-act form is in the tradition of the great Spanish dramatists. The small number of characters and the development of the thesis through dialogue rather than through lengthy sermonizing, lend the play a dramatic concentration unequaled in the 18th century theater.

Cf. *Obras,* in *BAE,* II; *Teatro,* (Ed.) Ruiz Morcuende, F., Madrid, 1924; idem, *Vocabulario de las obras de Moratín,* Madrid, 1946.

Moratín, Nicolás Fernández de. See under *Moratín, Leandro Fernández de.*

Morel-Fatio, Alfred (1850-1924). French hispanist. Together with Mérimée, the most eminent Spanish scholar in France at the close of the 19th century. He was instrumental in founding the French hispanic journal, *Bulletin hispanique.* His special field was Spanish-French-Italian literary relations during the Renaissance *(L'Espagne au XVIe et au XVIIe siècles,* Heilbronn, 1878). His pioneering critical editions of Spanish works were Calderón's *El mágico prodigioso* (Heilbronn, 1877), and *El Libro de Alixandre* (Dresden, 1906). A collection of his important research articles was *Études sur L'Espagne* (3 vols., Paris, 1888-1904), in which his work on *Lazarillo de Tormes* (Vol. I, 1895) and Tirso de Molina (Vol. III, 1904) are outstanding.

Cf. Martinenche, E., *Les études hispaniques,* Paris, 1915.

Moreno Villa, José (1887-1955). Postmodernist poet, artist, editor and lecturer. Born in Málaga. Studied in Germany and at the University of Madrid. Associated with the Fine Arts Section of the *Centro de Estudios Históricos.* Traveled widely and lectured in Europe and North America. He was a friend and associate of Juan Ramón Jiménez, who influenced him considerably. His work also shows the influence of Machado and of Unamuno. Notable in the hispanic field are his critical editions (in the *Clásicos Castellanos* series) of Espronceda (1923) and Lope de Rueda (1924). In the field of art, his outstanding contributions are his study of Velásquez and his translation of Wölfflin's *Kunstgeschichtliche Grundbegriffe (Los conceptos fundamentales de la historia del arte).* He lived as an exile in Mexico from 1937 on. Moreno Villa's poetry *(Garba,* 1913; *El pasajero,* 1914; *Carambas,* 1931; etc.) is delicate, subtle and intellectual. It is the reflection of a sensitive, artistic and complex personality, expressing a pervasive sense of the sadness of existence in a contemporary poetic idiom which, at times, verges on surrealism.

Cf. Del Río, A., *Historia de la literatura española,* N. Y., 1948.

Moreto, Agustín (1618-1669). Outstanding dramatist of the Golden Age. Born in Madrid; died in Toledo. Descended from an Italian mercantile family, his full name was Agustín Moreto y Cavanna (Cabaña). He was educated at the University of Alcalá, where he received his degree in 1639. He served as a soldier in Flanders, and upon his return to Spain, took minor orders in 1642. Enjoying the friendship of Calderón, who introduced him to literary circles at the court, and the patronage of the Cardinal of Toledo, who appointed him to a benefice, Moreto devoted himself to clerical tasks and to writing. His literary activity dwindled after he was ordained in 1657. The rest of his life was spent as a priest in Toledo. Most of his plays were published in three volumes (1654, 1676, 1681). He was the author of about 70 dramatic works, some in collaboration with other authors. Moreto's masterpiece was *El desdén con el desdén* (1654). Deftly interweaving situations borrowed from Lope de Vega and Tirso de Molina, the comedy is still enjoyable today. Its plot is that of a haughty young lady who disdainfully rejects all offers only to succumb to the first suitor whose haughtiness and disdain exceed her own. Molière attempted a less successful imitation of this comedy in his *La Princesse d'Élide* (1664). Moreto was at his best in the genre known as the *comedia de figurón,* or type-caricature. His outstanding play of this kind was *El lindo don Diego* (1662), which ridicules the mincing dandy and fop. Interesting among his historical plays was *El valiente justiciero* (1657), based on a legend about Pedro el Cruel (1350-1369) and his victorious proceedings against an arrogant nobleman. In addition to these, Moreto essayed almost every genre of the classical theater: burlesques, masque farces *(mojigangas), entremeses, autos, loas,* etc. For his plots he borrowed freely, but he was such an accomplished dramaturgist that he actually improved on his borrowings. Next to Ruiz de Alarcón, he was the best portrayer of character in the Golden Age drama. His style was simple, his verse deft, and his wit ingratiating. Unlike the writers of his time, he rarely belabored the moral lesson of his plays.

Cf. *Obras,* in *BAE,* XXXIX, (Ed.) Fernández Guerra, L.; *Comedias escogidas de Moreto,* (Ed.) Alonso Cortés, N., Madrid, 1922; Crawford, J. P. W., *Spanish Drama Before Lope de Vega,* Phila., 1922; Chaytor, H. J., *Dramatic Theory in Spain,* Cambridge, 1925; Kennedy, R. L., *The Dramatic Art of Moreto,* Phila., 1932.

moriscos. See under *romance.*

Moro expósito (El). See under *Saavedra, Ángel de.*

Moros, Lope de. See under *Razón de amor.*

Moscas (Las). See under *Azuela, Mariano.*

Mosquea. A burlesque epic by José de Villaviciosa (1589-1658). It was written in 1615 and tells of a war in the insect world. See under *Villaviciosa.*

mosqueteros. The "musketeers". A term applied to the standees in the *corral* (courtyard), or early Spanish theater. The *mosqueteros* were a rowdy element, voicing their disapproval by hissing and whistling *(silbos).* They were the terror of the actors in Lope de Vega's day.

mozárabe. (1) The name given to Spaniards of the Christian faith in southern and central Spain under the rule of the Moors (8th to

15th centuries). (2) The group of Romance dialects spoken by such Spaniards. Specimens of the language are preserved in *aljamiada* literature; i.e. transcribed in Arabic or Hebrew characters. An example of *aljamiada* literature is the *Poema de Yuçuf* (14th century). See also under *jarcha; muwassaha.*

Cf. González Palencia, A., *Historia de la literatura arábigo-española,* Barcelona, 1928; Nykl, A. R., *Hispano-Arabic Poetry . . .,* Baltimore, 1946.

Mucáddam de Cabra. See under *muwassaha.*

Mudarra. See under *Infantes de Lara.*

Muérete y verás. See under *Bretón de los Herreros.*

Muerte del cisne (La). See under *González Martínez, Enrique.*

Murguía, Manuel. See under *Castro, Rosalía de.*

Museo universal (El). See under *Bécquer.*

muwassaha. The Arabic name for a verse form consisting of five or six stanzas written in classical Arabic or Hebrew, with a rhyme scheme of AA BBBAA CCCAA. The *muwassaha* terminates with a stanza of three or four lines written either in popular Arabic or in Mozarabic and known as the *jarcha.* The form was invented by an Andalusian-Arabic poet, Mucáddam de Cabra (9th century). The *jarcha* termination of the *muwassaha* is a source for the study of *aljamiada* literature. See also *jarcha.*

Cf. Stern, S. M., "Les vers finaux en espagnol dans les muwassahas hispano-hébraïques," *Al-Andalus,* XIII, 1948; García Gómez, E., "Nuevas observaciones sobre las jarchas romances en muwassahas hebreas," *Al-Andalus,* XV, 1950; Spitzer, L., "The Mozarabic Lyric. . . ," *Comparative Literature,* IV, 1952.

mysticism. The experience of direct communication with God, culminating in the *unio mystica,* or merging of individual consciousness with the Supreme Consciousness. The roots of mysticism in Spanish literature have been traced to Platonism, Neo-Platonism (Plotinus), the influence of medieval mystic treatises by way of France (Bernhard de Clairvaux), Germany (Eckehard, Thomas à Kempis), England (Anselm of Canterbury), the Netherlands (Ruysbroeck), and the spreading of Franciscan doctrines into the Iberian Peninsula (through Ramón Lull). The fact that Spanish mysticism flourished in the 16th century rather than in the Middle Ages has not yet been satisfactorily explained (*Cf.* Green, O. H.,

"The Historical Problem of Castilian Mysticism," *Hispanic Review,* IV, 1939). Two salient facts seem pertinent: the revolt against the paganism of the Renaissance (expressed in asceticism and in the glorification of God), and the spread of Franciscan and Erasmian doctrines (expressed through internal religious reform and through the "psychologizing" of religious experience). In some of the Spanish mystics the "soul-saving" and ascetic strain is predominant (fasting, prayer, criticism of loose manners and sensuality; *e.g.* Luis de Granada, *Guía de pecadores,* 1556). In others the Platonist influence is evident *(e.g.* Luis de León, *Los nombres de Cristo,* 1583-1585). But the notion of "stages" on the way to the mystical union is first developed in Francisco de Osuna's *Tercer abecedario* (1527), which describes the way to God as beginning with self-denial and prayer, leading to "recognition" and the pervasion of the soul with Divine ecstasy. The notion of the mystical union was later treated by Juan de los Ángeles in his *Triunfos del amor de Dios* (1589). However, the fullest elaboration of the mystical experience was described by Santa Teresa de Jesús in her *Camino de perfección* (1585), and *El castillo interior o Las moradas* (1588); and by San Juan de la Cruz in his poems, *Cántico espiritual, Noche oscura del alma, Llama de amor viva* (publ. 1618-1627), and in his prose commentary, *La subida del monte Carmelo* (1578-1583). As summarized by Menéndez y Pelayo *(De la poesía mística),* the mystic "ways" of the soul to God are: 1. *vía purgativa* (purification through prayer, self-discipline, obliteration of the senses and of the material world); 2. *vía iluminativa* (inward contemplation, concentration of mind, will and feeling on "recollection"—*recogimiento* —of God); *vía unitiva* (spiritual union with God). In addition, San Juan de la Cruz introduces the "dark night of the soul" *(Noche oscura del alma),* i.e. the distraction of the senses, for which the only saving "way" is faith. The Spanish mystics balanced their instrospection with good works and with efforts at internal religious reform. In their preoccupation with the Divine Vision and the achievement of grace, they produced the most impassioned lyrics and most subtle prose of the Golden Age.

Cf. Menéndez y Pelayo, M., "De la poesía mística," *Estudios de crítica literaria,* Madrid, 1884; Peers, E. A., *Studies of the*

Spanish Mystics, N. Y., 1927; Sáinz Rodríguez, P., *Introducción a la historia de la literatura mística en España,* Madrid, 1927; Green, O. H., "The Historical Problem of Castilian Mysticism," *Hispanic Review,* IV, 1939; Chuzeville, J., *Les mystiques espagnols,* Paris, 1952.

N

Nación (La). Influential Argentine newspaper. Founded in 1869 by Bartolomé Mitre, the first President of Argentina (1862-1868). See under *Mitre.*

Narrationes. See under *Libro de los gatos.*

naturalism. (1) A philosophical system which attributes all causes to nature or environment as a first principle; determinism. (2) A literary movement in the 19th century, developing from realism and opposed to romanticism. The theory of naturalism in literature was elaborated by Emile Zola (1840-1902) in his *Le roman expérimental* (1880), in which the novelist is conceived as a laboratory technician impassively recording data on human behavior within a given social environment. Although the notion of an impersonal, "scientifically" documented novel is contradictory to the creativeness of the writer, naturalism achieved a European vogue because of its exposure of the sordid aspects of 19th century society. In Spain, the naturalist theory was espoused by Pardo Bazán in her critical work, *La cuestión palpitante* (1883), and practised in her novels *(Los pazos de Ulloa; La madre naturaleza;* etc.). Other Spanish novelists went through a naturalistic phase before developing in other directions: Galdós *(La desheredada; Tormento);* Clarín *(La Regenta);* Palacio Valdés *(La espuma; La fe);* and above all, Blasco Ibáñez *(La barraca; La catedral; La horda).* In South America, the chief exponent of naturalism was the Argentine novelist, Eugenio Cambacèrés (1843-1888).

Cf. Del Río, A., *Historia de la literatura española,* N. Y., 1948.

Naufragios. See under *Núñez Cabeza de Vaca.*

Navarrete collection. See under *Prescott.*

Navarro-Aragonese. See under *Spanish.*

Navarro Tomás, Tomás (1884). Philologist and linguistic scientist. The most eminent contemporary authority on Castilian phonetics.

Born in La Roda de la Mancha, Albacete. Studied at Valencia and at Madrid. A pupil of Menéndez Pidal at the University of Madrid. Director of the phonetics laboratory at the *Centro de Estudios Históricos*. Associated with the *Cuerpo de Archivos, Bibliotecas y Museos* and with the *Archivo Histórico Nacional*. In 1912 he received a government grant for foreign study (with Rousselot and Grammont in France; with Viëtor and Sievers in Germany). Managing editor of the *Revista de filología española*. Elected to the *Real Academia Española* in 1935. Professor at Columbia University and Director of Publications of the *Hispanic Institute*. Director of research for the *Atlas lingüístico* of Spain and of Puerto Rico. Besides critical editions (Santa Teresa, Garcilaso), he has produced innumerable articles and monographs on linguistics, phonetics, dialect geography, literary criticism, *etc.* His *Manual de pronunciación española* (Madrid, 1918), *El acento castellano* (Madrid, 1935; inaugural address to the *Real Academia Española)*, and *Manual de entonación española* (N. Y., 1944) are the definitive works in their field.

Nazarín. See under *Pérez Galdós.*

NBAE. Abbreviation of *Nueva Biblioteca de Autores Españoles*. See under *Biblioteca de Autores Españoles.*

Nebrija, Antonio de (1444-1522). Spain's greatest Renaissance humanist. Born in Lebrija, Seville; died in Alcalá de Henares. His full name was Elio Antonio Martínez de Jarabe (or Martínez de Cala). Since his native town "Lebrija" is "Nebrissa" in Latin, his name of Nebrija (Nebrixa) has persisted, as befits the great Latinist. He studied at Salamanca and at Bologna, Italy. After some ten years of humanistic study in Italy, he returned to Spain, where his accomplishments in Latin scholarship gained him a professorship of grammar and rhetoric at the University of Salamanca. Here he reformed Latin studies in the spirit of Italian humanism. His Latin grammar, *Introductiones latinae* (1481), and his lexicon, *Vocabulario latínoespañol* (1492), were widely used throughout Spain and Europe. His greatest achievement, however, was his *Gramática castellana* (1492), a milestone in linguistic history as the first scientific grammar of a vernacular language in Europe. This work, together with his *Reglas de orthografía castellana* (1517), performed an invaluable function in standardizing Castilian usage and spelling. Recognition of his great scholarship came in 1509, when he was appointed *Cronista real.* Nebrija was one of the illustrious group of scholars who came to Alcalá in 1502 at the behest of Cardinal Cisneros to work on the first polyglot Bible to be printed *(Biblia poliglota complutense,* 1514-1517).

Cf. *Gramática castellana,* (Ed.) Galindo, P. & Ortiz, L., Madrid, 1946; Olmedo, P. F., *Antonio de Nebrija,* Madrid, 1942.

neoclassicism. (1) The literary and artistic trend toward imitation or revival of the spirit of Greco-Roman classicism. (2) In Spain, applicable to the dominating tendency of 18th century literature (Moratín, Iriarte, etc.).

Cf. Pellissier, R. E., *The Neo-Classic Movement in Spain During the 18th Century,* (Diss.), Harvard U., 1913.

neoplatonism. See under *platonism.*

Neruda, Pablo (1904). Chilean diplomat, essayist and poet. Pablo Neruda is the pseudonym of Neftalí Ricardo Reyes. Traveled widely in the diplomatic service of his country (China, Ceylon, Burma). Chilean Consul in Spain (1934-1938). Elected Senator of the Chilean Republic in 1945. Influenced by García Lorca, he developed through a phase of modernism to an independent and highly subjective style combining romantic and dramatic elements. His themes are romantic love and universal despair. The most gifted of contemporary Latin American poets, Neruda has been second only to Rubén Darío in his influence on the development of post-modernist poetry. Chief works: *Crepusculario,* 1919; *La canción de fiesta,* 1921; *Veinte poemas de amor y una canción desesperada,* 1924; *Residencia en la tierra,* 1933; *España en el corazón,* 1937; *Odas elementales,* 1954.

Cf. Alonso, A., "Algunos símbolos insistentes en la poesía de Pablo Neruda," *Revista Hispánica Moderna,* V, 1939; Sanhueza, J., *Bibliografía de Pablo Neruda, 1917-1954,* University of Chile, Santiago, 1954.

Nervo, Amado (1870-1919). Mexican diplomat and poet. A journalist at the beginning of his career, he achieved a *succès de scandale* with his naturalistic novel, *El bachiller* (1896). Identified with the modernist movement, he contributed to the *Revista azul,* and at its demise, founded the *Revista moderna* (1898) with the collaboration of Valenzuela. In Paris as a representative of the Mexican press (1900), he met Rubén Darío. He was secretary of the

Mexican legation in Madrid (1905-1918) and Mexican Minister to Argentina and Uruguay (1919). Although he wrote short stories and essays, he was primarily a poet. Nervo's poetry reveals modernist stylistic traits superimposed on a fundamental attitude of profound religious feeling. There is an exalted mysticism in his notion of the sanctity of all nature and in his serene acceptance of death as well as life. Many critics have pointed out Nervo's kinship with East Indian philosophy. Among his chief works were: *El bachiller,* 1896; *Perlas negras,* 1898; *Poemas,* 1901; *Los jardines interiores,* 1905; *Las almas que pasan,* 1906; *Juana de Asbaje,* 1910; *Serenidad,* 1912; *Elevación,* 1916; *Plenitud,* 1918; *El estanque de los lotos,* 1919; *La amada inmóvil* (posthumously, 1920). *Obras completas* (Ed. by Alfonso Reyes), Madrid, 1920-1928; *Obras completas,* Mexico, 1938.

Cf. Blanco-Fombona, R., *El modernismo y los poetas modernistas,* Madrid, 1929; Wellman, E. T., *Amado Nervo, Mexico's Religious Poet,* N. Y., 1936; Reyes, A., *Tránsito de Amado Nervo,* Santiago de Chile, 1937.

Nevares, Marta de. See under *Vega, Lope de.*

Niebla. See under *Unamuno.*

Nieremberg, Juan Eusebio. See under *Granada, Luis de.*

Niña de los embustes (La). See under *Castillo Solórzano.*

Niño de la bola (El). See under *Alarcón y Ariza.*

Noche oscura del alma. See under *Cruz, San Juan de la.*

Noche serena. See under *León, Luis de.*

Noches lúgubres. See under *Cadalso.*

Nombres de Cristo (De los). See under *León, Luis de.*

novecentismo. A term first used as the title of a review, edited by the Italian writer, Massimo Bontempelli (b. 1884), to designate the spirit of the 20th century. The term was popularized in Spain by the Catalán critic, Eugenio d'Ors (1882-1954). Spanish writers exemplifying this new spirit of the 20th century are Ortega y Gasset, Pérez de Ayala, Gerardo Diego, Jorge Guillén, Pedro Salinas, etc.

Cf. Del Río, A., *Historia de la literatura española,* N. Y., 1948.

novela bizantina. Milesian tale. A tale of romantic adventures dealing with distant travels, shipwrecks, pirates, the separation and miraculous reunion of lovers, *etc.* The type first occurs in late Greek fiction; e.g. *Teágenes y Cariclea* (3rd century), by Heliodorus, a Greek writer from Syria, widely translated and imitated in 16th century Spain. The earliest Spanish example of this type is the *Libro de Apolonio* (13th century). Cervantes' *Persiles y Sigismunda* (1617) is one of the best. In English literature the type is represented by Shakespeare's *Comedy of Errors,* and *Pericles, Prince of Tyre.*

novela bucólica. See *pastoral novel.*

novela experimental. A reference to Emile Zola's theoretical work on naturalism in the novel: *Le roman expérimental* (1880). See under *naturalism.*

novela pastoril. See *pastoral novel.*

novela picaresca. See *picaresque novel.*

Novelas ejemplares. See under *Cervantes.*

Novelas poemáticas. See under *Pérez de Ayala.*

Nuevo don Juan (El). See under *López de Ayala.*

Núñez, Hernán. See under *Mena, Juan de.*

Núñez, Cabeza de Vaca, Alvar (early 16th century). Spanish explorer. Born in Jerez de la Frontera; died in Seville. The exact dates of his birth and death are not known (1490? or 1507?-1559? or 1564?). A grandson of Pedro de Vera, conqueror of the Canary Islands. Cabeza de Vaca was a member of the ill-fated Florida expedition led by Pánfilo de Narváez (1528), which he vividly described in his *Naufragios* (1542). His experiences as "adelantado" of Paraguay were recounted by his scribe, Pero Hernández, in *Los Comentarios.* A recent edition of both works was published in Madrid in 1922 *(Naufragios y comentarios, con dos cartas).*

Cf. Bishop, M., *The Odyssey of Cabeza de Vaca,* N. Y., 1933.

Núñez de Arce, Gaspar (1834-1903). Post-romantic poet and dramatist. Born in Valladolid; died in Madrid. As a correspondent, he reported the events of the African campaign (1859-1860). Active in politics, he was at various times civil governor of Barcelona, legislative deputy, senator and minister. He became a member of the *Academia Española* in 1874. He wrote several plays early in his career but without success, except for one, *El haz de leña* (1872), dealing with the tragic death of Carlos, son of Philip II, who had been imprisoned by his inexorable father. It was as a poet that Núñez de Arce excelled, his best volume of lyrics being the virile *Gritos del combate* (1875), in which he cynically assailed the extremists and the tyranny of both right and left.

Among his other notable poetic works were *La visión de Fray Martín* (1880), a flattering portrait of Martin Luther as a disciple of doubt, and *La pesca* (1884), a romantically tragic love story of idyllic charm. Núñez de Arce shared the prevalent 19th century conflict between faith and science. Although his work is replete with social and political consciousness, his attitude is frequently one of romantic despair and disillusionment, often tendentious in its querulous outbursts. As a poet he displayed great formal versatility, expressing romantic ideas in a neoclassic style. Chief works: (plays) *Deudas de la honra,* 1863; *Quien debe paga,* 1867; *Justicia providencial,* 1872; *El haz de leña,* 1872; (poems) *Raimundo Lulio,* 1875; *Gritos del combate,* 1875; *La última lamentación de Lord Byron,* 1879; *La selva oscura,* 1879; *La visión de Fray Martín,* 1880; *La pesca,* 1884; *Maruja,* 1886.

Cf. Plays, in *Obras dramáticas,* Madrid, 1879; Poems, in *Poesías completas,* N. Y., 1920; Menéndez y Pelayo, M., "Núñez de Arce," in *Estudios de crítica literaria,* Madrid, 1893; Castillo Soriano, J. del, *Núñez de Arce,* Madrid, 1904; Romo Arregui, J., *Vida, poesía y estilo de don Gaspar Núñez de Arce,* Madrid, 1946.

Nuño Salido. See under *Infantes de Lara.*

O

OAS. Organization of American States. See under *Pan American Union.*

Obligado, Rafael (1851-1920). Argentine poet. Born in Buenos Aires and educated at the Colegio Nacional. Influenced by Echeverría and other romanticists, he composed patriotic odes, nature lyrics and Argentine folk legends in verse form. The most famous of his poetic legends is that of *Santos Vega,* composed in *décimas* and divided into four cantos. His other important works were: *El alma del payador,* 1877; *La prenda del payador,* 1885; *La muerte del payador,* 1887; *Leyendas argentinas,* 1905; *Poesías completas,* 1923.

Cf. Rojas, R., *La literatura argentina,* Buenos Aires, 1924-1925.

Ocampo, Florián de (1495?-1558). Chronicler and historian. Born in Zamora. The place of his death is unknown. Studied with Nebrija at Alcalá (1509-1514). Appointed Court Chronicler by Charles I (1539). Canon of Zamora (from 1547). Ocampo edited and printed a version of Alfonso X's *Crónica general,* using as a source one of the manuscripts of the *Tercera crónica general.* Ocampo's version was entitled, *Las quatro partes enteras de la crónica de España* (Zamora, 1541). His chief work as a historian was *Los quatro libros de la crónica general de España* (Zamora, 1543), which begins with the Creation and goes up to the early Romans. It contains anecdotes, legends and fantastic narratives, some of Ocampo's own invention. His attempt to prove the Spanish monarchy as the most ancient in Europe detracts from his factual accuracy. Ocampo's importance in the history of Spanish literature is due to the success of his edition of Alfonso's chronicle. It was reprinted and imitated a great many times and was the chief popular source of epic themes for writers from the 16th through the 19th century. See also under *crónica.*

Cf. *Obras,* (Ed.) Cano, B., Madrid, 1791; Bataillon, M., "Sur Florián de Ocampo," *Bulletin hispanique,* XXV, 1923; Cotarelo, E., "Varias noticias acerca de Florián de Ocampo," *Boletín de la Real Academia Española,* XIII, 1926.

Ocantos, Carlos María (1860-1949). Argentine novelist and career diplomat. Served with the Argentine diplomatic service in Madrid and in the Scandinavian countries. In 1915 he settled near Madrid and devoted himself to writing novels. His novel, *La cola de paja* (1923), received an award from the *Real Academia Española.* A prolific writer, Ocantos excelled in portraying the broad panorama of Argentine society and manners, his characters and plot being of secondary importance. Among his chief works are: *La cruz de la falta,* 1883; *León Zaldívar,* 1888; *Don Perfecto,* 1902; *La cola de paja,* 1923; *Fray Judas,* 1929; *Entre naranjas,* 1936.

Cf. Andersson, T., *Carlos María Ocantos, Argentine Novelist,* New Haven, 1934 (Sp. trsl., *Carlos María Ocantos y su obra,* Madrid, 1935).

Ocho comedias y ocho entremeses. . . . See under *Cervantes.*

octava. Any stanza of eight lines.

octava aguda. The same as *octava italiana.*

octava bermudina. The same as *octava italiana.*

octava de arte mayor. A stanza of eight 12-syllable *arte mayor* lines (*i.e.* with middle caesura and two accented syllables in each half line). The number of syllables may vary because the *arte mayor* line is rhythmic rather than syllabic. Frequent rhyme schemes in this form are: ABBAACCA, or ABABBCCB. Most notably the form was used by Juan de Mena (1411-1456), and hence it is also called *octava de Juan de Mena.*

octava de arte menor. See *octavilla.*

octava de Juan de Mena. The same as *octava de arte mayor.*

octava heroica. The same as *octava real.*

octava italiana. A stanza of eight 11-syllable lines, of which the fourth and eighth rhyme on the terminal syllable *(rima aguda).* With this exception, the rhyme scheme may vary. A frequently occurring pattern is ABBCDEEC. Also called *octava aguda, octava moderna,* or *octava bermudina* (after Salvador Bermúdez de Castro, 1814-1883).

octava italiana de pie quebrado. See under *pie quebrado.*

octava moderna. The same as *octava italiana.*

octava real. The "royal octave". A stanza of eight 11-syllable lines rhymed ABABABCC. It was the metrical form of the Italian epic poets, Ariosto (1474-1533) and Tasso (1544-1595), and the first adapted to Spanish poetry by Boscán (1493?-1542). It became the favorite meter of the Spanish erudite epic poets; *e.g.* Ercilla (1533-1544); and was also used in lyrical poetry. Because of its use in the epic, it is sometimes referred to as the *octava heroica.* Also called *octava rima* (from It. *ottava rima).*

octava rima. The same as *octava real.*

octavilla. A stanza of eight lines which are shorter than those of the *octava real.* Also called *octava de arte menor.*

octonario. A metrical line or verse of 16 syllables, variously stressed. The *octonario* frequently consists of two *octosílabos.*

octosílabo. A metrical line or verse of eight syllables, variously stressed. The *octosílabo* may also be one half of a 16-syllable line, called an *octonario.*

Odo de Cheriton. See under *Libro de los gatos.*

Oelschläger, Victor R. B. (1909). Romance philologist and authority on medieval Spanish literature. Teaching posts at University of Wisconsin, Tulane University, University of Southern California. Professor of Spanish and Head of Department, Modern Languages, Florida State University, since 1953. Editorial Consultant, *Britannica World Language Dict.* Editor, *Comparative Romance Linguistics Newsletter.* Author, *A Medieval Spanish Word List,* U. of Wisconsin Press, 1940; *Poema del Cid in Verse and Prose,* New Orleans, 1940. Articles on Juan Manuel, Cervantes, Alfonso Reyes, Salas Barbadillo, *etc.* Book reviews in *Hispania, Romance Philology, etc.*

Ojeda, Diego de. See *Hojeda, Diego de.*

Oligarquía y caciquismo. See under *Costa y Martínez.*

Olivares. See under *Quevedo.*

Ollanta. A Peruvian verse drama in Quechua dialect, supposedly written before the Spanish conquest of Peru. It was discovered by a priest, Antonio Valdés, between 1770 and 1780. *Ollanta (Ollantay?)* takes its name from the protagonist, an Indian, whose presumptuous love for an Incan princess supplies the dramatic conflict. *Ollanta* is the first important example of native American Indian literature.

Cf. Hills, E. C., "The Quechua Drama *Ollanta*," *Hispanic Studies*, Stanford University, California, 1929; Rojas, R., *Un titán de los Andes*, Buenos Aires, 1939.

Olmedo, José Joaquín (1780-1847). Ecuadorian statesman, diplomat and poet. Born in Guayaquil. Educated at the University of San Marcos in Lima, Peru. Although a doctor of jurisprudence, he devoted himself to literature, composing verse in the classical Latin tradition. He represented Guayaquil in the Spanish Cortes (1812) and was a member of the governing *Junta* of Guayaquil. As the result of political differences, he went to Peru (1822), where he was associated with Bolívar. After diplomatic service in England and in France, he was elected the first Vice-President of Ecuador (1830). Olmedo's most famous poem was inspired by Bolívar's triumph at Junín *(A la victoria de Junín*, 1825). Bolívar himself supplied the details of the action. The result was a heroic ode that transcends its classical form by the romantic intensity of its lyrical and descriptive passages.

Cf. Barrera, I. J., *Literatura ecuatoriana*, Quito, 1939.

Onís, Federico de (1885). Hispanist, literary critic, essayist, professor and editor. Born in Salamanca. Doctorate in literature at the University of Madrid. A pupil and associate of Menéndez Pidal at the *Centro de Estudios Históricos*, and a friend and associate of Américo Castro. Professor of Spanish Literature at the Universities of Oviedo and Salamanca. Professor of Spanish Literature and Head of the Spanish Department, Columbia University. Head of the Department of Hispanic Studies, University of Puerto Rico. Director of the *Hispanic Institute in the United States*, Columbia University. Editor of *Revista de Filología Española*, Madrid; *Romantic Review*, N. Y.; *Revista de Estudios Hispánicos*, Puerto Rico; *Revista Hispánica Moderna*, N. Y. Editor of a series, "Contemporary Spanish Texts," Boston, 1918 *et seq*. Critical editions: *Vida, Torres Villarroel*, Madrid, 1912; *Los nombres de Cristo, Luis de León*, Madrid, 1914. Author of *Disciplina y rebeldía*, Madrid, 1915; *Fueros leoneses*, Madrid, 1916; *El español en los Estados Unidos*, Salamanca, 1920; *Jacinto Benavente*, N .Y., 1923; *Martín Fierro y la poesía tradicional*, Madrid, 1924; *Ensayos sobre el sentido de la cultura española*, Madrid, 1932; *An-*

tología de la poesía española e hispanoamericana, Madrid, 1934. See also under *Hispanic Institute.*

Cf. Del Río, A., *Historia de la literatura española,* N. Y., 1948.

Oña, Pedro de (1570-1643?). The first distinguished poet to be born in Chile. Studied at the University of San Marcos in Lima, Peru (1590-1592). His most famous work is the *Arauco domado (primera parte,* 1596), a verse epic in rhymed octaves celebrating the deeds of the Marquis of Cañete. Oña used the *Araucana* of Ercilla as a model. Although he did not attain the epic stature of his master, his realism and poetic skill make him the foremost Chilean poet of the colonial period. He also wrote religious poems, one eulogizing Loyola *(Ignacio de Cantabria)* and one about the earthquake of Lima *(Temblor de Lima en 1609).* A critical edition of the *Arauco domado* was published by the Chilean Academy (Ed. Medina, J. T., Santiago, 1917).

Cf. Solar Correa, E., *Semblanzas literarias de la colonia,* Santiago, 1933; Caillet-Bois, "Dos notas sobre Pedro de Oña," *Revista de Filología Hispánica,* I, IV, 1942.

Oráculo manual. See under *Gracián y Morales.*

Ordóñez de Montalvo. See under *Amadís de Gaula.*

Orfeo (El divino). See under *Calderón.*

Orígenes de la novela. See under *Menéndez y Pelayo.*

Orígenes del español. See under *Menéndez Pidal.*

Orígenes del teatro español. See under *Moratín.*

Ors, Eugenio d' (1882-1954). Essayist, esthetician, lecturer and critic. Born in Barcelona. Studied at the University of Barcelona and at the Sorbonne, as well as in Germany and Switzerland. His full name was Eugenio d'Ors y Rovira. He occupied various public posts and represented Spain at international cultural conferences. He was a member of the *Academia Española.* Until 1916, he wrote in Catalán (under the pen name of *Xenius);* thereafter the bulk of his writing was in Castilian, although some of his essays were in French. Among his important works in Catalán were his *Glossari* (1906), and a novel, *La ben plantada* (1911). In Castilian, some of his chief works are: *El nuevo glosario* (1916-1920); *De la amistad y del diálogo* (1914); *Poussin y el Greco* (1922); *Tres horas en el Museo del Prado* (1923); *El arte de Goya* (1924); *Ecos de los destinos* (1943); *El secreto de la filosofía* (1947); etc. Eugenio d'Ors was most influential in the 1920's as an intellectual and cultural exponent of the spirit of the 20th century, which he called *novecentismo.* Like Ortega y Gasset, he was given to philosophical speculation, although more inclined to esthetics than to metaphysics or sociology. His endeavor was to identify and interpret permanent (classical) values or norms in the heterogeneous confusion of modern artistic and intellectual movements. A consummate stylist, at times verging on *conceptismo* in the gnomic manner of his *glosas,* he was often impressionistic in his judgments. His range of themes was comprehensive, evidence of a fertile imagination and a profound personal culture. See also under *novecentismo.*

Cf. Del Río, A., *Historia de la literatura española,* N. Y., 1948.

Ortega Munilla, José. See under *Ortega y Gasset.*

Ortega y Gasset, José (1883-1955). Philosopher, journalist, literary critic and lecturer. Born in Madrid. The son of José Ortega Munilla (1856-1922), famous journalist and novelist. Studied at the Jesuit College in Miraflores del Palo, Málaga, and at the University of Madrid (Ph.D., 1904). Further studies (1905-1907) at Leipzig, Berlin and Marburg (under Hermann Cohen, the great Kantian). Professor of Metaphysics at the University of Madrid (1910-1936). Elected to the *Real Academia de Ciencias Morales y Políticas* (1916). Founder of Spain's most eminent intellectual journal of modern times, the *Revista de Occidente* (1923-1936). Deputy in the Cortes (1931). From 1936 to 1945 he lived in France, Holland, Argentina and Portugal, returning to Spain in 1945. After that he made frequent lecture tours (U. S., Germany, Switzerland, Scotland). He founded the *Instituto de Humanidades* (Madrid, 1948). Ortega expounded his philosophy of vitalism chiefly in *El tema de nuestro tiempo* (1921). His system is thus described in the *Dictionary of Philosophy* (N. Y., 1942): "Although brought up in the Marburg school of thought, Ortega is not exactly a neo-Kantian. At the basis of his *Weltanschauung* one finds a denial of the fundamental presuppositions which characterized European rationalism. It is life and not thought which is primary. Things have a sense and a value which must be affirmed independently. *Things,* however, are to be conceived as the totality of situations which constitute the circumstances of a man's life; hence, Ortega's first philosophical principle: 'I am myself plus my circumstances'. Life as a problem, however, is but one of the poles of his formula; reason is the other. The two together function not by dialectical opposition but by necessary co-existence. Life, according to Ortega, does not consist in being, but rather, in coming to be, and as such it is of the nature of direction, program building, purpose to be achieved, value to be realized." Although this philosophy was essentially optimistic, in *La rebelión de las masas* (1929) Ortega seemed to share with Spengler the conviction of cultural decline, which he ascribed to totalitarian trends of the left and of the right. As a literary critic Ortega combined a vast erudition with an acute mind and a sense of positive values. Because of his cultural cosmopolitanism and his sensitive reactions to changes in the temporal scene, some critics consider him an inspired journalist rather than a philosopher. However, it must be admitted that he was one of the few modern Spanish intellectuals to have achieved a world view. Chief works: *Meditaciones del Quijote,* 1914; *El Espectador* (8 vols.), 1916-1935; *El tema de nuestro tiempo,* 1921; *España invertebrada,* 1922; *Kant,* 1924; *La deshumanización del arte,* 1925; *Espíritu de la letra,* 1927; *La rebelión de las masas,* 1929; *Goethe desde dentro,* 1934; *Estudios sobre el amor,* 1939; *Ensimismamiento y alteración,* 1939; *El libro de las misiones,* 1940; *Ideas y creencias,* 1940; *Historia como sistema,* 1941; *Obras completas,* 6 vols., Madrid, 1946-1947.

Cf. Barja, C., *Libros y autores contemporáneos,* Madrid, 1935; Iriarte, J., *Ortega y Gasset: su persona y su doctrina,* Madrid, 1942; Sánchez Villaseñor, J., *Ortega y Gasset: pensamiento y trayectoria,* Mexico, 1945; Marías, J., *Ortega y el vitalismo,* Madrid, 1948.

Ortiz, Fernando (1881). Cuban essayist, literary scholar and polygraph. Editor of *Revista Bimestre Cubana; Archivos del Folklore Cubano.* General editor of the series *Colección cubana de libros inéditos y raros; Colección de libros cubanos.* Principal works: *Los negros brujos; Glosario de afronegrismos; Contrapunteo cubano del tabaco y el azúcar; Los negros esclavos.*

Cf. *Hispania,* XXXVI, 1953.

Osorio, Elena. See under *Vega, Lope de.*

Osuna, Francisco de. See under *mysticism.*

ovillejo. A metrical form consisting of ten lines, of which the first, third and fifth are octosyllabic, each followed by a short line *(pie* *quebrado),* and concluding with a quatrain *(redondilla)* consisting of three octosyllabic lines and a final line incorporating the previous short lines of *pie quebrado.* A common rhyme scheme for this form is AABBCC–CDDC.

oxítona. (Eng. *oxytonic).* A word which has its major stress on the last syllable. Compare *rima aguda.*

P

Pablos de Segovia. See under *Quevedo.*
Paces de los reyes (Las). See under *Vega, Lope de.*
Pacheco, Francisco. See under *Escuela sevillana.*
Padre Las Casas (El). See *Casas, Bartolomé de las.*
Palabra sincopada. See under *syncope.*
Palacio Valdés, Armando (1853-1938). Novelist, short-story writer and essayist. Born in Entralgo, Asturias; died in Madrid. He took his degree at Oviedo and then studied law at Madrid. Completely devoted to a life of letters, he was active in the *Ateneo* of Madrid and in its celebrated *tertulia,* "La Cacharrería". He wrote for several newspapers *(El Imparcial, La Correspondencia de España),* edited the *Revista Europea,* and published several volumes of literary studies of contemporary writers *(Semblanzas literarias,* 1871; *Los oradores del Ateneo,* 1878; *Nuevo viaje al Parnaso,* 1879). He was elected to the *Academia Española* in 1906. In collaboration with his close friend, "Clarín" (Leopoldo Alas y Ureña), he produced a volume of critical essays, *Literatura en 1881.* Autobiographical elements predominate in his novels, *Riverita* (1886), *Maximina* (1887), and later, in *La novela de un novelista* (1921), with its posthumous sequel of essays, *Album de un ciego* (1940). Palacio Valdés published his first novel in 1881 *(El señorita Octavio).* Although of slight merit, it already displayed his talent for character delineation and his Dickensian humor. He achieved fame in 1885 with his novel of fishermen and the sea, *José,* together with Pereda's *Sotileza,* the best of this genre in the contemporary Spanish novel. He went through a temporary phase of naturalism during which he probed the seamier aspects of upper-class society *(La espuma,* 1890) and the problem of religious sham *(La fe,* 1892). His earlier novel, *Marta y María* (1883), had already explored religious and mundane life

as symbolized in two sisters; and although he had shown a realistic bent in preferring María, the embodiment of mundane virtues, the treatment had been more artistic than in his naturalistic novels. The power of the press is the theme of his social novel, *El cuarto poder* (1888). However, his best novels are those evoking regional atmosphere, Seville in *La hermana San Sulpicio* (1889), Valencia in *La alegría del capitán Ribot* (1899), and Asturias in *La aldea perdida* (1903). These represent his most enduring work, his contribution to the *novela de costumbres.* For the rest, he specialized in the gay, frivolous comedy of manners, projected on a shallow, upper middle-class background, charming but insubstantial.

Cf. *Obras completas,* (Ed.) Astrana Marín, L., Madrid, 1945; Cruz Rueda, A., *Armando Palacio Valdés,* Paris, 1925; Pitollet, C., "Palacio Valdés", *Bulletin hispanique,* XL, 1938; Narbona, R., *Palacio Valdés o la armonía,* Madrid, 1941.

Palma, Ricardo (1833-1919). Peruvian short-story writer. Born and died in Lima. Before beginning his literary career he was a sailor, journalist, and politician. Although he did not complete his university education, he was an omnivorous reader and naturalborn scholar. Appointed director of the *Biblioteca Nacional* in 1889, he rendered invaluable service in preserving the heritage of his country by restoring the library after it had been damaged during the wars with Chile. Palma's early literary influences were the romanticists, Scott and Heine, whose works he translated; but he outgrew his romanticism as his critical powers developed. His great contribution to Spanish American letters was his creation of a new literary genre known as the "tradición," a type of historical sketch or anecdote which, in his hands, became a distinctive art-form, reviving an entire era or a personage with a few deft strokes. Chief works: *Poesías,* 1855; *Anales de la Inquisición en Lima,* 1863; *Armonías, libro de un desterrado,* 1865; *Pasionarias,* 1870; *Rodil,* 1872; *Tradiciones peruanas,* 1872-1910 (complete edition, 1939); *La bohemia de mi tiempo,* 1886; *Apuntes para la historia de la Biblioteca de Lima,* 1912.

Cf. Leavitt, S. E., "Ricardo Palma," *Hisp. Amer. Hist. Rev.,* III, 1920; Palma, A., *Ricardo Palma,* Buenos Aires, 1933; Sánchez, L. A., *La literatura del Perú,* Buenos Aires, 1939; Bazin, R., "Les trois crises de la vie de Ricardo Palma," *Bulletin Hispanique,*

LVI, 1954; Miró, C., *Don Ricardo Palma, el patriarca de las tradiciones,* Buenos Aires, 1953.

Palmerín cycle. (Sp. *Palmerines).* Next to the *Amadís* cycle, the most important of the Renaissance romances of chivalry. The first of this cycle was *Palmerín de Oliva* (Salamanca, 1511), the love story of the titular hero and Polinarda. It was a poor imitation of *Amadís de Gaula.* The author is unknown, although thought to be a woman. The second in this cycle was *Primaleón* (Salamanca, 1512), which recounts the exploits of Palmerín's sons, Primaleón and Polendos, as well as those of Prince Edward of England *(Don Duardos de Inglaterra).* These were the chivalric romances so severely castigated by Cervantes in *Don Quijote* (Pt. I, Chap. XLVII) for their poor style and incredible exploits. However, he praised the greatest of the cycle, *Palmerín de Inglaterra* (Toledo, 1547), for its unity of development and for the beauty of some of its passages. An acrostic in the first edition attributed the work to Luis Hurtado de Toledo (d. 1590), but later research disclosed that it had originally been written in 1544 by a Portuguese author, Francisco de Moraes (d. 1572). The Portuguese version was not published until 1567. Like the other chivalric romances, the *Palmerines* enjoyed a great vogue despite official disapproval. They provided a source for Spanish authors *(e.g.* Vicente, Paravicino, and others), and were avidly read in translation in France, Italy and England.

Cf. *Palmerín de Inglaterra,* (Ed.) Bonilla y San Martín, A., *NBAE,* XI; Givanel Mas, J., *La novela caballeresca española,* Madrid, 1912; Thomas, H., *Spanish and Portuguese Romances of Chivalry,* London, 1920.

Palmerín de Inglaterra. See under *Palmerín cycle.*

Palmerín de Oliva. See under *Palmerín cycle.*

Pamphilus. See under *Ruiz, Juan.*

Pan American Union. Since 1948, the General Secretariat of the Organization of American States (OAS), with headquarters in Washington, D. C. The OAS developed from the Union of American Republics established by the first International Conference of American States, convened in 1890 by Secretary of State James G. Blaine. Its inspiration goes back to 1826, when Simón Bolívar called the first inter-American conference in Panama City. Among its many functions, the Pan American Union promotes the cultural development of the 21 South American Republics and the United States. Many of its publications, divisions, and services are of value to the teacher and student of Hispanics; in particular, the periodical *Americas* and the division known as "The Columbus Memorial Library," with its books, monographs and bibliographies dealing with the literature, science and philosophy of the American Republics.

Cf. Babcock, C. E., *Fifty Years of the Library of the Pan American Union (1890-1940),* Pan American Union, Washington, D. C.

panentheism. The philosophical system of Karl Friedrich Krause (1781-1832), the intellectual godfather of the Spanish *krausistas.* The word is a blend of pantheism and theism, and indicates Krause's attempt to reconcile these two concepts in his philosophy. See under *Krause; krausismo.*

Panorama matritense. See under *Mesonero Romanos.*

parábola. Parable. A narrative of an imaginary event from which a significant truth or moral lesson may be inferred.

Pardo, Miguel Eduardo. See under *criollismo.*

Pardo Bazán, Emilia (1852-1921). Novelist, short-story writer, critic and travel diarist. Born in La Coruña; died in Madrid. Her full name was Emilia Pardo Bazán de Quiroga. The only daughter of the Count and Countess of Pardo Bazán, she was a precocious child and improved her natural talents by wide reading. After her marriage to don José Quiroga in 1868, she traveled in Europe and then settled in Madrid, where she maintained a literary salon and devoted herself to writing. Although very plain in appearance, she had intelligence, wit and vivacity. She was quite proud of her noble title and eager for public acclaim. In 1916 a professorship in Romance literature was especially created for her at the University of Madrid, and a statue was erected in her honor in her native La Coruña; but the ultimate honor of election to the *Academia Española* eluded her. In the beginning, she was more conversant with European literature than with that of her own country. Her inspiration as a novelist derived from the French and Russian naturalists *(La cuestión palpitante,* 1883; *La revolución y la novela en Rusia,* 1887). The critical theories propounded in the above works can be described as a modified naturalism, her chief concern being with the socio-ethics of the naturalist movement. These theories she attempted to project in her best novels: *Los pazos de Ulloa* (1886), and its sequel, *La madre naturaleza* (1887), two Zolaesque studies of social decay and human degeneracy in a rural Galician setting. Among her other works were *La quimera* (1905), an autobiographical novel; *Cuentos trágicos* (1916), the last in a series of short stories, in which she excelled; her travel books on France, Italy, Germany and Spain; and her literary essays on Feijóo, Hojeda, Rivas, Zorrilla, Valera, Alarcón, and others. A center of controversy because of her defense of naturalism, Pardo Bazán was the butt of extremes in critical evaluation. Her enduring fame rests on the two Galician novels mentioned above.

Cf. *Obras completas,* (Ed.) Sáinz de Robles, F. C., Madrid, 1947; Brown, M. G., *La vida y las novelas de Doña Emilia Pardo Bazán,* Madrid, 1940; Hilton, R., "Doña Emilia Pardo Bazán, Neo-Catholicism and Christian Socialism," *The Americas,* July, 1954; Osborne, R. E., "Emilia Pardo Bazán y la novela rusa," *Revista Hispánica Moderna,* XX, 1954.

pareado. Referring to a pair or couplet of rhymed verses.

Paris, Gaston. See under *cantar de gesta.*

Parnasillo. See under *tertulia.*

Parnaso salmantino. See *Escuela de Salamanca.*

paroxítona. In metrics, a word which has its accent on the penultimate *(i.e.* next to last) syllable.

Parra, Teresa de la (1895-1936). Venezuelan novelist. Daughter of a noted Venezuelan family, she was educated in Paris, spent most of her life in Europe, and died in Spain. Her remains were reinterred in Venezuela in 1947. Awarded a prize in Paris for the best American novel *(Ifigenia,* 1924). She is chiefly noted for her fictionalized accounts of childhood experiences amid country surroundings in Venezuela *(Las memorias de Mamá Blanca,* 1929). Her original style reflects the ingratiating charm of her personality and makes her one of the most significant prose stylists of Latin American literature.

Cf. Ratcliff, D. F., *Venezuelan Prose Fiction,* N. Y., 1933.

paso. Passage or procession. (1) One of the incidents of the Passion of Christ in religious plays or processions. (2) A short dramatic sketch, farce or interlude; e.g. *Las aceitunas* (1548) by Lope de Rueda (d. 1565). The *paso* was the forerunner of the *entremés,* or interlude, later cultivated by Cervantes. The term *paso* was first used by Lope de Rueda to designate his short prose farces intended as comic relief in longer verse plays. Inspired by the Italian *commedia dell'arte,* Rueda used stock characters (the *bobo,* or clown, the barber, etc.), but recast them into racy Spanish types. See also *entremés; género chico; Rueda, Lope de.*

pastoral novel. (Sp. *novela bucólica* or *pastoril).* A type of novel in which the characters generally represent real persons in the guise of shepherds and shepherdesses. It grew out of the poetic eclogue, of classical origin, and developed into a medley of verse and prose (Boccaccio's *Ameto,* 1341). Sannazaro's imitation of Boccaccio, *Arcadia* (1504), was the Italian pastoral that influenced Spanish and European writers. The Spanish pastoral novel flourished in the 16th and early 17th centuries, after the decline of the chivalric novel. Jorge de Montemayor initiated the type in Spain with his *Diana* (ca. 1559), not only the first but also the best Spanish pastoral. It influenced Gaspar Gil Polo's *Diana enamorada* (1564), as well as Sidney's *Arcadia* (1590), Shakespeare's *Two Gentlemen of Verona* (1595), and d'Urfé's *Astrée* (1607-1624). It also inspired Cervantes' first considerable work, *Galatea* (1585), and Lope de Vega's *Arcadia* (1598). The idyllic characters and background as well as the magical and supernatural elements of the genre soon hardened into uninspired conventionality despite the frequently charming bucolic lyrics interspersed in the narrative and the interest created by thinly disguised contemporary personages and allusions.

Cf. Menéndez y Pelayo, M., "Orígines de la novela," *NBAE,* I, Chap. 8; Rennert, H., *The Spanish Pastoral Romances,* Philadelphia, 1912.

pastorela. A type of Provençal or Gallego poem in pastoral style. The theme is usually a debate between a suitor and a shepherdess (cow girl, goatherdess, *etc.),* wherein the girl's arguments prevail, as a rule. The *serranilla* is supposed to have originated from this form. See under *serranilla.*

pastourelle. A lyrical poem of Provençal and Galician origin, dealing with shepherdesses or cowgirls. It was the prototype of the Castilian *serranilla,* or pastoral love lyric. See under *serranilla.*

Pata de la raposa (La). See under *Pérez de Ayala.*

patraña. A fictitious tale or story.

patrañuelo. A collection of *patrañas,* or fictitious tales.

Patrañuelo (El). See under *Timoneda.*

payada. A song or poem composed by a gaucho minstrel *(payador),* often with guitar accompaniment. Also a song contest between gaucho minstrels. See also *payador.*

payador. The gaucho minstrel who improvised songs *(payadas)* to his own guitar accompaniment as he wandered from place to place like a troubadour of old. See also *gaucho literature; payada.*

Payró, Roberto J. (1867-1928). Argentine journalist, translator of Zola, short-story writer and dramatist. A socialist and ardent opponent of militarism. His plays emphasize social and ethical themes. His forte, however, is the "costumbre criolla," the short sketch of local manners and morals *(Historia de Pago Chico).* Payró's best known work is his "novela picaresca," *El casamiento de Laucha.* Chief works: (novelettes and sketches) *El casamiento de Laucha,* 1906; *Historia de Pago Chico,* 1908; *Violines y toneles,* 1908; (plays) *Canción trágica,* 1900; *Sobre las ruinas,* 1904; *Vivir quiero conmigo,* 1913; *Fuego en el rastrojo,* 1925.

Cf. Larra, R., *Payró, el hombre y la obra,* Buenos Aires, 1938.

Paz en la guerra. See under *Unamuno.*

Pazos de Ulloa (Los). See under *Pardo Bazán.*

Pedraza, Juan de. Author of *Farsa llamada danza de la muerte* (1551), one of the outstanding treatments of the *danse macabre* theme. See under *Danza de la muerte.*

Pedro de Urdemalas. See under *picaresque novel; Salas Barbadillo.*

Peers, Edgar Allison (1890-1952). British hispanist, literary scholar and translator. Professor of Spanish literature at the University of Liverpool. Founder and Editor of *Bulletin of Hispanic Studies,* U. of Liverpool. Among his many translations were the works of Ramon Llull and of Santa Teresa. He also translated Piñeyro's *El romanticismo en España* (Paris, 1904): *The Romantics of Spain,* Liverpool, 1934. His major fields of interest were Spanish mysticism and romanticism. Chief publications: *Spanish Mysticism,* London, 1924; *Studies of the Spanish Mystics,* London, 1926; *Ramon Llull: A Biography,* London, 1929; *Saint John of the Cross,* Cambridge, 1932; *A Handbook to the Study and Teaching of Spanish,* London, 1938; *A History of the Romantic Movement in Spain,* 2 vols., Cambridge, 1940; *Antonio Machado,* Oxford,

1940; *A Critical Anthology of Spanish Verse,* U. of California Press, 1949.

Cf. *Hispania,* XXXVI, 1953.

Pelayo. See under *Quintana.*

Pensador mexicano (El). See *Fernández de Lizardi.*

pentasílabo. A poetic line or verse consisting of five syllables.

Peñas arriba. See under *Pereda, José María de.*

Peonía. See under *criollismo.*

Pepita Jiménez. See under *Valera, Juan.*

Per Abbat. See under *Cantar de Mío Cid.*

Peralta Barnuevo, Pedro de (1663-1743). Peruvian scholar, historian, dramatist and poet. Of Spanish and Creole descent. Remarkable for his linguistic accomplishments and prolific output on a vast range of subjects (rhetoric, law, theology, mathematics, military engineering, metallurgy, astronomy). Author of many occasional poems *(loas, actos, entremeses, bailes).* His most sustained poetic work was *Lima fundada,* an epic in royal octaves and baroque style. His dramas show the influence of Calderón *(Afectos vencen finezas)* and of Corneille *(Rodoguna).* Although interesting as a personality and for the fact that his occasional poems reveal the colloquial speech and popular customs of colonial Peru, his work is replete with the gongoristic excesses of his time. Among his chief works were: *Rodoguna,* 1708; *Triunfos de amor y poder,* 1710; *Afectos vencen finezas,* 1720; *Historia de España vindicada,* 1730; *Lima fundada o conquista del Perú,* 1732.

Cf. Leonard, I. A., "A Great Savant of Colonial Perú, Don Pedro de Peralta," *Philological Quarterly,* XVII, 1933.

Pereda, José María de (1833-1905). One of the great regional novelists of the 19th century. Born and died at his ancestral estate in Polanco, Santander. His full name was José María de Pereda y Sánchez de Porrúa. Born into a noble and religious family, he was the youngest of 22 children. He took his degree at the *Instituto Cántabro* in Santander. Then he went to Madrid to prepare for entrance to the Artillery School of the Military Academy; but after a few years of literary-bohemian dawdling, he dropped his studies and spent the rest of his life managing his estate and writing. He was married in 1869; traveled in France and Spain; served as a Deputy to the Cortes; and, for a short time, was active in the Catalán separatist movement. He was elected to the

Academia Española in 1897, sponsored by his intimate friend, Pérez Galdós. Pereda's first important works were *costumbrista* sketches: *Escenas montañesas* (1864) and *Tipos y paisajes* (1871). His most popular novel was *Sotileza* (1884), a portrayal of the fishermen of Santander. His best *cuadros de costumbres* of the mountain region of Santander appeared in his *Peñas arriba* (1893). In portraying the fisherfolk and mountaineers of Santander, Pereda also projected his social and religious conservatism. To him the roots of Spanish tradition are fostered in the provinces. His pictures of the semi-feudal system of landholders and tenant farmers are idyllic; his antipathy to urban society is profound (Cf. his *Pedro Sánchez* 1883, a study of social and political life in Madrid). His vivid style, colored by native idiom, and his realistic portrayal of types and landscapes make him the classical representative of the regional novel.

Cf. *Obras completas,* (Ed.) Cossío, J. M. de, Madrid, 1934; Montera, J., *Pereda: biografía crítica,* Madrid, 1919; Camp, J., *José María de Pereda, sa vie, son oeuvre, et son temps,* Paris, 1937.

Pérez de Ayala, Ramón (1881). Novelist, poet and critic. Born at Oviedo, Asturias. Studied at the Jesuit schools in Gijón and in Carrión de los Condes. Took his law degree at Oviedo. World War I correspondent for *La Prensa* of Buenos Aires. Traveled widely (France, Italy, England, U. S. and South America). Elected to the *Academia Española* in 1928. Spanish Ambassador to England during the Second Republic. Now resident in Argentina. His three major poetic works respectively treat the themes of the country, the sea and the river *(La paz del sendero,* 1903; *El sendero innumerable,* 1916; *El sendero andante,* 1921). They reveal an intellectual poet, whose emotions pass through a filter of abstract symbols. His chief critical works appear in *Política y toros* (1918), satirical essays on politics and manners, and in *Las máscaras* (1918), a book of dramatic criticism. Pérez de Ayala is most original in his novels, beginning with *Tinieblas en las cumbres* (1907); *AMGD,* (1910), [*i.e.,* the Jesuit motto, *Ad majorem gloriam Dei*]; *La pata de la raposa* (1912); and *Troteras y danzaderas* (1913). These novels are partly autobiographical, the first dealing with erotic awakening in adolescence; the second, with unhappy reactions to Jesuit education; the third, with a pathological case of *abulia;* and the fourth, with literary bohemian life in Madrid. Outstanding among the novels of his mature period are: *Belarmino y Apolonio* (1921), a symbolic portrayal of the conflict between faith and reason; *Luna de miel, luna de hiel* (1923) and its sequel, *Los trabajos de Urbano y Simona* (1923), showing the contrast between the realities of love and idealistic innocence; *Tigre Juan* (1926) and its sequel, *El curandero de su honra* (1926), on the Don Juan theme. Also notable are his three novelettes of reality and disillusionment (*Novelas poemáticas,* 1916), respectively entitled *Prometeo, Luz del domingo,* and *La caída de los Limones.* A disciple of Clarín (Leopoldo Alas) and an admirer of Galdós, Pérez de Ayala developed into a consummate master of characterization and of novelistic technique. These factors, plus his wide culture, polished style and wry humor make him one of the greatest contemporary exemplars of the novel of ideas.

Cf. *Obras completas,* Madrid, 1923-1927; *Selections from Pérez de Ayala,* (Ed.) Adams, N. B. & Stoudemire, S. A., N. Y., 1934; *Poesías completas,* Buenos Aires, 1942; Agustín, F., *Ramón Pérez de Ayala. Su vida y sus obras,* Madrid, 1927; Balseiro, J. A., "Ramón Pérez de Ayala, novelista," *El vigía,* II, Madrid, 1928.

Pérez de Guzmán, Fernán (1376?-1460?). Court poet and biographer. Born and died at Batres. Nephew of López de Ayala *(El Canciller),* and uncle of the Marqués de Santillana. He served Henry III as ambassador to Aragón. His early poems are represented in the *Cancionero de Baena.* His most important prose work is the *Mar de (h)istorias* (written in the 1440's; publ. Valladolid, 1512), a collection of biographies in three parts: (1) emperors and princes; (2) savants and saints; (3) Enriquez III, Juan II, prelates, noblemen and other illustrious contemporaries. It is the third part of the *Mar de historias* which is of chief interest to literary historians. Its title is *Generaciones y semblanzas* (first published separately in 1516 at Logroño). Its brief biographies, teeming with vivid character insights and devoid of pedantry, created a modern style of succinct biographical portraiture.

Cf. *Mar de historias,* (Ed.) Foulché-Delbosc, R., *Revue hispanique,* XXXVIII, 1913; *Generaciones y semblanzas,* (Ed.) Domínguez Bordona, J., Madrid, 1924; Foulché-Delbosc, R., "Étude bibliographique sur Fernán Pérez de Guzmán," *Revue hispanique,* XVI, 1907.

Pérez de Hita, Ginés (1544?-1619?). Historian, poet and novelist. The only facts known of his life have been inferred from scattered evidence. His birthplace is thought to be the town of Mula, Murcia; he probably died in Barcelona. He took part in the war against the rebellious Alpujarra Moors (1568-1571). In about 1592 he wrote a verse adaptation of the *Crónica troyana,* entitled *Bello troyano.* The work for which he is chiefly noted is the *Historia de los bandos de los Zegríes y Abencerrajes* (Pt. I, Zaragoza, 1595; Pt. II, Alcalá, 1604), generally referred to as *Guerras civiles de Granada.* It is one of the first historical novels of Spanish literature and, after *Abindarráez y Jarifa,* the first of the Moorish romance cycles. The first part is more imaginative and relates events culminating in the fall of Granada (1492); the second part is more historical and relates events of the Morisco rebellion mentioned above. Although based on historical fact, the work abounds in fantastic episodes and introduces many fictitious characters. However, it contains vivid descriptions of local Granada scenes, and the narrative is interspersed with picturesque ballads of frontier warfare. The work enjoyed great popularity and went through innumerable editions both in Spain and abroad. Among the foreign authors it inspired were: Mlle de Scudéry (*Almahide,* 1660); Mme de la Fayette (*Zaïde,* 1670); Chateaubriand (*Aventures du dernier Abencérage,* 1826); and Washington Irving (*Chronicle of the Conquest of Granada,* 1829).

Cf. "Guerras civiles de Granada," *BAE,* III; Menéndez y Pelayo, M., "Orígines de la novela," *NBAE,* I; Festugiere, P., "Ginés Pérez de Hita, sa personne, son oeuvre," *Bulletin hispanique,* XLVI, 1944.

Pérez de Miranda. See *López Soler.*

Pérez Galdós, Benito (1843-1920). Spain's outstanding novelist in the 19th century. Born in Las Palmas, Canary Islands; died in Madrid. Of a large and well-to-do middle class family, he received his early education at English schools in the Canary Islands and then studied law in Madrid (1863). He never married, but had several mistresses, one of whom bore him children. After an unsuccessful start as a dramatist, he turned to the novel, beginning with *La fontana de oro* (1870), and shortly thereafter, continuing with his monumental historical series, *Episodios nacionales,* of which the first was *Trafalgar* (1873). Galdós participated actively in the literary and intellectual life of Madrid, frequenting the *Ateneo,* writing for various journals (*El Debate, La Nación, Revista de España,* etc.), and forming intimate friendships with eminent writers and critics, Pereda, Menéndez y Pelayo, etc.). He traveled to France and to England, the countries of his chief literary influences, Balzac, Zola and Dickens. He served several times as Deputy to the Cortes (1886, 1890, 1907), and was elected to the *Academia Española* in 1897. His declining years were saddened by ill health, blindness, political enmity and occasional financial difficulties. Galdós never really mastered the art of dramaturgy. Though some of his plays were well received, he was on the whole unsuccessful as a dramatist, most of his plays being dramatizations of his novels (*Realidad,* 1892; *La loca de la casa,* 1893; *El abuelo,* 1904; etc.). He owes his fame to his historical novel cycles, his social thesis novels and his panoramic novels of social and ethical themes. An extraordinarily fecund writer, spurred by financial necessity, he produced at the rate of several novels a year. His *Episodios nacionales* (1873-1912) were conceived on a grand scale, designed to illustrate the destiny of Spain and the lessons to be learned from her history. They have been classified into five groups comprising a total of 46 novels. Based on 19th century Spanish history, they cover the period from the naval battle of Trafalgar (1805) to the beginning of the reign of Alfonso XII (1875). The novels are carefully documented and realistic in treatment. Galdós succeeded in painting an objective picture of historical events as they must have appeared to those participating in them. Most vivid are his scenes of mass conflict, mobs, riots, street fighting and looting. However, his characterization is frequently weak and certain absurd episodes detract from the undoubted greatness of the series. Galdós was preeminent in novels of social reform and enlightenment. He fought clericalism and bigotry in his *Doña Perfecta* (1876), *Gloria* (1877) and *La familia de León Roch* (1878). One of his greatest novels is *La desheredada* (1881), inspired by *Don Quixote.* The heroine's delusion that she is of noble birth leads her ultimately to a life of degradation. The great masterpiece of his mature period is *Fortunata y Jacinta* (1886-1887), a four-volume series which is a social study of two unhappily married women, Fortunata, a proletarian, and Jacinta, a bourgeoise. The former is the mistress of the latter's husband and bears him a child, whereas the latter is barren. The symbolism indicates that the creativeness of Spanish society lies in the lower classes. Another of his longer novels is *Ángel Guerra* (1890-1891), treating the theme of religious conversion. It was the prelude to the Tolstoyan phase in Galdós. The four books of his *Torquemada* series (1889-1895) treat of the ethical decay of character as the result of avarice. In 1895 he wrote *Nazarín* and in 1897 *Misericordia,* the former about a Christ-like priest who aids the poor; the latter, a study of a beggar woman who is a kind of proletarian saint.

Cf. *Obras completas,* (Ed.) Sáinz de Robles, F. C., Madrid, 1942-1945; Menéndez y Pelayo, M., "Don Benito Pérez Galdós considerado como novelista," *Estudios de crítica literaria,* V, Madrid, 1908; Clarín, *Galdós,* Madrid, 1912; Madariaga, S., "Benito Pérez Galdós," *Semblanzas literarias contemporáneas,* Madrid, 1924; Walton, L. B., *Pérez Galdos and the Spanish Novel of the 19th Century,* N. Y., 1928; Casalduero, J., *Vida y obra de Galdós,* Buenos Aires, 1943; Eoff, S. H., *The Novels of Pérez Galdós,* St. Louis, 1955; Pattison, W. T., *Benito Pérez Galdós and the Creative Process,* Minneapolis, 1954; Río, A. del, *Estudios galdosianos,* Zaragoza, 1953.

Perfecta casada (La). See under *León, Luis de.*

Peribáñez. See under *Vega, Lope de.*

Periquillo sarniento (El). See *Fernández de Lizardi.*

Pero Abad. See under *Cantar de Mío Cid.*

perqué. (1) A type of poem employing the technique of query and response. (2) A defamatory book using the query and response technique.

Persiles y Sigismunda. See under *Cervantes.*

petrarquismo. (Eng. *petrarchism*). The style of the Italian Renaissance humanist and poet, Francesco Petrarch (1304-1374), especially in his *Rime* (to Laura), which achieved European-wide influence in the 15th and 16th centuries. Characteristic of *petrarquismo* are personalized feeling and a mannered or *culto* style. A predilection for autobiographical detail, the facets of human nature and the cult of classical antiquity are other features of the style. In Spain the influence of Petrarch was evidenced by the many translations of his works and by the imitations of Spanish poets. Chief among them were Santillana (1398-1458); Boscán

(1490-1542); Garcilaso de la Vega (1503-1536); and Herrera (1534-1597). Petrarch's influence is also evident in *La Celestina* (1499) and in Montemayor's *Diana* (1559). See also under *Renaissance.*

Cf. Berdan, J. M., "A Definition of Petrarchism," *Publications of the Modern Language Association,* XXIV, 1909; Fucilla, J. G., *A Study of Petrarchism in Spain During the 16th Century,* (Diss.), U. of Chicago, 1929.

petrarquista. An imitator or admirer of the style of Francesco Petrarch (1304-1374), Italian Renaissance poet and humanist. See *petrarquismo.*

Philip II. See under *Prescott.*

Philip V. See under *Biblioteca Nacional.*

Pi y Margall, Francisco. See under *krausismo.*

pícara. A female rogue. See under *pícaro.*

Pícara Justina (La). See *Justina.*

picaresca. (1) A band or guild of rogues. (2) The profession of roguery. (3) Picaresque literature. (4) Feminine form of the adjective *picaresco,* pertaining to rogues or roguery.

picaresco. (Fem. *picaresca*). Pertaining to rogues or roguery, or to literature dealing with these subjects.

picaresque novel. (Sp. *novela picaresca*). An episodic narrative dealing with the life of a *pícaro,* or rogue. (For different types of rogues, see under *pícaro*). The rogue is usually the servant of several masters in turn, each representative of a different class or calling, thus affording the rogue the opportunity of satirizing a wide cross-section of society. The picaresque novel is usually told in the first person and may contain elements of satire, caricature, more or less sham moralizing, and parodies of idealistic fiction. As a distinct genre it originated in Spain in the 16th century. It served as a realistic reaction against the fantastic romances of chivalry with their preposterous array of fabulous characters. Among the earliest of these novels are *La Lozana andaluza* (1528), by Francisco Delicado, and the great anonymous masterpiece of the type, *La vida de Lazarillo de Tormes* (1554). Ranking next to it is Mateo Alemán's *Guzmán de Alfarache* (Pt. I, 1599; Pt. II, 1604). *La pícara Justina* (1605), by López de Úbeda, introduces the female rogue. Cervantes' contribution to the genre uses animal satirists in his *Coloquio de los perros;* and introduces boy rogues and the rogues' guild in his *Rinconete y Cortadillo* (both in

Novelas ejemplares, 1613). *Marcos de Obregón* (1618), by Vicente Espinel, is an example of realistic autobiography. Traces of its influence are to be found in Le Sage's *Gil Blas.* Among the other writers of rogue romances were Quevedo (*Vida del buscón llamado don Pablos de Segovia,* 1626); Salas Barbadillo (*La ingeniosa Elena,* 1612; *Pedro de Urdemalas,* 1620; and *Don Diego de noche,* 1623, an example of the epistolary rogue novel); Castillo Solórzano (*Teresa del Manzanares,* 1632); and Vélez de Guevara (*El diablo cojuelo,* 1641, the prototype of Lesage's *Le diable boiteux*). See also *pícaro* and the various authors under their separate listing.

Cf. Chandler, F. W., *Literature of Roguery,* Boston, 1907; DeHaan, F., *Outline of the History of the Novela Picaresca in Spain,* N. Y., 1903; Suárez, M., *La novela picaresca y el pícaro en la literatura española,* Madrid, 1926; Bataillon, M., *Le roman picaresque,* Paris, 1931; Pereda Valdés, I., *La novela picaresca en España y América,* Montevideo, 1950.

pícaro. A rogue or knave. (Eng. *picaroon*). According to *DRAE,* as a noun: an impudent, saucy and dissolute character given to riotous living or evil ways; as an adjective: base, wicked, deceitful, crafty, sly, mischievous, knavish or roguish. The word first occurs in Spanish texts at about the middle of the 16th century (1541? 1548?), in the meaning of "tatterdemalion" in reference to ragged boys of the streets. Its etymology is uncertain. Various proposed derivations are: *picar,* to chop or mince (meat, *etc.*), as in *pícaro de cocina,* kitchen knave or scullion; *picard,* a soldier of Picardy; *bigardo,* a licentious cleric; *etc.* The *pícaros* were usually street urchins, errand boys or porters, kitchen help, personal servants, wandering rogues or adventurers. Living on the fringes of a caste-ridden society which spawned and then ignored them, they got by on their wits, flattering, lying, cheating and stealing. They were a distinct social class in 16th and 17th century Spain, often organized into rogues' guilds *(picarescas).* In literature the *pícaro* came into his own with the development of the picaresque novel *(novela picaresca).* In addition to the types mentioned above, the *pícaro* could be a female rogue *(La pícara Justina,* 1605); an animal (*El coloquio de los perros,* 1613); or a disembodied soul reincarnated in various characters (*El siglo pita-*

górico, 1644). The term "anti-hero" is often used to describe the *pícaro* of literature, since he usually serves as a foil to an honorable character and lacks the noble qualities ordinarily identified with a hero. See also *picaresque novel.*

Cf. Chandler, F. W., *Literature of Roguery,* Boston, 1907.

Picón-Febres, Gonzalo. See under *criollismo.*

pie quebrado. "Limping verse." (1) The short line interspersed in a series of long lines within a stanza. (2) A metrical form comprising short lines interspersed at intervals in a series of long lines. This metrical form has a long history, beginning with Berceo and the poets of the *Cancioneros* and going up to modern times. It reached its greatest vogue in the 15th century in the poetry of the Marqués de Santillana (1398-1458), Jorge Manrique (1440-1479), Juan del Encina (1468?-1529), Gil Vicente (d. 1536?), and others. The pattern established by these poets had eight syllables for the long lines and four syllables for the short lines. Later the syllabic ratios varied (16—8; 12—6; *etc.*). In the 18th century an Italianate form of *pie quebrado* was introduced by Manuel de Arjona (1771-1820), namely the *octava italiana de pie quebrado,* comprising eleven and seven syllable lines rhymed ABBCADDC.

Pío Cid. See *Ganivet, Ángel.*

Pipa de Kif. See under *Valle-Inclán.*

Píramo y Tisbe. See under *Góngora.*

Piscator de Salamanca. See under *Torres Villarroel.*

Pitcher, Stephen L. (1885). American hispanist. Supervisor, Foreign Languages, St. Louis Public Schools, 1928-1942. Principal of various secondary schools, and Lecturer, St. Louis University. Editor, school edition of Isaac's *María,* N. Y., 1922. Author of *The Teaching of Spanish and Portuguese,* N.E.A., Washington, D. C., 1943; Co-author, *A Survey of Language Classes in the A.S.T.P.,* Modern Language Association, N. Y., 1944. President, American Association of Teachers of Spanish and Portuguese, 1942-1944.

Pitollet, Camille (1876). French hispanist, literary critic and historian. Former editor of *Revue des langues vivantes.* Principal works: *V. Blasco Ibáñez: sus novelas y la novela de su vida; Hispania; Morceaux choisis de prosateurs et de poètes espagnols.*

Author of numerous articles in the *Bulletin hispanique* and the *Revista de Filología Española.*

Cf. *Hispania,* XXXVI, 1953.

Plácida y Vitoriano. See *Encina, Juan del.*

Plácido. See *Valdés, Gabriel de la Concepción.*

plateresco. A style of ornamentation used by Spanish silversmiths in the 16th century in imitation of the classic architecture typical of Spanish Renaissance façades. Because of the ornate filigree work of these silversmiths *(plateros),* the term is used in literary criticism to designate the style of writing in Spanish romances of the 16th century, before Cervantes. Compare *churrigueresco.*

platonism. The influence of Plato's doctrines was most prominent in Spanish literature during the Renaissance. The immediate sources of *platonismo* in Spanish poetry were the Italian Renaissance poets, Dante Alighieri (1265-1321) and Francesco Petrarch (1304-1374), widely translated and imitated in Spain during the 15th and 16th centuries. Also influential in disseminating platonic doctrines among Spanish writers and poets was León Hebreo's *Diálogos de amor* (first Spanish translation, 1582). The chief platonic ideas taken up by Spanish poets were those of ideal beauty and spiritual love. They are reflected in the poetry of Boscán (d. 1542) and Santillana (1398-1458); in the mystical writing of Luis de León (1522-1591), and in the humanistic works of Luis Vives (1492-1540). See also under *mysticism; humanism; Renaissance.*

Cf. Del Río, A., *Historia de la literatura española,* N. Y., 1948.

playera. A distinctive popular song of Andalusia, in its form a variant of the *seguidilla.*

pliegos sueltos. See under *suelto.*

Pobrecito hablador (El). See *Larra, Mariano José de.*

Poema de Alfonso Onceno. The last example of *mester de juglaría* poetry, composed before the middle of the 14th century. It is attributed to an unknown poet, Rodrigo Yáñez (Ruy Yannes), although internal evidence would seem to indicate that he was merely the translator, the original probably having been written in *gallego.* The manuscript was discovered in 1573 by Hurtado de Mendoza, and is now preserved in the *Escorial.* The poem consists of 2,456 quatrains of 8-syllable lines (many irregular) rhymed ABAB. It is a chronicle of the reign of Alfonso XI (1312?-

1350), and hence is frequently referred to as the *Crónica rimada de Alfonso Onceno.* The highlights of the poem are the episodes recounting Alfonso's heroic exploits against the Moors of Andalusia. The poem represents a transitional stage between the folk epic and erudite epic balladry. Alfonso XI himself is noted in Spanish literature as the probable author of the first examples of *juglaría* poetry (represented in *Canzionere portoghese della Biblioteca Vaticana).*

Cf. *Poema de Alfonso Onceno,* in *BAE,* LVII; Menéndez Pidal, *Poema de Alfonso XI: fuentes, dialectico, estilo,* Madrid, 1953.

Poema de Fernán González. See *Fernán González.*

Poema del Cid. See *Cantar de Mío Cid.*

Poema de Mío Cid. See *Cantar de Mío Cid; Cid (El).*

Poema de Yuçuf. The chief example of *aljamiada* literature, *i.e.* Spanish transcribed in the Arabic or Hebrew alphabet. The oldest preserved manuscript (incomplete) dates from the end of the 14th century, but the poem was probably composed much earlier (13th or early 14th century). It consists of 312 stanzas in *cuaderna vía.* The author is unknown, but he was probably a Moor and, to judge from the dialect, an Aragonese. The hero is Yuçuf (Yoçef, Yusuf) or José, the Biblical Joseph; however, the episodes recounted are not based on the Bible but on the Koran, rabbinical writings and Islamic legends. The story follows Joseph's adventures up to the time of his final triumph over his brothers. The highlight is the episode of Joseph and Potiphar's wife. The poem is also referred to under the titles of *Coplas de Yoçef,* and *Libro de Yusuf.* See also *aljamiada literature.*

Cf. *Poema de Yuçuf,* (Ed.) Menéndez Pidal, R., *Revista de archivos, bibliotecas y museos,* VII, 1902; *Coplas de Yoçef: A Medieval Spanish Poem in Hebrew Characters,* (Ed.) González Llubera, I., Cambridge, 1935.

poemas aljamiados. See *aljamiada literature.*

Poesía de la Edad Media. See under *Alonso, Dámaso.*

poesía gauchesca. See *gaucho literature.*

poesía gnómica. See *literatura gnómica.*

Poesía juglaresca y juglares. See under *Menéndez Pidal.*

Poética (de Luzán). See under *Luzán Claramunt de Suelves.*

Polendos. See under *Palmerín cycle.*

Polifemo y Galatea. See under *Góngora.*

Polinarda. See under *Palmerín cycle.*

Política de Dios. See under *Quevedo.*

Política y toros. See under *Pérez de Ayala.*

Político Fernando (El). See under *Gracián y Morales.*

Polo, Gaspar Gil. See under *Montemayor.*

Pombo. The famous literary *tertulia* founded by Gómez de la Serna at the Madrid Café Pombo. See under *Gómez de la Serna; tertulia.*

Porfiar hasta morir. See under *Vega, Lope de.*

Porvenir de España (El). See *Ganivet; Unamuno.*

postmodernismo. The contemporary period of Spanish literature, from about 1910 to 1936.

Prado, Pedro (1886-1952). Chilean artist, diplomat, novelist and poet. Former Chilean Minister to Colombia. Founded the artistic and literary society, *Los diez* (1915), and the literary journal, *Revista moderna,* exercizing in both a decisive influence on the esthetic theories and literary practice of his country. Awarded a poetry prize in 1935 and the National Literary Prize in 1949. An experimentalist in forms and styles, Prado wrote free verse, poems in prose and symbolic novels, his best work of the latter type being *Alsino* (1920). Among his chief works are: *Flores del cardo,* 1908; *La reina de Rapa Nui,* 1914; *Los pájaros errantes,* 1915; *Alsino,* 1920; *Un juez rural,* 1924; *Androvar,* 1925; *Las horas,* 1935.

Cf. Torres Ríoseco, A., *Novelistas contemporáneos de América,* 379-409, Santiago, 1940.

préciosité. See *gongorism.*

pregunta. Query-and-response verses, often in the form of a riddle. It occurs in early Spanish literature as a form of catechetical instruction or of entertainment.

Premio Fastenrath. A literary award of the *Academia Española,* sponsored in 1899 by a celebrated German hispanist, Johannes Fastenrath (1839-1908).

Prescott, William Hickling (1796-1859). Influenced by George Ticknor, Prescott began the study of Spanish in 1824, determined to make Spanish history his life work. He devoted three years to the gathering of materials and seven years to the writing of his first work, *Ferdinand and Isabella* (1837). In similar fashion he continued with *The Conquest of Mexico* (1843); *The Conquest of*

Peru (1847); and *Philip II* (vols. 1 and 2, 1852-55; vol. 3, 1858; vols. 4 and 5 incomplete). Of the 19th century school of American Hispanist historians (Irving, Motley), Prescott was the most thorough scholar, sparing no pains in documenting his work from original sources (the Navarrete collection of Mexican and Peruvian manuscripts, material from the Spanish Academy, unpublished Spanish archives, etc.).

Cf. Ticknor, G., *Life of William Hickling Prescott,* Philadelphia, 1875; Brooks, Van Wyck, *The Flowering of New England,* N. Y., 1936.

Primaleón. See under *Palmerín cycle.*

Primavera y flor de . . . romances. See under *romance.*

Primera crónica general. See under *crónica.*

Príncipe constante (El). See under *Calderón.*

Proa. See under *Güiraldes.*

Proemio e carta. See under *Santillana.*

progressive assimilation. See under *assimilation.*

Prontuario de Ortografía. See under *Real Academia Española.*

Propaladia. See under *Torres Naharro.*

proparoxítona. In metrics, a word which has its accent on the antepenultimate (*i.e.* third from last) syllable.

Prosas profanas. See under *Darío.*

Protestant Reformation. See under *Reformation.*

Proverbios morales. See under *Sem Tob.*

proverbs. See under *folklore.*

Prudencia en la mujer (La). See under *Tirso de Molina.*

psycho-zoological tale. See under *Arévalo Martínez.*

Pueblo (El). See under *Blasco Ibáñez.*

Pulgar, Hernando del (1430?-1493?). Historian and biographer. He was a court chronicler, serving in turn Juan II and Enriquez IV. His *Claros varones de Castilla* (Toledo, 1486) is a collection of biographies of illustrious men at the court of Enriquez IV (ruled 1454-1474). In a sense it was the continuation of a similarly-entitled poetic work by Pérez de Guzmán and of the latter's prose work, *Generaciones y semblanzas,* although considered superior to both. As Spanish ambassador to France (1474) and as official chronicler of Ferdinand and Isabella (ruled 1474-1504), Pulgar was ideally situated to write the authentic account of their reign (up to 1490): *Crónica de los Reyes Católicos* (published 1545 in a Latin translation by Nebrija; in Spanish, 1565). Pulgar also edited the *Coplas de Mingo Revulgo* (Seville, 1506). His *Letras* (Burgos, 1485-1486) show him as a man of classical learning, a keen judge of character and a concise stylist.

Cf. *Claros varones de Castilla,* (Ed.) Domínguez Bordona, J., Madrid, 1923; *Crónico de los Reyes Católicos,* in *NBAE,* LXX; *Letras,* in *BAE,* XIII.

pundonor. Point of honor. An expressed or implied challenge to personal or family virtue or integrity. The theme of *pundonor* occurs frequently in the Spanish drama. It was first made a primary dramatic factor by Bartolomé de Torres Naharro (d. 1524?) in his play *La Himenea* or *Ymenea (ca.* 1525). The *pundonor* is frequently the catastrophic element that precipitates the tragedy, since a stain on one's honor, however slight, must be wiped out whatever the cost, be it the death of the perpetrator and/or the compromised female, and the sacrifice of love, fortune and even one's own existence. The *pundonor* theme is common in the *capa y espada* comedy, and also occurs in Lope de Vega and in Calderón. The term is somewhat similar to the French expression *noblesse oblige.*

Puñal del godo (El). See under *Rodrigo el godo; Zorrilla y Moral.*

Purgatorio de san Patricio. One of the few examples of minor novelistic prose in the Middle Ages. It is believed to have been composed in the 13th century. The author is unknown. The story is adapted from a Latin original of the late 12th century, written by Henry of Saltrey. It relates the visions of Hell which St. Patrick experienced during a penitential retreat in a grotto in Ireland. The theme was later treated by Lope de Vega, Calderón, and others.

Púrpura de la Rosa. One of Calderón's musical plays. See under *zarzuela.*

Puyol y Alonso, Julio (1865-1937). Historian and literary scholar. Among his notable contributions is the three volume critical edition, with commentary and notes, of Úbeda's *La pícara Justina,* Madrid, 1912. Chief publications: *El Arcipreste de Hita,* 1906; *La crónica particular del Cid,* 1911; *Cantar de gesta de don Sancho II de Castilla,* 1911; *Elogio de Cervantes,* 1916; *Los cronistas de Enrique IV,* 1921.

Q

Quechua. (Also spelled *Quichua*). (1) The name of a Peruvian Indian tribe which, at the time of the Spanish conquest, inhabited the region northwest of Cuzco. (2) The language spoken by these Indians at the time of the Inca Empire, and still used today by Indians of Peru, Ecuador and Bolivia. The *Quechua* language comprises eight major dialects: quiteño, lamaño, chinchaya, huancayo, ayacucho, cuzqueño, boliviano and tucumano. The native verse drama, *Ollanta* (discovered *ca.* 1770), is written in *Quechua* dialect. See also under *Ollanta.*

quentos. See under *Libro de los gatos.*

querella calderoniana. See under *Schlegel; Böhl von Faber.*

Quevedo, Francisco de (1580-1645). Satirical poet, scholar, philosopher, caustic wit and critic of court corruption. Born in Madrid; died in Villanueva. His full name was Francisco Gómez de Quevedo y Villegas. He was an aristocrat, both his parents serving at the court. Orphaned at an early age, he was entrusted to the Jesuits in Madrid for his early education, then studied the humanities at Alcalá, and theology at Valladolid. He was noted for his classical scholarship. His first poems appeared in *Flores de poetas ilustres de España* (Ed. by Pedro Espinosa, 1605). As the result of a duel, he fled to Italy (1611), where he was employed as a diplomatic counselor by the Spanish Viceroy, the Duke of Osuna. Involved in the Venetian conspiracy of 1618, he shared Osuna's disgrace and, on his return to Spain, was confined to his estate at Torre de Juan (1620). After the death of Philip III, Quevedo returned for a while to royal favor, but not to the favor of the royal minister, Olivares. Under suspicion as the presumed author of some caustic verses placed on the king's table and reflecting against Olivares and court corruption, Quevedo was imprisoned for four years (1639-1643) at the Monastery of San

Marcos in León. Broken in health, he died a few years later. Quevedo was an accomplished scholar and philosopher, a subtle stylist and a satirical wit. In his fight against the influence of Góngora, he edited the poems of Luis de León in 1613; yet he himself was given to *conceptista* excesses. Although he was extremely versatile and essayed almost every literary form, his greatest work was in the field of the picaresque novel. His *Vida del buscón, llamado don Pablos de Segovia,* published at Saragossa in 1626 (referred to as "Buscón"), was a brilliant although cynical and, at times, repulsive novel, its milieu a student boarding house at Salamanca, peopled by unsavory characters. It is supposed to contain many autobiographical episodes. A broader social satire was his *Sueños y discursos de verdades y engaños en todos los oficios y estados del mundo,* published at Valencia in 1627 (referred to as "Sueños"). It consists of a series of five visions of hell, visited by the author in his dreams. He encounters people of various social classes and professions being punished for their sins, and he ridicules them mercilessly with his mordant wit. This work is the bitterest and most amusing social satire of the Golden Age. It enjoyed an enormous vogue and was translated and imitated throughout Europe. Among Quevedo's theological and philosophical works were *La cuna y la sepultura* (1612); *Constancia y paciencia del Santo Job* (1633); and *Vida de San Pablo Apóstol* (1643), all displaying stoicism and asceticism. His *Marco Bruto* (1631) and *Política de Dios* (I, 1617; II, 1635) show Quevedo as a political philosopher and moralist. His polemics against gongorism are contained in *La aguja de navegar cultos con la receta para hacer Soledades en un día* (1613). See also *conceptismo; gongorismo.*

Cf. *Obras completas,* in *BAE,* XXIII, XLVIII, LXIX; *idem,* (Ed.) Astrana Marín, L., 2 vols., Madrid, 1932; Mérimée, E., *Essai sur la vie et les oeuvres de Francisco de Quevedo,* Paris, 1885; Juderías, J., *Don Francisco de Quevedo y Villegas: la época, el hombre, las doctrinas,* Madrid, 1923; Spitzer, L., "Die Kunst Quevedos in seinem *Buscón,*" *Archivum Romanicum,* 1927; González Palencia, A., *Del "Lazarillo" a Quevedo,* Madrid, 1946.

quietismo. A mystical doctrine emphasizing attainment of Divine Grace through absolute passiveness rather than through works. Its chief exponent was the Spanish mystic, Miguel de Molinos

(1628-1696), in his *Guía espiritual* (1675). The doctrine exercized considerable influence on contemporary French writers, but was banned in Spain. Also called *molinosismo.*

Quijote. See under *Cervantes.*

Quintana, Manuel José (1772-1857). Poet, dramatist, and biographer. Born and died in Madrid. Studied under Meléndez Valdés at Salamanca. An ardent patriot, he was subject to the vicissitudes of Spanish politics during the reigns of Carlos IV (1788-1808) and Fernando VII (1808-1833). During the War of Liberation, he espoused the national cause, occupied a post in the *Junta Central,* edited the *Semanario Patriótico,* and published his stirring *Poesías patrióticas* (all in 1808). He was elected to the *Academia Española* in 1814. After the accession of Fernando VII and the trend to absolutism, Quintana, as a liberal constitutionalist and propagator of 18th century Enlightenment, was imprisoned at Pamplona (1814-1820). After the ensuing liberal reaction, he was appointed Minister of Education (1820). He suffered another period of imprisonment (1823-1828) during the reign of Fernando VII. Not until the accession of Isabel II (1833) was he restored to favor. He was appointed tutor to the royal family and was publicly honored by the Queen as the first poet laureate of Spain (1855). Although the Romantic movement reached its peak in his time, Quintana was hostile to it, his best work being in classical form; *e.g.* his patriotic odes: *Al armamento de las provincias españoles contra los franceses* (1808); *A España después de la revolución de marzo* (1808). As a dramaturgist he wrote a didactic poem, *Las reglas del drama* (1791), in which he championed the neo-classic theories of Boileau; and he put these theories into practice in his neo-classic tragedies: *El duque de Viseo* (1801) and *Pelayo* (1805), the latter more successful than treatments of the same theme by Moratín and Jovellanos. His outstanding prose work is his series of biographies, *Vidas de los españoles célebres* (1807-1833), dealing with the lives of the Cid, Guzmán el Bueno, Roger de Lauria, El Príncipe de Viana, Gonzalo Fernández de Córdoba ("El Gran Capitán"), Álvaro de Luna, Balboa, Pizarro, and Bartolomé de las Casas.

Cf. *Obras completas,* in *BAE,* XIX; Piñeyro, E., *Manuel José Quintana: ensayo crítico y biográfico,* Paris-Madrid, 1892; Mérimée, E., "Les poésies lyriques de Quintana," *Bulletin hispanique,*

IV, 1902; Menéndez y Pelayo, M., "Don Manuel José Quintana, considerado como poeta lírico," *Estudios de crítica literaria (5a. serie)*, Madrid, 1908; Blanco, R., *Quintana*, Madrid, 1910.

Quintero. See *Álvarez Quintero.*

quinteto. A stanza of five alternately rhymed lines in *arte mayor* (i.e. 12 syllables). A frequently occurring rhyme scheme is ABBAB. It differs from the *quintilla* in the length of its lines. See also *quintilla.*

quintilla. A stanza of five lines in *arte menor* (i.e. not exceeding 8 syllables). The rhyme scheme varies with individual poets. Frequently occurring patterns are: ABAAB, or ABABA. It differs from the *quinteto* in the length of its lines. Occasionally two *quintillas* may be combined to form a *décima.* See also *quintilla real.*

quintilla real. A stanza of five rhymed lines of eleven syllables. Except for the longer line it is the same as the *quintilla.*

Quiñones de Benavente, Luis (1589?-1651). Dramatist. Born in Toledo; died in Madrid. He was an ordained priest and a friend of Lope de Vega. Quiñones specialized exclusively in short plays *(entremeses, loas, jácaras)* in which he satirized social types and manners. He was a prolific writer and produced some 900 dramatic compositions of various sorts. The first collection of his playlets, numbering 48, was published in 1645. Next to Cervantes he is considered the outstanding writer of *entremeses.* See also under *entremés.*

Cf. *Colección de entremeses,* (Ed.) Cotarelo y Mori, E., *NBAE,* XVII, XVIII; Rouanet, L., *Intermèdes espagnoles du XVIIe siècle,* Paris, 1897.

Quiroga, Horacio (1878-1938). Uruguayan short-story writer. Born in Salto, Uruguay. Educated at the University of Montevideo. At various times a teacher, farmer, entrepreneur and government official. He lived most of his life in Argentina, in the province of Misiones, which furnished the background for his best stories. Influenced by the French Parnassians, by Poe and by Lugones, he was allied with the *modernista* group, his first book of tales and poems *(Los arrecifes de coral)* showing its characteristic style. Like his master, Poe, Quiroga was a neurotic with a penchant for morbid themes. He is best known for his collection of fifteen tales written in Misiones between 1910 and 1916 and published in 1917 under the title of *Cuentos de amor, de locura y de muerte.* A master of style and technique, his genius is revealed in the poetic evocation of the local atmosphere of the wild jungle region along the Paraná River. Many critics consider Quiroga the best *cuentista* in all South American literature. Among his chief works were: *Los arrecifes de coral,* 1901; *El crimen del otro,* 1904; *Los perseguidos,* 1905; *Historia de un amor turbio,* 1908; *Cuentos de amor, de locura y de muerte,* 1917; *Cuentos de la selva para niños,* 1918; *El salvaje,* 1920; *Anaconda,* 1921; *El desierto,* 1924; *Los desterrados,* 1926; *Más allá,* 1934.

Cf. Delgado, J. M. and Brignole, A. J., *Vida y obra de Horacio Quiroga,* Montevideo, 1939; Spell, J. R., *Contemporary Spanish-American Fiction,* Chapel Hill, N. C., 1944; Crow, J. A., *Horacio Quiroga—sus mejores cuentos,* Mexico City, 1943.

quiteño. A *Quechua* dialect. See under *Quechua.*

R

Raimundo, Archbishop (d. 1150). The Archbishop of Toledo, who assembled a group of scholars for the purpose of translating Arabic works into Latin. See under *escuela de traductores de Toledo.*

Ramón. See *Gómez de la Serna.*

ramonismo. See under *Gómez de la Serna.*

Raquel. See under *García de la Huerta.*

Razón de amor. The full title of this work is *Razón de amor con los denuestos del agua y el vino.* It is an early example of medieval *juglaría* poetry. Composed by an unknown author at about the beginning of the 13th century, it was probably of Provençal origin. The manuscript, preserved at the *Bibliothèque Nationale,* Paris, consists of two poems written together with very little continuity from one to the other. Despite references to the second half which appear in the first half, some authorities consider them two distinct works. The name of the copyist is given as Lope de Moros. The entire manuscript comprises 264 short lines of irregular length rhymed in couplets. The first part, *Razón de amor,* is interesting as the earliest example of a Castilian love lyric. It is a poetic dialogue between a medieval scholar and his damsel who encounter each other in a field of flowers, and who declare their love for each other, concluding with their reluctant separation amid protestations of eternal fidelity. The second part, *Los denuestos del agua y el vino,* is a debate between water and wine, a common medieval theme. Water's claim to preferment is its baptismal function; wine's claim is its symbolism in the communion. The outcome is inconclusive.

Cf. "Razón de amor . . .," (Ed.) Menéndez Pidal, R., *Revue hispanique,* XIII, 1905.

Real Academia de la Historia. See under *Montiano y Luyando.*

Real Academia Española. The Spanish National Academy of Language and Letters. Founded in 1713 by a Spanish nobleman, Juan Manuel Fernández Pacheco, during the reign of Felipe V (1700-1746), and approved by royal decree in 1714. The founder served as its first director. The original number of statutory members was 24; this was increased to 36 in 1847. Among the famous directors and secretaries of the *Real Academia* have been such writers and scholars as Martínez de la Rosa, the Duque de Rivas, Bretón de los Herreros, Rodríguez Marín, Menéndez Pidal, *et al.* In 1778, literary contests and awards were instituted by the Academy. Since 1847, the custom of having new entrants present an inaugural dissertation to be answered by a present member has been in effect. Many of these *discursos de ingreso* and *contestaciones* have become invaluable aids in the study of Spanish literature. The aim of the *Real Academia Española* was and is to study and foster the Spanish language. To this end, it began a compendious dictionary (*Diccionario de la lengua castellana,* 6 vols., 1726-1739) based on the authoritative usage of 100 great literary masters of the Spanish Language. Since 1780, a one-volume version of this dictionary has gone through 17 revised editions. A new version of the larger original edition is now in progress. The *Real Academia Española* also concerned itself with orthography and grammar (*Ortografía,* 1741; *Gramática,* 1771). Several revised editions of these works, for practical use, have been published (*Prontuario de Ortografía, Epítome de Gramática, Diccionario manual e illustrado de la lengua española,* etc.). The *Real Academia Española* also published critical and facsimile editions of the Spanish classics (Lope de Vega, Cervantes, etc.). This work is still carried on in a series entitled *Biblioteca selecta de clásicos españoles.* The Academy's journal, *Boletín de la Real Academia Española (BRAE;* or *BolReAc),* was founded in 1914. All of these activities are now under the supervision of Menéndez Pidal, Director of the *Real Academia Española* from 1925 to 1939, and from 1947 to date.

realismo. A reference to the group of 19th century post-romantic novelists or to their style. The originator of *realismo* was Fernán Caballero (1796-1877). Other precursors were the *costumbristas,* Larra (1809-1837), Mesonero Romanos (1803-1882), and Estébanez Calderón (1799-1867). Belonging to the earlier group of realistic novelists were: Pedro Antonio Alarcón (1833-1891), Juan Valera (1824-1905), and José María de Pereda (1833-1906). The later group comprises Emilia Pardo Bazán (1851-1920), Leopoldo Alas (Clarín) (1852-1901), Armando Palacio Valdés (1853-1938), and Vicente Blasco Ibáñez (1867-1928). The greatest representative of *realismo* was Benito Pérez Galdós (1843-1920). Characteristics of the Spanish realistic novel were its regionalism, its description of manners and types *(costumbrismo)*, its humor and general note of optimism.

Cf. Del Río, A., *Historia de la literatura española,* N. Y., 1948.

Rebelión de las masas (La). See under *Ortega y Gasset.*

reciprocal assimilation. See under *assimilation.*

Recuerdos del tiempo viejo. See under *Zorrilla y Moral.*

redondilla. A quatrain, or stanza of four variously rhymed lines of eight syllables *(arte menor).* A usual rhyme scheme for the *redondilla* is *ABBA*. Compare *cuarteta; cuarteto.*

Reformation. The Protestant Reformation had only an indirect influence on the literature of Spain. At the court of Charles V, the humanistic and reformist ideas of Erasmus (1466-1536) for a time held sway. Among the outstanding Spanish *erasmistas* were Luis Vives (1492-1540) and the brothers Alfonso (1490?-1532) and Juan (d. 1541) de Valdés. Certain reformist tendencies in the Spanish mystics also were inspired by Erasmian ideas (*e.g.* Fray Luis de León). However, Erasmian notions of reconciliation with the Protestants, externalized by Catholic attempts at the same objective (Diet of Worms, 1521; Diet of Augsburg, 1530) ended unsuccessfully. Reform of the Church thenceforth was to come from within, but coupled with stern measures against heresy. Foremost in the fight against Protestantism was the Jesuit Order, or Society of Jesus, founded in 1538 by Ignatius Loyola (1491-1556). The Catholic Reformation (Counter-Reformation) set in with the Council of Trent (1545-1563), which, together with its internal reforms, tightened the reins on orthodoxy. Strict limits were set on critical inquiry, and the sanctity of the Vulgate Bible was reaffirmed. In the latter part of the reign of Charles V and throughout the reign of Philip II, the decrees and suggestions of the Council of Trent were rigorously enforced; the *Index Librorum Prohibitorum* was instituted (banning the works of Erasmus, among others), the Inquisition was revived, and Spaniards were forbidden to study at foreign universities. The followers of Erasmus were dubbed "*alumbrados*" and the Erasmian movement, "*iluminismo*," derogatory epithets linked with Protestant heresy. Nevertheless, Erasmian notions echoed from the works of Gil Vicente, Torres Naharro, and others. See also *humanism; mysticism.*

Cf. Bataillon, M., *Erasme et L'Espagne,* Paris, 1937.

refrán. Proverb, adage, wise saying. (Not to be confused with the English word "refrain"). The *refrán* is a repository of folk wisdom and, as such, is a part of the study of folklore. It is often encountered in literary works (e.g. *Don Quijote*), and hence is of importance in the study of stylistics and metrics. See also under *folklore; refranero.*

refranero. A collection of *refranes,* or proverbs; e.g. *Refranes que dicen las viejas tras el fuego* (Marqués de Santillana); *Refranes glossados en verso* (Sebastián de Horozco); *etc.* See also under *folklore; refrán.*

Refranero español. See under *folklore.*

Refranes que dicen las viejas. See under *folklore.*

regeneracionismo. See under *europeızación.*

Regenta (La). See under *Clarín.*

Regimento de los príncipes. See under *Amadís de Gaula.*

regional novel. A type of novel confined to the language, characters, landscape and problems of a particular region or city; *e.g.* the mountains of Asturias, the arid plateaus of Castilla, the lush verdure of Andalusia, *etc.* Preceded by the *artículos de costumbres,* the regional novel flourished in the late 19th century. The chief regions and writers exemplifying the type are: Andalusia—Fernán Caballero, Juan Valera; Galicia—Pardo Bazán; Valencia Blasco Ibáñez; Madrid—Alarcón, Granada, Galdós; *etc.* Palacio Valdés chose various backgrounds: Asturias, Andalusia, Valencia. Corresponding to historical, topographical and ethnic factors, all making for individualism, the regional novel is a reflection of an inherent Spanish characteristic marked by realism, picturesque language, earthiness and humor.

Cf. Balseiro, J. A., *Novelistas españoles modernos,* N. Y., 1933; Northup, G. T., "The 19th Century Regional Novel," (pp. 368-385), *Introduction to Spanish Literature,* 2nd ed., Chicago, 1936.

Reglas del drama (Las). See under *Quintana.*

Reglas de orthografía castellana. See under *Nebrija.*

regressive assimilation. See under *assimilation.*

Reid, John T. (1908). American hispanist. Authority on Latin American literature. Instructor and Assistant Professor at Rice Institute, Duke University, and University of California. U. S. Foreign Service, since 1941. Author of *Modern Spain and Liberalism*, Stanford, 1936. Co-author of *Outline History of Spanish American Literature*, N. Y., 1942; *Anthology of Spanish American Literature*, N. Y., 1944.

Reinaldos. See under *Roncesvalles.*

Reinar después de morir. See under *Vélez de Guevara.*

Reinoso, Félix José. See under *Escuela sevillana.*

relación. (1) a report, memoir, account or narrative, usually of significant historical events. (2) An extended narrative speech in a drama.

Reloj de príncipes. See under *Guevara.*

Renacimiento. A literary review. See under *Martínez Sierra.* See also *Renaissance.*

Renaissance. The Renaissance in Spain *(Renacimiento)* began about the middle of the 15th century. Its origins were already evident at the end of the reign of Juan II (1454), as shown in Italian and humanist influences in the work of Santillana and Mena. The reigns of Fernando and Isabel (1474-1504) and of Carlos V (1516-1556) saw the Renaissance at its height in Spain. The period was marked by the rise of Spain as a dominant world power and by her achievement of political, religious and linguistic unity. Many trends emerged in Spanish literature during this period: humanism, platonism, Petrarchism, Erasmism, etc. The Renaissance traits of individualism, realism and interest in popular culture are present in the Spanish Renaissance as traditional Spanish characteristics. Because of Spain's religious orthodoxy, the secular features of the Renaissance, although present in Spanish literature, are relatively minor. In art, the *plateresco* style with its imposition of Renaissance décor on a medieval base symbolized the fusion of medieval and modern culture. In lyric poetry, Petrarchism was introduced by Juan Boscán and Garcilaso de la Vega. Interest in popular poetry and ballads was evinced by the collection and publication of the various *cancioneros.* The height of the Spanish Renaissance drama was reached by Tirso, Lope and Calderón. The 16th and early 17th centuries also saw the development of new types of prose fiction, from the romances of chivalry and the picaresque novel to their great synthesis in Cervantes' *Don Quijote,* the greatest work of Spanish Renaissance literature. See also *humanism; Petrarchism; Reformation.*

Cf. Bell, A. F. G., "Notes on the Spanish Renaissance," *Revue hispanique,* XXX; Onís, F. de, "El concepto del Renacimiento aplicado a la literatura española," *Ensayos sobre el sentido de la cultura española,* Madrid, 1932; Hatzfeld, H., "Italienische und spanische Renaissance," *Jahrbuch der Görres-Gesellschaft,* I, 1926.

Rennert, Hugo Albert (1858-1927). American hispanist. Professor of Spanish, University of Pennsylvania. Editor of many critical editions of Spanish classics and frequent contributor to hispanic journals. His most important work was *The Life of Lope de Vega,* N. Y., 1904, later amplified and translated with the collaboration of Américo Castro: *Vida de Lope de Vega,* Madrid, 1919. His other significant contributions to the history of Spanish literature were: *The Spanish Stage in the Time of Lope de Vega,* N. Y., 1909; and *The Spanish Pastoral Romances,* Philadelphia, 1912.

Repertorio Americano. One of the most influential literary reviews of Latin America. Founded in 1919. Published and edited by Joaquín García Monge, in Costa Rica.

Representaciones. See under *Encina, Juan del.*

Reprobación del amor mundano. See under *Arcipreste de Talavera.*

República literaria. See under *Saavedra Fajardo.*

Resende, García de. See under *cancionero.*

Residencia de Estudiantes. Another name for the *Centro de Estudios Históricos.* See under *Giner de los Ríos; krausismo.*

Resplandor de la hoguera. See under *Valle-Inclán.*

Retrato de la lozana andaluza. See under *Delicado, Francisco.*

retruécano. (1) The inversion of the terms of a proposition. (2) A figure of speech involving such inversion. (3) A play on words involving inversion of meanings.

Revelación de un ermitaño. See under *Disputa del alma y el cuerpo.*

Rev. Hisp. Abbr. of *Revue Hispanique.* See under Foulché-Delbosc.

Revista Azul. See under *Gutiérrez Nájera.*

Revista de América. A literary journal founded in 1896 by Rubén Darío and Ricardo Jaimes Freyre. See under *Darío; Jaimes Freyre.*

Revista de Filología Española (Abbr. *RFE).* See under *Menéndez Pidal.*

Revista de Filología Hispánica. (Abbr. *RFH).* A philological journal founded by Amado Alonso in 1939. See under *Alonso, Amado; Hispanic Institute.*

Revista de Occidente. See under *Ortega y Gasset.*

Revista Europea. See under *Palacio Valdés.*

Revista Hispánica Moderna. (Abbr. *RHM).* A scholarly journal published quarterly by the Hispanic Institute in the United States. Its aim is to study and propagate hispanic culture. It contains articles, reviews, literary notes, folklore studies, hispanic American bibliography, and a section for students of Spanish. See also under *Hispanic Institute.*

Revista Iberoamericana. A scholarly journal devoted to hispanic American literature. The organ of the *Instituto Internacional de Literatura Iberoamericana.* Editors: Julio Jiménez Rueda, Universidad Nacional de México, and Fernando Alegría, University of California.

Revista Interamericana de Bibliografía. A scholarly journal published three times a year by the Department of Cultural Affairs of the Pan American Union, Washington, D. C. It contains articles, reviews and bibliographies pertaining to Latin America.

Revista Moderna. See under *Nervo, Amado; Prado, Pedro.*

Revue Hispanique. (Abbr. *Rev. Hisp.*). See under *Foulché-Delbosc.*

Revulgo. See under *copla.*

Rey, Agapito (1892). American hispanist. Born in Spain; naturalized U. S. citizen, 1918. Associated with the University of Indiana since 1925; Professor of Spanish, since 1944. Author: *Leomarte-Sumas de Historia Troyana,* Madrid, 1932; *Cultura y costumbres del siglo XVI,* Mexico, 1944; *Ensayo de una bibliografía de las leyendas troyanas* (in collaboration with Solalinde, A. G.), Bloomington, Indiana, 1942. Critical ed., *Castigos e documentos,* Bloomington, Indiana, 1952; and many works on the early history of New Mexico.

Reyes, Alfonso (1889). Mexican scholar, critic, translator and poet. Born in Monterrey. A diplomatic and cultural representative of his country, he served in France (1913-1914) and in Spain (1920-1927), where he engaged in literary and scholarly activity, collaborating with Menéndez Pidal at the *Centro de Estudios Históricos.* He was also ambassador to Argentina and to Brazil (1927-1938). As director of the *Colegio de México,* he exercised a profound influence on his country's intellectual development. Reyes is a versatile scholar, being an authority on Spanish literature of the Golden Age and on Greek classicism. He has issued critical editions of the Spanish classics (Ruiz de Alarcón, Quevedo, Gracián, Lope de Vega, Góngora, *etc.)* and has done masterful translations of Mallarmé, Sterne, Chesterton, *etc.* In 1945 he was awarded the National Prize of Arts and Sciences for his work on classical criticism. Reyes is a giant among contemporary representatives of the humanist tradition in Spanish and Mexican letters. Chief works: *Rubén Darío en México,* 1916; *Visión de Anáhuac,* 1917; *El plano oblicuo,* 1920; *Huellas,* 1922; *Simpatías y diferencias,* 1921-1923; *Los dos caminos,* 1923; *Ifigenia cruel,* 1932; *Versos sociales,* 1932; *Yerbas de Tarahumara,* 1934; *Cantata en la tumba de García Lorca,* 1937; *Capítulos de literatura española,* 1938; *Algunos poemas,* 1941; *La experiencia literaria,* 1942; *El deslinde,* 1944; *La crítica en la edad ateniense,* 1945; *Homero en Cuernavaca,* 1949; *Árbol de pólvora,* 1953; *El suicida,* 1954; *Trayectoria de Goethe,* 1954.

Cf. González Peña, C., *Historia de la literatura mexicana,* Mexico, 1940; Jiménez Rueda, J., *Historia de la literatura mexicana,* Mexico, 1942.

Reyes, Neftalí Ricardo. See *Neruda, Pablo.*

Reyes de Oriente. See *Libro de los tres reyes de Oriente.*

Reyles, Carlos (1868-1938). Uruguayan novelist. Lecturer in philosophy and literature at the University of Montevideo. Of independent means, he devoted his entire life to travel and literature. Reyles was a poetic stylist despite his naturalistic leanings. For a time he was identified with the modernist trend *(El embruja de Sevilla).* However, he is at his best in his realistic novels *(El terruño)* depicting gaucho life on the *estancias.* Chief works: *Beba,* 1894; *La raza de Caín,* 1900; *El terruño,* 1916; *El embrujo de Sevilla,* 1922; *El gaucho Florido,* 1932.

Cf. Zum Felde, A., *Crítica de la literatura uruguaya,* Montevideo, 1921; Torres-Ríoseco, A., *Grandes novelistas de la América hispana,* U. of California Press, Berkeley, Cal., 1941.

RFE. Abbr. of *Revista de Filología Española.* See under *Menéndez Pidal.*

RFH. Abbr. of *Revista de Filología Hispánica.* See under *Alonso, Amado; Hispanic Institute.*

RHM. Abbr. of *Revista Hispánica Moderna.*

Ribaldo (El). Roboan's peasant squire in the *Caballero Cifar.* Ribaldo was an early prototype of Sancho Panza. See under *Caballero Cifar.*

Ribera, Julián (1858-1934). Spanish literary historian and Arabic scholar. Professor of Arabic literature at the University of Zaragoza and of Madrid. A member of the Spanish Academy. Outstanding modern authority on medieval Spanish-Arabic culture. Editor of *Biblioteca Arábico-Hispana,* and of a critical edition and translation of the *Crónica de Abenalcotía.* Author of *Cancionero de Abencuzmán,* 1912; *La épica entre los musulmanes españoles,* 1915; *La música de las cantigas,* 1922. See also under *cantar de gesta.*

rima aguda. Terminal-accent rhyme; e.g. *balcón-corazón.* See *octava italiana.*

Rimado de palacio. See under *López de Ayala.*

Rimas. See under *Bécquer.*

Rinconete y Cortadillo. See under *Cervantes; picaresque novel.*

Río, Ángel del (1901). Literary scholar, hispanist, editor and professor. Born in Spain; naturalized as a U. S. citizen, 1941. *Lic. en Letras,* U. of Madrid, 1920; *D. en H.,* 1924. Studied at the *Centro de Estudios Históricos,* 1920-1921. Lecturer and professor, U. of Strasbourg, France; U. of Puerto Rico; U. of Miami, Fla. Professor of Spanish, Columbia U., 1929-1950. Professor and Chairman, Spanish Dept., New York University, 1950-1953. Director of the *Hispanic Institute,* Columbia University, 1954. Editor, *Revista Hispánica Moderna,* 1954. Author of "Federico García Lorca. Vida y obra," *RHM,* VI, N. Y., 1940; "El poeta Pedro Salinas. Vida y obra," *RHM,* VII, N. Y., 1941; *Del solar hispánico* (with Amelia A. de del Río) N. Y., 1945; *El concepto contemporáneo de España* (with Bernadete, M. J.), Buenos Aires, 1946; *Tratadistas españoles del Siglo de Oro,* Buenos Aires, 1948; *Historia de la literatura española,* 2 vols., N. Y., 1948; *Antología general* *de la literatura española,* 2 vols., (with Amelia A. de del Río), N. Y., 1954; *Vida y obras de Federico García Lorca,* Zaragosa, 1952.

Río de la Plata. See under *Hernández, José.*

Ríos, Blanca de los (1862). Poet, novelist and literary scholar. Born in Seville. Chiefly known as an authority on Tirso de Molina and Golden Age literature. Her *Estudio biográfico y crítico de Tirso de Molina* received an award from the *Real Academia Española* in 1889. Her other principal critical works are: *Las mujeres de Tirso; Del Siglo de Oro* (1910); *De la mística y de la novela contemporánea.* Critical edition: *Obras dramáticas completas, Tirso de Molina,* 2 vols., Madrid, 1947.

Cf. *Hispania,* XXXVI, 1953.

Rivadeneyra, Manuel. See under *Biblioteca de Autores Españoles.*

Rivas, Duque de. See *Saavedra, Ángel de.*

Rivera, José Eustasio (1889-1928). Colombian lawyer, poet and novelist. Born in Neiva, a port on the Magdalena River, he painted exquisite word-pictures of his native region's tropical beauty in a collection of sonnets which are among the most noteworthy of South American literature *(Tierra de promisión,* 1921). In 1922 he was appointed secretary of a commission to settle the boundary dispute between Colombia and Venezuela. The experiences in traveling through the Amazon jungle inspired his *La vorágine* (1924), one of the great American novels of our time (English translation by E. K. James, *The Vortex,* N. Y., 1935). The greatness of the novel lies in its magnificent descriptions of the vast Colombian plains and the dense tropical jungles of the Amazon. It was also of great social significance in its exposure of the cruel peonage to which the Amazon rubber gatherers were subjected.

Cf. Spell, J. R., *Contemporary Spanish-American Fiction,* University of North Carolina Press, Chapel Hill, N. C., 1944.

Rixa animi et corporis. See under *Disputa del alma y el cuerpo.*

Roboan. One of the sons of the *Caballero Cifar.*

Rocinante. The decrepit hack chosen by Don Quijote to be his noble steed.

Rodó, José Enrique (1872-1917). Uruguayan essayist and philosopher. Born in Montevideo; died in Sicily. The leading prose stylist and thinker of the modernist group. One of the founders of

La revista nacional de literatura (1895), in which many of his essays appeared. His first major essay was a penetrating critical study of Rubén Darío (preface to *Prosas profanas,* 2nd ed., 1899). His greatest work was *Ariel* (1900), an ethical admonition to the youth of South America to cultivate spiritual values (Ariel) rather than material values (Caliban, *i.e.,* the United States). Rodó's basic philosophy is one of humanistic idealism, accepting the notion of dynamic change as the essence of life. His allegorical style and seminal ideas exercised a profound influence on his own and succeeding generations of Spanish American writers. His important works were: *Ariel,* 1900; *Los motivos de Proteo,* 1909; *El mirador de Próspero,* 1914; *El camino de Paros,* 1918; *Hombres de América,* 1920.

Cf. *Obras completas,* Montevideo, 1945; Zaldumbide, G., *José Enrique Rodó,* Madrid, 1919; Zum Felde, A., *Proceso intelectual del Uruguay,* Montevideo, 1930.

Rodrigo de Toledo. See under *Bernardo del Carpio; crónica.*

Rodrigo Díaz de Vivar. See under *Cid; Cantar de Mío Cid.*

Rodrigo el godo. One of the lost epics in the Cid cycle, preserved only in a "prosification" in the *Crónica de 1344.* It deals with the early exploits of the Cid, and is more romantic and contains many more fictitious episodes than the *Poema de Mío Cid.* However, it introduces for the first time certain themes in the Cid cycle; *e.g.* the Cid's encounter with a leper who turns out to be St. Lazarus. In addition it introduces the conflict between love and honor in Ximena, who marries her father's slayer, the Cid. This was the theme that attracted many subsequent authors. The subject from which the work derives its title concerns the exploits of Rodrigo, the last of the Visigothic kings, who is portrayed as a seducer and a moral weakling, and who loses Spain to the Moors (711), ending as a repentant sinner. Hence this epic is also referred to as *Las mocedades de Rodrigo,* and the reconstruction of Rodrigo themes is called the *Cantar de Rodrigo.* Derived from *Rodrigo el godo* is *La crónica rimada del Cid* (early 15th century), a fragment of 1,132 irregular lines. Thus the only extant poetic version containing the Rodrigo theme already belongs to the declining period of the epic, the period of "epic degeneration". The Rodrigo theme was treated in Guillén de Castro's *Mocedades del Cid* (1618), the source of Corneille's *Cid* (1636). It also occurred in the romantic drama, *El puñal del godo* (1842), by José Zorrilla y Moral. See also under *cantar de gesta; Cid.*

Cf. *Rodrigo el último godo,* (Ed.) Menéndez Pidal, R., 3 vols., Madrid, 1925, 1926, 1927.

Rodríguez de la Cámara, Juan (died *ca.* 1450). Early Renaissance poet. Also referred to as Juan Rodríguez del Padrón. Little is known of his life. He seems to have been a page at the court of Juan II. Some of his shorter poems are included in the *Cancionero de Baena.* Among his more extended poems are one in praise of women *(Triunfo de las donas)* and one in praise of nobility *(Cadira del honor).* He is chiefly known for his allegorical and romantic autobiography, *El siervo libre de amor (ca.* 1440), inspired in part by Boccaccio's *Fiammetta.* The book contains chivalric, sentimental and homiletic elements and is an early example of the Renaissance *novela sentimental.*

Cf. *Obras,* (Ed.) Paz y Mélia, A., Madrid, 1884; Pidal, J. P., "Vida del trovador Juan Rodríguez del Padrón," in *Estudios literarios,* Madrid, 1890; Menéndez y Pelayo, M., "Orígines de la novela," *NBAE,* I.

Rodríguez de Montalvo. See *Amadís de Gaula.*

Rodríguez Marín, Francisco. See under *folklore.*

Roger de Flor. See under *Tirant lo Blanch.*

Rogers, Paul Patrick (1900). Professor of Romance Languages, Oberlin College. Authority on 18th and 19th century Spanish literature. Author of *Pre-Romantic Drama of Spain,* 1928; *Goldoni in Spain,* 1941.

Rojas, Fernando de. See under *Celestina.*

Rojas, Manuel (1896). Chilean journalist and short-story writer. A sombre realist, his stories are based on the personal experiences of a checkered career as a laborer and sailor. His best known works are: *Hombres del sur,* 1926; *Lanchas en la bahía,* 1932.

Cf. Silva Castro, Raúl, *Retratos literarios,* 163-179, Santiago, 1932.

Rojas, Ricardo (1882). Argentine poet, professor, literary historian and critic. Professor of national literature at the University of Buenos Aires. General Editor of the *Biblioteca Argentina* publications. The dean of Argentina's literary scholars and a creative writer of marked ability. His greatest achievement is as a philosophical analyst, interpreter and historian of Argentine culture and literature *(La argentinidad, Eurindia).* In 1921 he was awarded the Argentine Grand Prize of Literature for the first four volumes of his monumental *La literatura argentina* (8 vols., Buenos Aires, 1924-1925). Chief works: *La victoria del hombre,* 1903; *El país de la selva,* 1907; *La argentinidad,* 1916; *Poesías,* 1923; *Discursos,* 1924; *Eurindia,* 1924; *La literatura argentina,* 1924-1925; *Ollontay,* 1939.

Cf. Sánchez, L. A., *Historia de la literatura americana,* Santiago, 1940.

Rojas Villandrando, Agustín de (1572-163-?). Novelist, actor-author, and gentleman of fortune. Born in Madrid; died in Paredes de Nava. The date of his death is not known. A contemporary dramatist called him the "*caballero del milagro*", for he led a picaresque existence, frequently living from hand to mouth. He fought in France, was a prisoner at La Rochelle, joined the crew of a pirateer preying on English shipping, was a fugitive from justice after having killed a man at Málaga, wandered through Spain as a strolling actor, wrote several brilliant theatrical prologues *(loas)* and a single play, *El natural desdichado.* His satire on government, *El buen repúblico,* was banned by the Inquisition. His chief work was a picaresque novel, *El viaje entretenido* (1603), a rambling miscellany interspersed with tales, dialogues and *loas.* It is a story of adventures in the theater, describing in detail the actor's life, dramatic troupes, the organization of the early Madrid theater, practical aspects of staging, costuming, *etc.* It has great documentary value for historians of the 17th century Spanish theater. Traces of its literary influence are to be found in Calderón's *La vida es sueño,* in Scarron's *Le roman comique,* in Shakespeare's prologue to *The Taming of the Shrew,* in Goethe's *Wilhelm Meister,* and in Hauptmann's *Schluck und Jau.*

Cf. *El viaje entretenido,* in *Colección de libros picarescos,* Madrid, 1901; Alonso Cortés, N., "Agustín de Rojas," *Revista Castellana,* VII, 1923; Cirot, G., "Valeur littéraire du Viaje entretenido," *Bulletin hispanique,* XXV, 1923.

Rojas Zorrilla, Francisco de (1607-1648). Outstanding dramatist of the Calderón school. Born in Toledo; died in Madrid. Studied the humanities at Toledo, Salamanca and Tormes, but without taking a degree. He led a bohemian existence as a wandering student until he took up residence in Madrid in 1631, abandoned all pretense at being a scholar and devoted himself to poetry and the theater. He wrote plays for the royal theater, *Buen Retiro;* was a friend and collaborator of Antonio Coello, Pérez de Montalbán and Calderón de la Barca, with whom he wrote *El monstruo de la fortuna;* and towards the end of his career was awarded a knighthood of the Order of Santiago (1643) by Philip IV. During his lifetime he published two volumes, each containing twelve plays (1640; 1645), of which the best known are *No hay ser padre siendo rey* (1635); *Donde hay agravios no hay celos, y amo criado* (1637); and *Entre bobos anda el juego,* or *Don Lucas del cigarral* (1638). His great masterpiece, still performed today, is *Del rey abajo ninguno,* or *El labrador más honrado García del Castañar* (1650), usually called *García de Castañar* after its chief character. It has a *pundonor* theme. García, a nobleman and farmer, suspects that the king has compromised his wife. Although García adores her, the code of honor requires that he put her to death. However, the suspected lover turns out to be a courtier, whom García kills. His honor is preserved, and a royal pardon follows. Conventional in its plot, the play is superior in its natural action and its subdued lyrical tone. Rojas Zorrilla stands apart from others of the Calderón school in his lighter plays *(Abre el ojo; Lo que son mujeres,* as well as those mentioned above). In his comedies he expanded the role of the *gracioso* to include a variety of fools, taken from real life, thus creating a new type of *comedia de gracioso.* Although his poetic style was sometimes gongoristic, he excelled in humor, *costumbrista* touches, and impassioned dramatic effects. His plays were widely imitated and translated, especially in France (Scarron, Le Sage, Corneille) and in Italy (Alfieri, Goldoni).

Cf. *Comedias escogidas,* in *BAE,* LIV; *Teatro,* (Ed.) Morcuendo, R., Madrid, 1917; Cotarelo y Mori, E., *Don Francisco de Rojas Zorrilla,* Madrid, 1911; Sáinz de Robles, F. C., *Dramaturgos de la escuela de Calderón: Rojas Zorrilla,* Madrid, 1947.

romance. The Spanish lyrical ballad, of which the earliest examples are descended from anonymous folksongs and from the *cantares de gesta.* Usually epic in character, the *romance* occurs in various metrical patterns. The typical *romance* verse has eight syllables and penultimate stress. Stanza groupings vary, but the even verses generally end in assonant rhyme while the odd verses are generally blank. At a later stage in the development of the *romance,* the quatrain becomes a usual feature. *Romances* have been variously classified. The broadest grouping distinguishes between the *romance viejo* and the *romance artístico,* i.e. between the primitive ballad and the modern art-ballad. To the former belong the *romances históricos,* dealing with national heroes of the 12th and 13th century epics (El Cid, Bernardo del Carpio, etc.), the *romances juglarescos* or *caballerescos,* dealing with romantic 14th century epic themes (Arthurian and Carolingian cycles, the Crusades, etc.), the *romances fronterizos* or *moriscos,* dealing with the border strife between Christians and Moors in the 15th century *(Poema de Alfonso XI,* etc.), the *romances eruditos* or *cultos* or *antiguos,* dealing with themes from 16th century chronicles (from the *Crónica general* of Alfonso X, especially from Ocampo's edition) and composed by known authors (Lope de Vega, Góngora, Quevedo, etc.). The latter form a transition between the primitive ballad and the art ballad which is cultivated by authors from the 18th century on (Rivas, Zorrilla, Lorca, etc.). The folk ballad also continues to flourish in Spain and in South America. Collections of *romances* began to appear in about the 16th century under the collective titles of *romancero* and *cancionero,* e.g. *Cancionero sin año* (before 1550); *Silva de varios romances* (1550); *Romancero general (*1600); *Primavera y flor de los mejores romances* (1621); *Rosa de romances* (1572); etc. For the ballad in America, see under *gaucho literature.*

Cf. Collections of *romances:* Morley, S. G., (Ed.), *Spanish Ballads: romances escogidos,* N. Y., 1911; Menéndez Pidal, R., (Ed.), *Flor nueva de romances viejos,* Madrid, 1938; Entwistle, W. J., (Ed.), *European Balladry,* Oxford, 1939; González Palencia, A., (Ed.), *Romancero general (1600, 1604, 1605),* Madrid, 1947.

Critical works: Menéndez y Pelayo, M., "Tratado de los romances viejos," *Antología de poetas líricos castellanos,* XI, XII, Madrid, 1914-1916; Bédier, J., *Les légendes épiques,* Paris, 1914-1921; Menéndez, Pidal, R. *El romancero español,* N. Y., 1910; *Poesía popular y poesía tradicional en la literatura española,* Oxford, 1922; *Poesía juglaresca y juglares,* Madrid, 1924; *El romancero: teorías e investigaciones,* Madrid, 1928; Menéndez Pidal, R., *Romancero Hispánico,* 2 vols., Madrid, 1953.

romance corto. A ballad written in verses of less than eight syllables. The same as *romancillo.*

Romance de lobos. See under *Valle-Inclán.*

romance heróico. A metrical form consisting of 11-syllable lines with alternating assonance. See also under *Saavedra, Ángel de.*

romancero. (1) A collection of *romances,* or ballads. (2) A ballad singer. See also under *romance.*

Cf. Menéndez Pidal, R., *Romancero Hispánico,* 2 vols., Madrid, 1953.

Romancero de Durán. See under *Durán, Agustín; folklore; romance.*

Romancero del Cid. See *Cid (El).*

Romancero general. See under *Durán, Agustín; folklore; romance.*

Romances históricos. See under *Saavedra, Ángel de.*

romances of chivalry. Prose narratives of the adventures of knightly heroes. The type originated in the 14th century, generally as anonymous prose versions of earlier epics. It flourished during the Renaissance (16th century *libros de caballerías)* and faded out during the Golden Age (late 16th and early 17th centuries). The subject matter of these romances of chivalry dealt with: 1. Arthurian legends *(Tristán, Lanzarote);* 2. Legends of Charlemagne *(Roncesvalles, Maynete);* 3. Classical legends *(Historia troyana);* 4. The Crusades *(La gran conquista de ultramar*—in which appears the Lohengrin motif); 5. The Milesian tale *El caballero Cifar);* 6. The *Amadís de Gaula* and the *Palmerín* cycles. The earlier types of chivalric romances, based on epic material, sentimentalized the primitive strength of epic heroes. They introduced love motifs and elements of the supernatural. During the Renaissance the chivalric romances became the most popular type of fiction, and their exotic and adventurous elements increased. They were read by all classes (Loyola and St. Teresa adored them). At its best, the type glorified knightly virtues, the institution of chivalry *(caballeresco)* and high ethical principles *(Amadís de Gaula);* at its worst, it was crudely realistic and often verged on the burlesque *(Tirant lo Blanc).* It was as a satire on the worst features of the type that Cervantes began his *Don Quijote.*

Cf. Thomas, H., *Spanish and Portuguese Romances of Chivalry,* Cambridge, 1920; Entwistle, W. J., *The Arthurian Legend in the Literatures of the Spanish Peninsula,* London, 1925; Ruiz-de-Conde, J., *El amor y el matrimonio secreto en los libros de caballerías,* Madrid, 1948.

romancillo. A *romance corto,* or ballad written in verses of less than eight syllables.

Roman d'Alexandre. See under *Libro de Alexandre.*

Roman de Troie. See under *Historia troyana.*

roman expérimental. See *novela experimental.*

Romanticism. The dates of the Romantic Movement in Spanish literature are approximately from 1830 to 1850. The movement began as a reaction against Neoclassicism, and was in turn superseded by Realism. The literary production of the Romanticists was chiefly in lyric poetry (Espronceda, Bécquer, Campoamor, etc.), the drama (Rosa, Rivas, Zorrilla, Gutiérrez, etc.), and the historical novel (Larra, Espronceda, Rosa, etc.). Most of the Romantic theories came from Germany (Herder, Schlegel via J. N. Böhl von Faber and A. Durán), France (Victor Hugo via López Soler), and England (Byron via Espronceda; Scott via López Soler). The Barcelona periodical *El Europeo* (1823-1824) also did much to propagate European romantic theories and literature in Spain through translations of Byron, Schiller and Scott. The adoption of these theories (individualism, freedom from established forms, nature as reflecting the moods of man, irony and pessimism, political freedom, medievalism, folklore, etc.) resulted from the exile of Spainsh liberals during the absolutist reign of Fernando VII (1808-1833). In 1833, the return of these *emigrados* to Spain ushered in the Romantic Movement. While foreign in theory and inspiration, the Spanish Romantic Movement achieved indigenous status in its return to national tradition: historical legends, folksongs, ballads, local-color writing, i.e. the *costumbrista* trend (Larra, Romanos, Estébanez Calderón, etc.), and religious philosophy (Jaime Balmes, Donoso Cortés).

Cf. Peers, E. A., *A History of the Romantic Movement in Spain,* 2 vols., Cambridge, 1940; Díaz-Plaja, G., *Introducción al estudio del romantismo español,* 2a ed., Madrid, 1942.

Romera-Navarro, Miguel (1888-1954). Literary scholar, hispanist, editor and professor. Born in Almería, Spain; died in Austin, Texas. Naturalized as a U. S. citizen, 1927. *Lic. en Leyes,* U. of Madrid, 1908. Sec'y, *Sección de Ciencias Morales y Políticas* of the *Ateneo de Madrid,* 1909-1910. Ph. D., U. of Pennsylvania,

1927. Professor of Spanish, U. of Pa., 1927-1947. Professor of Spanish, U. of Texas, 1947-1954. Editor (1933-1954) of the *Hispanic Review,* U. of Pa. Founder of the *University of Texas Hispanic Studies,* 1949. Corresponding member, *Real Academia Española, Hispanic Society of America,* etc. Chief publications: *El hispanismo en Norte América,* Madrid, 1917; *Historia de la literatura española* (1927), 2a. ed., Boston, 1949; *Miguel de Unamuno, novelista, poeta, ensayista,* Madrid, 1928; *Antología de la literatura española,* Boston, 1933; *La preceptiva dramática de Lope de Vega,* Madrid, 1935; Critical edition of Baltasar Gracián's *El criticón,* 3 vols., Philadelphia, 1938-1940; and *Oráculo manual y arte de prudencia,* Madrid, 1954; "Estudios sobre Gracián," *U. of Texas Hispanic Studies,* II, 1950; *Regístro de lexicografía hispánica,* Madrid, 1951.

Cf. *Bibliography of Romera-Navarro,* Philadelphia, 1947; "Necrology: Miguel Romera-Navarro (1888-1954)," *Hispanic Review,* XXII, U. of Pa., 1954.

Romero, José Rubén (1890-1951). Mexican poet, novelist and diplomat. Participated in the Madero revolt (1911). Former ambassador to Brazil and to Cuba. Chiefly known as the author of *La vida inútil de Pito Pérez* (1938), an original adaptation of the picaresque novel in modern style. Colorfully depicting the types and scenes of his native Michoacán, Romero is one of the outstanding representatives of contemporary South American regionalism. Among his important works are: (poems) *Fantasias,* 1908; *La musa heroica,* 1912; *Apuntes de un lugareño,* 1932; (novels) *Desbandada,* 1934; *El pueblo inocente,* 1934; *La vida inútil de Pito Pérez,* 1938; *Anticipación de la muerte,* 1939; *Rosenda,* 1946; (memoirs) *Breve historia de mis libros,* 1942; *Algunas cosillas de Pito Pérez,* 1945.

Cf. Moore, E. R., *Novelistas de la Revolución Mexicana: J. Rubén Romero,* Habana, 1940.

Romero, García, Vicente. See under *criollismo.*

Roncesvalles. A fragmentary epic poem, of 100 irregular lines, on the theme of the Battle of Roncesvalles (778). It was composed by an unknown *juglar* (probably Navarrese, to judge from the dialect) in about the middle of the 12th century. The manuscript, dating from about 1310, was discovered in 1917 among the archives of Pamplona by Menéndez Pidal. Unlike the French

Chanson de Roland, this version follows the Spanish tradition in the Carolingian Cycle *(e.g.* reference to Reinaldos, a Spanish chieftain in Charlemagne's army). The fragment deals with the episode in which Charlemagne reaches the scene of Roland's defeat at Roncesvalles and mourns for his slain heroes. The work is important as the only extant poem in medieval Spanish literature based on the Carolingian Cycle. The *Bernardo del Carpio* epic, which also touches upon this theme, is only known through prose versions in the *Crónicas.* The theme later received epic treatment during the Golden Age in Balbuena's *Bernardo* (1624). See also under *Balbuena, Bernardo de; cantar de gesta.*

Cf. "Roncesvalles", (Ed.) Menéndez Pidal, R., *Revista de filología española,* IV, 1917.

rondeña. (1) A song or melody characteristic of Ronda. (2) The words to such a song, generally in stanzas of four octosyllabic verses or lines.

Roo, Andrés Quintana (1787-1851). Mexican statesman, journalist and poet. A Father of the Republic, he aided the Mexican War of Independence through his political journalism and patriotic poetry. His verse is classical in style.

Cf. Menéndez y Pelayo, M., *Antología de poetas hispanoamericanos,* Madrid, 1893-1895.

Rosa de romances. See under *Timoneda; romance.*

Rosana en los fuegos. See under *Meléndez Valdés.*

Rouanet, Léo. See under *auto sacramental.*

royal octave. See *octava real.*

Rueda, Lope de (1510?-1565). Creator of the popular, realistic drama as playwright and manager of a strolling troupe of actors. Born in Seville; died in Córdoba. He influenced Cervantes, who greatly admired him (Cf. *Prólogo, Ocho comedias,* Madrid, 1615). After a long career of staging plays at inns and market places in the cities and towns of Spain, Rueda achieved widespread fame in 1554 when the Conde de Benavente engaged him to stage a series of elaborate festivals in honor of Philip II. His collected plays were published in Valencia (1567-1570) by his friend, Juan de Timoneda (1490?-1583). Rueda wrote several comedies in prose and one in verse, pastoral dialogues *(coloquios pastoriles),* and short sketches or farces *(pasos),* in which he excelled. He wrote some 40 *pasos,* many of them interspersed in his longer plays, but actually independent comedy playlets which have outlived their context. Inspired by the Italian *commedia dell'arte,* Rueda created the Spanish counterparts of its stock characters: the *bobo,* or clown, the *fanfarrón,* or braggart, the *rufián,* or pimp, etc. The most famous of his *pasos* is entitled *Las aceitunas* (1548) (Cf. *The Olives,* Lewis, G. H., London, 1845), a farce in which a husband and wife quarrel about the value of a crop of olives that they may have in 30 years if their seedlings prosper. Others of his better known *pasos* are *El convidado, El rufián cobarde, Cornudo y contento, Los lacayos ladrones, Pagar y no pagar,* etc. Rueda's type characters, vivid, realistic dialogue, and comic spirit diverted the Spanish drama from its erudite and religious channels and brought it into the market place, directly to the people. With his *pasos* he began a trend toward the lighter dramatic genres now traditional in the modern Spanish theatre as the *género chico.* See also *género chico; paso.*

Cf. *Obras,* (Ed.) Cotarelo y Mori, E., 2 vols., Madrid, 1908; Cotarelo y Mori, E., *Lope de Rueda y el teatro español de su tiempo,* Madrid, 1901; Salazar, S., *Lope de Rueda y su teatro,* Santiago de Cuba, 1911; Northup, G. T., *Ten Spanish Farces,* Boston, 1922.

Rueda, Salvador (1857-1933). Modernist poet. Born and died in Málaga. Of humble origin, he was self-educated while working as a journalist and librarian. His genius was first recognized by Núñez de Arce, who assisted him in his career. Later, he won the friendship of Darío, Clarín, Unamuno, and other great writers of his generation. His first important volume of poetry was entitled *En tropel* (1892). His best known poetic works were: *El país del sol,* 1901; *Fuente de salud,* 1906; *Trompetas de órgano,* 1907; *Lenguas de fuego,* 1908; and *Cantando por ambos mundos,* 1914. His best novel was entitled *La cópula* (1906), an idyllic love story. He also wrote some dramatic poems *(La musa,* 1901; *Vaso de rocío,* 1908). Salvador Rueda was an elemental and untutored genius with remarkable poetic facility and amazing versatility. A bold experimenter in metrical forms, he also excelled in colorful description and musical rhythms. Although his poetry was often uneven and his sense of good taste questionable, his sheer lyrical passion and exuberance submerged his defects. His influence was considerable on Rubén Darío, Ramón Jiménez, Villaespesa, Martínez Sierra and on other *modernista* poets. Some critics consider Salvador Rueda to have been the true creator of *modernismo,* rather than Rubén Darío.

Cf. *Poesías escogidas,* Madrid, 1912; Prados, M., *Salvador Rueda, el poeta de la raza. Su vida y su obra.,* Málaga, 1941.

Ruedo ibérico. See under *Valle-Inclán.*

rufián. Pimp, pander. A type character in the *pasos* of Lope de Rueda. See under *Rueda, Lope de.*

ruido. See *comedia de ruido.*

Ruiz, Juan (1283?-1350?). "El Arcipreste de Hita". The greatest poet of the medieval *mester de clerecía* school. Nothing is known of his life except from internal evidence of his autobiographical *Libro de buen amor* (ca. 1330), and from various indications on the three 14th century manuscripts in which it is preserved (Cf. the edition of Ducamin, Toulouse, 1901). He was probably born at Alcalá and was Archpriest in the town of Hita. He was a cleric who wrote verses for *juglares.* His superior was Gil de Albornoz, Archbishop of Toledo (1337-1367), to whom the poet ascribes his "unmerited" imprisonment (probably for his licentious verses), during which he is supposed to have composed his masterpiece. Since the records of Hita show the name of another as the archpriest in 1351, it is inferred that Juan Ruiz died before that date. That he was well-versed in medieval literature appears from various episodes in his book adapted from other sources; *e.g.* Don Melón's wooing and seduction of Doña Endrina, based on a 13th century Latin play, *De Amore,* by Pamphilus; the tale of *Don Pitas Payas, Pyntor de Bretaña,* based on a French *fabliau;* the allegories of the Twelve Seasons, based on the *Roman de la Rose* or on the *Libro de Alexandre;* etc. *El libro de buen amor* is essentially a collection of twelve narrative poems, each recounting a different love affair. The poem is written in *cuaderna vía,* interspersed with lyrics in various meters *(serranillas,* or *canticas de serrana, canticas de loores de Santa María, cantares de ciegos* etc.). The *"buen amor"* of the title refers to spiritual love, as contrasted with *"loco amor",* carnal love. Although nominally favoring the former, the author makes a concession to human frailty by dwelling in great detail on the latter. His aim is to provide for the reader an education in both types of love. This tacit acceptance of carnal love is ascribed by critics to general medieval licentiousness and to the influence of Arabic rather than Christian mores. Juan Ruiz goes far beyond his theme of love, introducing humorous satire of medieval life and manners. Of particular interest is his description of types of the lower classes. Memorable characters are Trotaconventos, an old hag who is the hero's panderess, the prototype of Celestina; and Don Furón (the "Weasel"), who is the hero's rascally servant. It is the autobiographical element that is unique in the book. For the first time in Spanish literature a vivid personality, human in his contradictions, reveals himself in artistic form.

Cf. *Libro de buen amor,* (Ed.) Cejador, J., Madrid, 1913; Puyol y Alonso, J., *El Arcipreste de Hita,* Madrid, 1906; Lecoy, F., *Recherches sur le "Libro de buen amor" de Juan Ruiz,* Paris, 1938.

Ruiz de Alarcón y Mendoza, Juan (1581?-1639). Dramatist of the Spanish classical period. Born in Mexico; died in Madrid. Educated at the University of Salamanca, Spain (1600 *et seq.)* and at the University of Mexico (1608 *et seq.).* Lived in Spain from about 1614 on. Held governmental administrative and business positions. Writing for his own edification rather than for gain, he was subjected to merciless satire by his rivals who callously dwelt on the fact that he was bow-legged, a hunchback and a scarecrow lover. Ruiz de Alarcón was the 17th century's greatest writer of thesis plays, achieving a European influence that extended to Corneille, Molière, and Goldoni. Less prolific than most of the dramatists of his day, he produced about twenty plays (published in two volumes, 1628 and 1634). His forte, like that of Molière, was the development of character types that represent vices and illustrate moral truths. Thus, *La verdad sospechosa, ca.* 1619, exposes the vice of lying (Cf. Corneille's *Le Menteur,* 1642); *Las paredes oyen, ca.* 1622, assails the vice of slander; *Mudarse por mejorarse, ca.* 1622, inveighs against inconstancy in love; *etc.* An artist in combining entertainment with ethical teaching, Alarcón was the most modern of his contemporaries and the greatest moralist of the Spanish classical theater.

Cf. Works, in *BAE,* XLIII; Ureña, P. R., *Don Juan Ruiz de Alarcón,* Havana, 1915; Reyes, A., *Páginas selectas de Ruiz de Alarcón,* Madrid, 1918; Jiménez Rueda, J., *Juan Ruiz de Alarcón y su tiempo,* Mexico, 1939.

Ruiz-de-Conde, Justina (1909). Literary scholar and educator. Born in Spain; naturalized, U. S. citizen, 1944. *Profésora de Instituto Nacional de Segunda Enseñanza,* Valdepeñas, Madrid, Barcelona, 1934-1939. Associate Professor, Wellesley College. Author of *El amor y el matrimonio secreto en los libros de caballerías,* Madrid, 1948.

Ruysbroeck. See under *mysticism.*

Ruy Velásquez. See under *Infantes de Lara.*

S

Saavedra, Ángel de (1791-1865). Duque de Rivas. Dramatist, poet and ballad writer of the Romantic School. Born in Córdoba; died in Madrid. The younger son of an affluent aristocratic family, his full name was Ángel de Saavedra Ramírez de Baquedano. In histories of literature he is frequently referred to as "El Duque de Rivas", the title to which he succeeded after his older brother died without leaving any heirs. As a child he was tutored privately in Latin, French, history, mathematics, painting and other subjects; so that, in 1805, when he entered the *Seminario de Nobles* in Madrid, he amazed his teachers by his precocious knowledge. At 17, he became an officer in the Royal Guards and distinguished himself in action against the French during the War of Independence, being wounded several times. As a patriotic liberal in the Cortes (1822), he gained the enmity of the royal faction and was condemned to death by Fernando VII. Forced to flee for his life, he spent a 10-year exile in England, Italy, Malta and France. In England he read Shakespeare, Byron and Scott. In France he exercised his talent for painting. In 1834, like the other *emigrados,* he returned to Spain during the amnesty following the death of Fernando VII (1833). He devoted himself to politics and writing and occupied several diplomatic and cultural posts: Ambassador to Naples, 1848; to France, 1849; President of the Council of State, 1863; Director of the *Academia de la Lengua,* 1864. Rivas began as a neoclassic writer and dramatist (1810-1820), but turned into a typical romantic during and after his exile. His most famous drama was *Don Álvaro, o La fuerza del sino* (in prose, France, 1831; rewritten in prose and verse, Spain, 1835). The play inspired Verdi's opera, *La forza del destino* (1862). *Don Álvaro* is an example of the melodramatic fate-drama, depicting a hero harassed by Fate until, in desperation, he does away with himself. It is romantic in its appeal to the emotions rather than to the mind. Also romantic, in its medievalism, is Rivas' verse epic, *El moro expósito, o Córdoba y Burgos en el siglo XI* (1834), written in the heroic ballad meter *(romance heróico;* i.e. 11-syllable lines with alternating assonance). *El moro expósito* incorporates old epic material *(Infantes de Lara)* which Rivas derived from early Spanish folk ballads. Its contrasting scenes of Moorish (Córdoba) and Christian (Burgos) civilization are romantically picturesque. Rivas excelled in the *romance* form (i.e. 8-syllable assonating lines), reviving the early Spanish historical ballads in his *Romances históricos* (1841), which deal with subjects culled from the whole range of Spanish history. His talent as a painter is reflected in his colorful word-pictures of dramatic historical scenes. The Preface to these ballads has become famous as one of the most significant expositions of romantic theory.

Cf. *Obras completas,* Madrid, 1945; Peers, E. A., *Rivas and Romanticism,* London, 1923; "Azorín", *Rivas y Larra,* Madrid, 1916; Díaz-Plaja, G., *Introducción al estudio del romanticismo español,* Madrid, 1936.

Saavedra Fajardo, Diego de (1584-1648). Historian, political theoretician and diplomat. Born in Algezares, Murcia; died in Madrid. Studied at Salamanca. Active as a church official and as a diplomat. Ambassador to Rome (1631). One of the last great stylists of the baroque period, he was famous for his work on political theory, *Idea de un príncipe político-cristiano representada en cien empresas* (1640), usually referred to as *Empresas políticas;* and for his imaginative interpretation of the culture of his time, *República literaria* (posthumously published, 1655). In the former, Saavedra Fajardo emphasized the ethics of statesmanship as opposed to Machiavellianism; in the latter, he used the Lucian device of a dream city peopled by artists, scientists and writers. Many of his literary judgments were of unusual acuity for his time. Also of interest is his work entitled *Locuras de Europa* (posthumously, 1748), a Lucian dialogue in which the modern idea of universal peace among nations is elaborated.

Cf. *República literaria,* (Ed. Diego, G. de), Madrid, 1923; *Obras completas,* (Ed. González Palencia), Madrid, 1946; Ayala, F. de, *El pensamiento vivo de Saavedra Fajardo,* Buenos Aires, 1941.

Sacrificio de la misa (El). See under *Berceo.*

saeta. A short song chanted or sung in religious processions, especially during Holy Week *(Semana Santa).* Its metrical form varies, consisting of stanzas of from two to as many as six octosyllabic verses.

sáfico. (1) Referring to a verse of Greek origin, used by the poetess Sappho *(ca.* 600 B.C.) and introduced into Latin poetry by Catullus and Horace. (2) Referring to the Castilian adaptation of this verse, consisting of a stanza *(estrofa sáfica)* of three 11-syllable verses *(sáficos)* and one 5-syllable verse *(adónico).* The form was used by Santillana (1398-1458), Villegas (16th century), and other Spanish poets. See under *endecasílabo.*

sainete. A one-act, comic dramatic sketch; one of the minor dramatic genre known as *"el género chico".* The *sainete* is frequently in verse and depicts or satirizes folkways and folk-types. Like its predecessors, the *entremés* and the *paso* of the 16th century, the *sainete* of the 18th century was often presented as an extra feature together with a full-length play. The great exemplar of this dramatic form was the Madrid playwright, Ramón de la Cruz (1731-1794). The word *sainete* is a diminutive form of *saín,* an appetizing sauce used to flavor certain dishes. See also *Cruz, Ramón de la; género chico.*

Sainte-More, Benoît de. See under *Historia troyana.*

Sáinz de Robles, Federico Carlos (1899). Literary critic, historian of Madrid, editor and lexicographer. Archivist of the Municipality of Madrid and an official of the Madrid Library and Museum. A versatile and gifted writer, he is the author of poems, novels, plays, literary studies, biographies and histories. He has produced critical editions, anthologies and dictionaries. Among his more important works on literature are: *Vida, pasión y muerte de don Rodrigo Calderón,* 1936; *Historia del Teatro español,* 7 vols., 1943; *Galdós: su vida, su época y censo de sus personajes,* 1941; *Historia y antología de la poesía castellana,* 1946; *Lope de Vega: vida, horóscopo y transfiguración,* 1947; *Ensayo de un diccionario de la literatura,* 2a. ed., 2 vols., I. Términos, conceptos, "ismos" literarios, Madrid, 1954; II. Escritores españoles e hispanoamericanos, Madrid, 1953.

Salas Barbadillo, Alonso Jerónimo (1581-1635). Picaresque novelist, playwright and poet. Born and died in Madrid. The son of a commercial agent for colonial affairs, he received his early schooling at Madrid and then studied canon law at Alcalá and at Valladolid; however, he never completed his studies. Unsuccessful in his father's business, he became embroiled in law suits and ended as a failure burdened with debt. He turned to writing as a livelihood, producing verse, short plays *(entremeses)* and novels. A friend of Cervantes, he contributed to the programs of the Madrid literary academies. Because of his satires of officials, he was fined and exiled repeatedly. His greatest work was a picaresque novel, *La hija de Celestina,* or *La ingeniosa Elena* (1612), in which a female rogue dupes and satirizes her lovers. Elena is a beautiful, clever and corrupt creature, the embodiment of all the evil and vice of her time, mercilessly exposed by the author. She meets a well-deserved end on the gallows. Because of its interesting autobiographical elements, its unity and clarity of style, this novel is considered among the best of the picaresque type. It influenced Scarron's *Hypocrite* (1654) and Molière's *Tartuffe* (1664). Among Salas Barbadillo's other noted novels was *El subtil cordobés, Pedro de Urdemalas* (1620), a picaresque tale in which the characters organize a literary academy, spin yarns, sing songs and perform a play. Also interesting was his *Don Diego de noche* (1623), an account of nine nocturnal adventures of the hero. This work marks the introduction of the epistolary form in the picaresque novel. See also under *picaresque novel.*

Cf. *Obras,* 2 vols., (Ed. Cotarelo y Mori, E), Madrid, 1907-1909; also in *NBAE,* XVII, 1911; Valbuena Prat, A., "Estudio y notas," *La novela picaresca española,* Madrid, 1946; Place, E. B., "Salas Barbadillo, Satirist," *Romanic Review,* XVII; LaGrone, G. G., "Salas Barbadillo and the *Celestina,*" *Hispanic Review,* IX.

Salinas, Pedro (1892-1951). Modern lyric poet. Born in Madrid; died in Boston. Studied at the University of Madrid. Lectured on Spanish literature at the Sorbonne (1914-1917). Ph.D. in literature at the University of Madrid (1917). Professor of Spanish language and literature at the University of Seville (1918). Lecturer in Spanish at Cambridge (1922-1923). Associated with the *Centro de Estudios Históricos* in Madrid, he came to America during the Spanish Civil War. He lectured at the University of Puerto Rico and at Johns Hopkins University. From 1936 on, he was Professor of Spanish at Wellesley College. Together with Jorge Guillén, Gerardo Diego, Dámaso Alonso, García Lorca, and others, Salinas was one of the creators of the poetic revival in Spain in the 1920's. Influenced by Juan Ramón Jiménez, he rapidly developed a style of his own. His one theme was love, in all its phases. His predilection for free verse in short meters and his reference to everyday situations lend an air of naturalness and simplicity to his style that belies its subjective complexity. He characterized his own poetry as "una aventura hacia lo absoluto". Salinas wrote a modern ballad version of the *Poema del Cid* and a critical study of the *Poesías de Meléndez Valdés* (both in 1925). He also published crtical essays on modern Spanish literature, on Jorge Manrique, Rubén Darío, *etc.* Among his volumes of poetry are: *Presagios* (1923), *Seguro azar* (1929), *Fábula y signo* (1931), *La voz a ti debida* (1934), and *Razón de amor* (1936).

Cf. *Poesía junta,* Buenos Aires, 1942; Diego, G., *Poesía española,* Madrid, 1934; Del Río, A., and Spitzer L., "Pedro Salinas: Vida y obra," *Revista Hispánica Moderna,* N. Y., 1942; Ferrandiz Alborz, F., "Pedro Salinas," *Ibérica,* N. Y., Sept., 1954.

Samaniego, Félix María (1745-1801). Next to Iriarte, Spain's most noted writer of fables. Born and died at La Guardia, Alava, in the Basque region. Of an affluent and noble family, he studied at Valladolid and then traveled in France, coming under the influence of the Encyclopedists. Having acquired decidedly heterodox views, he returned to Spain, became the president of the *Sociedad Vascongada,* and also spent some time at the *Seminario de Vergara.* To the pupils of this school he dedicated his most famous work, *Fábulas morales* (1781-1784). Despite his friendship with Iriarte, Samaniego engaged in polemics with him regarding his priority in the field of the literary fable in Spain. In producing his work, Samaniego translated, imitated and appropriated outright some of the fables of Aesop, Fedro, Gay and Lafontaine; however, a great many in his collection were original. The *Fábulas morales* were an enormous success and for over a century were required reading and memory work in the schools of Spain.

Cf. Navarette, F. de, "Prólogo," *Obras inéditas . . . del insigne fabulista don Félix María Samaniego,* Vitoria, 1886.

Sánchez, Florencio (1875-1910). Uruguayan dramatist. Born in Argentina; died in Italy. After a checkered career as a journalist, office-holder and revolutionary, he found his true calling as a dramatist, producing more than twenty plays from 1903 to 1909.

Showing promise as a realistic observer in his early plays *(Ladrones, Canallitas),* he first achieved widespread fame with his *M'hijo el dotor* (1903), a dramatic father-and-son conflict, contrasting gaucho ideals with those of urban life. His socialistic and patriotic message found its natural vehicle in the thesis play, a genre which he cultivated with marked success. The foremost dramatist of the "teatro rioplatense" school, and perhaps the greatest in contemporary Spanish-American dramatic literature, Sánchez nevertheless was essentially a local writer. Chief works: *M'hijo el dotor,* 1903; *La gringa,* 1904; *Barranca abajo,* 1905; *Los muertos,* 1905.

Cf. Giusti, R. F., *Florencio Sánchez, su vida y su obra,* Buenos Aires, 1920; Richardson, R., *Florencio Sánchez and the Argentine Theatre,* N. Y., 1923; Flores, A., "Florencio Sánchez, Uruguayan Playwright," *Panorama,* Jan., 1944.

Sánchez, José (1905). Literary scholar. Born in Spain; naturalized, U. S. citizen, 1912. Assistant Professor and Chairman of the Spanish Department, University of Illinois, since 1947. Author of Spanish textbooks and anthologies. Articles on Cervantes, Alarcón, Pereda, *etc.,* and especially, *El periodismo español y su relación con la literatura,* 1944; *Circulos literarios de Iberoamérica,* 1945; *Academias y sociedades literarias de México,* 1951.

Sánchez, Luis Alberto (1900). Peruvian critic and literary historian. A political exile, he is now teaching at the University of Puerto Rico. Principal works: *La literatura peruana; Panorama de la literatura actual; Vida y pasión de la cultura en América; Nueva historia de la literatura americana; Indice de la poesía peruana contemporánea.*

Cf. *Hispania,* XXXVI, 1953.

Sánchez, Tomás Antonio. See under *Biblioteca Nacional; Cantar de Mío Cid.*

Sánchez de Badajoz, Diego. See under *juegos de escarnio.*

Sánchez de Calavera, Ferrán. See under *decir.*

Sánchez de las Brozas, Francisco (1523-1601). Better known by his Latinized name, *El Brocense.* See under *humanism.*

Sánchez de Vercial, Clemente. See under *ejemplo.*

Sancho II de Castilla. See under *Cantar de Zamora.*

Sancho Panza. The ignorant, selfish and materialistic, yet loyal and shrewd peasant whom Don Quijote chooses as his squire.

Sancho Saldaña. See under *Espronceda y Delgado.*

Sandoval, Prudencio de (1553-1620). Historian. Born at Valladolid; died at Estella, Navarra. He entered the Benedictine Order in 1569; became Bishop of Tuy in 1608, and of Pamplona in 1611. A Royal Chronicler under Felipe III, Sandoval's most famous work was his *Historia de la vida y hechos del emperador Carlos V* (Pt. 1, 1604; Pt. 2, 1606); which, although not entirely objective, is still a valuable historical source of many previously unpublished original documents. Among his other historical works were a *Crónica del inclito emperador Don Alfonso VII de Castilla* (Madrid, 1600), and a *Historia de los reyes de Castilla y de León* (Pamplona, 1615).

Cf. Castañeda, V., *El cronista Fr. Prudencio de Sandoval,* Madrid, 1929.

Sangre y Arena. See under *Blasco Ibáñez.*

San Juan de la Cruz. See *Cruz, San Juan de la.*

Sannazaro. See under *pastoral novel.*

San Pedro, Diego de (late 15th century). Renaissance poet and novelist. Very little is known of his life except that it must have been amorously eventful, judging from his writing. He held various minor positions, among them that of Judge-Auditor in the Royal Council of Enrique IV of Castile. His name appears in the *Catálogo de autoridades* of the *Academia Española.* The author of some poems which appear in the *Cancionero General,* of a novel, *Tratado de amor* (1491), and of a *Sermón de amor* (1511), San Pedro is chiefly known for his *Cárcel de amor* (1492), the most popular *novela sentimental* of the Renaissance. Influenced by Dante's *Vita Nuova* and Boccaccio's *Fiammetta,* the novel had an extraordinary vogue (over 25 editions in the 15th and 16th centuries; over 20 foreign translations, of which the English *[ca.* 1540] by Lord Berner introduced the trend to Euphuism). In turn, the *Cárcel de amor* influenced Rojas *(Celestina)* and Cervantes *(Novelas ejemplares; Quijote).* The novel is in epistolary form, relating the amorous adventures of the hero and heroine, Leriano and Laureola. Some of the episodes are autobiographical and some the product of the author's imagination. Among the features of the book are a eulogy of women and various allegorical elements. The hero's slow suicide by starvation captured the sentimental imagination of his readers, much as Goethe's *Werther* was to do in the 18th century. The book became the *breviario de amor* of its time, despite the disapproval of outraged moralists.

Cf. *Obras,* (Ed. Gili Gaya), Madrid, 1950; *Cárcel de amor,* in *NBAE,* VII; Cotarelo y Mori, E., "Nuevos y curiosos datos biográficos de . . . Diego de San Pedro," *Boletín de la Real Academia Española,* XIV, 1927.

Santa María Egipcíaca. A medieval narrative poem (late 12th or early 13th century), based on a Provençal source and relating episodes from the life of an Egyptian Magdalen, who, after a sinful life, repented and turned to holy ways. The poem comprises 1,451 lines of irregular metrical form, although 9-syllable lines predominate. Among the episodes recounted are those dealing with the Egyptian's youthful experiences, her conversations with holy men, her penance and her performance of miracles. Parallel episodes in a contemporary *Vie de Sainte Marie l'Egyptienne,* attributed to Robert Grosseteste, Bishop of Lincoln, seem to indicate this work as the source. The Spanish version is interesting in that it contains both *clerecía* and *juglaría* elements; the pious theme typical of the former, and the mundane treatment and metrical irregularity typical of the latter.

Cf. Text in *BAE,* LVII, (Ed. Menéndez Pidal, R.).

Santillana, Marqués de (1398-1458). Early Renaissance poet, critic, soldier and statesman. Born in Carrión de los Condes; died in Guadalajara. Of an eminent aristocratic and literary family—his father was Diego Hurtado de Mendoza, Admiral of Castile, and his uncle was the great Chancillor, López de Ayala—his full name was Íñigo López de Mendoza, but he is commonly known by his title, El Marqués de Santillana, conferred upon him by Juan II of Castile for his military triumphs at Huelva (1436) and at Olmedo (1445). A cultured gentleman, noted bibliophile and patron of letters, he was also active in the political and literary life of his time. As a politician, he opportunely changed from one faction to another; and after his preferment by Juan II, he wrote a philippic *(El doctrinal de privados)* exulting over the downfall of his enemy, Álvaro de Luna. In his sonnets *(Sonetos fechos al itálico modo)*—the first ever written in Spain—Santillana shows himself an imitator of Petrarch and Dante. Although theoretically opposed to the popular poetry of his day, his best lyrics were inspired by folk themes and forms derived from Galician poetry (*canciones, decires, serranillas* and *villancicos*). As a lyric poet, Santillana is distinguished for his delicate grace and sentiment expressed in simple form. His longer poems in *arte mayor* are allegorical and show Italian influence. Inspired by Petrarch was his dramatic *Comedieta de Ponza,* containing allegorical visions and telling of the disastrous defeat of the kings of Aragón and Navarra in the naval battle against Genoa (1435) near the Island of Ponza. Similarly allegorical and containing dreams and visions is his *Infierno de los enamorados,* modeled after Dante's *Inferno.* Aside from his lyric poetry, Santillana is most significant as a pioneer historian and critic of Castilian literature. In his *Proemio e carta* (1449), which prefaces his poems addressed to Don Pedro, Constable of Portugal, he acknowledges the inspiration of Gallego-Portuguese poetry, professes disdain for popular poetry, preferring strict form and classical models, and expresses his admiration for the Italian poets. The *Proemio e carta* is the first important *ars poetica* in Spanish literature.

Cf. *Obras* (Ed. Amador de los Ríos, J.), Madrid, 1852; *Proemio* (Ed. Sorrento, B.), *Revue hispanique,* LV; *Poesías* (Ed. Foulché-Delbosc), *NBAE,* XIX; *Canciones y decires* (Ed. García de Diego), Madrid, 1913; Pérez Curís, M., *El Marqués de Santillana,* Montevideo, 1916; Trend, J. B., *Marqués de Santillana, Prose and Verse,* Oxford, 1940.

Santob. See *Sem Tob.*

Santo Domingo de Silos. See under *Berceo.*

Santos Vega. See under *Ascasubi; Obligado.*

Sanz del Río, Julián. See under *krausismo.*

Sarmiento, Domingo Faustino (1811-1888). Argentine educator, journalist, statesman and writer. Noted in Argentine literature as one of the "proscriptos", he was an exile from 1829 to 1852, except for a brief interim (1837-1840), during which he was jailed for his anti-Rosas sentiments. After a political career as deputy, senator, and governor, he was elected President of the Argentine Republic, serving from 1868 to 1874. For the remainder of his career he returned to his earliest interest in the promotion of popular education. In literature Sarmiento is known for his translations of Scott's novels and his essays in defense of romanticism. His greatest achievement was a unique work of mixed literary genres, entitled *Civilización y barbarie: Vida de Juan Facundo*

Quiroga (1845), subsequently referred to simply as *Facundo.* It is a combination of novel, essay and history dealing with the career of a Rosas minion, General Quiroga, as it unfolds within the ethnic, social and scenic milieu of the Argentine dictatorship. Another notable work of Sarmiento was his *Recuerdos de provincia* (1850), containing memorable descriptions of the pampas and of Argentine types.

Cf. Rojas, R., *La literatura argentina,* Buenos Aires, 1924-1925; Nichols, M. W., *Sarmiento,* Washington, D. C., 1940.

Sarria, Luis de. See *Granada, Luis de.*

saudade. A term of Portuguese origin, designating melancholy solitude or nostalgic longing, especially as a characteristic of medieval Gallego-Portuguese verse. In Gallego, *soedade* or *soidade.* See also *soledad.*

sayagués. See under *Encina, Juan del.*

Sbarbi y Osuna, José María. See under *folklore.*

Schevill, Rudolph (1874-1946). American hispanist. Professor of Spanish, University of California. Eminent Cervantes scholar. Editor, complete works of Cervantes in collaboration with Bonilla y San Martín *(Obras completas de Miguel de Cervantes Saavedra,* 19 vols., Madrid, 1914-1941). Critical editions of the works of Timoneda, Lope de Vega, Vélez de Guevara, Núñez de Arce, and other Spanish classics. Author of *Ovid and the Renaissance in Spain,* Berkeley, 1913; *Cervantes,* N. Y., 1919.

Schlegel, August Wilhelm von (1767-1845). Eminent German philologist and a leader in the German romantic movement. In his lectures, *Über dramatische Kunst und Literatur* (1808), he emphasized the important role of Calderón in the Spanish and European theater. This idea was propagated in Spain by Johann Nikolaus Böhl von Faber, the father of Fernán Caballero, in *Reflexiones de Schlegel sobre el teatro* (1814), and gave rise to the famous controversy *(la querella calderoniana)* between pro- and anti-Calderonians during the early romantic period in Spain. See also under *Böhl von Faber.*

Cf. Del Río, A., *Historia de la literatura española,* N. Y., 1948.

secentismo. See under *gongorismo.*

Segadoras de Vallecas. A musical play by Ramón de la Cruz (1731-1794), composed in 1768. It is an example of the revival of the *zarzuela* with modern instead of mythological characters. See under *zarzuela.*

seguidilla. (1) A metrical form consisting of four-line stanzas, in which the first and third lines have seven syllables, and the second and fourth lines have five syllables. The second and fourth lines rhyme, whereas the first and third are unrhymed. The pattern is as follows: A_7 B_5 C_7 B_5. (2) In another form the *seguidilla* stanza consists of seven lines, of which the first four are called the *copla* and the last three, the *estribillo* or *bordón.* The pattern of this form is A_7 B_5 C_7 B_5 D_5 E_7 D_5. (3) A popular song or dance, occasionally improvised, corresponding to the above. The form of the *seguidilla* was established in the 16th century. The term was probably derived from the phrase, "*gente de la vida seguida*", the reference being to a song sung by wayfaring folk.

Segunda crónica general. See under *crónica.*

Segunda parte de la Diana. A sequel to Montemayor's *Diana (ca.* 1559), written by Alonzo Pérez in 1564. At the end of his work, Montemayor had referred to a continuation, but did not live to write it. The *Diana* of Alonzo Pérez was inferior in style to its original. See also under *Montemayor, Jorge de.*

Segura de Astorga, Juan Lorenzo. See under *Libro de Alexandre.*

Semanario Patriótico. See under *Quintana.*

Semanario pintoresco español. See under *Mesonero Romanos.*

Semblanzas literarias. See under *Palacio Valdés.*

Semblanzas literarias contemporáneas. See under *Madariaga.*

Sem Tob (1290?-1369?). Medieval poet. Born at Carrión de los Condes. Referred to as *El rabí Sem Tob del Carrión.* He was a converted Jew who enjoyed the patronage of Pedro I, El Cruel (1350-1369). The first of his religious origin to write in Castilian, he was also the first writer of gnomic verse in Spanish literature. His masterpiece is the *Proverbios morales* (bet. 1350 and 1369), a poem of concentrated ethical wisdom consisting of 686 quatrains in verses of seven syllables *(heptasílabos).* The work influenced Santillana, Gómez Manrique, Pérez Guzmán, and other early Spanish poets. See also under *poesía gnómica.*

Cf. *Proverbios morales,* (Ed. Llubera, I. G.), Cambridge, 1947.

Sender, Ramón José (1902). Novelist, editor, literary critic and professor. Born in Spain; naturalized U. S. citizen, 1946. Editor, *El Sol,* Madrid, 1925-1930. Free-lance writer in Spain, 1930-1936.

Participated in the Spanish Civil War, 1936-1939. Resided in Mexico, 1939-1942. Various teaching posts in the U. S. since 1942: Amherst College, Denver University, Ohio State University. Professor of Spanish Literature, University of New Mexico, since 1947. Chief works: *Imán,* Madrid, 1929; *Teresa de Jesús,* Madrid, 1931; *Siete domingos rojos,* Barcelona, 1932; *Mister Witt en el cantón,* Madrid, 1935; *El lugar del hombre,* Mexico, 1939; *Epitalamio del prieto Trinidad,* Mexico, 1942; *Crónica del Alba,* Mexico, 1942; *La esfera,* Buenos Aires, 1947; *El verdugo afable,* Santiago de Chile, 1952; *Ariadna,* Mexico, 1955. Sender is one of the few contemporary Spanish novelists who have won a world-wide audience. His works have been widely translated. In 1935 he received the National Prize of Literature in Spain. Master of a vigorous, realistic technique, his humanitarian ardor and the intensity of his social compassion raises the substance of his work far above the deficiencies of style noted by certain critics.

Cf. Río, A. del, *Historia de la literatura española,* N. Y., 1948.

Sentimiento trágico de la vida (Del). See under *Unamuno.*

Señora ama. See under *Benavente.*

Señora Cornelia (La). See under *Cervantes.*

Señor de Bembibre (El). See under *Gil y Carrasco.*

septisílabo. Referring to a verse of seven syllables; the same as *heptasílabo.*

Serafina. See under *Torres Naharro.*

serena. A Provençal poem or song, intended to be chanted or sung at night; a serenade or *serenata.*

serenata. A serenade or night song, of Provençal origin.

Sergas de Esplandián. See under *Amadís de Gaula.*

Serís, Homero (1879). Literary scholar and bibliographer. Born in Spain; naturalized U. S. citizen, 1941. Professor of Spanish at the Université de Dijon (1923-1924). Secretary, *Revista de Filología Española,* 1924-1931. Head of Department of Bibliography, *Centro de Estudios Históricos,* 1925-1936. In the United States, he has taught at the University of North Carolina, Duke University, and Brooklyn College. Professor of Spanish, Syracuse University, 1943-1952. Director of the *Centro de Estudios Hispánicos,* Syracuse University, since 1945. Chief publications: *La colección cervantina de la Sociedad Hispánica,* Illinois, 1918; *Indice de materias de la Revista de Filología,* Madrid, 1929-1936; *Biblio-*

grafía de Don Ramón Menéndez Pidal, Madrid, 1931; *Sinónimos*, (in collaboration), 5a. ed., Barcelona, 1932; *Manual de bibliografía de la literatura española*, Primera parte, Syracuse, 1954.

Sermón de amor. See under *San Pedro, Diego de.*

Sermón de amores. See under *Castillejo.*

serventesio. (1) A stanza of four 11-syllable lines rhymed ABAB, derived from the Provençal through the Italian. (2) A Provençal poetic form dealing with moral and political themes, sometimes in a satirical vein. Also called *sirventés.*

serrana. (1) A shepherdess or cowgirl. (2) A pastoral poem, or *serranilla.*

serranilla. A lyrical poem or ballad in rustic or pastoral style, written in short verses. Of Provençal and Galician origin, it deals with the poet's encounter *(lucha)* with a shepherdess or cowgirl *(serrana).* The type appears in the *Libro de buen amor* of the Archpriest of Hita (14th century) and in the lyrics of Santillana (1398-1458).

Seven Wise Masters. See under *Libro de los engaños. . . .*

Sevillan school. See *Escuela sevillana.*

sexta rima. A poem written in stanzas of six verses of *arte mayor.*

sextilla. A stanza of six verses in *arte menor (i.e.* fewer than 11 syllables).

sextina. (1) A poem consisting of six stanzas, each having six verses, and a final stanza having three verses. (2) A stanza of six rhymed verses either in *arte mayor* or in *arte menor.* The *arte menor* type is called the *sextilla.* A commonly occurring rhyme scheme for this form is ABABCC.

Sierra, Justo. See *Gutiérrez Nájera.*

Siete infantes de Lara. See *Infantes de Lara.*

Siete infantes de Salas. See *Infantes de Lara.*

Siete libros de la Diana. See under *Montemayor.*

Siete partidas. See under *Alfonso X.*

Siete virtudes. See under *decir.*

Siglo de Oro. The Golden Age of Spanish literature *(ca.* 16th to mid-17th century). The *Siglo de Oro* coincides approximately with the reigns of Ferdinand and Isabella (1474-1504) and Charles V (1516-1556), when Spain reached its apogee as a world power; and with the reign of Philip II (1556-1598), towards the end of which began Spain's decline. Three divisions of *Siglo de Oro* literature are generally distinguished: 1. *ca.* 1500 to *ca.* 1550, the Renaissance and Italianate phase; 2. *ca.* 1550 to *ca.* 1600, the late Renaissance phase; and 3. *ca.* 1600 to *ca.* 1650, the baroque or decadent phase. The characteristics of *Siglo de Oro* literature are: national consciousness, religious fervor, humanism, neoplatonism and individualism. The culmination of the Golden Age is represented by Miguel de Cervantes (1547-1616) and Lope de Vega (1562-1635), in whom the Renaissance spirit reaches its full fruition and in whom the seeds of the baroque spirit are already evident. The *Siglo de Oro* begins with an efflorescence of lyrical poetry as the result of the introduction and adaptation of Italian meters (Boscán, d. 1542; Garcilaso de la Vega, 1501?-1536; Luis de León, 1527-1591; Herrera, 1534?-1597; *etc.);* and its decadence is marked by the excesses of baroque *culteranismo* and *conceptismo* (Góngora, 1561-1627; Quevedo, 1580-1645; *etc.).* Other poetic forms which flourished during this period were the art ballad *(romance artístico),* as represented in the *Romancero general* (1600); and the erudite epic (Ercilla's *Araucana,* 1569; Balbuena's *Bernardo,* 1624; Lope de Vega's *Jerusalén conquistada,* 1609; *etc.).* The Spanish drama was created and developed to its fullest during this period (Juan de la Cueva, 1543-1610; Lope de Vega, 1562-1635; Tirso de Molina, 1583?-1648; Juan Ruiz de Alarcón, 1581-1638; Calderón, 1600-1681; *etc.).* The *Siglo de Oro* also witnessed the development of the picaresque novel *(La lozana andaluza,* 1528; *Lazarillo de Tormes,* 1554; *Guzmán de Alfarache,* 1599; *La pícara Justina,* 1605; *Vida del buscón,* 1626; *etc.).* Reflecting the religious spirit of the Golden Age are the lyrics and prose of the great Spanish mystics (San Juan de la Cruz, 1542-1591; Santa Teresa de Jesús, 1515-1582; Luis de Granada, 1504-1588; Luis de León, 1527-1591; *etc.).* Also called the *Edad de Oro.*

Cf. Kane, E. K., *Gongorism and the Golden Age,* Chapel Hill, 1928; Pfandl, L., *Historia de la literatura nacional en la Edad de Oro,* Barcelona, 1933; Vossler, K., *Introducción a la literatura española del Siglo de Oro,* Madrid, 1934; Davies, R. T., *The Golden Century of Spain (1501-1621),* London, 1937; González Palencia, A., *La España del Siglo de Oro,* N. Y., 1939; Valbuena Prat, A., *La vida española en la Edad de Oro,* Barcelona, 1943.

Siglo pitagórico, (El). See under *pícaro.*

Sigma Delta Pi. United States national honorary Spanish society. Official publication: *Entre Nosotros.*

Sigüenza y Góngora, Carlos de (1645-1700). Mexican scientist, historian and poet. Of Spanish and Creole descent. Related to Don Luis de Góngora and a friend of Sor Inés de la Cruz. Studied arts and sciences at the Jesuit College, where he took his vows, but left the Order temporarily for a professorship of astronomy and mathematics at the University of Mexico. As a Royal Geographer, he surveyed and mapped Pensacola, Florida. Considered the foremost savant of colonial Mexico, his writings include a panegyric to the Virgin Mary *(Triunpho Parthénico,* ca. 1682), an epic poem *(Piedad heroica de don Hernando Cortés,* ca. 1690), and a chronicle *(Paraíso occidental).* His picaresque narrative, *Infortunios de Alonso Ramírez* (ca. 1690), can be considered a forerunner of the Mexican novel.

Cf. Leonard, I. A., *Don Carlos de Sigüenza,* California, 1929.

silbos. See under *mosqueteros.*

Silva, José Asunción (1865-1896). Colombian poet. Born and died in Bogotá. An adverse fate brought him financial reverses, the death of his loved ones, and the loss of his manuscripts in a shipwreck. Little wonder that he committed suicide at the age of 32, ending a brief ten-year span of brilliant poetic creation that had not yet reached its zenith. Influenced by Heine, Poe, Baudelaire and Bécquer, Silva's lyrics are marked by romantic nostalgia, pessimism, frustration and irony. He is a poet of melancholy shadows and sombre grief, as indicated by the titles of his most famous poems: *Crepúsculo, Nocturnos, Día de defuntos,* etc. As a metrical and stylistic innovator he was a precursor as well as an exemplar of modernist poetry.

Cf. King, G. G., *A Citizen of the Twilight: José Asunción Silva,* N. Y., 1921; Blanco-Fombona, R., *El modernismo y los poetas modernistas,* Madrid, 1929; García Prada, C., *José Asunción Silva. Prosas y versos,* Mexico, 1942.

silva. (1) A miscellany. (2) An irregular metrical form consisting of a combination of verses of eleven and of seven syllables. The form was used by Góngora (1561-1627) in his *Soledades* (1613).

Silva de varios romances. See under *folklore; romance.*

Simón Bocanegra. See under *García Gutiérrez.*

sinalefa. See *synalepha.*

sincopa. See *syncope.*

Sindibad. See under *Libro de los engaños. . . .*

sinéresis. See *syneresis.*

Sireno. See under *Montemayor.*

sirventés. See *serventesio.*

Smith, Abiel. See under *Smith Professorship.*

Smith Professorship. The most famous professorship in the annals of Spanish studies in the United States. Established 1816 at Harvard on the basis of a bequest of $20,000 from Abiel Smith. The chair is known as the "Smith Professorship of the French and Spanish Languages and Literatures." It was occupied in turn by George Ticknor (1819-1835); Henry Wadsworth Longfellow (1836-1854); James Russell Lowell (1854-1891); J. D. M. Ford (1907-1943).

Cf. Doyle, Henry Grattan, "Spanish Studies in the United States," *Bulletin of the Pan American Union,* LX, March 1926. Doyle, Henry Grattan, "George Ticknor," *Modern Language Journal,* XXII, October 1937.

Society of Jesus. See under *Reformation.*

soidade. See *saudade.*

Soldadesca. See under *Torres Naharro.*

soledad. (1) Solitude; nostalgic longing. (2) A melancholy song of Andalusia. (3) A verse form consisting of stanzas of three octosyllabic verses.

Soledades. See under *Góngora; Machado y Ruiz.*

Solís, Antonio de (1610-1686). Historian and dramatist. Born in Alcalá de Henares; died in Madrid. His full name was Antonio de Solís y Rivadeneyra. He was educated at Alcalá and at Salamanca. In 1637 he entered the service of the Count of Oropesa, Viceroy of Navarre. He was appointed to the staff of the secretary of state by King Philip IV in 1654. In 1665 he was named by the Queen Regent, Mariana of Austria, "cronista mayor de las Indias," a post which he held until 1667, when he took Holy Orders. He wrote a number of minor plays in the style of Calderón; his poetry shows the influence of Góngora. His chief work was his *Historia de la conquista de México* (1519-1521), covering a period of three years, from the beginning of the conquest until the fall of the city. Using previous accounts *(e.g.* those of Cortés, Díaz del Castillo, *etc.*), Solís produced a masterpiece of prose style and vivid historical narrative. For all its copious documentation, it rises to dramatic and epic heights in its depiction of scenes and characters. The book became a standard work and Solís was chosen by the compilers of the *Academia Española* as one of the "autoridades de la lengua."

Cf. Text in *BAE,* XXVIII.

"Solitario (El)." See *Estébanez Calderón.*

Sombrero de tres picos (El). See under *Alarcón y Ariza.*

Sonata de otoño, de estío, etc. See under *Valle-Inclán.*

sonetillo. A poem in sonnet form but with verses in *arte menor* (*i.e.* shorter than eleven syllables). Compare *soneto.*

soneto. Sonnet. A verse form of Italian origin, consisting of fourteen 11-syllable verses divided into two quatrains and two triplets. The most frequent rhyme scheme is ABBA-ABBA-CDC-DCD. In Spanish verse the sonnet is sometimes supplemented by an *estrambote* (three verses, of which the first has seven, and the other two, eleven syllables). See also under *estrambote.*

Sonetos de muerte. See under *Mistral, Gabriela.*

Sonetos fechos al itálico modo. See under *Santillana.*

sonido asimilado. In phonetics, the "assimilated sound." See under *assimilation.*

sonido asimilador. In phonetics, the "assimilatory sound." See under *assimilation.*

sonido epentético. Epenthetic or excrescent sound. The interpolated sound in the phonetic phenomenon known as "epenthesis" *(epéntesis.)* See *epenthesis.*

Sotileza. See under *Pereda, José María de.*

Spanish. The national language of Spain, spoken in one form or another by approximately 115,000,000 people in Spain, North Africa (Tangiers and other Spanish protectorates), Central and South America, Mexico, Cuba, Puerto Rico, Santo Domingo, the southeastern United States, and the Philippine Islands. Spanish is a Romance language which developed from the Vulgar Latin of the Iberian Peninsula and which achieved independent status by about the 10th century. In addition to Latin, Spanish contains elements of Arabic, Greek, French and Italian. In early medieval times, Spanish consisted of three major dialect groups: (1) Catalan, or Catalonian (including Valencian, Andorran and Balearic); (2) Navarro-Aragonese (including Castilian, Leonese and Mozarabic); (3) Gallego-Portuguese. (An unclassifiable anomaly is Basque, believed to be derived from pre-Roman Iberian, or Aquitanian). With the unification of Castile and Aragon (1469), Castilian (*Castellano*) emerged as the predominant Spanish dialect, accounting for the present-day interchangeability of the terms "Spanish" and "Castilian" (*Español-Castellano*). Literary scholars use *Castellano* to distinguish that dialect from others (Aragonese, Leonese, *etc.*) in reference to works antedating the dominance of Castilian as the literary language of Spain (*i.e.* before the end of the 15th century). Since 1924, the *Diccionario de la Real Academia Española* has preferred the term *la lengua española* to that of *la lengua castellana.*

Cf. Spaulding, R. K., *How Spanish Grew,* Berkeley, 1943; Fernando Lázaro Carreter, *Diccionario de términos filológicos,* Madrid, 1953; Pei, M. A., and Gaynor, F., *Dictionary of Linguistics,* N. Y., 1954; Trend, J. B., *The Language and History of Spain,* London, 1953.

Spaulding, Robert Kilburn (1898). American hispanist, Romance philologist and authority on the history of the Spanish language. At University of California since 1920; Professor of Spanish since 1948; Head of Department of Spanish and Portuguese, since 1953. Author of *Syntax of the Spanish Verb,* N. Y., 1930; *How Spanish Grew,* Berkeley, 1943; and of many textbooks, articles and book reviews in *Hispanic Review, Hispania, etc.*

Spell, Jefferson Rea (1886). American hispanist. Authority on Latin American literature. Associated with the University of Texas since 1920; Professor of Romance Languages. Diploma de Honor, *Academia Mexicana.* Publications: *The Life and Works of José Joaquín Fernández de Lizardi,* Philadelphia, 1931; *Rousseau in the Spanish World Before 1833,* Austin, Texas, 1938; *Contemporary Spanish-American Fiction,* Chapel Hill, 1944. Editor: *Don Catrin de la Fachenda,* Mexico City, 1944; *Tres Comedias de Eusebio Vela,* Mexico City, 1948; *El periquillo sarniento,* Mexico City, 1949.

Spitzer, Leo (1887). Romance philologist. Born in Austria; naturalized U. S. citizen, 1945. Professorships at Vienna, Bonn, Marburg, Cologne, Istanbul. Professor of Romance Philology, Johns Hopkins University, since 1936. Author of *Aufsätze zur romanischen Syntax und Stilistik,* Halle, 1918; *Stilstudien,* Marburg, 1928;

Romanische Stil- und Literaturstudien, Bonn, 1932; *Essays in Historical Semantics,* N. Y., 1948; *Linguistics and Literary History,* Princeton, 1948. Articles in *Revista Hispánica Moderna, Modern Language Journal, Romance Philology, etc.*

Stern, S. M. See under *jarcha.*

stichomythia. See *esticomitia.*

Storni, Alfonsina (1892-1938). Argentine schoolmistress and poetess. Born in the Italian part of Switzerland but lived in Argentina from childhood on. Taught school in Buenos Aires. Incurably ill, she committed suicide in 1938. A poetess of great sensitivity, her lyricism was essentially feminine, treating the emotion of love and desire with rare intellectual insight. Her collected poems were published in Barcelona (*Las mejores poesías,* 1923) and in Buenos Aires (*Antología poética,* 1940). Among her chief works were: *La inquietud del rosal,* 1916; *Mascarilla y trébol,* 1938.

Cf. Mañach, Jorge, "La liberación de Alfonsina Storni," *Revista iberoamericana,* I, 1939.

Stúñiga, Lope de. See under *cancionero.*

Subida del Monte Carmelo (La). See under *Cruz, San Juan de la.*

Subtil cordobés (El). See under *Salas Barbadillo.*

suelto. "Broadside." A printed sheet of an actor's script, of a popular ballad, *etc.* Such sheets are a source of some early plays and ballads. In the printers' trade they were called *pliegos sueltos.* Some of them were pirated extracts from plays, copied in haste during a performance, or from memory afterwards. They are frequently unreliable as sources because they were cheaply printed without corrections.

Sueños. See under *Quevedo.*

Sueños morales. See under *Torres Villarroel.*

Suma de enxemplos por A.B.C. See *ejemplo.*

Swain, James O. (1896). American hispanist. Professor, University of Tennessee. Editor, *Hispania,* 1937-1942. Authority on 19th century Spanish and Spanish American novel. Articles on Pereda, Ibáñez, Concha Espina, *etc.*

synalepha. (Sp. *sinalefa*). In metrics, (1) the blending into a single syllable of two successive vowels of different syllables; (2) the elision of a final vowel before a following word beginning with a vowel or mute *h.*

syncope. (Sp. *sincopa*). The dropping out or disappearance of a medial sound, letter or syllable, resulting in the contraction of a word. The resulting form is known as a "syncopated word" (*palabra sincopada*). Example: calidus > *caldus* > *caldo.*

syneresis. (Sp. *sinéresis*). In metrics, the blending of two vowels or syllables, usually pronounced separately, into a single syllable.

Syntipas. See under *Libro de los engaños.*

T

Talavera. See *Arcipreste de Talavera.*

Tamayo y Baus, Manuel (1829-1898). Actor, dramatist and critic. Born and died in Madrid. Both his parents were actors, a vocation which he also followed in his youth. His practical experience in the theater was later reflected in his dramaturgical skill and in his theories on dramatic art, presented in his *discurso de ingreso* (1858) to the *Academia Española (De la verdad como fuente de belleza en la literatura).* Beginning at the age of eleven, when he translated and adapted a French play, Tamayo wrote continuously for the theater until his last play, *Los hombres de bien* (1870). For the rest of his life he was employed in research as Secretary of the *Academia Española* and as Director of the *Biblioteca Nacional.* His reasons for deserting fame and the theater for the last 28 years of his life are still a mystery. Tamayo's versatility as a playwright is shown in the wide range of literary styles and genres which his plays encompass: sentimental, romantic comedies, classical tragedies, historical dramas, comedies of manners, thesis plays, *etc.* His best play was *Un drama nuevo* (1867), a prose tragedy of infidelity, set in Elizabethan England. The action involves a clown (Yorick) in Shakespeare's company of players; and the great English bard himself plays an important role. It is a play within a play, the imaginary betrayal and murder becoming tragically real. The play appears to have been suggested by Kyd's *Spanish Tragedy,* and in turn influenced Leoncavallo's *Pagliacci.* Tamayo's other notable tragedy was *Virginia* (1853), a Classical theme treated in Romantic fashion. Outstanding among his historical dramas was *La locura de amor* (1855), a study of pathological jealousy involving Doña Juana de Castilla (1479-1555), the daughter of Fernando and Isabel. Tamayo's thesis plays were directed against personal and social vices:

(jealousy) *La bola de nieve* (1856); (materialism) *Lo positivo* (1862); (duelling) *Lances de honor* (1863); *etc.*

Cf. *Obras dramáticas,* 4 vols., Madrid, 1898-1900; Siscar y Salvado, N., *Don Manuel Tamayo y Baus, estudio crítico-biográfico,* Barcelona, 1906.

Tanto por ciento (El). See under *López de Ayala.*

Tarsiana. See under *Libro de Apolonio.*

Tassis Peralta, Juan de. See *Villamediana.*

Teágenes y Cariclea. See under *novela bizantina.*

Teatro crítico universal. See under *Feijóo y Montenegro.*

Teatro de la Zarzuela. See under *género chico.*

Teatro de los niños. See under *Benavente.*

Teatro del Recreo. See under *género chico.*

Teatro Eslava. See under *Martínez Sierra.*

Teatro Español. The Spanish National Theater, located in Madrid. It is reputed to have the oldest continuous tradition of any theater in the world. It was erected on the site of the *Teatro del príncipe,* the same place where performances were presented in the *Corral de la Pacheca* as early as 1568. See also under *Benavente.*

Tejado de vidrio (El). See under *López de Ayala.*

Téllez, Gabriel. See *Tirso de Molina.*

Tema de nuestro tiempo (El). See under *Ortega y Gasset.*

Tenorio, Don Juan. See under *Tirso de Molina.*

tensón. A form of troubadour poetry *(poesía trovadoresca)* in which two or more troubadours *(trovadores)* engage in a debate, generally on a love theme. Also spelled *tensión* or *tensó.* See also under *trovador.*

Tercer abecedario. See under *mysticism.*

Tercera crónica general. See under *crónica.*

tercerilla. A stanza of three lines in *arte menor:* i.e. seven to nine syllables in length. The rhyme scheme is similar to that of the *terceto.* See under *terceto.*

terceto. "Triplet." A metrical stanza consisting of three 11-syllable lines, rhymed ABA. The rhyme of the middle line is used for the first and third lines of the following *terceto:* e.g. ABA, BCB, etc. *Tercetos* thus rhymed are called *tercetos en cadena* or *tercetos encadenados,* and the process is referred to as *encadenamiento.*

The form originated from the Italian *terza rima,* and was popular in Spain during the Golden Age. See also *tercerillo.*

Teresa de Jesús, Santa (1515-1582). Great mystic of the Spanish Counter-Reformation. Of noble lineage, her name was Teresa Sánchez de Cepeda y Ahumada. The exact place of her birth is a matter of dispute, some authorities citing Avila, and others the town of Gotarrendura, to the north of Avila. She died at Alba de Tormes, Salamanca. Sickly as a child, she had many visions and spells of religious ecstasy. At the age of seven, she ran away with her brother to seek martyrdom. Aside from an adolescent addiction to romances of chivalry, for the most part she read devotional literature, for she knew no Latin. By the age of 19, she was already a Carmelite nun, rising eventually to become Mother Superior of the Order. She founded and governed no less than 17 new convents before her death. She was beatified in 1614 and canonized in 1622. Combining introspection with activity, she spent most of her life in reading, meditation, writing, organizing the reform of the Carmelite Order and founding many convents. These achievements are related in her *Libro de las fundaciones* (1573). Many of the external facts of her life are revealed in a charming personal style in a collection of over 400 of her letters covering the period from 1561 to 1582; but unfortunately, her correspondence with San Juan de la Cruz has not been preserved. Her inner life is revealed in her introspective autobiography, *Libro de su vida* (1562-1565; pub. Salamanca, 1588). Her greatest mystical work is *Las moradas,* or *El castillo interior* (Salamanca, 1588), in which are described the seven "abodes" corresponding to seven degrees of prayer, the last of which leads to union with God. Also important in the exposition of her mystical visions and philosophy are her *Camino de perfección* (1585), a guide for nuns, and her *Conceptos del amor de Dios* (1611), a commentary on the *Song of Songs.* In these works Santa Teresa opened up new vistas of mystical experience, at times creating her own terminology to express spiritual subtleties. Her basic message was extinction of self and submergence into the Divine Essence. Yet her style was conversational and full of native humor and pungency.

Cf. *Obras completas,* Madrid, 1951; Peers, E. A., *Studies of the Spanish Mystics,* London, 1927; Castro, A., *Santa Teresa y otros ensayos,* Madrid, 1929; Hoornaert, R., *Saint Teresa in her Writings,* London, 1931.

Teresa del Manzanares. The heroine of Castillo Solórzano's picaresque novel, *La niña de los embustes* (1632).

Teresa Mancha. See under *Espronceda y Delgado.*

Terralla y Landa, Esteban de (latter 18th century). Peruvian poet who wrote under the pen name of "Simón Ayanque." Of Spanish birth, he came to Peru in 1787. He is chiefly known for his verse satire, *Lima por dentro y fuera,* a merciless commentary on society and manners in the Peruvian capital.

Cf. Palma, R., *Apéndice a mis últimas tradiciones peruanas,* Barcelona, 1910; Menéndez y Pelayo, M., *Antología de poetas hispanoamericanos,* vol. III, Madrid, 1927-1928.

tertulia. A social gathering for discussion or entertainment. Beginning with the academies of the Golden Age, the institution of the *tertulia* has been inseparable from the development of Spanish literature, and of Spanish culture in general. The *tertulia* is usually held in a café, a club, a library, editorial meeting rooms, or in some cultural center. Among the more modern famous literary *tertulias* of Spain have been *El Parnasillo, El Ateneo, El Gato Negro, Pombo, etc.*

Cf. Williams, E. M., *The Development of the Literary Tertulia,* (Diss.), Cornell U., 1935.

terza rima. See *terceto.*

Tesoro de la lengua castellana. See *Covarrubias y Orozco.*

tetrasílabo. A poetic line or verse of four syllables. Also called *cuatrisílabo.*

tetrástrofo. A stanza of four lines; the typical form of *cuaderna vía* as written by medieval *clerecía* poets. See also *cuaderna vía; mester de clerecía.*

Thomas à Kempis. See under *Granada; mysticism.*

Ticknor, George (1791-1871). The first hispanist of international reputation in the United States. Occupied the Smith Professorship at Harvard (1819-1835). Traveled to France, Spain, Portugal, Italy and Germany (1815-1819) in preparation for his Harvard lectures, during which time he also studied at Göttingen. Later he traveled to Europe (1856-1857) on behalf of the Boston Public Library. Chief works: *Syllabus of a Course of Lectures on the History and Criticism of Spanish Literature,* Cambridge, 1823.

Lecture on the Best Methods of Teaching the Living Languages, Boston, 1833. *History of Spanish Literature,* 3 vols, N. Y., 1849. Successive revised and enlarged editions of the same, 1854, 1863, 1872, 1879, 1891. First edition in England, 1849. Foreign editions: *Historia de la literatura española,* 4 vols., Madrid, 1851-56. *Histoire de la littérature espagnole,* 3 vols., Paris, 1864-72. *Geschichte der schönen Literatur in Spanien,* 2 vols., Leipzig, 1867.

Cf. Brooks, Van Wyck, *The Flowering of New England,* N. Y., 1936; Doyle, Henry Grattan, "George Ticknor," *Modern Language Journal,* XXII, October, 1937; Hart, T. R., Jr., "George Ticknor's History of Spanish Literature: The New England Background," *Publications of the Modern Language Association,* March, 1954.

Tierra vasca. See under *Baroja.*

Tigre Juan. See under *Pérez de Ayala.*

Timoneda, Juan de (1490?-1583). Dramatist, short-story writer, poet, ballad collector and bibliophile. As a dramatist, he wrote comedies, *pasos, entremeses* and *autos sacramentales* in the manner of Lope de Rueda. His *Rosa de romances* (Valencia, 1573) was a collection of ballads grouped according to theme: love, classical antiquity, Spanish history and royal heroes. His best known collection of tales was *El patrañuelo* (Valencia, 1567), the first successful Spanish imitation and adaptation of the Italian *novela* form. See also under *Rueda; entremés.*

Cf. *Obras,* 3 vols., (Ed. Juliá, E.) Madrid, 1947-48.

Tinelaria. See under *Torres Naharro.*

Tipos y paisajes. See under *Pereda.*

Tirano Banderas. See under *Valle-Inclán.*

Tirant lo Blanch. A monument of medieval Catalonian literature, it was the best known romance of chivalry after the *Amadís* and the *Palmerín* cycles. The first three parts are by Johanot Martorell; the fourth by Martí Johán de Galba. It was begun in about 1460 and first appeared in 1490 (Valencia) in Catalan. The first Castilian translation was published in 1511 (Valladolid). The work shows the influence of the English romance, *Guy of Warwick,* and of the works of Dante, Petrarch and Boccaccio. In turn it influenced Cervantes, among others. The story is based on the historical exploits of Admiral Roger de Flor during an expedition to the Orient. Unlike the other chivalric romances,

Tirant lo Blanch reflects middle class rather than aristocratic ideals. It eschews the fantastic and supernatural episodes typical of the other romances; it is realistic, obscene, and contains burlesque elements; *e.g.* a duel in underwear, obviously a parody on the ideals of chivalry. Like Don Quijote, the hero Tirant dies in bed.

Cf. *Tirant lo Blanch,* (facsimile, ed. of 1490), Hispanic Society of America, N. Y., 1904; (Castilian ed. by Riquer, M. de), Barcelona, 1947-1948; Vaeth, J. A., *Tirant lo Blanch,* N. Y., 1918; Givanel Mas, J., *El "Tirant lo Blanch" y D. Quijote de la Mancha,* Barcelona, 1922.

Tirso de Molina (1584?-1648). Chief dramatist of the Lope de Vega school. Born in Madrid; died in Soria. Tirso de Molina was the pseudonym of Gabriel Téllez, a Mercedarian friar. Little is known of his family origin beyond one disputed theory that he was the natural son of the Duke of Osuna. Tirso was educated at Alcalá and entered the Order of Mercy in 1601. He became Chronicler of the Order in 1637, and Prior of the Monastery of Soria in 1645. He is said to have written over 400 plays, but only 86 are extant. Five volumes of his works were published between 1624 and 1633; but he stopped writing for the theater in 1625 after having been censured by the Council of Castile for the over-realistic portrayal of vice in his plays. Tirso's most famous play was *El burlador de Sevilla y convidado de piedra* (publ. 1630), the first Don Juan drama in world literature. Tirso's hero, Don Juan Tenorio, became a universal type second only to Don Quijote; it was the inspiration for Molière's *Festin de Pierre* (1665), Mozart's *Don Giovanni* (1787), and Byron's *Don Juan* (1819-1824), among other famous treatments of the theme. Don Juan Tenorio, in Tirso's version, is a titanic character whose reckless defiance of the moral code reaches a level of superhuman courage which, to some extent, redeems his libertinism. Tirso's dramatic theories are contained in a rambling work of miscellaneous content, *Los cigarrales de Toledo* (1624). In it he rejects the traditional unities of time and place and champions the mixed genre of tragi-comedy, in accordance with Lope de Vega's theories. He is a staunch believer in verisimilitude, unhampered by conventional rules. Tirso excelled in all the dramatic types of his day: "cape and sword" (*El burlador de Sevilla,* 1630); religious (*El condenado* *por desconfiado,* 1635); historical (*La prudencia en la mujer,* 1633); folk legend (*Los amantes de Teruel,* 1635); palace play (*El vergonzoso en palacio,* 1621); *etc.* Outstanding among the above is the religious play which treats the metaphysical problem of grace and free will and demonstrates the necessity of faith and repentance. In general, it can be said that Tirso, in his radical dramatic theories, anticipated the romantic drama. He was a great stylist and showed remarkable skill in his plots. He was a master of psychological characterization, especially in the portrayal of his women and his *graciosos.* However, he injected so little of his own personality into his plays that scholars cannot positively verify his authorship of some of the most important plays attributed to him. See also under *Don Juan.*

Cf. *Obras dramáticas completas,* (Ed. Ríos, B. de los), 2 vols., Madrid, 1947; Muñoz Peña, P., *El teatro del maestro Tirso de Molina,* Valladolid, 1889; Bushee, A. H., *Three Centuries of Tirso* de Molina, Oxford, 1939.

Tob, Sem. See *Sem Tob.*

tonadilla. (1) A light and gay popular air. (2) A fifteen-minute miniature operetta which succeeded the *zarzuela grande* towards the end of the eighteenth century. The *tonadilla* was so-called because it contained popular airs, such as *seguidillas.* See under *zarzuela.*

Torquemada. See under *Pérez Galdós.*

Torre, Francisco de la. See under *Escuela de Salamanca.*

Torre, Guillermo de (1900). Essayist, literary and art critic, poet, editor and translator. Born in Madrid. A resident of Argentina from 1927 to 1932, and again since 1937. He was the chief theoretician of the literary and artistic movement known as *ultraísmo,* elaborated in his *Manifiesto vertical ultraísta* (1920). His collected poems, *Hélices,* appeared in 1923. In 1927 he founded the vanguardist periodical *La Gaceta Literaria* in collaboration with Ernesto Giménez Caballero. The most eminent Spanish authority on modern literary and artistic movements, his most important book of literary criticism is *Literaturas europeas de vanguardia* (1625). Among his other important works are: *Examen de conciencia,* 1928; *Itinerario de la nueva pintura española,* 1931; *Vida y arte de Picasso,* 1936; *La aventura y el orden,* 1943; *Guillaume Apollinaire: su vida, su obra y las teorías* *del cubismo,* 1946. He has also edited the *Obras completas* of Federico García Lorca (Buenos Aires, 1940). See also under *ultraísmo.*

Torre de los Panoramas. See under *Herrera y Reissig.*

Torres Bodet, Jaime (1902). Mexican poet, novelist, critic, professor and diplomat. Professor of French Literature at the University of Mexico. Director of the National Library of Mexico. Diplomatic service in Spain, Holland and France. President of UNESCO. A prolific writer, Torres Bodet began as a modernist poet in 1918, went through ultraist and surrealist phases, finally achieving a personal creative synthesis. He has also made his mark as a critic of contemporary literature. Among his chief works are: (poems) *Fervor,* 1918; *Canciones,* 1922; *Poemas,* 1924; *Biombo,* 1925; *Destierro,* 1930; (novels) *Margarita de Niebla,* 1927; *La educación sentimental,* 1929; (criticism) *Contemporáneos,* 1927; *Perspectiva de la literatura mexicana,* 1928; *Fronteras,* 1954; *Tiempo de arena,* 1955.

Cf. Llanos, A., "La poesía de Torres Bodet," *Abside,* II, Mexico, 1938.

Torres Naharro, Bartolomé de (d. 1524?). Dramatist and poet. Little is known of his life beyond the few details given in the preface of his collected plays, *Propaladia* (Naples, 1517). He was born at Torre de Miguel Sexmero, a small town in Badajoz, where in later life he officiated as a priest. The place of his death is not known. Educated in the humanities at Salamanca, he was conversant with the Latin, Italian, French and Portuguese languages and literatures. As a youth he was a soldier, was captured by pirates and sold into slavery in Algiers. After being ransomed, he went to Rome, where he was ordained and began his career in letters. Both in Rome and in Naples he became the protégé of popes and cardinals. His first play, *Comedia Trofea,* was performed before Leo X in 1512. Reacting against the corruption of 16th century Rome, he wrote a scathing dramatic satire entitled *Comedia Tinelaria* (from *tinelo,* servants' mess hall). In it he exposed the immorality and intrigue of a Roman palace as revealed through the conversations of servants. His early experiences as a soldier were realistically portrayed in his *Comedia Soldadesca.* His best play, *Comedia Himenea,* is ingenious in its plot and masterly in its characterization. It is the first "cape and sword" play in Spanish literature and contains what were later to become typical elements of love, intrigue, honor, *etc.* In this play the family honor is preserved by a brother who spares his sister's over-impetuous suitor when the latter's matrimonial intentions are revealed. Another of his plays of love and intrigue, *Comedia Serafina,* also ends happily when the hero conveniently falls in love with his brother's rejected sweetheart and prevents an impending catastrophe. Torres Naharro's importance in the development of the Spanish drama is not only due to the example of his own plays, which were more original than those of Encina, but also to the dramatic theories set forth in the prologue *(prohemio)* to his *Propaladia.* These represent the first attempt at dramatic criticism in Spanish literature. Torres classified the drama into *comedias a noticia* (realistic observations of life) and *comedias a fantasía* (imaginative creations). He adhered to the Horatian precept of five acts *(jornadas)* and drew a sharp distinction between comedy and tragedy. Among his other principles of dramatic composition are those of truth, verisimilitude, concentration of plot by limiting the number of characters, and observance of decorum. Significant is his failure to mention the Aristotelian unities. A master of versification and of satire, Torres Naharro did much toward the development of the secular drama. His later influence was considerable. See also under *jornada.*

Cf. *"Propaladia" and Other Works of Bartolomé de Torres Naharro,* (Ed. Gillet, J. E.), 3 vols., Bryn Mawr, Pa., 1943-1946-1952; Menéndez y Pelayo, M., "Prólogo," *Propaladia,* Tomo II, "Los libros de antaño," Madrid, 1900.

Torres Villarroel, Diego de (1693-1770). Picaresque personality, mathematician and writer. Born and died in Salamanca. The son of a bookseller, he studied the humanities at Salamanca, but soon embarked on an eccentric career. He was in turn pamphleteer, bullfighter, soldier, charlatan, quack, soothsayer, dancing master, beggar, duellist, thief and what not. He traveled widely and lived by his wits, managing to become for a time the protégé of the Countess of Arcos and of the Duchess of Alba. As he matured, he achieved respectability. Having taken minor orders in 1715, he was ordained in 1745. He became professor of mathematics at the University of Salamanca in 1726. His collected works were first published in 1752. Most of this biographical data comes from his own *Vida* (1743-1758), a picaresque autobiography, reflecting the chaotic and obscurantist state of the society in which he lived. Among the more successful of his miscellaneous publications was a series of *Almanaques* written under the pen name of *El gran Piscator de Salamanca.* In addition to presenting a medley of fabulous lore, he managed to predict the death of King Luis I, and the coming of the French Revolution, thus gaining his reputation as a soothsayer. His *Sueños morales, visiones y visitas de Torres con don Francisco de Quevedo por Madrid* (1743) were an imitation of his favorite author, Quevedo, and showed an ethical trend in his writing. He also published a volume of plays, *Juguetes de Talía* (1738).

Cf. *Obras,* 15 vols., Madrid, 1794-1799; *Vida (*Ed. Onís, F.), Madrid, 1912; García Boiza, A., *Don Diego de Torres Villarroel,* Salamanca, 1911.

Trabajos del Pío Cid (Los). See under *Ganivet.*

Trabajos de Persiles y Sigismunda (Los). See under *Cervantes.*

tradición. A Spanish-American literary art form, essentially an anecdote or sketch based on history or legend. The *tradición* derives from the *costumbrista* sketch, but was developed into an independent genre by Peru's greatest writer, Ricardo Palma (1833-1919), in the ten volumes of his *Tradiciones peruanas* (1872-1910). Palma's *Tradiciones* are remarkable for their vivid evocation of historical atmosphere achieved with great economy of literary means.

Cf. *Tradiciones peruanas,* Buenos Aires, 1941; Sánchez, L. A., *La literatura del Perú,* Buenos Aires, 1939.

Tradiciones peruanas. See under *Palma, Ricardo; tradición.*

Traductores de Toledo. See under *Escuela de traductores de Toledo.*

Trafalgar. See under *Pérez Galdós.*

Tragicomedia de Calisto y Melibea. See *Celestina.*

Trapaza. See under *Castillo Solórzano.*

Tratado de amor. See under *San Pedro, Diego de.*

Trend, John Brande (1887). British hispanist, literary scholar and translator. Professor of Spanish, Cambridge University. Emeritus, 1953. Author of articles on Spanish literature in the *Encyclopedia Britannica.* Translator of Calderón's *La vida es sueño,* and of the poems of Juan Ramón Jiménez. Editor, revised edition, *Oxford*

Book of Spanish Verse, 1949. Critical edition, *Marqués de Santillana, Prose and Verse,* Oxford, 1940. Author of *Alfonso the Sage and Other Essays,* London, 1926; *Berceo,* Cambridge, 1952; *Antonio Machado,* Oxford, 1953; *The Language and History of Spain,* London, 1953.

Trescientas (Las). See under *Mena, Juan de.*

Tres reyes de Oriente. See *Libro de los tres reyes de Oriente.*

Tribuna nacional. See under *Andrade.*

trisílabo. A poetic line or verse consisting of three syllables.

Tristán. See under *romances of chivalry.*

Triunfos del amor de Dios. See under *mysticism.*

trobador. The same as *trovador.*

trobar. The same as *trovar.*

trobar clus. See *trovar cerrado.*

Trobes en lahors de la Verge Marie. The title of the first book printed in Spain (Valencia, 1474). It is a collection of hymns in praise of the Virgin Mary.

Trofea. See under *Torres Naharro.*

Trotaconventos. See under *Ruiz, Juan.*

trova. (1) A verse or poetic line. (2) A poem written in imitation of another. (3) A poem to be sung or chanted. (4) A love lyric composed or sung by a medieval *trovador.*

trovador. (1) Troubadour; a medieval French poet who composed in the *langue d'oc* of La Provence. (2) A Spanish *mester de clerecía* poet. Compare *juglar.*

Trovador (El). See under *García, Guitérrez, Antonio.*

trovadoresco. Referring to the poetry or style of medieval troubadours *(trovadores).* See *trovar; trovador.*

trovar. (1) To compose verses; to create poetry. (2) To write in the style of the Provençal troubadours *(trovadores).*

trovar cerrado. The highly formal and complex art *(trobar clus)* which was a later development of Provençal troubadour poetry.

Turiana. See under *entremés.*

Turk, Laurel Herbert (1903). American hispanist. Professor, DePauw University. Author of many Spanish textbooks. Articles and book reviews: *Modern Language Journal, Hispania, Books Abroad,* etc. Co-editor, *Cuentos y comedias de América,* Boston, 1950; *Cuentos y comedias de España,* Boston, 1951.

Tuy, Lucas de. See under *Bernardo del Carpio; crónica.*

U

Úbeda, Francisco López de. See under *Justina.*

Ugarte, Eduardo. See under *García Lorca.*

Ugarte, Manuel (1878). Argentine political propagandist, novelist, critic and short-story writer. Since the age of twenty, a resident of France. A militant opponent of so-called "Yankee imperialism," he is known as the creator of the expression "el coloso del norte" in reference to the United States. His best creative achievement is to be found in his short stories. Chief works: *Cuentos de la Pampa,* 1903; *Cuentos argentinos,* 1908; *El porvenir de la América latina,* 1911; *El destino de un continente,* 1923.

Cf. Sánchez, L. A., *Historia de la literatura americana,* Santiago, 1940.

Ultra. One of the most important literary reviews associated with the ultraist movement. It was published in Seville from 1921 to 1922. One of its collaborators was Guillermo de Torre (b. 1900). See also under *ultraísmo.*

ultraísmo. One of the many vanguardist esthetic and literary movements, such as cubism, futurism and dadaism, of French and Italian origin, which flourished in Spain and in Spanish America during the 1920's. The chief theoretician of this movement in Spain was the journalist and poet, Guillermo de Torre (b. 1900), generally considered the coiner of the terms, *ultraísmo* and *ultraísta* (cf. his *Vertical, manifiesto ultraísta,* Madrid, 1920). The most important literary organs of the movement were the periodicals *Grecia* (1919-1920) and *Ultra* (1921-1922), published in Seville. Poets who, at one time or another, were briefly associated with the movement were Gerardo Diego, Pedro Salinas, Jorge Guillén, Vicente Huidobro, Federico García Lorca and Rafael Alberti. Not all were avowed *ultraístas.* The outstanding representative of *ultraísmo* in South America was the Argentine poet, Jorge Luis Borges. The program of *ultraísmo* was to effect a literary regeneration, particularly in poetry, through eschewal of all non-poetic elements; *i.e.* rhetorical embellishments and traditional romantic love themes. Narrative was also considered peripheral to the essential core of poetry. The image and the metaphor were to reign supreme. *Ultraísmo* also extended its revolutionary program to the lexical, orthographic and thematic features of poetry. Although of short duration, the movement helped poets achieve a more refined sensitivity, a more creative language and more modern themes. See also under *Torre, Guillermo de.*

Cf. Torre, G. de, *Literaturas europeas de vanguardia,* Madrid, 1925; Brussot, M., "Was ist ultraismus?", *Die Literatur,* Berlin, Nov. 1933; Gómez de la Serna, R., *Ismos,* 2a. ed., Buenos Aires, 1943; "El ultraísmo y el creacionismo español," *Revista Nacional de Cultura,* Caracas, Enero-Febrero, 1955.

Unamuno y Jugo, Miguel de (1864-1936). Popular philosopher, Greek philologist, philosophical-literary essayist, and creative writer. Born at Bilbao; died at Salamanca. Of a Basque family, he received his early education in Bilbao. From 1880 to 1884 he pursued philosophical and literary studies at the Central University of Madrid. In 1901 he became Professor of Greek at the University of Salamanca, where he remained for most of his life except for brief sojourns in Madrid, Portugal and France (as an exile, 1924-1930, during the Primo de Rivera dictatorship). From 1931 on, he was Professor of the History of the Spanish Language at the University of Salamanca. Twice in his career he served as Rector of his University. He died in the opening days of the Spanish Civil War. Among his most important works were the following: *Paz en la guerra,* 1897; *De la enseñanza superior en España,* 1899; *En torno al casticismo,* 1902; *Amor y pedagogía,* 1902; *Vida de don Quijote y Sancho,* 1905; *Mi religión y otros ensayos,* 1910; *Soliloquios y conversaciones,* 1912; *Contra esto y aquello,* 1912; *Ensayos,* 7 vols., 1916-1920; *Del sentimiento trágico de la vida,* 1914; *Niebla,* 1914; *La agonía del Cristianismo,* 1930; *etc.* Unamuno's philosophy can be summarized under three main categories: (1) the doctrine of man as an end in himself and not as a means; (2) man's intuitive awareness of the world as expressed by word and deed (theory of the *Logos*); (3) an extra-rational faith in immortality. Unamuno's thought and personality have been said to embody, or symbolize, the cultural crisis which marks the Spanish character; namely, a paradoxical radicalism (he advocated socialism and individualism); eclecticism (he favored both a European and a traditional Spain); preoccupation with the conflict between faith and reason, life and thought, culture and civilization *(Del sentimiento trágico de la vida).* Basically an idealist and a humanitarian, Unamuno's entire personal, intellectual and literary life was an unrelenting battle against materialism, against those forces which would make of men an abstract integer *(Vida de don Quijote y Sancho).* All of these ideas run through his creative works. Although his poetry has some merit, his novels *(Paz en la guerra; Niebla;* etc.) are little else but philosophical dialogues in which the characters voice the author's ideas. He is at his best in his critical essays, in which he treats the subjects of education, politics, religion, literature, etc., with an unorthodox and not always consistent independence of judgment expressed in a vigorous, trenchant style. Although criticized for his paradoxical principles, Unamuno was a liberal in the best sense of the word. His idealism influenced a whole generation of Spanish youth.

Cf. Barja, C., *Libros y autores contemporáneos,* Madrid, 1935; Romera Navarro, M., *Miguel de Unamuno,* Madrid, 1928; Marías, J., *Miguel de Unamuno,* Madrid, 1943; Harris, M. T., *The Technique of Unamuno's Novels,* (Diss.), Wellesley, 1952; Clavería, C., *Temas de Unamuno,* Madrid, 1953.

Un drama nuevo. See under *Tamayo y Baus.*

Urbina, Isabel de. See under *Vega, Lope de.*

Urdemalas, Pedro de. See under *Salas Barbadillo.*

"utile dulci." Luzán's literary principle of combining the utilitarian (moral) with the "sweet" (the appeal of beauty and interest), as expounded in his *poética.* See under *Luzán Claramunt de Suelves.*

V

Valbuena Prat, Ángel (1900). Critic and literary historian. Professor at the Universities of Barcelona and Murcia. Visiting Professor, University of Wisconsin, 1951. He has lectured in England, Puerto Rico and Brazil, and is one of the outstanding literary scholars of modern Spain. Principal works: "Los autos sacramentales de Calderón," *Revue Hispanique,* LXI, 1924; *Literatura dramática española,* 1930; *La poesía española contemporánea,* 1930; *La vida española en la Edad de Oro,* 1943; *Historia de la literatura española,* 3 vols., 3rd ed., 1950.

Cf. *Hispania,* XXXVI, 1953.

Valdés, Alfonso de (d. 1532). Humanist and prose satirist. He was the most prominent Spanish Erasmist of his time and was said to have been more Erasmist than Erasmus himself. The brother of Juan de Valdés, he was born in Cuenca and died in Vienna. Alfonso de Valdés was one of the so-called "heterodox" personalities of the Spanish Renaissance. He maintained an extensive correspondence with Erasmus and with Melanchthon, was vitriolic in his condemnation of clerical venality and papal ineptitude in politics, but nevertheless died within the Catholic Church. As secretary and counsellor of Carlos V, he wrote an anticlerical political tract defending his royal patron in connection with the sack of Rome *(Diálogo de Lactancio, o Diálogo en que particularmente se tratan las cosas acaecidas en Roma en el año de 1527).* He also wrote a satire on European politics, once erroneously attributed to his brother, Juan (*Diálogo de Mercurio y Carón,* 1528). In this work he combined the style of Lucian with the ideas of Erasmus to produce one of the liveliest satirical dialogues of his time. See also under *humanism.*

Cf. *Diálogos,* (Ed. Montesinos), 2 vols., Madrid, 1928-1929; Bataillon, M., *Erasme et l'Espagne,* Paris, 1937.

Valdés, Antonio. See under *Ollanta.*

Valdés, Gabriel de la Concepción (1809-1844). Cuban poet. Pseudonym, Plácido. Of illegitimate birth, he spent his childhood in a foundling home. Without formal education, he earned his living at various trades, including those of carver and printer. He was executed in 1844 on the charge of revolutionary conspiracy. A protégé of Martínez de la Rosa, who praised his first poetic attempts (1834), Valdés developed into one of the true poets of the romantic period in South America. His humble origin, ardor for justice, and tragic end inspired many biographers and novelists. Among his better known poems are the ballad, *Jicotencal,* the *letrilla* verses of *La flor de la caña;* and his swan song, *Plegaria a Dios.* His complete works appeared in Havana in 1886 *(Poesías completas con doscientas diez composiciones inéditas).*

Cf. García Garófalo Mesa, M., *Plácido, poeta y mártir,* Mexico, 1938.

Valdés, Juan de (d. 1541). Humanist, religious writer and literary critic. Born in Cuenca; died in Naples. He studied Latin, Greek and Hebrew at Alcalá, where he was associated with the noted humanist, Juan de Vergara. Like his brother, Alfonso, he corresponded with Erasmus and became one of the latter's staunch adherents. His favorite author was Lucian, from whom he learned the technique of the dialogue. Of decidedly independent religious views, he developed a personal theological philosophy, Protestant in essence but different in many respects from the doctrines of Luther and Calvin. Fearing the Spanish Inquisition as the result of his unorthodox *Diálogo de la doctrina cristiana* (Alcalá, 1529), he went to Rome in 1531 and there continued his religious writing. He spent the last years of his life in Naples, where he attracted a select group of disciples, forming the chief center of heterodoxy in Italy. His unorthodox religious views on questions of dogma, salvation, church discipline and biblical exegesis are summarized in his *Ciento y diez consideraciones divinas* (1539; publ. in Basle, 1550). His greatest contribution to Spanish letters, however, was his critical dialogue on Spanish language and literature, *Diálogo de la lengua* (in mss. *ca.* 1535; first publ. 1737), wherein two learned Italians and two Spaniards discuss the origins of the Spanish language, questions of vocabulary, style, phonetics, orthography, *etc.,* illustrated by examples from Spanish literature. The critical judgments expressed have remarkably withstood the test of time. It is one of the basic documents of Spanish philology. Interesting also as a folklore source are the approximately 200 proverbs included in the dialogue. See also under *humanism; folklore.*

Cf. *Diálogo de la lengua,* (Ed. Montesinos), Madrid, 1928; *Diálogo de la doctrina cristiana,* (Ed. Bataillon), Coimbra, 1925; *Ciento diez consideraciones divinas,* (Ed. Boehmer), Leipzig, 1860; Wiffen, B., *Life and Writings of Juan de Valdés,* London, 1865; Caballero, F., *Alfonso y Juan de Valdés,* Madrid, 1875.

Valencia, Guillermo (1872-1943). Colombian diplomat and poet. Served in the administrative and diplomatic services of his country, at one time running as a candidate for the presidency. His aristocratic origin and classical education are reflected in his literary creation where the emphasis is on quality rather than on quantity. This is attested to by his only volume of poems, *Ritos,* 1899. A blend of humanistic classicism and French symbolism, Valencia's poetry represents one of the most successful achievements of *modernista* writing.

Cf. Ortiz Vargas, A., "Guillermo Valencia, Colombia's Master Poet," *Poet Lore,* XXXI, 1930.

Valencian. See under *Spanish.*

Valera, Juan (1824-1905). Regional novelist, poet, critic and diplomat. Born in Cabra, Córdoba; died in Madrid. Of an aristocratic family, his full name was Juan Valera y Alcalá Galiano. He received an excellent education, studying philosophy at Málaga (1837-1840) and taking his degree in law at Madrid (1846). Valera served in various diplomatic capacities in Naples, Lisbon, Brazil, Belgium, Germany, Austria, and Russia; and was Spanish Minister to the United States from 1883 to 1886. His first publication was a volume of *Ensayos poéticos* (1844). Having achieved prominence as a poet and critic, he was elected to the *Academia Española* in 1861. His first and most famous novel, *Pepita Jiménez,* was published in 1874. It is a delicate psychological study of the victory of carnal love over divine aspirations; the story of a youth who intends to become a priest, but who succumbs to the attractions of a designing widow. In *Doña Luz* (1879), Valera treats the same theme in reverse; this time the platonic love of a girl for an elderly priest marks the victory of spirit over flesh. *Las ilusiones* *del doctor Faustino* (1875) carries on Valera's dissection of psychological illusions, presenting a modern Faust with all of the problems of his medieval prototype but without the latter's supernatural aids. The same aura of illusion pervades his *Juanita la Larga* (1895), the story of an old man's love for a young girl. Valera has been called "the last humanist." His wide learning and cosmopolitanism combined with urbanity and philosophical detachment, and his re-creation of Andalusian background make him one of the best of Spain's 19th century regional novelists. His plots are classically simple and his style witty, limpid and refined. His insight into human motives and his broad humanity make him a moral philosopher through the medium of his novels.

Cf. *Obras completas,* (Ed. Araujo), Madrid, 1942; Azaña, M., *La novela Pepita Jiménez,* Madrid, 1927; Fishtine, S., *Don Juan Valera, The Critic,* Bryn Mawr, Pa., 1933; Romero Mendoza, P., *Don Juan Valera,* Madrid, 1940; De Coster, C. C., "Valera en Washington," *Arbor,* Feb., 1954.

Valiente justiciero (El). See under *Moreto, Agustín.*

Valle-Inclán, Ramón del (1866-1936). Galician novelist, poet and dramatist. Born in Villanueva, Pontevedra; died in Santiago de Compostela. His real name was Ramón del Valle y Peña, but he invented fantastic stories about his illustrious antecedents and adopted the aristocratic name of Ramón María del Valle-Inclán. After completing his studies at Pontevedra, he began to practise law in Santiago de Compostela, but soon abandoned the profession for a literary career. His first book, *Féminas, seis historias amorosas,* showing the influence of D'Annunzio and of Barbey d'Aurevilly, appeared in 1895. Valle-Inclán led a literary-bohemian existence interspersed with travels to Mexico, France and Rome. A striking, one-armed figure (he had lost an arm as the result of a fracas with a journalist) with a black beard and flowing hair, he impressed his contemporaries with his brilliant but eccentric conversation in his favorite haunts, cafés, salons, *tertulias,* backstage rooms, editorial offices and lecture halls. He was a theatrical manager in South America and a lecturer on esthetics in Rome and Madrid. In 1929 he was imprisoned for criticizing the dictatorship of Primo de Rivera. His last years were spent in his native Galicia. Valle-Inclán was a sensational writer with an exotic style and a penchant for erotic themes. The books which first brought him notoriety were the famous four *Sonatas,* which portray the different love affairs of the Marqués de Bradomín, each corresponding to a different season of the year: *Sonata de otoño, Sonata de estío, Sonata de primavera, Sonata de invierno* (1902-1905). The Marqués de Bradomín is a type of Don Juan, described as being *"feo, católico y sentimental"*; he was invariably irresistible to women, a projection, no doubt, of the author's wishful eroticism. The *Sonatas* are notable for their delicate musical style rather than for any intrinsic novelistic merit. Among the best of his other earlier novels were *Flor de Santidad* (1904) and *Romance de lobos* (1908), picturesque evocations of Galician life and background. These works were followed by a trilogy of historical novels based on the last of the Carlist wars (1870), and remarkable for their scenes of barbaric cruelty: *Los cruzados de la causa, El resplandor de la hoguera,* and *Gerifaltes de antaño* (1908-1909), of which the second is generally considered his best. Among his subsequent works were novels combining the satirical with the grotesque (a type which he designated *esperpentos*), the best of which was *Los cuernos de Don Friolera* (1921). Memorable for its pictures of bohemian life was *Luces de Bohemia* (1924), a novel in dialogue about a blind, frustrated poet. His final novels were *Tirano Banderas* (1926), a satire of a Mexican dictator; *La corte de milagros* (1927); and *Viva mi dueño* (1928); the last two about the court of Isabel II (part of a series entitled, *El ruedo ibérico*). Important among his verse plays was *Cuento de abril* (1910), the story of a Provençal troubadour and a cruel princess whom he loves in vain. His best prose play was *La cabeza del Bautista* (1924), a drama of modern life. As a poet Valle-Inclán was strongly influenced by Rubén Darío (*La pipa de Kif,* 1919; *El pasajero,* 1920) and the modernists. He was associated with the Generation of 1898, but with an esthetic detachment that distinguished him from the tumultuous agitation of the others. The hallmark of his work is exoticism and estheticism. He revolutionized the novel just as Ruben Darío revolutionized poetry. Today he is chiefly remembered as the outstanding prose stylist of the late 19th century.

Cf. *Obras completas,* 2 vols., Madrid, 1944; Fernández Almagro, M., *Vida y literatura de Valle-Inclán,* Madrid, 1943; Gómez de la

Serna, R., *Don Ramón María del Valle-Inclán,* Buenos Aires, 1944.

Valle y Caviedes, Juan del (1652-1695?) Peruvian poet. Born in a small town in Andalusia, Spain, but lived most of his life in Lima, Peru, except for a three-year sojourn in Spain at the age of twenty. Little is known of his life. Most of his poems were published long after his death. The best known collection is *Diente de Parnaso* (Ed. Palma, R., 1899). Although most of his poetry strikes a trenchant, satirical note interspersed with earthy humor, he also wrote a few lyrics and mystical poems.

Cf. Sánchez, L. A., *Historia de la literatura peruana,* Lima, 1921.

Valores literarios (Los). See under *Azorín.*

Van Horne, John (1889). Romance philologist. Authority on Italian and Spanish literature. Critical edition, *La grandeza mexicana de Bernardo de Balbuena,* 1930. Author of *Bernardo de Balbuena: Estudio biográfico y crítico,* 1940.

Varela, Juan Cruz. See *Cruz Varela, Juan.*

Vasconcelos, José (1882). Mexican lawyer, politician, journalist, educator, sociologist and philosopher. One time Rector of the University of Mexico. Minister of Public Education (1920-1925) under President Obregón. An unsuccessful candidate for the presidency, he lived in the United States during various periods of exile. Intensely nationalistic, Vasconcelos champions an indigenous culture for Mexico, independent of North American influence and based on the native Indian race *(La raza cósmica),* for which he envisions future cultural ascendancy. In Mexican literature he is best known for his four-volume autobiography (1935-1939), beginning with *Ulises criollo* and followed by *La tormenta, El desastre,* and *El proconsulado.* The *Ulises criollo* tetralogy belongs among the masterpieces of socio-cultural memoirs. It is an intimate account of the author's eventful life, seen against the social, political and cultural background of the Mexico of his era. Chief works: *La raza cósmica,* 1925; *Indología,* 1927; *Bolivarismo y Monroísmo,* 1934; *Ulises criollo,* 1935; *La tormenta,* 1938; *El desastre,* 1938; *El proconsulado,* 1939.

Cf. González Peña, C., *Historia de la literatura mexicana,* Mexico, 1940; Sánchez, L. A., *Historia de la literatura americana,* Santiago, 1940.

Vega, Garcilaso de la. See *Garcilaso de la Vega.*

Vega, Lope de (1562-1635). After Cervantes, Spain's greatest literary figure, and unquestionably her greatest dramatist. He was born (Nov. 25, 1562) and died (Aug. 27, 1635) in Madrid. Of humble origin, his full name was Lope Félix de Vega Carpio. His father was a gold filigree craftsman with a penchant for versifying. A precocious child, Lope was said to have dictated verses before he could write and to have written his first play *(El verdadero amante)* at the age of twelve. He received his early education at the Jesuit *Colegio de los Teatinos,* and later studied at the University of *Alcalá de Henares.* Among his patrons were the Bishop of Avila and the Duke of Alba. Of a passionate temperament, Lope led a tumultuous existence, crowded with many love affairs, abductions, elopements and two marriages. He was exiled from Madrid for having libeled the family of his first sweetheart, an actor's wife named Elena Osorio (the *Filis* of his pastoral ballads; also described in his last novel, *La Dorotea,* 1632). He spent his exile in Valencia, where he became prominent in the group of dramatic poets in that city. After returning to Madrid to elope with the girl who was to become his first wife, Isabel de Urbina, (the *Belisa* of his poems; cf. *Las bizarrerías de Belisa*), he left her almost immediately to embark with the ill-fated Invincible Armada in 1588 (cf. his poem on Sir Francis Drake, *La Dragontea,* 1598). His most productive period coincided with a time of domestic happiness at Alba de Tormes, which ended in 1595 with the death of his first wife, Isabel. Late in life, as the result of a religious crisis, he took holy orders (1614), but this did not end his profane writing nor his amorous susceptibilities. His last great love was Marta de Nevares, the *Amarillis* of his eclogues. The last years of his life were embittered by the insanity and death of his second wife, the death of his son and the elopement of his daughter. Lope de Vega died one of the most celebrated men of his time. His reputation was such that the phrase *"Es de Lope"* became a synonym for perfection; and his universality earned him the famous epithet by Cervantes, *"el monstruo de la naturaleza."*

Like Goethe, Lope is impressive for his fecund creativeness and infinite invention. His writings were said to total over a thousand, of which some 400 are preserved. His *Comedias* were published in 25 volumes (1604-1647) and at irregular intervals since then. Of his non-dramatic writings, his pastoral novel *Arcadia* (1598) is outstanding. In it he appears personally as *Belardo,* and his patron, the Duke of Alba, appears as *Anfriso.* Lope also excelled in the erudite epic: *Hermosura de Angélica* (1602); *Jerusalén conquistada* (1609); *Andrómeda* (1621); and in a burlesque of the Italian epic, dealing with feline love, *Gatomaquia* (1634). As a lyric poet, particularly in the sonnet form, Lope had few equals. However, his great achievement was the founding of the baroque drama. Ironically enough, he regarded his dramas as hack work. A key to Lope's dramatic theories (which, incidentally, he did not always observe) is his poem, *Arte nuevo de hacer comedias en este tiempo* (1609). His dramatic aims are determined by the audience, the common folk *(vulgo);* and his chief criterion is appeal, in terms which the *vulgo* can understand. He believes in variety, of genres (tragicomedy), of metrical forms, of themes. His principle of verisimilitude requires life-like situations and language appropriate to the characters. He recommends dramatic devices, such as word play, a good curtain, "deceiving with the truth." Influenced by Italian Renaissance critics, Lope discards all unities except that of action. The number of acts should be three, the climax being in the middle of the third act.

Lope's plays have been classified into (1) *Comedias de capa y espada* (love and honor intrigues against a background of aristocratic and middle class society and manners); (2) *Autos sacramentales* (religious allegories); (3) *Comedias históricas* (based on national tradition and derived from chronicles, ballads and chivalric romances); (4) *Comedias de carácter* (depicting type characters from the society of his time); (5) *Comedias mitológicas, pastoriles, picarescas, de santos,* etc.; (6) *Loas* and *entremeses.* Among his best historical plays were: *El mejor alcalde, el rey; Las paces de los reyes y judía de Toledo; El rey Don Pedro en Madrid, o el infanzón de Illescas; Peribáñez y el comendador de Ocaña; Los Tellos de Meneses; El caballero de Olmedo; Porfiar hasta morir; Fuente Ovejuna; La estrella de Sevilla* (authorship disputed); etc. Outstanding among his lighter comedies were: *El acero de Madrid; La moza de cántaro; Amar sin saber a quién; El perro del hortelano; La hermosa fea; Mila-*

gros del desprecio; La dama boba; El anzuelo de Fenisa; etc. Lope de Vega exploited a great variety of sources, some of them repeatedly. With extraordinary command of language and with amazing lyrical facility, he treated a universal array of themes, classical and contemporary, sacred and profane. Although at odds with Góngora, he made some concessions to the prevailing vogue of *conceptismo.* But in general he wrote simply and clearly. His work, like that of Shakespeare, was designed for the popular stage, without Aristotelean preconceptions.

Cf. *Obras,* (Ed. Academia, con prólogos de Menéndez y Pelayo), Madrid, 1890-1913; *idem.,* Nueva edición, (Ed. Cotarelo y Mori), Madrid, 1916-1931; *Obras no dramáticas, BAE,* XXXVIII; *Poesías líricas,* (Ed. Montesinos), Madrid, 1925-1926; Rennert, H. A. & Castro, A., *Vida de Lope de Vega,* Madrid, 1919; Schevill, R., *The Dramatic Art of Lope de Vega,* Berkeley, 1918; Icaza, F. A. de, *Lope de Vega, sus amores y sus odios,* Madrid, 1925; Romera-Navarro, M., *La preceptiva dramática de Lope de Vega,* Madrid, 1935; Vossler, K., *Lope de Vega y su tiempo,* Madrid, 1932; Morley, S. G. & Bruerton, C., *The Chronology of Lope de Vega's Comedias,* N. Y., 1940; Entrambasaguas, J. de, *Vivir y crear de Lope de Vega,* Madrid, 1947.

Vega, Ricardo de la. See under *género chico.*

Vélez de Guevara, Juan. See under *Vélez de Guevara, Luis.*

Vélez de Guevara, Luis (1579-1644). Dramatist and picaresque novelist. Born in Ecija, near Seville; died in Madrid. The son of a lawyer, his full name was Luis Vélez de Guevara Dueñas. Some of his earlier writings appeared under his maternal name of Vélez de Santander. After completing his studies at Osuna, he entered military service and saw action in Italy. Despite the patronage of various noblemen and of the King, Felipe IV, whom he served in the unsalaried post of usher to the privy bedchamber, he led an impecunious existence. He was married four times and had several children, of whom one, Juan Vélez de Guevara (1611-1675), also gained fame as a writer. As a dramatist, Luis Vélez de Guevara was influenced by Lope de Vega, from whom he borrowed extensively. His specialty was the sensational *teatro de ruido,* but he also wrote *autos sacramentales* and *entremeses.* In all he was supposed to have written some 400 plays. His most famous one was entitled *Más pesa el rey que la sangre,* based on the patriotic story of Guzmán el Bueno, whose loyalty to the king outweighed his love for his son. Rather than surrender the city of Tarifa to the Moors, who were holding his son as hostage, Guzmán elected to fight it out. Another noted play by Vélez de Guevara was *Reinar después de morir,* based on the Inés de Castro legend, which tells of a love that was faithful beyond death. The wife of a Portuguese prince, Inés is murdered in a conspiracy. Upon assuming the throne, the prince stages a posthumous coronation for his beloved wife. Vélez de Guevara's baroque style makes him a precursor of Calderón. Yet, although a celebrated dramatist in his time, today he is chiefly known for his picaresque novel, *El diablo cojuelo* (Madrid, 1641). Influenced by Quevedo's *Sueños,* he introduced a new technique for exposing the society of his day to satire; namely, the magical intervention of an imp (Asmodeo) who makes roofs transparent for the student (Cleofás) who has liberated him from a necromancer's bottle. This ingenious device was widely imitated, but it remained for Le Sage to give the story a European vogue in his *Diable boiteux* (1707).

Cf. *Obras* in *BAE,* XIV, XLV, LIV; *El diablo cojuelo,* (Ed. Bonilla y San Martín, A.), Madrid, 1910; Spencer, F. E. & Schevill, R., *The Dramatic Works of Luis Vélez de Guevara,* Berkeley, Cal., 1937; Muñoz Cortés, M., "Aspectos estilísticos . . . en *El diablo cojuelo,*" *Revista de filología española,* 1943.

Verdadero amante (El). See under *Vega, Lope de.*

Verdi. See under *Saavedra, Ángel de.*

Vergara, Juan de. See under *Valdés, Juan de.*

Vergonzoso en palacio (El). See under *Tirso de Molina.*

versificación irregular. See under *cantar de gesta; Henríquez Ureña.*

verso de arte mayor. See *arte mayor.*

versos de romance. See under *Cantar de Mío Cid.*

Vertical, manifiesto ultraísta. The program of the ultraist movement; published in Madrid (1920) by Guillermo de Torre (b. 1900). See also under *ultraísmo; Torre, Guillermo de.*

Viaje del Parnaso. Cervantes' versified critique (1614) of the writers of his day. See under *Cervantes.*

Viaje entretenido (El). See under *Rojas Villandrando.*

Viana, Javier de (1868-1926). Uruguayan politician, journalist and short-story writer. Studied languages and medicine in Montevideo. Lived in Buenos Aires from 1904 on. Most eminent in the regional tale, in which he reveals himself as a forerunner of the "criollo" school. He was the author of more than a dozen collections of stories, including one which appeared posthumously in Madrid. Among his important works were: *Campo,* 1898; *Yuyos,* 1912; *Leña seca,* 1913; *Gurí y otras novelas,* 1916.

Cf. Zum Felde, A., *Proceso intelectual del Uruguay,* II, 193-217, Montevideo, 1930.

Vicente, Gil (1470?-1536?). Renaissance dramatist and lyric poet. Although of Portuguese nationality, Vicente nevertheless wrote the greater part of his important work in Castilian, the chief language of the Portuguese poets of his day. Of his approximately 40 plays, only seven were entirely in Portuguese; twelve were entirely in Castilian; and the remainder in a mixture of the two. Very little is known of his life. He may have studied law at the University of Lisbon, but from the evidence of his plays, he seems to have been self-educated. Neither the dates nor the places of his birth and death are known exactly. His first known work dates from 1502 and his last play bears the date 1536. According to some authorities, he was a goldsmith and financial adviser to the Portuguese court. What we know definitely is that he lived at the court and dedicated his work to his royal patron, Juan III. The works of Gil Vicente were first published by his son, Luis, (Lisbon, 1562), under the following categories: (1) *Obras de devoción;* (2) *Comedias;* (3) *Tragicomedias;* (4) *Farsas;* (5) *Obras menudas.* Outstanding in the first group is a trilogy of three ships: *Auto da barca do Inferno* (1517); *Auto da barca do Purgatorio* (1518); *Auto da barca da Gloria* (1519); all on the medieval subject of the Dance of Death. Only the last of these *autos* is in Castilian. The protests and indignation of kings and clerics as they arrive in Hell make these plays Aristophanic satires in addition to moralities. Another of his religious plays, written in Castilian, is a kind of allegory of the Incarnation: *Auto da Sibila Casandra* (1509?). Casandra is a shepherdess who refuses to marry because she believes she is destined to be the virgin who will bear a Christ child. She is reproved for her conceit, and the play ends with the real Nativity scene. References to the Hebrew origin of Christianity (Casandra's uncles are named Abraham, Isaiah and Moses), and to corruption in Christendom, lend an Erasmian note of satire to the play. Among Vicente's lighter plays is the *Comedia do viuvo* (1514), in which a widower manages to marry off his two daughters to two brothers. His *Comedia de Rubena* is notable because it contains the first *bobo,* or clown, of the early Spanish drama. In it there also appears for the first time the element of magic. Vicente also gave the Spanish drama its first specimens of plays based on the romances of chivalry, the tragicomedies, *Don Duardos* (1525), based on the *Palmerín* cycle; and *Amadís de Gaula* (1533), based on the *Amadís* cycle. Gil Vicente was essentially a court poet, but he made use of popular lyric forms. His work represented an advance over that of Encina in its greater variety of themes and characters, but especially in its expression of ideas of the time.

Cf. *Obras completas,* (Ed. Braga), 6 vols., Lisbon, 1942-1944; Freire, A. B., *Vida e obras de Gil Vicente,* Oporto, 1920; Bell, A. F. G., *Gil Vicente,* Oxford, 1921; Alonso, D., "Estudio y notas," in *Tragicomedia de Don Duardos,* Madrid, 1942; Parker, J. H., "Gil Vicente: A Study in Peninsular Drama," *Hispania,* XXXVI, 1953.

Victoria de Junín. See under *Olmedo, José Joaquín.*

Victoria de Roncesvalles. See under *Roncesvalles; Balbuena, Bernardo de; cantar de gesta.*

Vida de don Diego de Torres Villarroel. See under *Torres Villarroel.*

Vida de don Quijote y Sancho. See under *Unamuno.*

Vida de Lazarillo de Tormes. See *Lazarillo de Tormes.*

Vida del escudero Marcos de Obregón. See under *Espinel, Vicente.*

Vida de Santa María Egipcíaca. See *Santa María Egipcíaca.*

Vida de Santo Domingo de Silos. See under *Berceo.*

Vida es sueño (La). See under *Calderón.*

Vida fantástica. See under *Baroja.*

Vida Literaria. A review. See under *Benavente.*

Vida Moderna. A literary review. See under *Martínez Sierra.*

Vida retirada. See under *León, Luis de.*

Vidas de los españoles célebres. See under *Quintana.*

Vidas de San Isidoro . . . See under *Arcipreste de Talavera.*

Vie de Sainte Marie l'Egyptienne. See *Santa María Egipcíaca.*

Villaespesa, Francisco (1877-1936). Andalusian poet, dramatist and novelist from Almería. He led a bohemian existence as a writer, editor, lecturer and theatrical producer. A friend of Salvador Rueda (1857-1933) and of Juan Ramón Jiménez (b. 1881), he began as a modernist poet but lapsed into neo-romantic vagaries for lack of poetic discipline. His favorite theme, like that of his model, Zorrilla, was the life of Moorish Spain *(Andalucía,* 1911; *Los nocturnos del Generalife;* 1915; etc.). Among his most representative verse were *Canciones del camino* (1906); *El jardín de las quimeras* (1909); and *Torre de marfil* (1911). He also essayed the poetic drama *(El alcázar de las perlas,* 1911), in which he achieved a degree of romantic color; but his plays were essentially of the chamber variety, suitable for reading but unsuccessful on the stage.

Cf. *Obras completas,* Madrid, 1916; *Poesías completas,* Madrid, 1954; Onís, F. de, "Francisco Villaespesa y el modernismo," *Revista Hispánica Moderna,* II, 1936-1937.

Villamediana, Conde de (1582-1622). Satirical poet and dramatist. Born in Lisbon; died in Madrid. Of noble origin, his name was Juan de Tassis y Peralta. His father occupied an important post at court, and the son was educated there by private tutors. The young Count led a tumultuous existence at court, being repeatedly exiled for gambling, various escapades and for his satirical verse directed against court favorites. During one of these periods of exile, he lived in Naples. Legend has it that he was the lover of Philip IV's first wife, Isabel de Bourbon, but this has not been substantiated by modern research. Nevertheless, the exact circumstances of his death at the hands of an assassin have never been satisfactorily cleared up. A friend and disciple of Góngora, Villamediana wrote in a *culto* style. His works were not published until after his death. He is known for his epigrams, sonnets, and longer poems in baroque style *(La fábula de Faetón).* His play, *La gloria de Niquea,* based on the Amadís theme, was presented at court in 1622.

Cf. *Poesías,* in *BAE,* XLII; Cotarelo y Mori, E., *El Conde de Villamediana,* Madrid, 1886.

villancete. The same as *villancico.*

villancico. A form of popular dance-song containing an *estribillo* (repeated and developed theme-verse or theme-stanza). It originated from the Arabic *zéjel* and was adopted by Spanish court poets at the end of the Middle Ages. It is still retained in its early form in Spanish Christmas carols. Hence, the current meaning of *villancico* is synonymous with the term, Christmas carol. In early works on metrics the word *villancico* is also encountered in a meaning synonymous with that of the *estribillo* alone, its most essential feature. See also under *estribillo; zéjel.*

Villasandino, Álvarez de. See under *Álvarez de Villasandino.*

Villaviciosa, José de (1589-1658). Poet and cleric in Cuenca. He was the author of an animal epic entitled *Mosquea* (1615), a poem in twelve cantos of octaves, which tells of a war in the insect world. It is a burlesque of the classical (Homer, Virgil) and the Italian (Dante) epic. Although inferior to Lope de Vega's *Gatomaquia* (1634), it is one of the most famous burlesque epics in Spanish literature.

Cf. Text in *BAE,* XVII; González Palencia, A., "José de Villaviciosa y *La Mosquea*", *Historias y Leyendas,* Madrid, 1942.

Villegas, Antonio de. See under *Abencerraje.*

Virginia. See under *Cueva; Tamayo y Baus.*

Visión de Fray Martín. See under *Núñez de Arce.*

Viva mi dueño. See under *Valle-Inclán.*

Vives, Juan Luis (1492-1540). Renaissance humanist and philosopher. Born in Valencia; died in Bruges. He studied at the Sorbonne in Paris (1509). Later he became a colleague of Erasmus at Louvain (1519). At the death of Nebrija (1522), Vives was offered the latter's post at Alcalá, but he refused and instead accepted a professorship at Oxford University. One of the most profound and learned humanists of his time, he sought to cast off the shackles of medieval scholasticism and developed an enlightened philosophy of his own, in many respects anticipating the ideas of Bacon, Locke, Descartes and Kant. His scholarly interests were universal, including philosophy, science, history, sociology, psychology, pedagogy, ethics and esthetics. Although he wrote all of his treatises in impeccable Latin, the many Spanish translations of his works (beginning with his *Diálogos,* Alcalá, 1574), assured his influence in Spain in succeeding centuries. Among his chief works were: *Introductio ad sapientiam,* 1524 *(Introducción a la sabiduría); De institutione feminae christianae,* 1528 *(De la instrucción de la mujer cristiana);* and *De anima et vita,* 1538 *(Del alma y de la vida).* See also under *humanism.*

Cf. *Obras completas,* (Ed. and trsl. by Riber, L.), Madrid, 1948; Bonilla y San Martín, A., *Luis Vives y la filosofía del Renacimiento,* Madrid, 1903; Watson, F., *Luis Vives,* Oxford, 1922;

Marañón, G., *Luis Vives. Un español fuera de España,* Madrid, 1942.

Vocabulario de refranes. See under *folklore.*

Vocabulario latínoespañol. See under *Nebrija.*

vocalization. (Sp. *vocalización).* The changing of a consonant to a vowel. Example: factum > *faitum* > *fecho* > *hecho.*

vocal anaptíctica. Anaptyctic vowel. See under *epenthesis.*

voluntad. The slogan of the Generation of 1898, indicated as the antidote to the Spanish trait of *abulia,* or loss of will-power, which accounts for Spain's decadence. The term achieved wide currency through its use in Ganivet's *Idearium español* (1897), and as the title of Azorín's novel, *La voluntad* (1902).

W

Wast, Hugo (1883). A pseudonym of Gustavo Martínez Zuviría, Argentine novelist. For many years Director of the Argentine National Library, he also served as Minister of Education. Hugo Wast is a prolific writer whose themes range from historical romance to *criollo* realism. Although his work is of uneven quality when judged by the highest esthetic standards, he is Argentina's most popular novelist. Among his important works are: *Flor de durazno,* 1911; *La casa de los cuervos,* 1916; *Desierto de piedra,* 1925; *Tierra de jaguares,* 1926-1927; *Lucia Miranda,* 1929; *Oro o el Kahal,* 1936; *Lo que Dios ha unido,* 1945.

Cf. Hespelt, E. H., "Hugo Wast, Argentine Novelist," *Hispania,* VII, 1924.

Whitmore, Katherine Reding (1897). American hispanist. Professor of Spanish, Smith College. Author of studies on Cadalso, Generation of 1898, *etc.,* in *Hispanic Review, Smith College Studies in Modern Languages, Columbia Dictionary of Modern European Literature, etc.*

Wilkins, Lawrence A. See under *American Association of Teachers of Spanish.*

William of Tyre. Guillermo de Tiro. See under *Gran conquista de ultramar.*

Wilson, E. M. (1906). Professor of Spanish at the University of London. Translator of Góngora's *Soledades (The Solitudes of Don Luis de Góngora,* Cambridge, 1931).

X

Xenius. The pen name of Eugenio d'Ors. See under *Ors; novecentismo.*

Ximénez de Rada, Rodrigo (d. 1247). The best known Spanish chronicler prior to Alfonso X. He was Bishop of Toledo, took an active part in church councils and wrote a compendious church history *(Breviarium Historiae Catholicae).* His most famous work was a history of Spain *(De rebus Hispaniae,* or *Historia Gothica),* commonly known in Spanish as the *Crónica del Toledano,* which became a source for many popular ballads. See also under *crónica.*

Y

yámbico. The type of eleven-syllable verse *(endecasílabo)* adapted to Castilian meters by Boscán and Garcilaso. It is accented on the 6th and 10th syllables. Also known as *endecasílabo heroico.* See under *endecasílabo.*

Yáñez, Rodrigo. See under *Poema de Alfonso Onceno.*

Yepes. See *Cruz, San Juan de la.*

Ymenea. See under *pundonor; Torres Naharro.*

Yoçef. See under *Poema de Yuçuf.*

Yuçuf. See *Poema de Yuçuf.*

Yxart, José (1852-1895). Journalist, poet and literary critic. Born and died in Tarragona. An authority on the Spanish theater from the 16th through the 19th centuries. His influential work was entitled *Arte escénico en España* (1893-1896).

Z

Zamora. See *Cantar de Zamora.*

Zamora, Antonio de. Author of the Don Juan drama, *No hay plazo que no se cumpla ni deuda que no se pague* (1722). See under *Don Juan.*

Zapaquilda. See under *Gatomaquia; Vega, Lope de.*

Zapatero y el rey (El). See under *Zorrilla y Moral.*

zarzuela. A musical comedy, or a play in which spoken parts alternate with songs. The music or lyrics of such a play. A forerunner of the opera, the *zarzuela* was first enacted at the Buen Retiro Palace in the 1630's. Later such light *divertissements* were performed at a royal hunting lodge near Pardo, known as *La Zarzuela,* whence the name. They were generally of a festive character with mythological content and allegorical elements. Among the earliest of the *zarzuelas* were Calderón's *Púrpura de la rosa, El laurel de Apolo,* and *Eco y Narciso* (ca. 1660's). One of the ablest librettists of the *zarzuela* in the 17th century was F. A. Candamo (1661?-1704). In the 18th century the type was revived by Ramón de la Cruz *(Las segadoras de Vallecas,* 1768), who replaced the original mythological personages with modern characters. Towards the end of the 18th century the *zarzuela* was succeeded by a short operetta form known as the *tonadilla,* consisting mainly of a brief libretto interspersed with popular airs. Such miniature operettas are referred to as the *zarzuela menor* or *género chico,* whereas the longer two or three-act form is known as the *zarzuela grande.* In the 19th century the *zarzuela* developed into musical comedy and light opera. See also under *género chico.*

Cf. Cotarelo y Mori, E., *Historia de la zarzuela,* Madrid, 1934; Subirá, J., *La historia de la música teatral en España,* Barcelona, 1946.

zéjel. An Arabic-Spanish popular song or verse form in which a theme verse *(matla)* or theme stanza is repeated and developed in subsequent stanzas. The *zéjel* ends with a repetition of the rhyme of the *matla.* The *zéjel* differs from the *muwassaha* in that the former is in popular, whereas the latter is in classical, Arabic. The *zéjel* is the prototype of the *villancico,* cultivated by Spanish court poets at the end of the Middle Ages. See also under *villancico; estribillo; muwassaha.*

Zifar. See *Caballero Cifar.*

Zorrilla de San Martín, Juan (1855-1931). Uruguayan jurist, professor, journalist, diplomat and poet. Born in Montevideo into a family of Spanish descent. Educated at various Jesuit colleges (Montevideo, Santa Fe, Santiago). Professor of literature at the University of Montevideo (1880). One time Minister to Portugal, France, Spain, and the Vatican. He is chiefly known for his patriotic ode, *La leyenda patria* (1879), and for his major work, *Tabaré* (1886), a verse epic inspired by a native legend. He also wrote political and cultural addresses, travel sketches and critical essays. His poetry is romantic in style, showing the influence of Bécquer. Among his chief works were: *Notas de un himno,* 1876; *La leyenda patria,* 1879; *Tabaré,* 1886; *Resonancias del camino,* 1895; *La epopeya de Artigas,* 1900; *Conferencias y discursos,* 1900.

Cf. Zum Felde, A., *Crítica de la literatura uruguaya,* Montevideo, 1921.

Zorrilla y Moral, José (1817-1893). Romantic dramatist and lyric poet. Born in Valladolid; died in Madrid. Details of his life are divulged in his autobiographical *Recuerdos del tiempo viejo* (1880-1882), a mixture of fact and fantasy. His father was an official in the royal chancelry at Valladolid and had no patience with his son's literary aspirations. When the family moved to Madrid, José was sent to the Jesuits at the *Real Seminario de Nobles* for his preliminary education. Later his father sent him to Toledo to study law, but José drifted into a bohemian, impecunious existence. Differences with his stern father and an unfortunate marriage with an older woman were the basic causes of his bohemian escape. Zorrilla first became famous as a poet when, at the age of twenty, he read a poetic tribute at Larra's grave (1837). He soon won the friendship of García Gutiérrez, Espronceda and other romantic writers. In France (1846) he made the acquaintance of Hugo, Sand and De Musset. In Mexico (1860) he became director of the National Theater under the patronage of Emperor Maximilian. In 1885 he was elected to the *Academia Española.* Although publicly honored towards the end of his life, he died in poverty. Besides the drama, Zorrilla also excelled in lyric poetry. His first poems appeared in the 1830's in various periodicals before publication as a whole (*Poesías,* 1837). Later collections of his verse were: *La flor de los recuerdos* (1859); *Album de un loco* (1867); *Ecos de las montañas* (1868); *El cantar del romero* (1883); etc. His forte was the verse *leyenda,* or ballad, based on national and religious themes. Outstanding among these were: *Cantos del trovador* (1841), containing legends of Old Spain; *María* (1849), on the life of the Virgin; *Granada* (1852), an unfinished poem about the conquest of Granada and containing legends of the Alhambra; *La leyenda del Cid* (1882), on the Spanish epic hero. Zorrilla's colorful evocation of the past made him one of the most popular poets of his day; but his frequently careless facility detracts from his stature as a poet. His best plays were likewise based on historical legends. *El zapatero y el rey* (1840) recreates the time of Pedro el Cruel (1350-1369); *El puñal del godo* (1842) deals with the epic hero Rodrigo. Zorrilla also wrote a number of three-act verse comedies patterned on the Golden Age *comedia de capa y espada: Cada cual con su razón* (1839); *Ganar perdiendo* (1839); *Más vale llegar a tiempo que rondar un año* (1845); etc. His greatest stage success—although he himself came to despise it—was *Don Juan Tenorio* (1844), a verse drama in seven acts. Zorrilla made his Don Juan a generous, sentimental and altogether sympathetic character; he also created a happy ending for him (salvation through love). The play is full of animation, color, emotion, fantastic elements and memorable characters. Despite its inconsistencies and exaggerations, it became the most celebrated of all Spanish romantic dramas and is still traditionally performed in Spanish theaters every autumn during the week of All Saints' Day (Nov. 1st). See also under *Don Juan.*

Cf. *Obras completas,* 2 vols., Valladolid, 1943; Alonso Cortés, N., *Zorrilla: su vida y sus obras,* 3 vols., Valladolid, 1916-1920.